Scripts and Calligraphy

Paths to the Soul

Scripts and Calligraphy

Paths to the Soul

SKIRA

وزارة الثقافة
Ministry of Culture

The exhibition *Scripts and Calligraphy: Paths to the Soul* and the publication that accompanies it are produced by the Ministry of Culture of Saudi Arabia:

HH. Prince Badr bin Abdullah bin Farhan Al Saud, Minister of Culture
HE. Hamed bin Mohammed Fayez, Vice Minister of Culture

The exhibition, presented at Irqah hospital, Riyadh from 10 June to 2 September 2023 and at Madina Arts Center, Medina from 15 October to 23 December 2023, is organized by the Cultural Assets & Centers Deputyship, Ministry of Culture:

Mona Khazindar
Deputy of Cultural Assets & Centers

Ibrahim Alsanousi
General Manager, Strategy, Design and Development

Dr. Virginia Cassola
Project Lead

Yassmeen Tukan
Project Lead

Hala Abuzeid
Project Coordinator

Hashim Alshaiban
Design and Development Director

Sara Alromaizan
Design Coordinator

Salwa Samargandi
Design Coordinator

Dr. Jana Jabbour
Communications Director

Production & Collection

Essa Alkhaldi
Monitoring Manager

Arjan Alahmadi
Monitoring Senior Specialist

Mohammad Alenezi
Monitoring Senior Specialist

Thamer Alhamidi
Monitoring Senior Specialist

Mohammed Sanousi
Monitoring Senior Specialist

Kristyna Storkova
Collection Manager

Yara Bana
Assistant Collection Manager

Daniah Alnabulsi
Administrative Officer

Hanadi Almuallem
Senior Executive Assistant

With the support
from the Communication
and Media Deputyship

Marketing Officers
Farah Alzayed
Hind Aldawish

Design Officers
Atheer Alkhashram
Ghada Almarshadi

Media Officers
Abdullah Alghannam
Djamila Benchaib

Digital Media Officers
Abdullah Alaqil
Bushra AlGhanim
Loujain Alsadhan

Editor
Wedad Aljamood

Translator
Ebaa Alturki

Photographers
Muath Alyahya
Saleh Althubaiti

Steering Committee
for the Exhibition

Dr. Huda Smitshuijzen AbiFarès
Founding Director of the Khatt Foundation, Amsterdam

Dr. Lotfi Abdeljaouad
Head of Research at the National Heritage Institute, Tunis

Eric Delpont
Islamic Art Specialist and Director of the Museum of the Institut du Monde Arabe, Paris

Nuria García Masip
Classically trained calligrapher

Dr. Issa Makhlouf
Poet and Writer

Nasser Al Maymoun
Classically trained calligrapher

Dr. Haytham Nawar
Associate Professor of Design, Department of the Arts, The American University in Cairo

Scenography
Pylône with Ideaa3
Jean-Paul Boulanger, Margo Renisio, Tang Tu

Graphic Design
Studio Nem / Naji El Mir

Lighting Design
ABRAXAS Concept

Mounting
AINU

TABLE OF CONTENTS

Preface

HH. Prince Badr bin Abdullah bin Farhan Al Saud

Apart from being a means of recording and documenting as well as a form to preserve culture, arts and science, Arabic calligraphy has acquired a special significance in Arab and Muslim civilizations as a tool that contributed to the transcription of the Holy Qur'an and an art that combines beauty with meaning, aesthetics with functionality. Moreover, Arabic calligraphy is a form of fine art that has played a pivotal role in transmitting knowledge and arts, advancing the Arabic language throughout history, and positioning it at the heart of Arab culture and identity.

Arabic calligraphy was born in the Arabian Peninsula and served as a means to instil traditions and values and enhance a sense of pride and belonging among Arabs. It was used across a broad range of mediums and fields, including manuscripts, paintings, architecture and sculptures. This art has been passed down from one generation to another as a unique form of expression.

The Kingdom of Saudi Arabia has dedicated considerable attention to Arabic calligraphy as a treasured aspect of the country's national identity and cultural heritage. In recognition of its cultural importance, the Ministry of Culture has launched an initiative to designate the years 2020 and 2021 as the "Year of Arabic Calligraphy". The initiative included a series of events and programmes aimed at celebrating this fine art, preserving it, and bolstering its presence in society. The Ministry has also revived the Dar Al-Qalam Complex in Medina to serve as a global platform for Arabic calligraphy, ensuring the survival and continuity of this art form. The Complex, which has been renamed the Prince Mohammed bin Salman Global Center for Arabic Calligraphy, aims to nurture talent and train a new generation of calligraphers in order to strengthen the Kingdom's pioneering stance in this field and position it as a global hub for Arabic calligraphy.

In 2022, following efforts led by the Kingdom of Saudi Arabia, in cooperation with fifteen Arab countries, Arabic calligraphy was inscribed on UNESCO's Intangible Cultural Heritage List, thus testifying to its immense value to humanity and consolidating its status as a global symbol of Arab culture.

In continuation of these efforts aimed at fostering interest in Arabic calligraphy, the Ministry of Culture has organized the second edition of the *Scripts and Calligraphy* exhibition. Following the first edition, *Scripts and Calligraphy: A Timeless Journey*, which showcased the roots of Arabic calligraphy and its historical development, the second, *Scripts and Calligraphy: Paths to the Soul*, sheds light on the spiritual dimension of Arabic calligraphy.

For this second edition of the exhibition, the Ministry of Culture has commissioned local, regional and international master calligraphers, as well as artists and designers. Through this unique collection of classical and contemporary artworks, *Scripts and Calligraphy: Paths to the Soul* is an invitation to embark on an immersive journey of discovery and reflection on the aesthetics of Arabic calligraphy. With this project, we hope to highlight the value of Arabic calligraphy as a cultural treasure and a manifestation of the culture and heritage of the Kingdom of Saudi Arabia.

Cultural Assets
& Centers Deputyship
Ministry of Culture

Scripts and Calligraphy: Paths to the Soul

In Arabic, writing and calligraphy are combined in the term *khatt* because of the sacred nature of the language of the Holy Qur'an, a word derived from the root *qara'a* referring to both recitation and reading. Many verses also refer to the surahs revealed to the Prophet (PBUH) as a Book, which provided writing with a unique role in Islamic arts, to the point where the use of writing is perceived as the unifying feature for both religions and cultures in the history and the geographical extent of the civilization generated by the advent of our father Abraham's religion.

The spiritual dimension of writing in its practice and perception is the theme of the second edition of the *Scripts and Calligraphy* exhibition, following the first edition, *A Timeless Journey*, which was presented at the National Museum in Riyadh in 2021, focused on the birth of Arabic writing and the rise of calligraphy. The art of calligraphy, codified in its learning and practice, has generated and perpetuated two distinguishing characteristics of the Islamic arts: their openness to changes in taste over time and their ability to satisfy the aesthetic expectations of varied populations, from North Africa to the Near East, from the Middle East to all of Asia.

The itinerary of the exhibition *Paths to the Soul* is built around four interconnected and complementary themes: Light, Letter, Space, and Poetry. These themes share a relationship that could be described as organic, in that they provide the keys to understanding the particular link that every Muslim – or anyone interested in the arts, regardless of the civilization they belong to – has with the written script.

Light refers to the cognitive and sensory abilities stimulated by writing. The light is that of spiritual and intellectual understanding, since the Holy Qur'an appeals many times to the reason of human beings so that they might apprehend God's message in its incommensurability. At the same time, the immateriality of light touches human beings' intuition and soul. The plastic and visual arts make light their raw material by capturing or transposing it. Surah *an-Nur*, the verse of Light (24:35), sets out this very polysemy of the word.

In turn, the light of the mind guides the drawing of the letters and then of the words, whether they are Qur'anic verses or prayers, to make the balance and harmony that God has conferred on Creation tangible. By mastering his gesture, the calligrapher shares with the reader the transmission of a content imbued with the sacred and enriches the act of reading with an invitation to meditation. The attention paid to the deciphering of graphemes becomes observation that leads to the enjoyment of calligraphy, which thus combines reason and feeling.

More than any other, the civilization of Islam focused on writing, extending it beyond the arts of the book to art curios made of ceramics, glass, metal, wood, textiles and architecture, moving it into the monumental format. All these productions are an exploration of ornament that differs from that developed at the same time in writing or calligraphy on parchment and paper. For a long time, the monumental epigraphy of places of prayer, pilgrimage and transmission of faith in the Arab world has favoured angular writing. Yet, more than reading them, believers recognize in the inscriptions a sign, maybe even a visual focus.

From the reign of the Abbasid dynasty (132–656 AH / 750–1258 AD), art curios were adorned with poems (also found in palaces such as the Alhambra in Granada, Spain), proverbs or good wishes, all testimonies of Arab sensitivity towards the arts of language to express collective ideals. Beautiful writing materializes the word (valued in jousts and oratorical meetings). It becomes the primary vehicle for introducing signs of belief and power in a society where mimetic images are banned. The inimitability of the literary form of the Holy Qur'an, sometimes rhyming and using assonance but freed from metrics, made poetry an autonomous discipline as well as an essential tool for a profound knowledge of classical Arabic, which allows the best understanding of the text of the Holy Qur'an. As a continuation of poetry, the *hurufiyya* creates a link between the drawing of the letters of the Arabic alphabet and a mode of informal expression while maintaining the representation of meaning, which requires intelligence and imagination. This modern artistic approach, which appeared in the second half of the twentieth century, was notably theorized by the Iraqi artist Shakir Hassan Al Said as the authentic spiritual aesthetics of Arab culture.

From this perspective, the exhibition *Paths to the Soul* combines and creates interaction between ancient and contemporary works, inviting visitors to engage in contemplation and introspection. Every visitor can reconnect with their experience and memory through their senses. Everyone is also free to interpret what they are looking at, be it akin to or far from the artist's vision. The enduring force of the Islamic arts from the past until this day, and calligraphy in particular, lies in allowing multiple interpretations.

Head of Research at the
National Heritage Institute, Tunis

Early Islamic Engravings and Inscriptions: Different Contents and Supports

Dr. Lotfi Abdeljaouad

Documenting was not a privilege exclusive to the Arab Islamic civilization; like its past or contemporary counterparts, it sought to immortalize architectural and artistic works and to register the names of people. However, this practice took writing well beyond its initial function, to the point where calligraphy itself morphed into a symbolic tool and an essential element of Islamic decoration on all types of supports. Documentation became all the more important as, after the Arab conquests, the various regions falling under Islamic rule experienced a marked political, urban and architectural development. This explains the vast number of Islamic inscriptions found to date on archaeological sites and during exploration missions. Islamic writings were a true expression of Man's inner and outer journey. Inscriptions are also the trace through which the Arabic calligraphy history and evolution can be studied along with its various styles.

To this day, the Library of Arabic Literature keeps a book by Abu al-Farag al-Isfahani (d. 356 AH / 967 AD), *Literature of Strangers*, through which one can partly understand the purpose behind one given type of inscriptions: graffiti written on walls, monuments or stones.

EARLY ISLAMIC INSCRIPTIONS: GRAFFITI

The earliest found Arabic inscriptions were undoubtedly spurred by the desire to leave a trace of one's passage or stay. Archaeological excavations and research have uncovered Arabic inscriptions in various scripts, the most recent of which being perhaps the Nabatean script used in the Namara inscription (328 AD), which commemorates the death of the Arab King Imru al-Qays ibn 'Amr and lists his many victories.

Other inscriptions in classical Arabic, dating back to the early first century AH, most of which were found in the Arabian Peninsula, most notably in Saudi Arabia, mention the names of famous Companions, such as the recently discovered stone inscription in the Najran region, carrying the name of the blessed Companion Yazid bin Mu'awiyah bin Hazan bin al-Muhajjal, a member of the Najran delegation that sought the Prophet (PBUH) in 10 AH / 630 AD. Other inscriptions discovered in Saudi Arabia include the Salma inscription, which commemorates the Prophet's (PBUH) name on a stone in the Muthallath region near Yanbu' and dates back to 23 AH / 643 AD, and the Zahir inscription, the second oldest dated Arabic text to date, which was discovered in a place near Qa'a al-Mu'tadil in the al-'Ula Province; it dates back to 24 AH / 644 AD and mentions the death of Caliph Omar bin al-Khattab.

QUR'ANIC INSCRIPTIONS

Qur'anic passages are perhaps the most widespread type of texts found among early inscriptions and throughout the ages. They were made by people who, through the act of writing, wished to be blessed by the verses contained in the Holy Book, sought to proclaim their adherence to the Islamic faith, and expressed their desire to disseminate the teachings and principles of the Holy Qur'an. Those who wrote Qur'anic inscriptions were keen to record those verses and put them into circulation, this being a clear indication that the Islamic faith had spread in the region. In the geographical areas covered by the Islamic conquests, these texts often contain answers to dogmatic postulates professed by the Peoples of the Book – Jews and Christians – such as

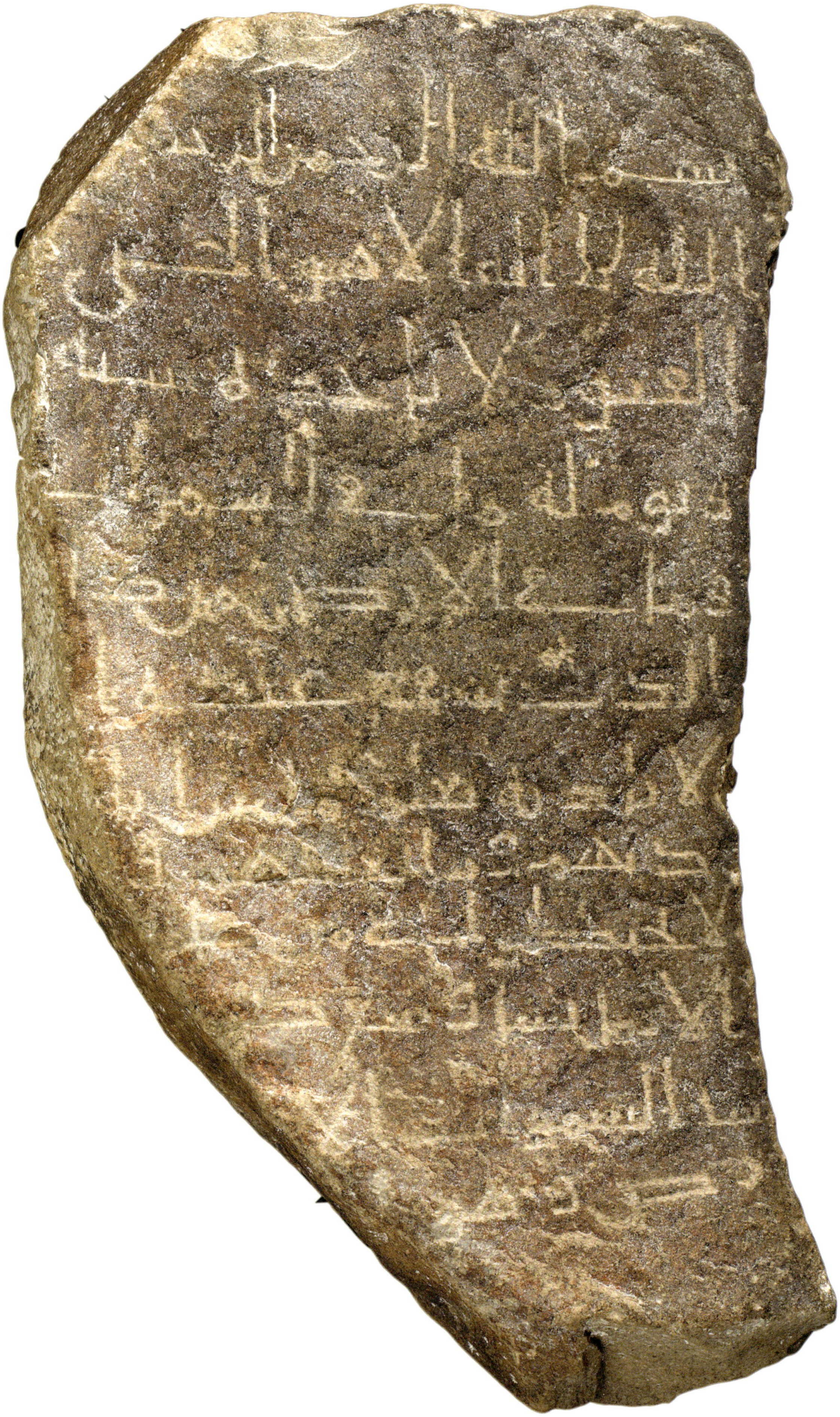

Inscription in kufi script engraved on an animal clavicle, second–third century AH / eighth–ninth century AD
Surah *al-Baqarah*, verse 255
Bone
The National Museum of Saudi Arabia, Riyadh

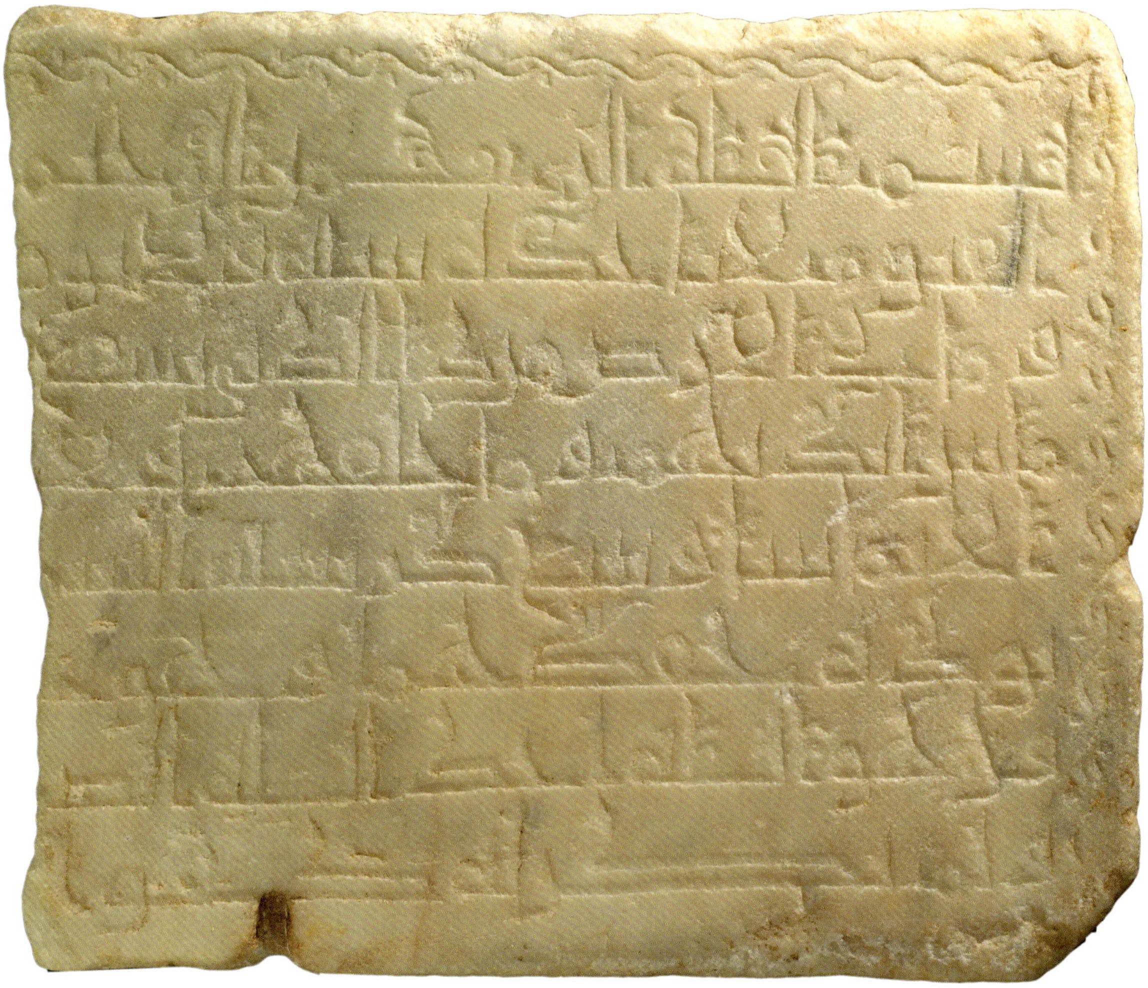

Lapidary inscription in kufi script carved on a quasi-square panel, second–third century AH / eighth–ninth century AD
Surah *al-Baqarah*, verse 255
Marble
The National Museum of Saudi Arabia, Riyadh

the issue of the Trinity, the nature of Christ and his death on the Cross. These inscriptions also mention the names of prophets and messengers of the faith in acknowledgement of their identities and of the books and messages they carried as they reaffirmed their adherence to the Islamic faith.

Stone surfaces, animal bones, palm tree fronds and animal skins were the most popular writing supports at the time. In the Mecca region, a stone inscription dated 80 AH / 699 AD was found with verse 87 of the surah *al-Nisa'* written on it. The National Museum in Riyadh houses a unique collection of such writings, including the one known as the Verse of the Throne engraved both on an animal bone clasp in simple *kufi* script (second–third century AH / eighth–ninth century AD) and on a rectangular stone tablet dating back to the same period. The museum also houses a Qur'anic inscription engraved on an unpolished stone containing the full text of the surah *al-Fatiha* and verse 21 of the surah *al-Hashr*. Texts like these can be found in all regions and on different types of supports right up to the contemporary period.

PILGRIMAGE ROUTE INSCRIPTIONS: SPONTANEOUS GRAFFITI

Pilgrimage to the Great Mosque in Mecca in order to perform the Hajj or the Umrah is regarded as the most important spiritual trip of all for Muslims. It used to be a long and perilous journey along travel routes that necessitated repeated stops, sojourning at hosting stations and interacting with people of various origins. Those stops were an opportunity to spontaneously scribble graffiti whose importance cannot be underestimated as they offer an insight into those times, the prevailing situation, people's desires and their religious sensitivities. Inscriptions on the Iraqi pilgrimage route known as the al-Zubaydah route attest to that. Some date back to 40 AH / 660–661 AD, others to 56 AH / 675–676 AD, such as the Khashna' inscription between Dhariba Dhat Irq and Mecca: "Oh Allah, forgive Hidbah / bin 'Ali bin Habira / written in the year 56 AH". Inscriptions along the Sham pilgrimage route abound with references to and testimonies of this holy practice; one of these, dating back to 97 AH / 716 AD, mentions the pilgrimage of the Commander of the Faithful, Sulayman bin 'Abdul-Malik: "Oh God, I testify and believe / that there is no God but You, written by Muhammad Ibn Abi Talha al-Homsi in 97 AH / (Pilgrimage of Sulayman the Commander of the Faithful)". They also include inscriptions dating back to the second century AH. Al-'Ula was a major pilgrimage hosting station on that route, where caravans stopped and stocked up on water and provisions, and where pilgrims could partly dispose of their belongings on their way to Mecca. The hosting stations on the Yemeni pilgrimage route are a veritable open-air museum full of these inscriptions. Perhaps the oldest of these is the text dated 98 AH / 716–717 AD found on the Najdi route near the station of Ghail al-Mundaj (al-Mubarrah) in the province of South Dhahran. There are also the Umm al-Ruha (141 AH / 758 AD) and the Umm Waqar inscriptions in the province of Bisha (226 AH / 840 AD). The most beautiful writings to be found on this road are probably the three inscriptions signed by Sa'id bin Salim al-Makki.

The National Museum in Riyadh is home to a stone engraving found at one of the hosting stations on the Egyptian pilgrimage route, which contains humorous testimonies of faith dating back to the year 160 AH / 777 AD.

PILGRIMAGE ROUTE INSCRIPTIONS: MILESTONES

Pilgrimage roads required planning, building and periodic maintenance under the supervision of the ruling authority of the time, whether it be the Caliphate central government or any peripheral authorities. The accuracy of the milestones stands as the best testimony to the attention given by rulers to building these roads. The texts inscribed on them are the expression of a continuous desire to influence and control space by delimiting distances, pointing to places and directions, indicating the following hosting station and sometimes even mentioning the facilities housed there. Most famous is the Darb al-Zubaydah milestone collection on the Iraqi pilgrimage route, of which the National Museum in Riyadh owns two specimens. Pilgrimage routes are strewn with milestone inscriptions but also commemorative texts to mark the construction and establishment of hosting stations for both ordinary travellers and pilgrims to the Great Mosque of Mecca.

The National Museum in Riyadh houses a foundation stone of the Green Pond on the Sham pilgrimage route. It was found south of Tabuk, with text written in a highly skilled *thuluth* script dating back to the Mamluk Period (817 AH / c. 1415 AD).

Religious land endowments (*wakf*) were concentrated along these roads and on hosting station locations, their purpose being to draw travellers near God, to have people's prayers answered and to earn them retribution for good deeds. The National Museum in Riyadh keeps a text engraved on a standing stone dating back to the third century AH / ninth century AD, commemorating the construction of a house and water point for pilgrims performing the Hajj and Umrah to the Great Mosque of Mecca.

FUNERARY INSCRIPTIONS

Funeral practices transpire through writings: they are spiritual journeys where worldly and otherworldly matters are inscribed on various supports. In either elaborate or simple language, they document events from the life and death of the departed: Who was he? What was his ancestry? Where did he come from?

Three lapidary inscriptions in kufi script carved on a stone, 160 AH / 777 AD

Discovered on the Egyptian Hajj Road, north-west of the Kingdom of Saudi Arabia
Basalt

Text 1 (right upper part of the stone) reads: "... and His angels and His books and His / prophets and the Qur'an and the Bible / and the Resurrection and the Judgement day / and Heaven and Hell /and rejecting / the first evil / ... / ... five".
Text 2 (left upper part of the stone) reads: "done ... / ... Said bears witness / that none has the right to be worshipped but Allah / alone Who has no partner / and that Muhammad is His slave and / Messenger".
Text 3 (lower part of the stone) reads: "None has the right to be worshipped but Allah alone, He brings life and He causes death / and He can do all things / And Ayub b. Khaled wrote knowing what was sent from God and his Prophet and wrote on the ... of Rabi', in the year One hundred and sixty. May the prayers of God be on his Prophet Muhammad".
The National Museum of Saudi Arabia, Riyadh

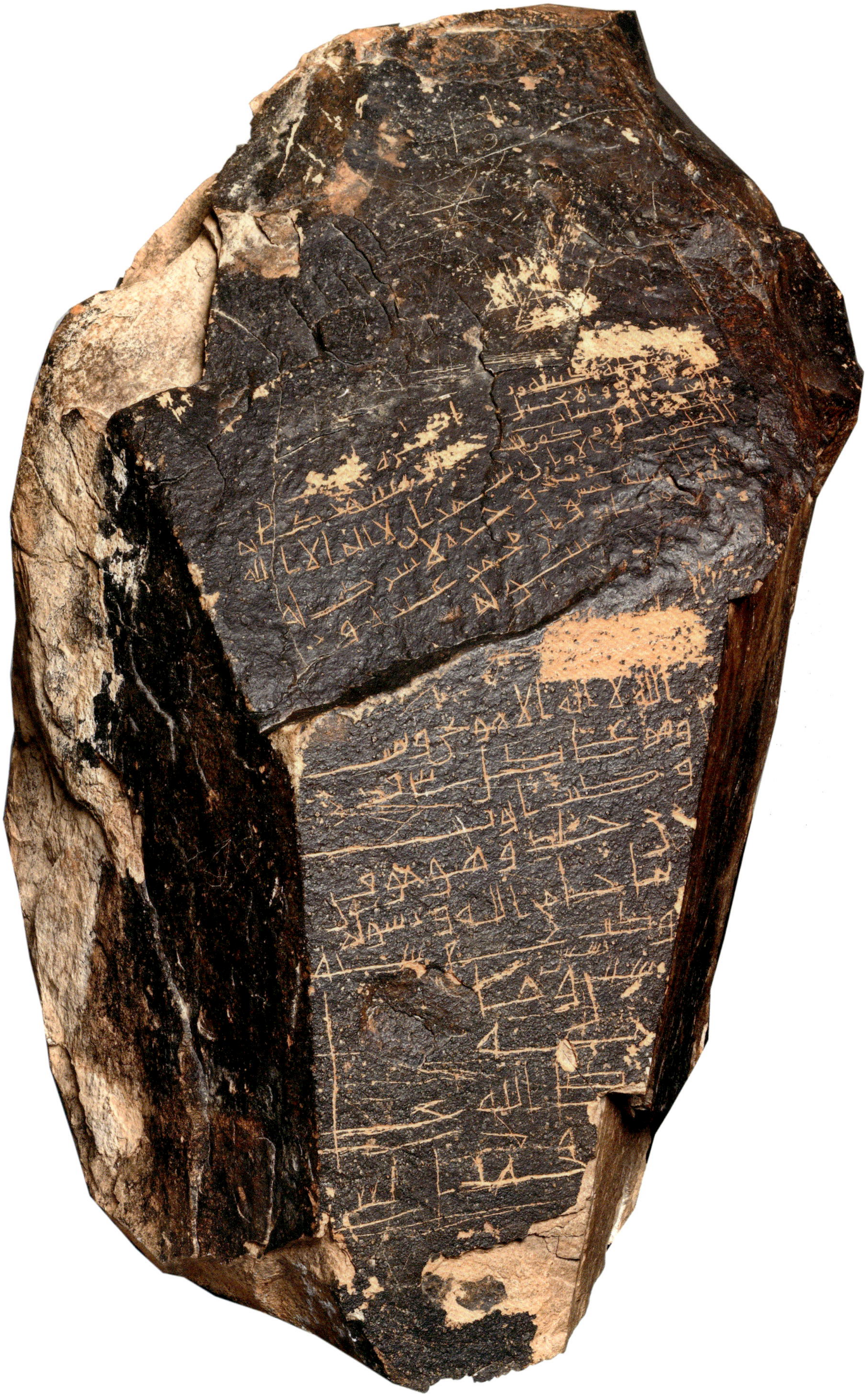

Milestone fragment bearing an inscription, 156–169 AH / 772–785 AD

Discovered between Al-Mughaytha and Al-Rabza region

Stone

The text reads: "... mile from /.../ 62 / ... / mile from / al-Kufa".

The National Museum of Saudi Arabia, Riyadh

What tribe did he belong to? What was his ethnicity or his religious affiliation? What was his legal status? What occupation, craft or public office did he hold? What official or honorary titles did he hold? What were his main qualities and traits of character?

Sometimes the date and cause of death appear on these inscriptions, which means they constitute an inexhaustible and irreplaceable source of social, economic, political and historical information. Funerary inscriptions are also a source of knowledge pinpointing to the religious faith: they contain references to beliefs and convictions, emerging from writings, on the journey of faith initiated during one's earthly life and stretching to the other world. Their impact can even be felt beyond death, as they can obtain graces for the departed by asking the reader for a prayer, or they can be a sermon on a gravestone that, once read, can be beneficial to the reader. Written on supports of different shapes and materials, this type of inscription is the most common and widespread of all. Saudi Arabia's museums abound in such funerary inscriptions, perhaps the most famous being the gravestone engravings discovered in the *al-Ma'alah* cemetery in Mecca.

Milestone fragment bearing an inscription indicating the two thirds of the road leading to Kufa, second century AH / eighth century AD

Discovered on the Iraqi Pilgrimage Road, Darb al-Zubaydah
Stone

The text reads: ". . . 8 / miles that is / two thirds of the road from / al-Kufa".
The National Museum of Saudi Arabia, Riyadh

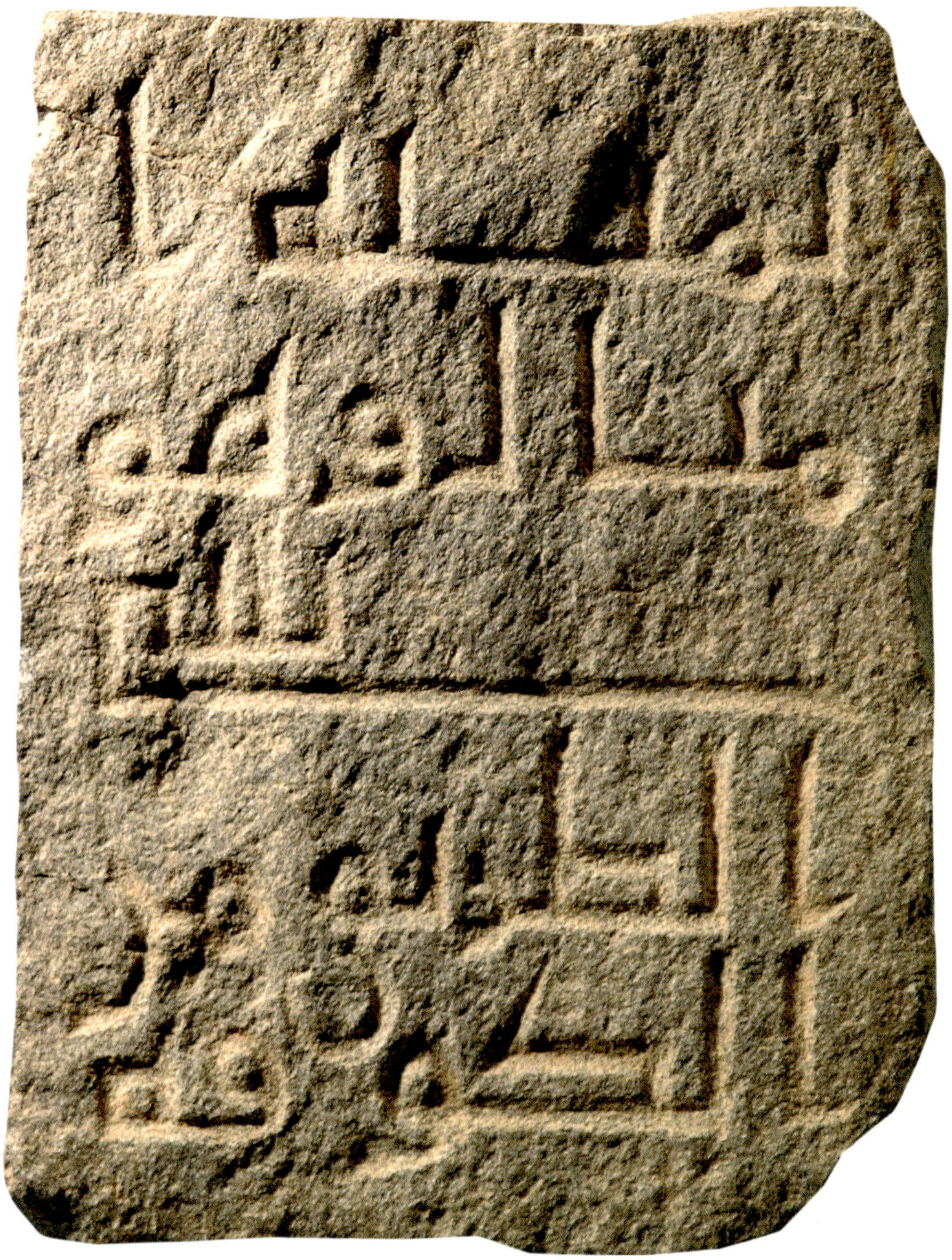

INSCRIPTIONS ON RELIGIOUS BUILDINGS

Most interesting in early writings are the inscriptions adorning the various structures in Islamic architecture, most notably religious buildings, especially mosques. These inscriptions were intended to document official and private acts of charity and to record sermons. Furthermore, Qur'anic verses and selected hadiths written on walls project an aura of sanctity; they can be sentences compatible with the teachings dispensed in any given religious place, or they can refer to a section of the building such as *mihrabs*, mosque libraries or places dedicated to the acquisition of knowledge. These inscriptions also include religious texts such as prayers, songs of praise, lists of the Holy Names of God and short statements expressing the positions of a given intellectual or doctrinal school on a specific issue. This spiritual dimension cannot be separated from its prominent ornamental one, the latter belonging to various schools depending on location and era. A number of short words and formulations received special recognition and were widely spread across all kinds of supports and instruments; examples include *al-mulk lillah* (kingship belongs to God), *al-'izza lillah* (glory to God), words related to prayer

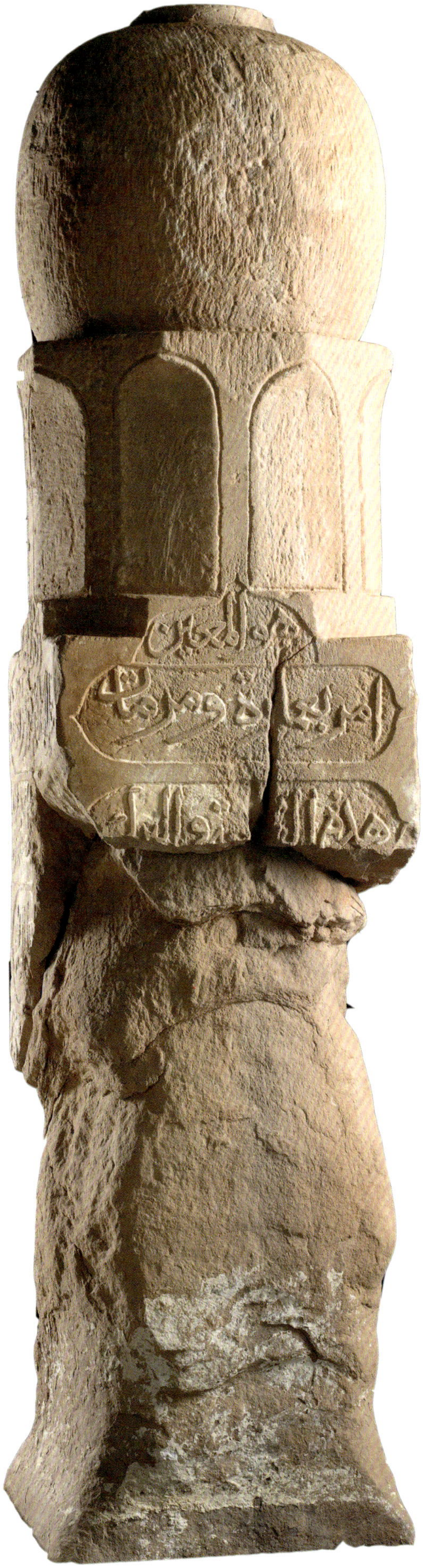

Foundation inscription for al-Akhdar Fountain, Mamluk Period, 817 AH / c. 1415 AD

Discovered south of Tabuq, Kingdom of Saudi Arabia

Stone

The text reads: "God is the only support / Ordered the construction and the . . . this . . ."
The National Museum of Saudi Arabia, Riyadh

such as *baraka* (blessing), *'afiya* (wellness), *salama* (safety), *iqbal* (good fortune), *nasr* (victory), *yumn* (success) and others. These words appear on weapons, utensils, clothes, walls, furniture, lighting, etc.

QUR'ANS

Parchment – and later paper – remain the most famous support for recording the most beautiful texts, especially the Holy Qur'an. Islamic libraries and museums abound with Qur'anic masterpieces.
From the earliest times onwards, Muslims deployed treasures of artistry in writing, ornamenting and annotating these texts. Earlier versions used the *hijazi* slanted script, then came the *kufi* and then other scripts following major developments in Arabic calligraphy at the hand of Ibn al-Bawwab, Ibn Muqla and those who followed in their footsteps.

A REFINED AND ADVANCED ARTISTIC TASTE

Writing is a journey of refined artistic taste. As a form of art, it represents a major development in the history of Islamic art. Through collections arranged by chronological order across different countries, a number of observations can be made about the evolution of the art of writing. The common denominator is the engravers' and/or calligraphers' constant preoccupation with balance, as the content of the page would need to be supplemented with lines, hence the persistent search for solutions in order to fill the gaps resulting from the differences in height within Arabic letters.

Attempts to resolve this issue can be seen as early as the first century AH: calligraphers would reduce the differences between letters by increasing their thickness and introducing broad curved lines above and below most of them. In addition, detached folial and geometrical ornamentations were introduced to fill the remaining empty spaces above the written script. Master calligraphers even went as far as embellishing ligatures between letters to reduce monotony and rigidity and increase the sense of movement. Then, this trend evolved into making denser letters with a more dynamic writing base, resulting in the addition of the "parting" element to the ligatures (a convex, concave, or sometimes triangular line or shape), thus adding beauty to the writing by extending letters with folial endings. *Kufi* writing reached its pinnacle of creativity. Various solutions were introduced to achieve the required balance, including increasing the amount of folial lines springing from letters, so much so that the interlacing of letters, lines and arabesques became so convoluted, and reading became a very complicated task. The very bodies of the letters and their tails were also put to use so as to bring balance about: the letter *jeem*, for instance, went beyond its original geometrical shape, i.e. from a sloping line to a curve and then an opposite upward curve; a leg was added to the *fa'* and the *qaf* in order to raise them; and the *meem*, the *waw*, the *ra'* and the *nun* had their short geometrical tails removed so as to rise above the line, their interlacing wreaths and braids now attracted, repelled or faced one other in the most beautiful of ways. In parallel to this evolution of the Arabic script, cursive scripts of various kinds were used, like the *naskh*, the *thuluth*, as well as others, depending on location and era. In addition, diacritical points, vowel signs (the *damma*, the *fatha*, the *kasra*, the *sukun*, the *shaddah* and the *tanwin*) and other markings were introduced above or under the letters to distinguish those with similar shape but different pronunciations from one another – like the *ha'* from the *jeem* and the *kha*. The same applies to the *seen* to be distinguished from the *sheen*. All of these markings have, to some extent, replaced the usual fill-in elements used in the *kufi* script without entirely eliminating them. Master calligraphers overcame imbalance in the writing space, among others, by using writing itself, i.e. inserting a second and sometimes third layer into the same writing field. Cursive scripts allow such a technique, resulting in a high degree of complexity and overlap despite the presence of the above-mentioned diacritical points and vowel signs.

Classically trained calligrapher

Paths to the Soul in Classical Arabic Calligraphy

Nuria García Masip

The word calligraphy comes from the Greek *kalos graphos*, beautiful writing, which corresponds to the same term in Arabic, *al-khatt al-jamil*. While the notion of beauty is intrinsically embedded in the art of calligraphy, its expressions fluctuate according to time periods, regions, aesthetic contexts, and systems of transmission. With the expansion of Islam from the seventh century across a wide geographical territory, the Arabic script was adopted to write different languages over this vast territory, from the Maghreb to Sub-Saharan Africa, across Central Asia and the Far East, giving rise to a plethora of different calligraphic styles.

From the earliest periods of the Islamic calligraphic tradition, calligraphers have endeavoured to define and codify what constitutes beautiful writing. Striving to understand, capture and transmit beauty through letterforms is the journey of every calligrapher. However, according to the classical tradition, calligraphy is not only a path to find perfection in exterior forms, but also an inward journey, where beautiful writing is linked to the beauty of character. The transformative effect of calligraphy on the soul is thus linked to the aesthetic norms and canons that rule this art as well as to the discipline and *adab* (etiquette) required for its practice and transmission.

BEAUTY AND PROPORTION

Abu Hayyan al-Tawhidi (d. 414 AH / 1023 AD), one of the most important philosophers of the tenth century, defined beauty as something "whose organs are perfect, whose parts are harmonious and which is pleasing to the soul".[1] Philosophical treatises produced during this period were influenced by Neoplatonic and classical Greek works on aesthetics and the arts translated into Arabic. Thus, beauty was equated with perfection and harmony, which were, in turn, associated with balance and proportion.[2] Classical Arab philosophers, often well-versed in the art of writing, used calligraphy to illustrate these aesthetic principles. Thus, according to Ibn al-Haytham (c. 354–430 AH / c. 965–1040 AD), "Calligraphy is not beautiful unless its letters are proportionately arranged in their forms, dimensions, positions, and order".[3] And in similar terms, al-Ghazali (450–505 AH / 1058–1111 AD) states: "Beautiful is every line of calligraphy that combines what is appropriate to calligraphy, such as proportionality of the letters, their spacing, the straightness of their order, and the beauty of their arrangement".[4] From the earliest periods, the search for proportion and balance was one of the primary concerns for calligraphers, who spent the following centuries building a system of proportion that would codify and beautify different calligraphic styles.

The first system of proportion appears already in the early *kufi* Qur'ans from the Abbasid period. Studies have shown that these Qur'ans were codified according to a complex system of geometric proportions in order to determine the page layout, text box and letter units.[5] Letterforms were developed according to a six-line grid system determined by the width of the pen, which in turn dictated the height of the ascenders.[6] In parallel, during the eighth and ninth centuries, a second system was developed for the round style, *mustadir*, which was destined for everyday use, official decrees and correspondence. Scribes in the chancellery codified standard sizes of pens for different round scripts, measured by the width of a workhorse's tail. These styles became known as "balanced calligraphy", *al-khatt al-mawzun*, and historian Ibn al-Nadim mentions 24 different pens being used during this time for different scripts.[7] Like for the *kufi* scripts, a proportional system was created in order to determine letterform proportions according to the pen, where the height of the letter *alif* (ا) was given by squaring the width of the pen nib.[8]

But perhaps the most transformative development in the history of calligraphy was brought about by Ibn Muqla (d. 328 AH / 939 AD) and Ibn al-Bawwab (d. 413 AH / 1022 AD),[9] who are credited with creating and refining what became known as the well-proportioned script, *al-khatt al-mansub*.[10] According to the tradition, Ibn Muqla developed a system in which the letters are proportioned according to the circle, its diameter given by the height of the letter *alif*. This system was further refined by the introduction of the *nuqta* measurement, the rhomboid point made by the nib of the pen to codify the measurements of each letterform according to each script.[11] The round styles were thus organized between the eleventh and twelfth centuries into six classical styles, known as the *al-aqlam al-sitta*, namely *thuluth*, *naskh*, *muhaqqaq*, *rayhani*, *tawqi'*, and *riqa'*. For the centuries that followed, *al-khatt al-mansub* became the basis for all classical scripts in the calligraphic tradition, and many later styles were codified according to the *nuqta* proportional system.[12]

In this articulation of proportion, every single letter and connection is ruled by a complex system of measurements that varies according to the script being practised. Calligraphic exercises and practice sheets by great masters, highly esteemed for their artistic value, can give us an inkling of what lies behind a well-calligraphed sentence. It is in this context that we can understand the saying by Euclid, often quoted in the calligraphic treatises, "Handwriting is spiritual geometry by means of a corporeal instrument". Beyond a mere unit of measurement, the *nuqta* carries a strong symbolical weight for calligraphers, in that it represents unity in multiplicity, containing in its essence all the letters before they unfold onto the page. Everything stems from the *nuqta*, and the *nuqta*, in turn, stems from the *qalam*, the symbol of the Primordial Pen.

Folio from the Holy Qur'an, first–second century AH / seventh–eighth century AD (detail of cat. 41)

MASHQ AND PRACTICE

As all calligraphers know well, the proportion is only one aspect of beautiful writing. Going back to Abu Hayyan al-Tawhidi, in his treatise on calligraphy he enumerates a series of principles of what constitutes beautiful calligraphy. These refer not only to accurate proportions but also to the harmony of line – balancing the negative and positive space, making elegant curves, spacing and arranging the line evenly, respecting the rhythm of the words on the page, the nuance and exactness of strokes – and to the pressure exerted on the calamus when writing. Other treatises on calligraphy mention other, more elusive notions such as the breath-like flow of strokes or the concept of *shan*, the energy transmitted to the viewer, which in fact constitute the greatest challenge for calligraphers. The secret of good calligraphy lies mostly on mastering the pen to create nuance, transmitting energy, and allowing the writing to present the effortless flow to which all calligraphers aspire. In essence, for the calligrapher's hand to disappear and for the letters to manifest onto the page in all their formal beauty. To transmit these elements, calligraphers must consecrate themselves to the path of *mashq*, or continuous practice.

Following the well-known saying by 'Ali Ibn Abi Talib, "The secret of calligraphy is hidden in the master's teaching, and its consistency is in its repeated practice [*mashq*]". Classical sources refer to three different types of *mashq*: the practice of the eye (*nazari*), the practice of the pen (*qalami* or *'amali*), and the practice of the imagination (*khayali*).[13] The first two are practised by the student from the earliest stages and under the close supervision of the master, who leads his pupil through the different levels of understanding. First, the students must observe the master's writing and models, concentrating on correct posture, how to hold and dip the pen into ink, the order and pressure of strokes, and the correct composition of letterforms, lines and text. They will also study models of great past masters, educating their eyes to distinguish the correct dimensions, nuance, and thickness of the stroke. In parallel, the students will concentrate on copying (*naql*) the teacher's models, exercising continuously with pen and ink in order to improve their skills and techniques. Thus, through continuous visual and pen practices, the students will eventually reach a stage where calligraphy permeates

واما اذا ما ابتله فقد
ر عليه رزقه فيقول ربى اهنن ۝ كلا بل لا تكر
مون اليتيم ولا تحضون على طعام المسكين
وتاكلون التراث اكلا لما ۝ وتحبو
ن المال حبا جما ۝ كلا اذا دكت الا
رض دكا دكا ۝ وجا ربك والملك صفا صفا
وجاى يومئذ بجهنم يومئذ يتذكر
الانسن وانى له الذكرى ۝ يقول يليتنى
قدمت لحياتى ۝ فيومئذ لا يعذب عذابه
احد ولا يوثق وثاقه احد ۝ يايتها
النفس المطمئنة ارجعى الى ربك
راضية مرضية فادخلى فى عبدى
وادخلى جنتى

فاتحة سورة لا اقسم وهي عشرو

بسم الله الرحمن الرحيم لا
اقسم بهذا البلد ۝ وانت حل بهذا ا
لبلد ووالد وما ولد ۝ لقد خلقنا الانسن

منتصب ومسطح اه وقال ابن

...لام ويكون المنتصب
...دار ثلث الف

في الفكر والنور
الرأي والتناسب
ما اشبههم من النسبة
لن يجعل لذلك اصلا
اليه في حروفه ولا يقصر دونه
...ت الفا وتجعل غلظة الذي هو عرضه مناسبا
مرات لن تجعل

قال ابن
مقلة هي شكل
مركب من خطين
منكب ونصف دائرة
وقطرها مساو للألف

نصف دائرة
بعينه
الفاضلة
ابني عليه
ومثال ذلك
لطوله والثمن
البركار على وسطها
وسط الالف

قال ابن مقلة هي
شكل مركب من
خطين

وللأثاري شعر يقول فيه
سبع من النقط للذي نصب جعل
من خطه الى رأسه منها علم
والباء قس في وسطها عليه
وكل ذي مثل اضيف اليه

ولا
يحتاج في
مقاييسك ما تقصدها الى شيء يخرج
عن الالف وعن الدائرة التي تحيط به
ثم قال ومن المقادير وكمية نسبة بعضها

Ahmed Fares Rezq
Ibn Muqla Theory, 2010
(detail of cat. 16)

their entire being and the letterforms enter their imagination. It is only at this stage that a calligrapher is able to write a piece without copying a model. As was beautifully described in the seventeenth century, "'Imaginative practice' is when the scribe writes not according to a model but with reference to the power of his own nature, and he writes every composition that appears [to him]. The benefit of this practice is that it makes the scribe a master of spontaneity (*tasarruf*)".[14]

Great masters of calligraphy are thus the ones who have acquired these different skills, being able to reproduce great calligraphic pieces from the masters of old as well as invent or create original pieces. For calligraphers, both exercises are equally valuable. For in the exercise of reproduction (*naql*) of an old masterwork, the calligrapher must, in fact, eliminate all sense of personal accent, imitating the spirit as well as the form of the original. In the case of an original composition stemming entirely from the calligrapher's imagination, he must create within the boundaries and rules of the classical canons, experimenting with new compositions while respecting the classical letterforms. For either of these genres, allowing for the breath of inspiration to manifest onto the page and infuse the letters with energy is one of the signs of a true masterpiece.

TEXT AND FORM

The final dimension of the calligraphic path is the combination of form and text as carriers of meaning. Indeed, the interaction of these two elements lies behind many of the styles that were developed throughout history. Certain scripts were conceived for the chancellery and administration, others were used for longer treatises, holy scripture, prophetic literature, poetry, and wise sayings. In the same way, certain styles were reserved almost exclusively for *mushafs*, others for architectural inscriptions, and others for everyday writing. Indeed, the relationship between text and script was also related to the level of readability intended – that is, the level of difficulty of the script was a direct reflection of the education of the intended reader. For example, early Qur'ans in the highly stylized *kufi* script can only be read by those who already know most of the Qur'an by heart, functioning basically as an *aide mémoire*. Equally difficult are the *diwani* or chancellery scripts, meant to be accessed only by the highly educated classes and often very tight-knit in order to prevent any changes or alterations in legal texts.

However, apart from these considerations, the sources tell us that calligraphers were meant to write texts that would elevate the viewer – and in turn, the calligrapher himself. Following the advice of the great Ibn al-Bawwab, "pray that the fingers of your hand will write only what is good for you to leave behind in the house of deception. Everything a man does, he will be confronted with on the morrow, when he is confronted with the written decree (on the Day of Resurrection)".[15] In fact, most classical calligraphers today derive their inspiration from holy scripture, hadiths, and poetry, aiming to convey the meaning of these texts with the most beautiful composition. Certain formulas are particularly dear to calligraphers, such as the testimonies of faith (*shahada*) or the *basmala*, for according to tradition, "If a man writes the *basmala*, and writes it very well and carefully, God will pardon him".[16] Another common piece is the *Hilyah*, or the calligraphic icon of the Prophet (PBUH), containing the hadith describing his appearance, as well as the Qur'anic verses that mention him. Qur'anic verses related to the remembrance of God, Divine Mercy and the beauty of Manifestation are meant to invite readers to reflect and be reminded of these passages. The calligraphy thus functions as a visual icon leading viewers to contemplate while reading the text, reflecting on how a particular meaning is transmitted through the chosen composition.

The classical calligraphy pieces presented in the exhibition *Paths to the Soul* illustrate the calligrapher's journey through the different sections of the exhibition. It leads the viewer through the various stages of *mashq*, including the articulation of proportion, calligraphic practice pages, the creation of words, lines and texts

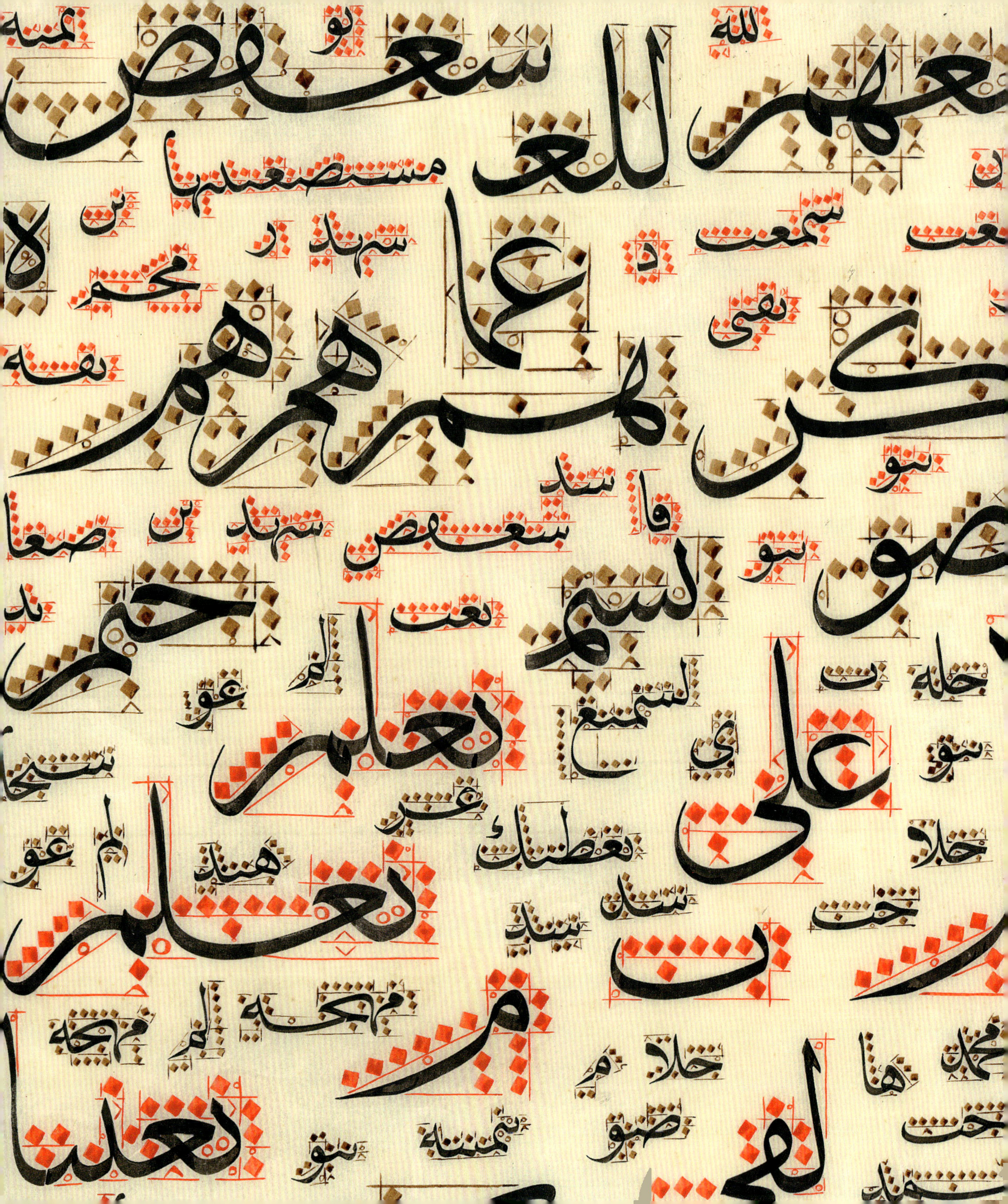

Ihab Thabet
Karalama, 2022
(detail of cat. 29)

in different calligraphic styles. Calligraphy gradually unfolds from the *nuqta* to script, manifesting onto different surfaces as a carrier of meaning through poetry, wise sayings and sacred scripture. We will thus finish with the words of ʿAbd al-Hamid ibn Yahya al-Katib (d. 132 AH / 749–750 AD): "The calamus is a tree whose fruit is the spoken word. Reflection is an ocean whose pearl is wisdom. Eloquence is a watering place where the thirsty intellects are watered. Handwriting is a garden whose flowers are instructive remarks".[17]

We invite viewers to journey inwards through the beauty of calligraphy, reflecting on the wisdom conveyed across the themes of light, prayer and poetry.

[1] J. M. Puerta Vilchez, *Aesthetics in Arabic Thought* (Leiden: Brill, 2017), p. 723.
[2] For the mentions of proportion in early Arabic texts, see A. George, *The Rise of Islamic Calligraphy* (London: Saqi, 2010), pp. 103–14.
[3] Ibid., p. 109; Ibn al-Haytham, *Kitāb al-manāzir*, ed. A. Sabra (Kuwait, 1983), p. 229; Puerta Vilchez, *Aesthetics in Arabic Thought*, p. 723.
[4] Puerta Vilchez, *Aesthetics in Arabic Thought*, p. 745.
[5] A. George, "The Geometry of Early Qur'anic Manuscripts", in *Journal of Qur'anic Studies* IX, 1 (2007): 78–110.
[6] Ibid.
[7] Ibn al-Nadīm, *The Fihrist of al-Nadīm*, trans. B. Dodge (New York: Columbia University Press, 1970), p 15.
[8] Documented by the fourteenth-century encyclopaedist al-Qalqashandī in *Ṣubḥ al-Aʿshá*, 2: 454–55, 3: 52–53. See the chart made by Nihad Çetin in "The Rise and Development of the Art of Calligraphy", in *The Art of Calligraphy in the Islamic Heritage* (Istanbul: IRCICA, 1998), p. 23.
[9] Only one *qasida* of 20 verses on calligraphy has been conserved by Ibn al-Bawwab: "Qaṣīda fi al-khaṭṭ wa adawātih wa taʿallumih wa taʿlīmih". This poem is quoted by Ibn Khaldun in his *Muqaddimah*. See Ibn Khaldun, *The Muqaddimah: An Introduction to History*, trans. F. Rosenthal (Princeton: Princeton University Press, 1967), 2, pp. 388–89. Later manuals compile the precepts of both Ibn Muqla and Ibn al-Bawwab.
[10] The treatise *Risāla fi'l khatt al mansūb* attributed to Ibn Muqla poses questions of authenticity, although his name is recurrent in early sources. For an analysis see George, *The Rise of Islamic Calligraphy*, pp. 134–37.
[11] For the ratios of these proportions see M. b. ʿAlī Al Rāwandī, "Faṣl fī maʿrifat uṣūl al-khaṭṭ min al-dāʾira wa al-nuqat", in *Kitāb-ārāyī dar tamaddun-i islām*, ed. N. Māyel-Hirawī (Mashhad, 1993), pp. 1–9.
[12] We wish to emphasize here that this system pertains only to the scripts known as the "classical" calligraphic styles; other scripts developed both in the Islamic West and the Far East were codified according to different criteria.
[13] For the translation and interpretation of one of the most important calligraphic treatises on this matter, see C. W. Ernst, "The Spirit of Islamic Calligraphy: Bābā Shāh Iṣfahānī's Ādāb al-mashq", in *Journal of the American Oriental Society* 112, 2 (1992): 279–86.
[14] Ibid., p. 284.
[15] From the poem by Ibn al-Bawwab cited in Franz Rosenthal's translation of Ibn Khaldun, *The Muqaddimah*, Book I, Chapter IV.
[16] F. Rosenthal, "Abū Ḥaiyān al-Tawḥīdī on Penmanship", in *Ars Islamica* 13–14 (1948): 10.
[17] Ibid., p. 286

Islamic Art Specialist and Director of the Museum
of the Institut du Monde Arabe, Paris

Reading Holy Architecture

Eric Delpont

The artistic creations of the Muslim world, like those related to science, reached the medieval West through the Crusades. What are known today as the "arts of Islam" (where "Islam" designates the civilization born after the advent of the eponymous religion) began to be analysed and theorized in Europe during the nineteenth century, when a number of collections of artworks made enthralling by a renewed taste for the Near and Middle East were created. They brought together items of furniture and architectural elements, which were qualified successively as "Arab", then "Islamic". Nevertheless, their study has long remained dependent on a Western conception of the arts founded on the image. Indeed, from Greco-Roman Antiquity and then from the Renaissance, mimetic reproduction in painting and sculpture established the criteria of taste and judgement in all of the West. These criteria, which became synonymous with *pompier* academicism, were called into question in the 1850s; the birth of photography challenged this unambiguous way of grasping the realities of the world and the imagery it aroused. At the same time, the discovery and examination of non-European arts opened new paths and perspectives.

It is in this context that the arts of Islam were credited with a strong decorative power, without this adjective being used in a pejorative sense, at a time when European industrial arts felt the need to resort to other repertoires of motifs to seduce a clientele that, thanks to the Universal Exhibitions, was growing curious about foreign cultures and lifestyles. Thus, alongside geometry and arabesque, the position and forms of writing in Arabic characters on objects – be they of the court or everyday items and, even more so, in architecture – captivated and fascinated the beholder. Indeed, no alphabet prior or contemporary to that in use in the Arab-Muslim world from the eighth century AD – Greek, Syriac, Cyrillic, or Latin – had generated such a profusion in terms of styles, formats and frames, to the point that the writing, often confused with calligraphy, is seen as a constant in the arts of Islam. And the written words would be attributed the functions assumed by the images of other civilizations.[1]

Our primary source for calligraphy is to be found in the Holy Qur'an, especially verses 3 to 5 of surah *al-'Alaq*, "Read! For your Lord is most Generous, [it is He] who teaches by the means of a pen, teaches man what he does not know", thus consecrating the status of the written word by seeming to confer on each word, even on each letter, a touch of the divine. Abbasid handwritten copies of the Holy Qur'an detail,[2] well before 'the advent of office automation, the number of surahs (114) and verses or *ayahs* (6,236), as well as that of words (77,439) and letters (323,015), according to the five philologists hired by the Iraqi governor al-Hajjaj (d. 95 AH / 714 AD).[3] Ibn al-Jawzi (510–597 AH / 1116–1201 AD) also counted the diacritics (1,015,030).[4]

Fixing in writing the text of the Revelation that the Prophet (PBUH) delivered orally in order to perpetuate the message without altering it gave rise to the need for an appropriate, legible and harmonious writing style, especially since making a copy by hand was equated with an act of piety. However, we must not lose sight of the fact that this spiritual necessity was part of the temporal dimension of the astounding expansion of Islam. In the century following the death of Prophet Muhammad (PBUH), the community of believers spread over a vast territory stretching from the shores of the Atlantic to the Great Wall of China, assimilating populations with varied languages and cultural heritages. The Umayyad Caliph 'Abd al-Malik (r. 65–86 AH / 685–705 AD) promoted Arabic as the language of administration (replacing the Greek and Persian used until that point by State services). As early as 77 AH / 696 AD, he minted a gold coin, the dinar, bearing exclusively Arabic legends including *shahada* and part of verse 33 of surah *at-Tawbah*, "He is the One Who has sent His Messenger with

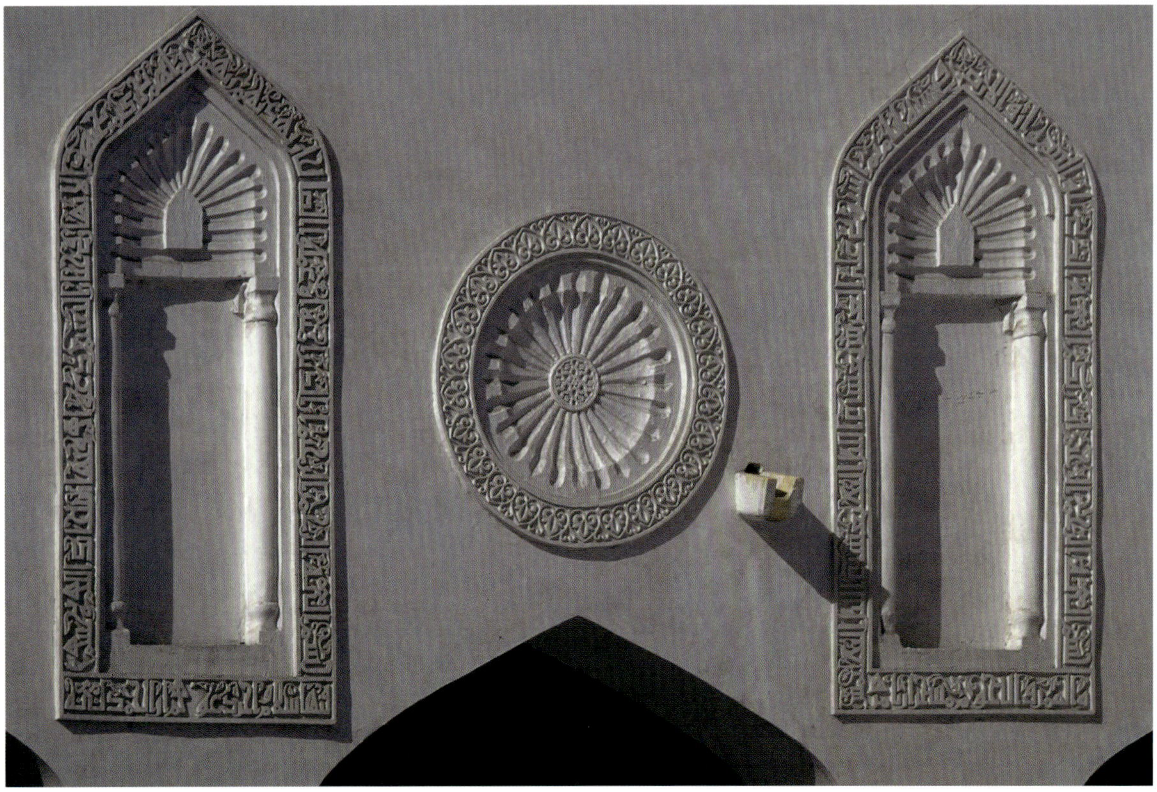

Inscribed niches of the façade in the courtyard of the al-Azhar Mosque in Cairo, built in 358 AH / 968 AD under the reign of the Fatimid Caliph al-Mu'izz

true guidance and the religion of truth, making it prevail over all others, even to the dismay of the polytheists", in an angular written form called *kufi* that was readable by all those who practised the Arabic language. In addition to coinage, which contributed to the dissemination of the Qur'anic message on a large scale and daily, even to non-Muslim populations, contemporary inscriptions on religious buildings, funerary stelae and milestones (the first milestone listed is dated back to Muharram 73 AH / May–June 692, found on the road linking Al-Quds to Damascus, the Umayyad capital) constitute the best-dated evidence of ancient written texts. As for the manuscripts or fragments of the Holy Qur'an from the first two centuries of Islam that have been passed down to us, they rarely bear the date of their copy; however, they used the same angular writing until the eleventh century AD and beyond in the Maghreb.

A SINGULAR MONUMENT, THE QUBBAT AS-SAKHRA (DOME OF THE ROCK)

The Holy Qur'an repeatedly alludes to architecture. Creation is the work of an architect, with the earth conceived as a dwelling and the firmament as a building without visible columns, as stated in verse 64 of surah *Ghafir*: "It is Allah Who made the earth a place of settlement for you and the sky a canopy", and in verse 2 of surah *ar-Ra'd*: "It is Allah Who has raised the heavens without pillars – as you can see". The perfect geometry of the Dome of the Rock – a rotunda topped with a cupola on an octagonal base – seems to echo this vision. Built by the Caliph 'Abd al-Malik and dated 72 AH / 691–692 AD in the dedicatory inscription (where his name was replaced by that of the Abbasid Caliph al-Ma'mun in 216 AH / 831 AD), it is the earliest surviving Islamic religious monument and contains the oldest known architectural inscription. In mosaic with a gold background, it displays its angular writing above the arcades of the ambulatory that surrounds the Rock, a place of mystical experience for the Prophet (PBUH), both the point of arrival of the *Isra* and the starting point of the *Mi'raj*.
In the mind of its founder, the building embodied the victory of Islam over the Byzantine enemy as well as over the Kharijite rebellion that he was then fighting. The meaning given by the founder to the motifs of trees laden with fruit and overflowing vases with clusters of gems that, inside the building, adorn the arcades of the

The first Islamic monumental inscription in the Dome of the Rock, Al-Quds, commissioned by the Umayyad Caliph in 72 AH / 691 AD

Following pages
The Ayyubid inscription on the lower drum mosaic band in the Dome of the Rock, Al-Quds, replacing a Latin inscription left by the Crusaders

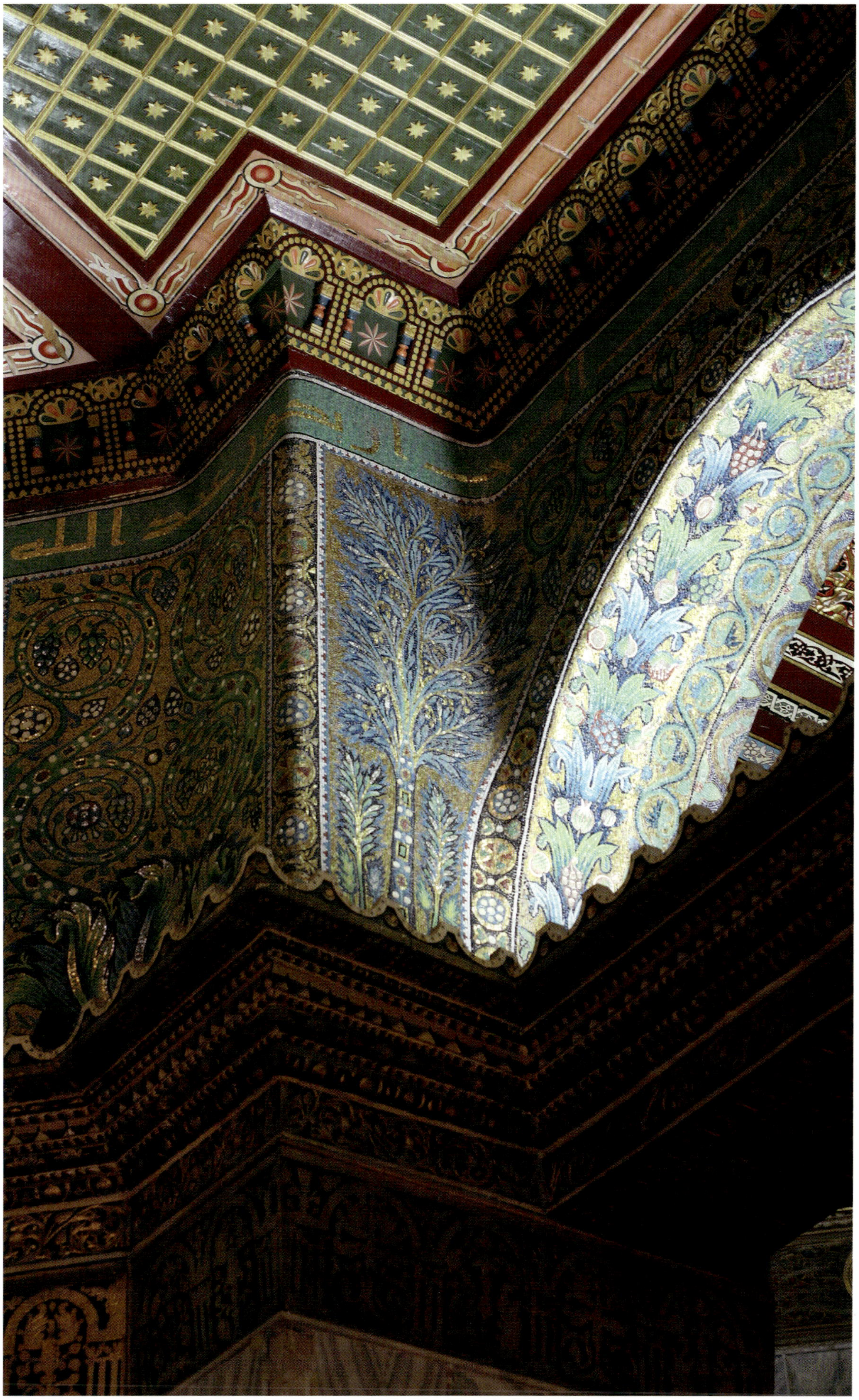

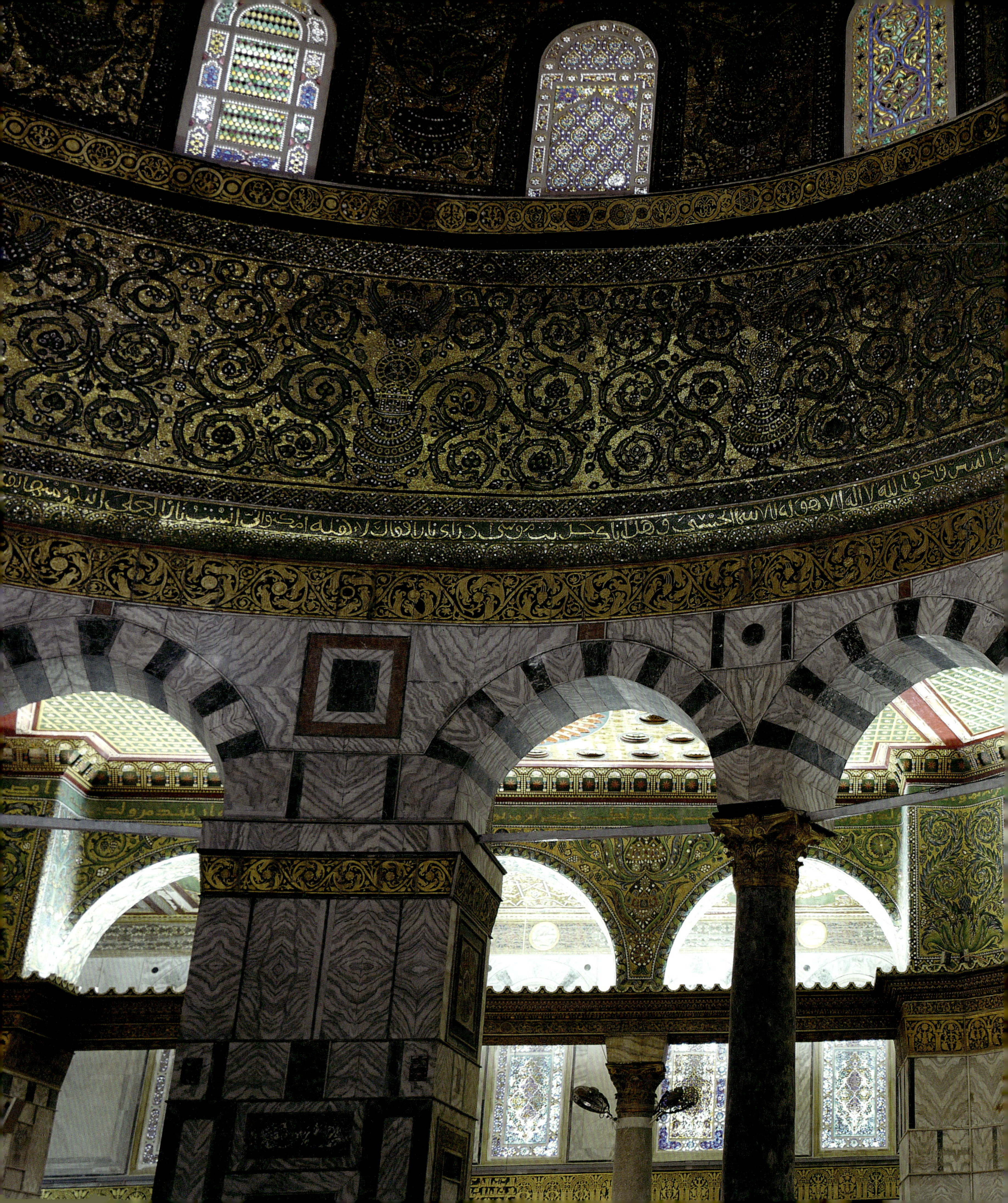

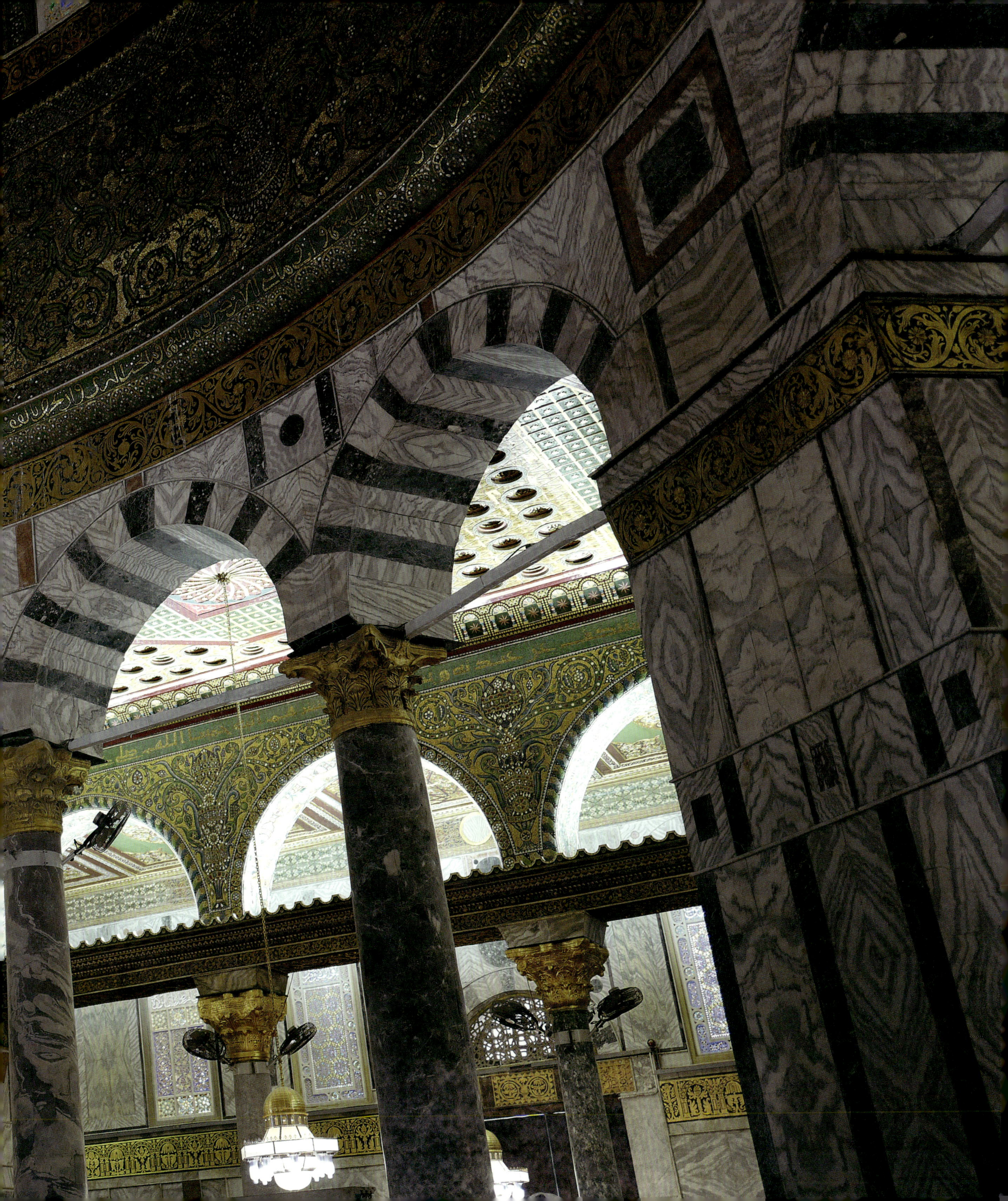

ambulatory, was soon lost. On the other hand, the inscribed bands are more explicit, with the *basmala* repeated several times, quotations of Qur'anic verses asserting God's omnipotence and the mission of His messenger (surahs *al-Baqarah* verse 255, *at-Tawbah* verse 33, *al-Qalam* verse 28, or even *as-Saff* verse 9), with whom the Caliph identifies as a successor of the Prophet (PBUH). The verses are arranged clockwise on the outer side of the arcades and counter-clockwise on their inner side. Either way, the inscription does not contain vowels and diacritical marks, which implies that it would have acted as a mnemonic sign for Muslims who had memorized passages from the Holy Qur'an. But on the other hand, it also invites a sense of circumambulation and actively participates in the architectural experience of the pilgrim/visitor.

The inscriptions dated 952 AH / 1545 AD on the external tile revetments of the octagon and drum of the Dome of the Rock, Al-Quds

Over the centuries, the Dome of the Rock has undergone multiple restorations led by the Abbasids (132–656 AH / 750–1258 AD), the Fatimids (297–567 AH / 909–1171 AD), the Ayyubids (564–659 AH / 1169–1260 AD) and the Mamluks (648–927 AH / 1250–1517 AD). These are documented in inscriptions mentioning the caliphs and sultans who commissioned them and testify to the concern that the Ayyubids and the Mamluks had to regenerate Islam and erase the imprint left on the building by the Crusaders. For example, the Ayyubid band in the lower part of the tambour that supports the dome quotes verses 1–21 of surah *Taha*, recalling the cosmological meaning of the Rock and the place of Moses in the manifestation of divine sovereignty. This mosaic inscription, in a common cursive script, would have replaced a text left by the Crusaders, who had made the Dome the place of coronation for their kings. These epigraphic testimonies also underline how the monument was perceived through the centuries, both a symbol of Islamic power and memorial for *Isra* and *Mi'raj*.

The renovation of the Dome undertaken from 935 AH / 1528 AD is however the most spectacular. While it did little to alter the interior decoration made of mosaics, engraved copper plates and marble slabs, it replaced the mosaic facing of the exterior walls, damaged over time, with a ceramic covering, which gives calligraphy a prominent place. The bands inscribed in a majestic *thuluth*, which run along the façades of the octagon and the drum of the dome, compose a real "epigraphic" programme, in which the word replaces the image.[5] The text reporting this restoration, dated 959 AH / 1552 AD, occupies the tympanum above the door on the north side of the Dome. The calligraphy is signed by 'Abd Allah al-Tabrizi. The set is completed by the four bronze-plated doors and the stained-glass windows, which are also inscribed. Singular in its form and decoration, in which calligraphy plays a major role, the Dome of the Rock remains unique in Islamic architecture.

THE EMBLEM OF THE ARAB-MUSLIM CITY: THE MOSQUE

Little is said about the actual building of mosques in the Holy Qur'an, apart from their orientation towards the *qibla*. No recommendation is given for their interior design; the sobriety of their forms and materials is rather implied. Pages of the Holy Qur'an, on parchment and on paper, found during renovation works in the Great Mosque of Sanaa some forty years ago,[6] and others preserved in the National Library of Cairo,[7] have the peculiarity of being illuminated with architectural motifs: columns supporting arches of different profiles – sometimes with "clusters" reminiscent of those of the mosaics on the Dome of the Rock – evoke the prayer rooms of the mosques known as "hypostyles", which were specifically developed by the Arab world. If specialists dispute their dates, between the eighth and tenth centuries AD, these sheets testify to an ancient link established between the text of the Revelation and architecture.

The first mosques would have followed the plan of the Prophet's (PBUH) residence, a covered space preceded by a courtyard. It is difficult to figure out today the appearance of the primitive arrangements of the Masjid al-Haram in Mecca or that of the Prophet's Mosque in Medina. Outside the Arabian Peninsula, the primitive mosques of Kufa, Wasit or Basra have disappeared. Was writing present in these buildings? From the ninth century AD, a more monumental trend established itself in the construction of places of worship in the cities that were conquered or founded as the Muslim community expanded. To the elements that mark

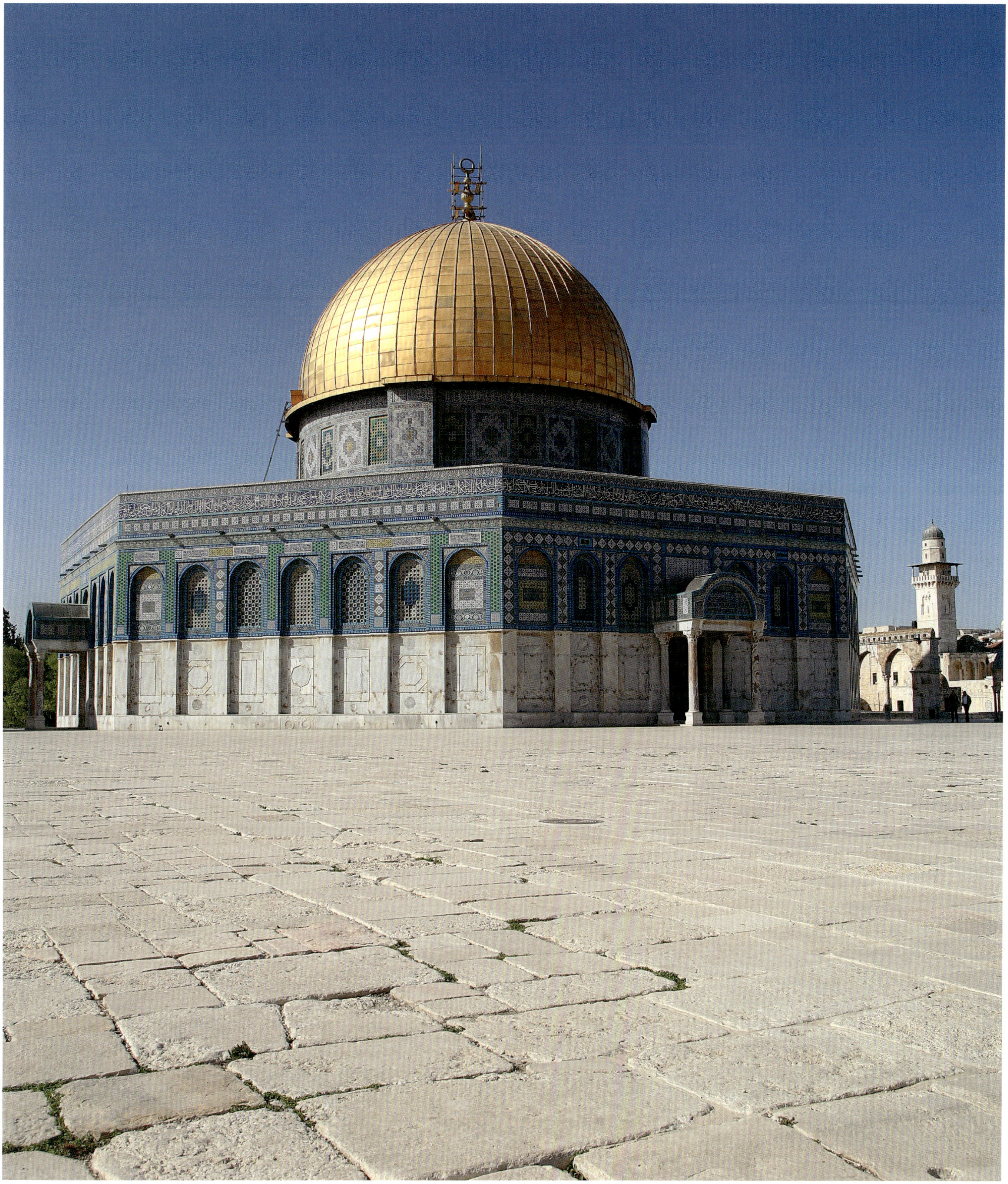

the mosque in the urban fabric – the dome surmounting the *mihrab*, the minaret and, to a lesser extent, the portal – is added the presence of script, most often in bands or panels variously distributed according to the morphology of the mosques as they were designed in space and time. However, the presence of Qur'anic inscriptions is more than tenuous in the Umayyad Mosque built in Damascus, beginning in 86 AH / 705 AD, by Caliph al-Walid I on the site of an old Christian basilica. The state of preservation of the two imposing Abbasid mosques of Samarra, in Iraq, does not allow us to appreciate the role given to quotations from the sacred text either. Inside the places of prayer, the *mihrab* and its cupola are the focal point of the deployment of the epigraphy; the inscriptions also run above the arcades of the naves in the hypostyle mosques, on the cornices, and even on the joists of the ceilings. Outside, the portal, as well as the minaret, serve as a support for the Qur'anic message. However, there are no established rules and no systematic approach to their distribution. Depending on the materials used for its construction and decoration, each mosque can be viewed as a sheet in a volume with its own particular layout. It should be remembered here that architectural practice in the classical Muslim world was a craft based on apprenticeship, as the absence of technical or theoretical writings suggests; in the Muslim world, architecture only became a professional discipline from a conceptual and practical standpoint in the sixteenth century AD.[8] It should also be noted that we do not know who then defined what is now called a commission and a programme, and how these were transmitted to artists and craftsmen. Such documents would start to appear in the royal courts from the fifteenth century AD onward.

The verses on the *mihrabs*, whether they take the form of a three-dimensional niche or a slab with a niche design, are inscribed in bands that form the niche frame and follow, or not, its profile. This is the case of the mosaic *mihrab* with a gold background in the Great Mosque of Cordoba, created during the third enlargement of the sanctuary undertaken in 350 AH / 961 AD by the Umayyad Caliph of Spain al-Hakam II, which has a double panel in *kufi* script. The stucco *mihrab* applied to one of the pillars in front of the original *mihrab* in Ibn Tulun Mosque in Cairo, commissioned by the vizier al-Afdal, probably in 491 AH / 1097 AD, is also framed by a *kufi* band and the arch of its niche is underlined by a double inscribed band. A similar arrangement prevails in the *mihrab* of other mosques either in stucco or ceramic tiles in Western and Central Asia. On the other hand, in Anatolia and Eastern Europe, the inscriptions upon and around the *mihrabs* remain scarce.

In addition to the *mihrab*, the writing emphasizes the lines of the interior architecture of the prayer halls. The morphology of the hypostyle mosque that prevails in the Arab world is characterized by colonnades establishing naves parallel or perpendicular to the wall of the *qibla*. It only has walls on three sides of the sanctuary, most often left bare, the fourth opening out onto the courtyard through a row of arcades. The inscriptions run on a single line and can be articulated with decorative bands. This is the case in the Ibn Tulun Mosque in Cairo, built in 264 AH / 878 AD: a strip of *kufi* writing, carved in wood, is placed at the top of the arcades at the junction with the flat ceiling, while the profile of the arches and their intrados are decorated with geometric and abstract vegetal designs sculpted in stucco. In 413 AH / 1022 AD, in the Great Mosque of Kairouan in Tunisia, inscriptions in foliated *kufi* were painted on the ceiling joists. It is the tie beams in pine wood linking the columns in the Fatimid Salih Tala'i Mosque, built in 555 AH / 1160 AD in Cairo, that bear the verses of the Holy Qur'an in a *kufi* script devoid of diacritics. Traces of polychromy suggest that these tie beams were originally painted, no doubt to enhance the legibility of their inscriptions. The interior space of these hypostyle mosques seems boundless horizontally, with a vertical dimension closer to the human scale, like a materialization of verses 109 and 136 of surah *al-Baqarah*.[9]

Since the beginning of the fourteenth century AD, a new type of mosque was developed whereby the prayer room was placed under several cupolas, and then under only a huge one. The inscriptions in *thuluth* or *muhaqqaq* were placed discretely on the exterior walls and distributed on the inside in rectangular panels and medallions, in ceramics or painted, which do not invite a linear reading – they lead the gaze more upwards.

In Western and Central Asia, the prayer hall was built within a hypostyle space with a wide span under a dome in the axis of the *mihrab*; it is the place where the written corpus is usually concentrated. Unlike what is observed in the Arab world, the inscriptions also cover the exterior surfaces: the cupolas and their tambours, the shafts of the minarets, the façade of the *iwans*, i.e. the rooms in half-vaulted arches on their side overlooking the courtyard of the mosque. All these inscriptions, often enhanced with a vivid polychromy unlike those of the Maghreb and the Near East, catch the eye in the environment in which the mosque stands. Another characteristic lies in the co-existence of *kufi* and cursive calligraphic compositions, all executed in brick (with or without glaze) as well as in ceramic mosaic, breaking with the unity of the style of writing prevailing elsewhere.

FOR READING AND ORNAMENTATION

In addition to mosques, other foundations contributed to the spiritual and physical well-being of the community: the *madrasa*, *zawiya* or *imaret* were created on the initiative of members of the ruling class or wealthy individuals who were sometimes buried in or near these buildings. The inscriptions on these buildings proclaim what could be termed the "social" piety of their patrons; the pious quotations were enriched with laudatory formulas to celebrate the memory of their founders, who were not always exempt from a certain worldly vanity. The bands inscribed on the façades and inside the complexes, which can combine a mosque and a hospital as in Divrigi in Anatolia (founded in 626 AH / 1228–29 AD), or a mosque, a *madrasa* and a tomb such as the Mamluk complexes that punctuate the Cairo sky with their domes and minarets, reflect the glory of their patrons engraved in stone. The legibility of the inscriptions is therefore necessary to properly identify them.

Whatever their calligraphic style, the monumental inscriptions in religious architecture seek to combine legibility with a formal play of letters in order to visually embellish the literalness of the divine message.[10] Thus, all the decorative effects that the *kufi* script generated as soon as it took over religious architecture must be reminded: the rigidity of the base line does not slow down the evolution towards very ornate forms of lettering, including the end of the upstrokes, and sometimes goes as far as to turn them into floriation in the form of leaves, palmettes or half palmettes. Those of a fragment of a stucco frieze, dated around 621 AH / 1225 AD and coming from the Dar al-Hadith founded in Cairo by the Ayyubid Sultan al-Kamil, really seem to be in motion against a background of foliated scrolls. These types of ornate *kufi* script, which are also found on funerary stelae, are not to be seen in the *kufi* used in manuscript copies of the Holy Qur'an, except, from time to time, in the titles of particularly illuminated surahs.

Arab treatises on geography and certain chronicles prior to the fifteenth century AD describe cities by considering their assets – that is to say, above all the illustrious men who were born there or practised their discipline there, in particular in the field of religious sciences. The monuments, cultural and secular, are not systematically mentioned and we learn little about those who designed and executed them. As for the monumental inscriptions, they are generally only noted by their date and the name of the sovereigns who sponsored or who reigned, without specifying their content or who made the choice when it came to Qur'anic verses. A resident of Cairo at the end of the reign of the Ayyubid sultans provides testimony to the discretion of the sources with regard to architecture.[11]

One could say that the greater or lesser ease of reading the inscriptions in pious architecture reflects the dual attitude towards the chosen texts. Their literal perception is coupled with an evocative function, appealing to the semantic memory and personal recollections of whoever looks at them and reads them.[12] In addition to conveying a message, writing in architecture provides a spiritual framework and generates a feeling of pleasantness and serenity. We can cite here the Qutb Minar erected in Delhi between 607 AH / 1211 AD

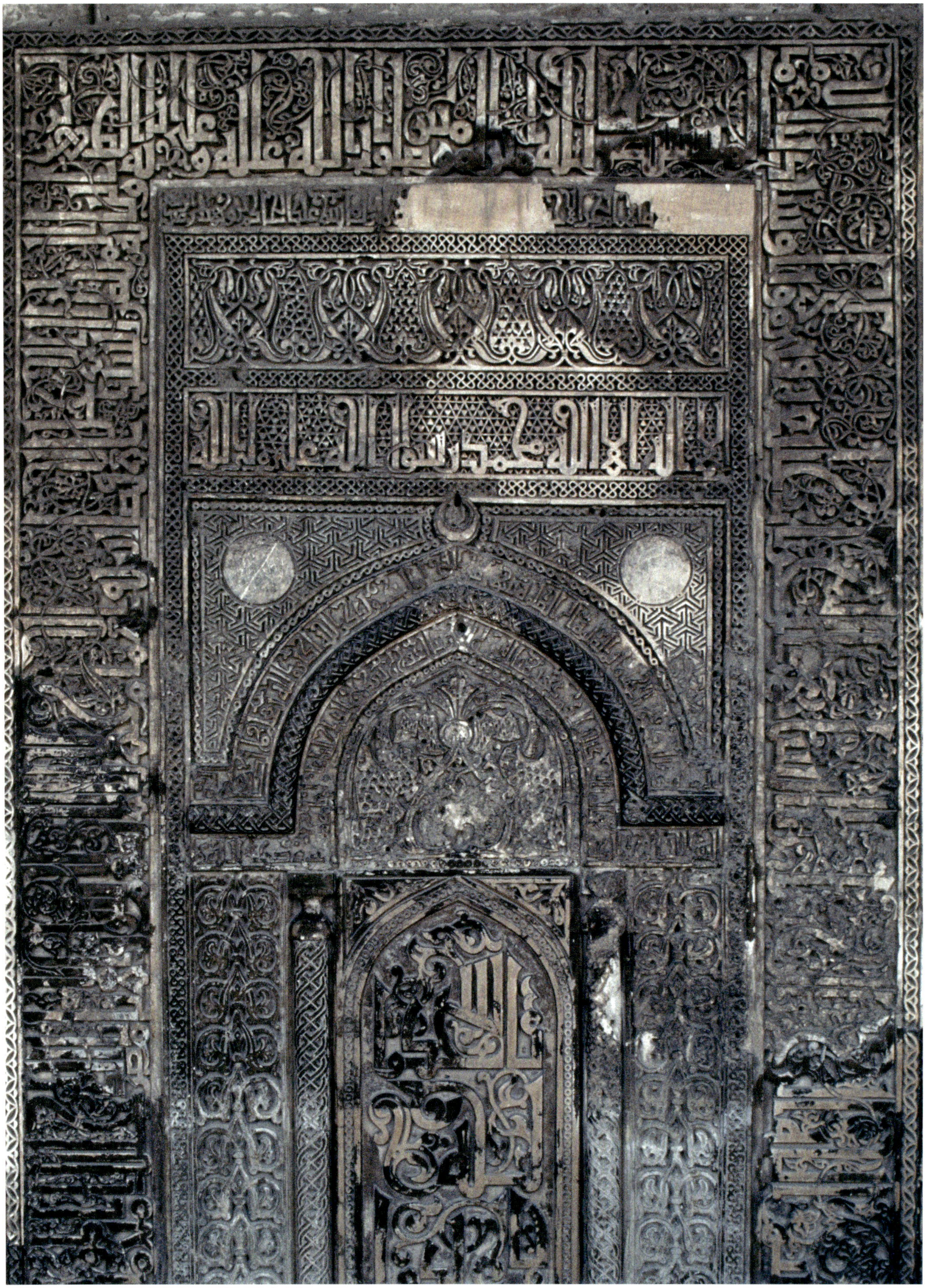

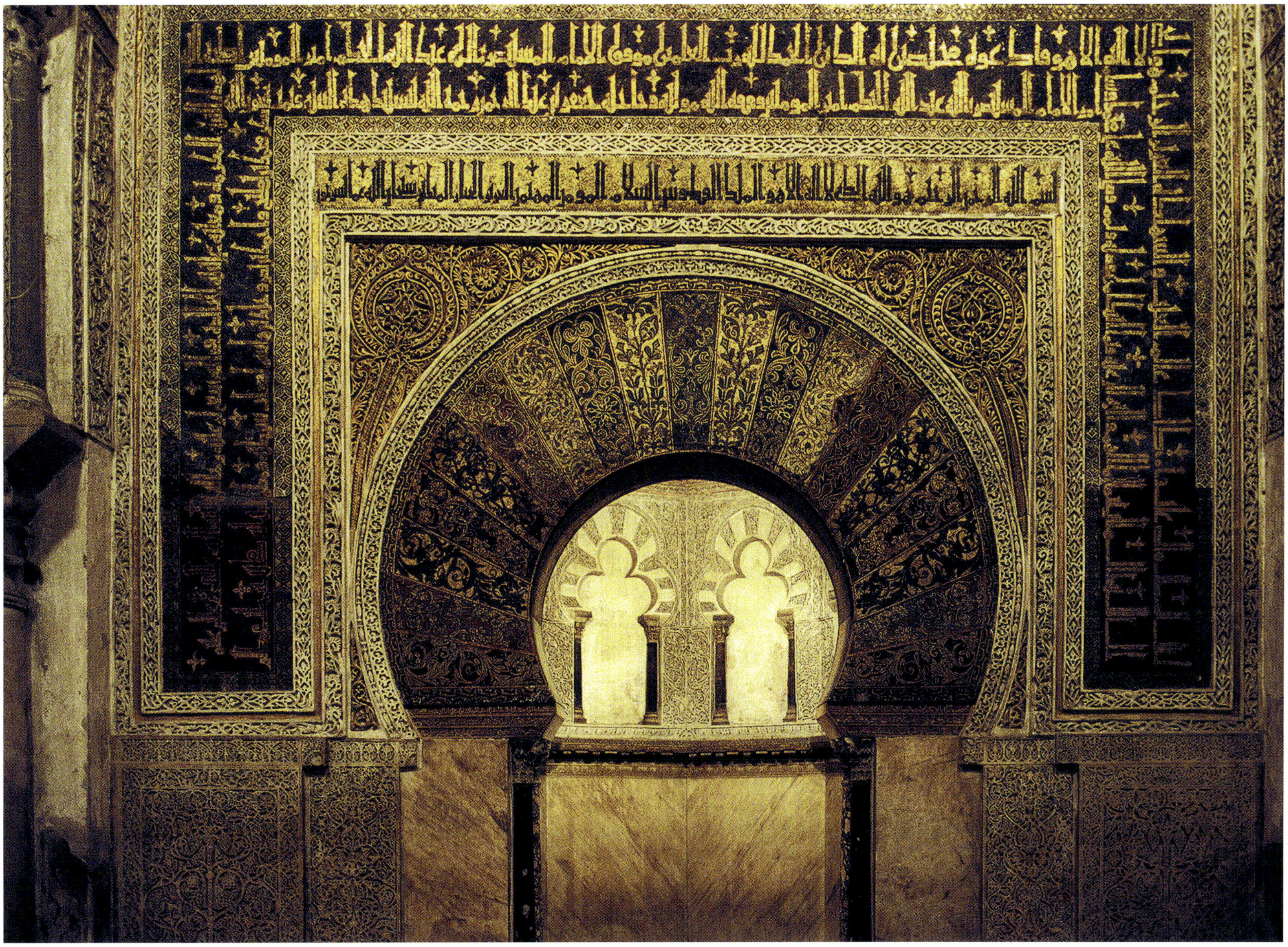

The stucco *mihrab* commissioned in 491 AH / 1097 AD by the vizier al-Afdal, installed in the Ibn Tulun Mosque of Cairo

The mosaic *mihrab* commissioned in 350 AH / 961 AD by the Umayyad Caliph of Spain al-Hakam II during the third enlargement of the Great Mosque of Cordoba

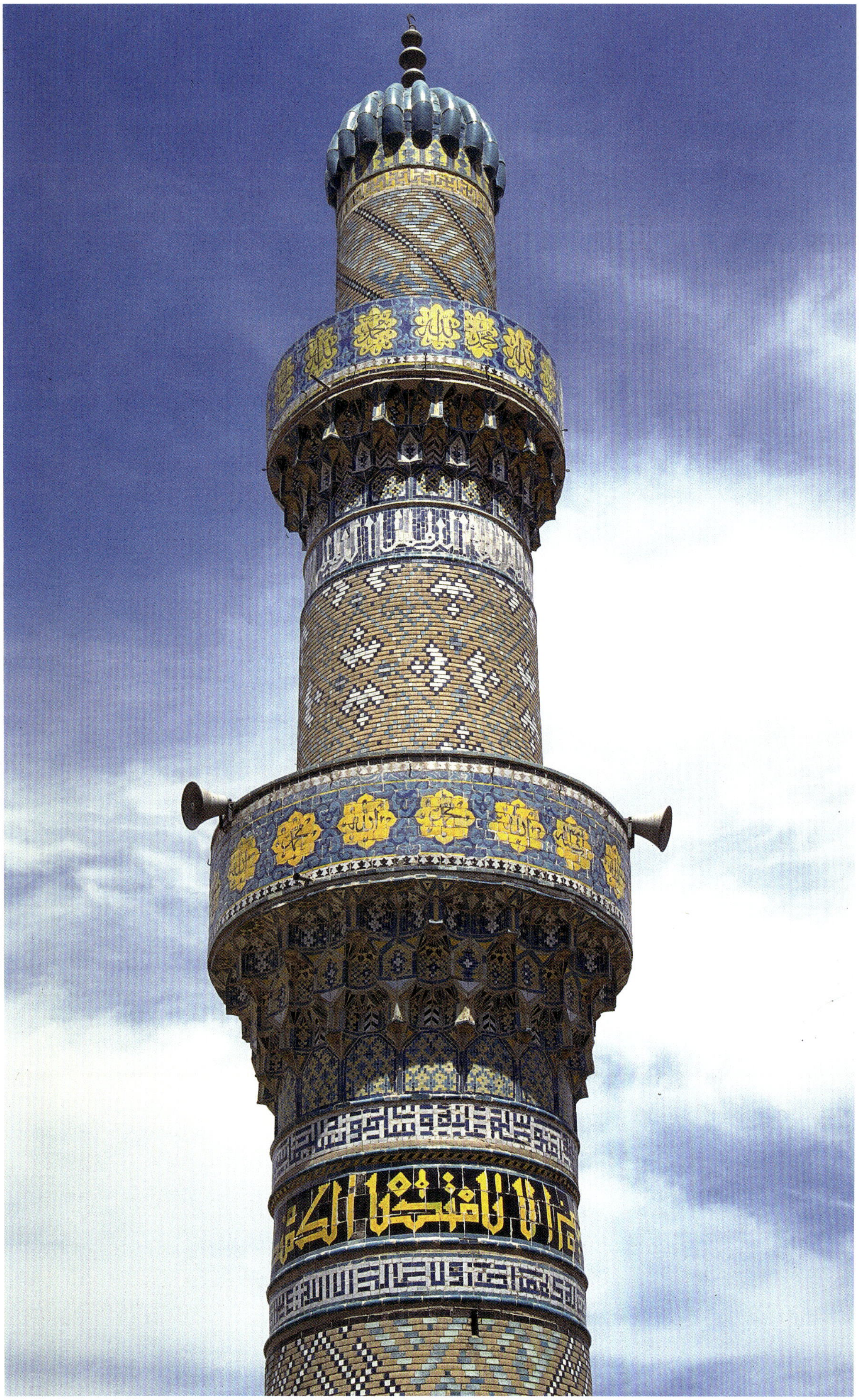

The brick tile inscribed compositions on the minaret of the al-Asafiyah Mosque and *madrasa* in Baghdad, rebuilt in 1004 AH / 1596 AD and renovated in 1241 AH / 1826 AD and 634 AH / 1236 AD, whose bands of Qur'anic verses in its upper part are no longer legible but exist as an affirmation of Islamic sovereignty. The writing also acts as a mediator, it accompanies the entry and the journey of those who go into a mosque, a *madrasa*. It awakens a feeling that goes beyond the content of the text itself.

The inscriptions of religious buildings are often associated with the art of calligraphy. This recognition is legitimate when the documentation confirms that a master drew the model that was then transposed by craftsmen working in wood, stucco, stone, brick and ceramics, mosaic. This pedigree remains rare for creations before the sixteenth century AD. We can also assume that the craftsmen, masters in their respective skills, had integrated the principles of *al-khatt al-mansub* as defined by the vizier Ibn Muqla (d. 328 AH / 939 AD), establishing a reproducible method thanks to a fixed canon for the construction of the letter. Ibn al-Bawwab (d. 413 AH / 1022 AD) had, for his part, developed types of script in a quasi-typographical sense, nevertheless allowing variations that would contribute to the existence of ornamental formulas specific to the whole Muslim world, with regional styles emerging from North Africa to China.

The piety of the faithful who frequent the monuments of pious architecture endows them with life. They are likely to undergo transformations in connection with the evolution of the practices and tastes of believers. Unlike objects that, faced with such an evolution, can be sold, stored, or destroyed, the investment required for a construction is a long-term commitment. The inscriptions are the first to bear witness to these transformations, through their content and their style. Modern mosque architecture also uses scripts, more or less successfully, with an often historicist tendency during the past century. Nowadays, the designers of contemporary places of worship remodel the calligraphic inscriptions, which turn out to be a structural element of space through materials and light. Their aim is to fulfil the faithful's expectations regarding readability and feeling.

[1] E. Dodd, "The Image of the World", in *Berytus* 18 (1969).
[2] O. Grabar, *L'Ornement. Formes et fonctions dans l'art islamique* (Paris: Flammarion, 2013), p. 96.
[3] F. Déroche, *The Abbassid Tradition: Qur'ans from the 8th to the 10th Centuries AD. The Nasser D. Khalili Collection of Islamic Art*, vol. 1 (London, 1992). Three Holy Qur'ans of this collection, copied respectively in the Near East or North Africa at the end of the ninth or the beginning of the tenth century AD (KFQ 45, folios 1b–2a), in Iraq around 1000–50 AD (QUR 284, folio 1a) and in Iran in the late eleventh century AD (QUR 89, folio 1a), give a detailed account of words and letters.
[4] Ibn al-Jawzī, *Funūn al-afnān fī 'uyūn 'ulūm al Qur'ān* (Beirut, 1987), pp. 245–52.
[5] G. Necipoğlu, "The Dome of the Rock as Palimpsest: 'Abd al-Malik's Grand Narrative", in *Muqarnas* XXV (2008): 17–107.
[6] Grabar, *L'Ornement*, pp. 215–30.
[7] B. Moritz, *Arabic Paleography* (Cairo, 1905; reprint Osnabrück, 1986), pls. III–IX.
[8] N. Rabbat, "Design without Representation in Medieval Egypt", in *Muqarnas* XXV (2008): 147–55.
[9] U. Vogt-Göknil, *Mosquées* (Paris: Chêne, 1975).
[10] Grabar, *L'Ornement*, pp. 114–16.
[11] Rabbat, "Design without Representation".
[12] O. Grabar, *Penser l'art islamique. Une esthétique de l'ornement* (Paris: Albin Michel, 1996).

Founding Director of the
Khatt Foundation, Amsterdam

The Spiritual Dimensions of Contemporary Art and Design

Dr. Huda Smitshuijzen AbiFarès

In the two years preceding this exhibition, human civilization has come face-to-face with its own vulnerability and fragility. Environmental as well as socio-political conflicts have flared all over the globe. The interdependence of nations across the world failed to secure permanent collaboration and stable relationships. At this particular moment in history, it is natural for people to seek solid and authentic values that can provide them with inspiration and motivation to persevere. Looking inwards and beyond the immediate present becomes a survival strategy for healing and rebuilding one's inner strength.

The endeavour to reconnect with one's cultural heritage, to re-engage and re-evaluate traditional and age-old social practices, has permeated the recent scene of contemporary art and design. The incorporation of traditional crafts in contemporary design and the reviving of collective creative practices in an ever more individualistic world have spawned new progressive collaborations. Designers and visual artists are often individuals who create work that both represents the pulse of their respective era and goes beyond it to imagine a better future. They engage with daily strife in their imagination, bringing forward unexpected solutions and uncovering often unnoticed concerns.

Spirituality and the power of belief uphold humanity's ability to endure, find peace, and recover. These are some of the underlying themes addressed in this exhibition. The notions of Light, Letter, Space, and Poetry embody universal and spiritual values that frame the works on display and group them together to spark a potent and thought-provoking dialogue. Arabic script and calligraphy play a central role as the binding agent of disparate objects, from different time periods and of diverse nature. This use of the Arabic script in contemporary art and design testifies to the lasting spiritual power we attribute to both the "word" and its visual embodiment into a "script" – for the Arabic script is both a medium for communication and a vehicle for beauty and spirituality.

The contemporary art pieces and design objects scattered amongst the classical Islamic artworks display an array of concepts and explore various media. They directly engage with the historical and classical calligraphy in their vicinity; they revisit ancient myths and demonstrate the continuum of spiritual concepts that have travelled across generations and cultural geographies; they demonstrate the continuity and the innovation of contemporary Islamic culture as they unveil lasting universal values.

MANIPULATING LIGHT

For most living beings, physical and material light is essential to their growth and health as well as their very existence. Like most living beings, humans are fascinated by light, which invariably draws them to itself. But for human beings, light possesses an additional spiritual dimension, for it is equated with enlightenment, wisdom and the soul; it is at the core of the myth of creation and marks the genesis of the world, giving it form and definition. The Holy Qur'an describes God (The Almighty) as "the light of the heavens and the earth" (surah *an-Nur*, verse 35).

Light seems immaterial, yet it travels at speeds faster than anything in the universe. According to Albert Einstein's theory, matter becomes infinite if its mass approaches the speed of light. People have tried since the dawn of human civilization to study light, slow it down, capture it, manipulate it, and eventually reproduce it in imaginative and man-made objects. Light art and calligraphy drawn with light are some of the ways employed by

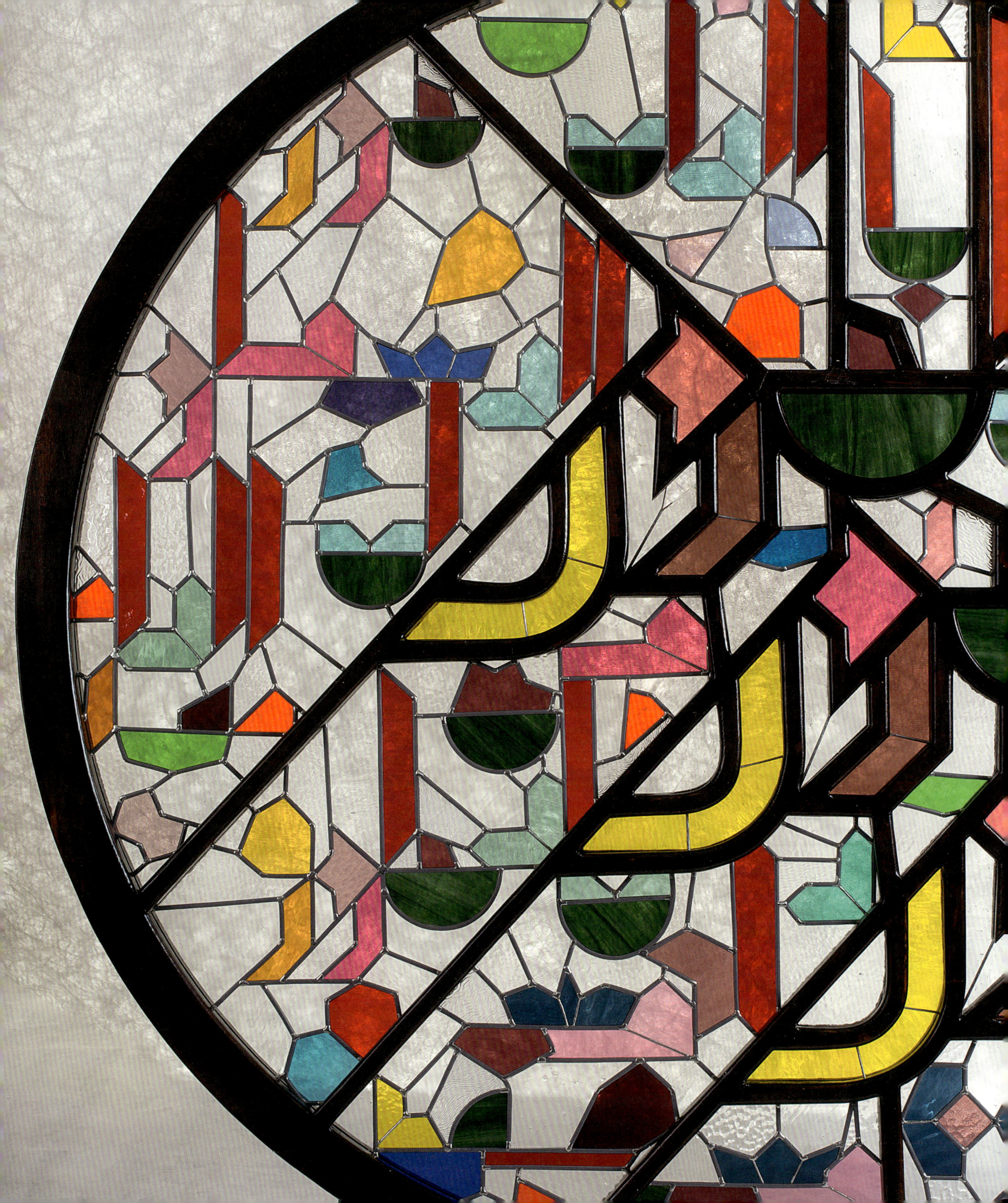

Sara Ouhaddou
An-Nur, 2022
(detail of cat. 1)

modern and contemporary artists and calligraphers to challenge our perception and experience of our own environment, exploring various materials from natural lights to man-made lights (led lights, screens, and neon) and coloured glass.

Light creates and diffuses or abolishes shadows; it represents the interdependence of body and soul, of the material and immaterial worlds. This duality of "physical" and "spiritual" in light is thoroughly explored in the contemporary arts and designs hosted by the exhibition, where the "personal" is connected with the "collective" to create poetic and thought-provoking works. Words like "*Allah*" (God), "*nur*" (light), "*ihna*" (Egyptian slang for *nahnu*, we), and various iterations of verses and prayers populate the works, establishing a dialogue between them through writing and calligraphy. Calligraphy presents itself here as a bridge that connects heaven and earth, past and present, spanning across styles and geographies, as it is embodied by way of immaterial light and supporting materials (like glass, wood, ceramics, and paper).

Working with light through glass, Sara Ouhaddou created a multi-coloured stained-glass disk that hovers in mid-air, generating coloured shadows of abstract shapes – in fact, Arabic letters – assembled out of modular parts of coloured glass held together by a complex structure made of cedar wood and metal that delineates the shapes of the letters and holds them in place. We perceive the meaning first and foremost through shapes and colours before we can recognize and read the letters. In this work, the Arabic letters' symbolic meaning is prioritized over their linguistic function. With this work simply entitled *An-Nur* (*al-nur*, light) (cat. 1), Ouhaddou refers to the Islamic stained-glass windows of mosques and palaces from across the historical Islamic world.

In traditional Islamic architecture, light does not only pass through the glass to create a spiritual space for contemplation, it is also manipulated to control how much of it gets through. In the traditional techniques of *mashrabiyya* and *mangur*, complex and intricately assembled wooden screens are used to shield from excessive light without blocking it completely. The light passing through them casts ornamental moving shadows that animate private inner spaces. They also provide one-way visibility, preserving the privacy of the personal space and allowing those inside the building to see without being seen. In the *mashrabiyya* of Susan Hefuna's work *Ihna* (We) (cat. 14), the artist refers to this duality of material (wood) versus immaterial (light) and the duality of the personal versus the collective identity. She explores collaborations with Egyptian artisans yet incorporates conceptual messages and written text into what is traditionally known as abstract arabesque motifs.

Light can also be explored in ceramics, where the white surfaces refract the light and create fascinating reflections that mirror the surrounding environment and change according to context. Khaled Ben Slimane's ceramic sculptures, inscribed in free-form calligraphy with the word *Howa* (He) (cat. 2) in reference to God (Allah, The Almighty), express his quest for spirituality. His calligraphy dances around the objects: the letters dripped and melted under the fired glaze seem to be in perpetual movement, and like the material itself, they obliquely allude to God – the source of eternal light.

UNPACKING THE LETTER

"Arabic calligraphy is the geometry of the Spirit."[1]

Arabic calligraphy, as practised by calligraphers, is a spiritual act of devotion as much as it is a performance of artistic discipline. It is characterized by a set of basic principles, some of which apply across regional contexts while others are more style-specific. Its visual fluidity masks the control and mastery it exacts from the calligrapher. It follows age-old conventions of harmonious proportions, repetitive shapes and balanced rhythms. The strife for perfection is matched with creative license and imagination. Islamic art's holistic tradition of inscribing everyday objects with calligraphic motifs and designs is founded on the notion of spiritual geometry, which is applied to both the basic elements of letterforms and the abstract modules that form arabesque patterns applied to architectural space as well as a wide range of materials. This holistic approach has returned in the form of a culturally grounded practice of contemporary art and design from the Arab/Islamic world. In this vein, the pieces in the exhibition explore the spiritual geometry inherent in the construction of Arabic letterforms and in the ubiquitous modular arabesque patterns.

Geometry stands as a universal value, bringing order to the universe and a mystical logic to astronomy. In Timo Nasseri's sculptures entitled *The Unknown Letters* (cat. 17), the letters are plucked from the stars, their geometry corresponding to that in the heavens. The artist explores the myth of the missing letters of the Arabic alphabet that remained in the mind of their creator, the ninth-century AD master calligrapher and vizier Ibn Muqla. This myth is rediscovered and reimagined centuries later, leading to the creation of four more letters that could have existed: Nasseri's hypothesis is that Ibn Muqla found the letters in constellations of stars. In order to reconstruct them, the artist researched the stars' ancient position in the sky above Baghdad using astronomical measuring tools from that period and attempting to extract the letterforms from those maps. This work thus creates a link between letters and the spiritual mathematics that govern the universe. They literally give body and physical presence to the immaterial world beyond. Cast in wood and standing tall, *The Unknown Letters* are a monumental veneration of the Arabic script and its mystical dimension.

Ibn Muqla had developed a system for proportional scripts that was based on sacred geometry. In this system, every Arabic letter is constructed in relation to a circle and its diameter (*nidham al-da'ira*) and the point (*nuqta*) traced by the pen (*qalam*), the latter being the ultimate means for precise measurement that defines the proportions of each letter. In his contemporary calligraphic piece, Nasser Al Salem hypothesizes, *What if the Circle Disappeared?* (cat. 55) – a philosophical question that goes well beyond the simplicity of its statement. He writes: "In Arab culture, the circle is the beginning and end of every shape" and the measure of all letters, "it is the initiator of countless different geometric shapes and is also the basis of the tool [that was] used in the study of the sky before the world was recognized as circular in shape". Al Salem selected the ancient *kufi mushafi* style that pre-dated diacritic dots and marks to write his question, which clearly transcends the obvious answer that without dots, the Arabic letters are difficult to read; he questions the possibility itself to communicate clearly and to connect to others via text and language. Is the circle meant for the dots on the letters, for the geometry of the universe, or for planet Earth? If one or all of these disappeared, then the calamity would be large, and creation itself would be threatened. This work alludes to the environmental and cultural issues we face today and uses mystical geometry to discuss universal themes.

Working with light and the spiritual geometry of the Arabic letterforms, Abdelrahman Elshahed's *Wise Text* (cat. 23) explores the creative potential and complexity of the Arabic script. The artist develops basic units of language, words written with light, words that transcend time and space and allude to a wide range of meditation and introspection practices. Enclosed in their circular space, *da'ira*, the words reference the sacred geometry and proportions established by Ibn Muqla. Lama Abdulrahman's piece *Noon* (cat. 18) exposes the underlying sacred geometry behind the construction of this Arabic letter, unpacking its essence and proposing an imaginary underlying structure that reveals an abstract work of art. While Lama's pieces are light and translucent, the letter *Noon* in Samir Sayegh's work (cat. 20) is solid and monumental; it dissolves into a pure abstraction of shapes and colours, implying a third dimension beyond the surface of what is represented. The letter becomes pure meaning of and by itself, it refers to itself and invites the viewer to contemplate it and extract from it a personal significance that speaks directly to the heart. His letter takes on a symbolic implication that goes beyond the linguistic sense to reveal a subtle cosmic spirituality.

The notion of spiritual symbolism is explored through imaginary, wordless manuscript-like compositions in Noor Saab's prints *The Voyage of a Word on a Spread* (cat. 21). The meaning of each piece is emphasized at the macro-level by the geometry and architecture of the page; then the geometry is further employed at the micro-level to create elaborate and complex arabesque patterns, each starting from a word: *qalam* (pen), *khatt*

Susan Hefuna
Ihna, 2009
(detail of cat. 14)

Following pages
Timo Nasseri
The Unknown Letters, 2015–17
(detail of cat. 17)

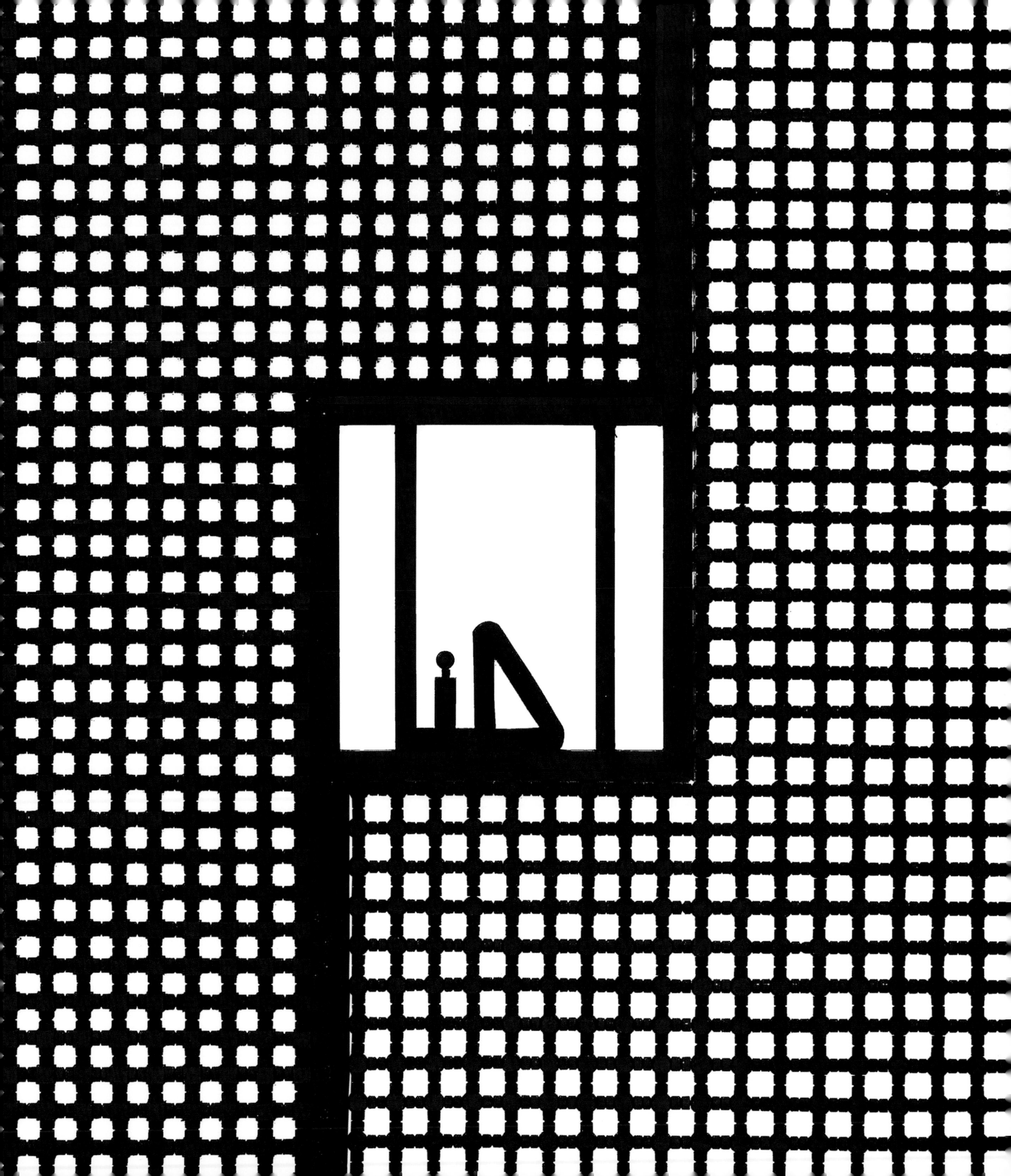

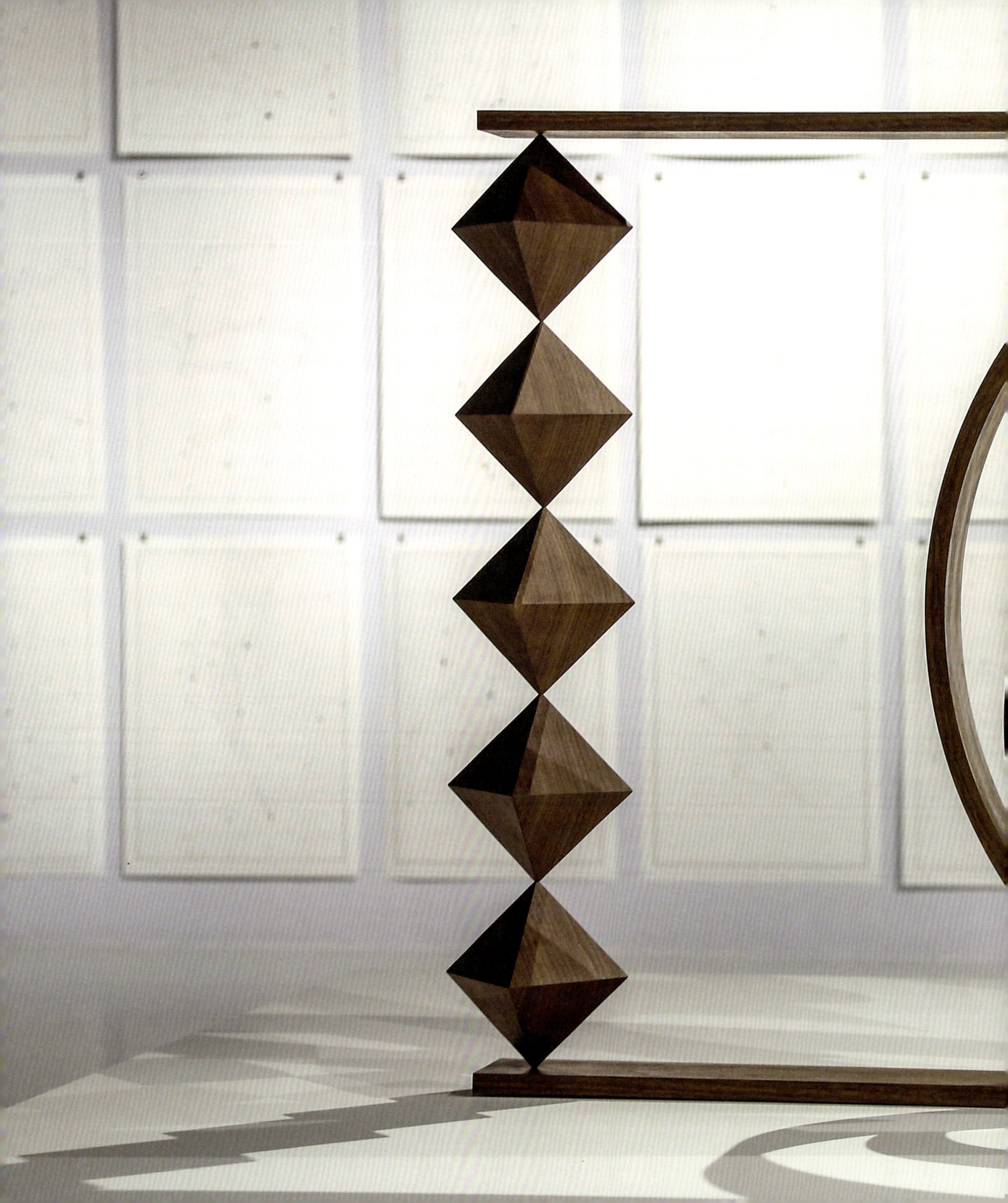

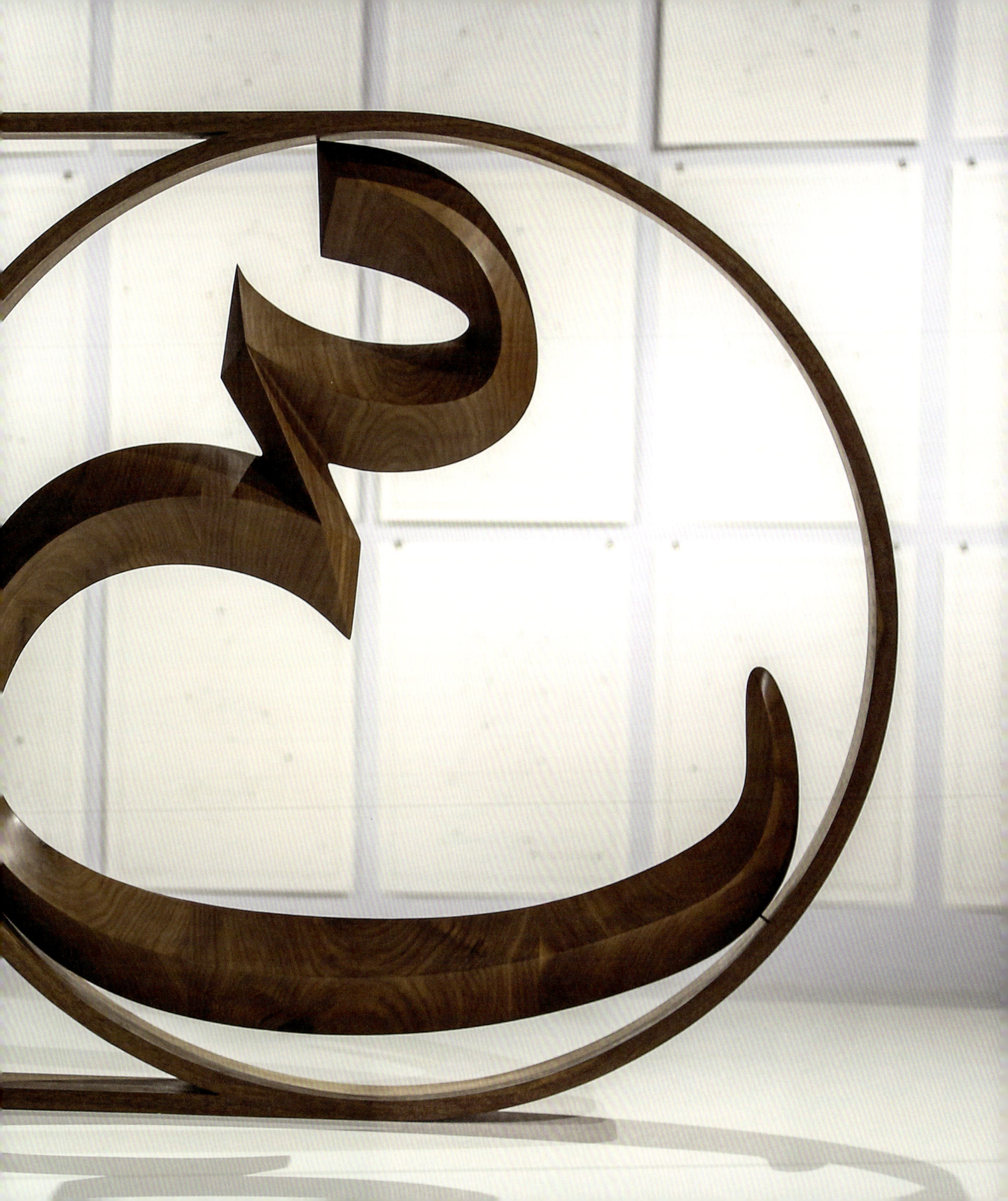

Lara Assouad
Companions of the Road, 2022
(detail of cat. 19)

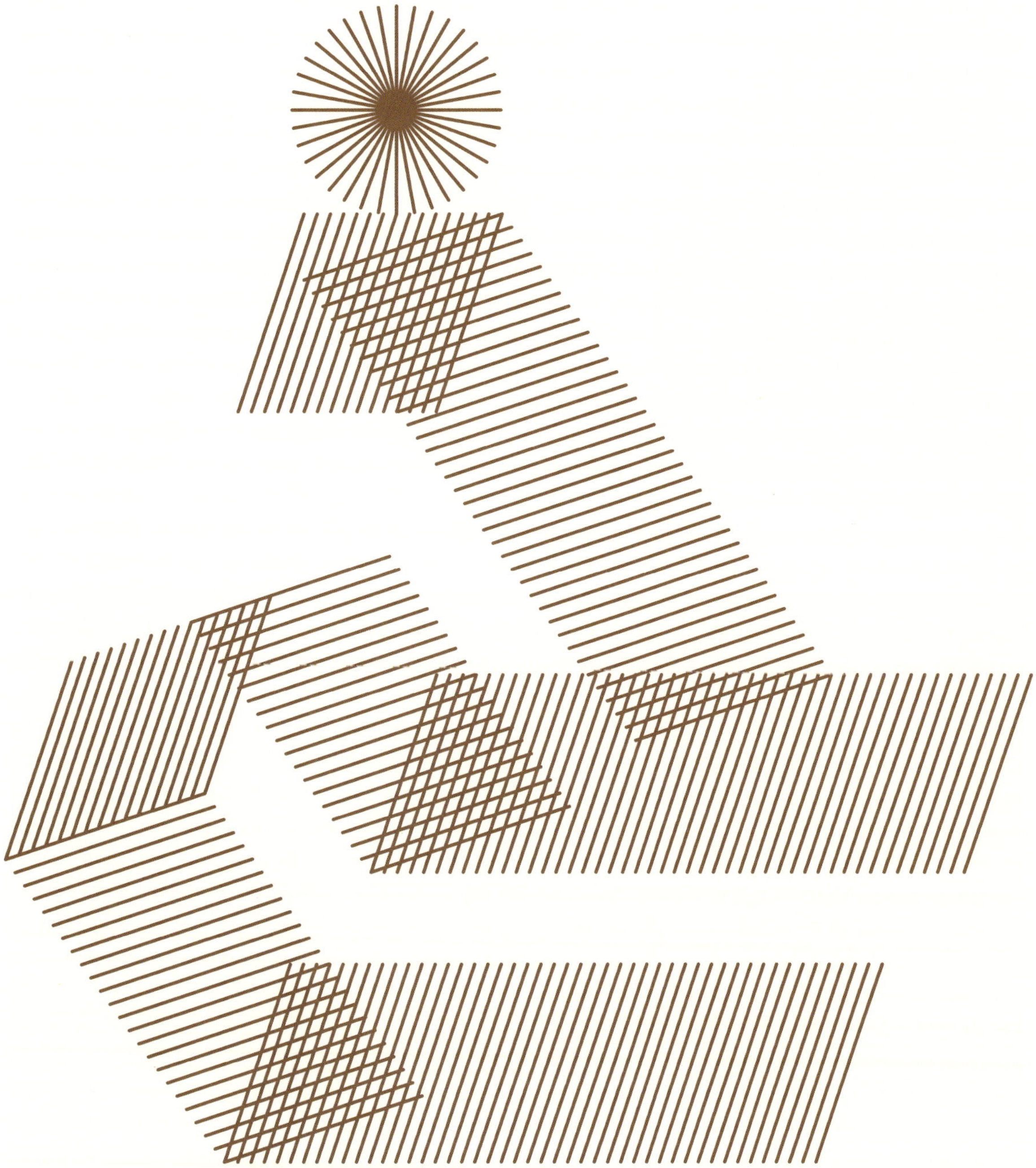

(calligraphy), *baraka* (blessing). We "read" the pages visually without recognizing that underlying the arabesque patterns is a module composed of one word, drawn in a modern ornamental square *kufi* style. By hiding the words in meditative and repetitive patterns, the artist invites viewers to enter a spiritual space and experience the message beyond the literal linguistic meaning of a text.

Similarly, Lara Assouad's work, *Companions of the Road* (cat. 19), takes on the intimate and emotional dimension of our relationship with the Arabic script as its point of departure. She presents us with "letters that we carry with us, on us, as a reminder of values we want to embody and live by". Her letters are like "loved ones we hold dear to our hearts and want to remember as we go through our lives' journeys". She plucks her letters from historical artefacts that have been used in personal and intimate ways (textiles, astrolabes, jewellery, miniature Qur'ans…), objects carried along or worn on the bodies of their owners along their travel routes and spiritual pilgrimages. Assouad's letters take their shapes from their material support and function; they link the spiritual with the secular, the holy with the human experience of it.

EXPANDING SPACE

Going beyond the page, letters in the Islamic tradition have been applied to all forms of support. They adorn various objects and endow public and private spaces with a poetic and spiritual dimension. The Arabic script has become emblematic of the Islamic built environment and continues to be so until today. In recent years a renewed interest in Arabic lettering and calligraphy has been embraced in all aspects of contemporary art and design. The works in this exhibition were selected to reflect this trend. They engage with the personal space of contemplation and meditation, the inner spiritual space invoked by holy scripture and prayer, the inner journey of the artist, and the collective space of places of worship.

Yusef Alahmad's silkscreen prints *Guide to Goodness* (cat. 81) take inspiration from the historical printed books and manuscripts of the *Dala'il al-Khayrat* (Guidelines to the Blessings and the Shining of Lights, giving the saying of the blessed prayer over the Prophet) (PBUH), a collection of prayers and a manual of devotion to the Prophet (PBUH); carrying the manuscript and reciting the prayers it contains is thought to provide blessing (*baraka*), good luck and protection. Alahmad remixes visual elements commonly found in these manuscripts, such as geometric interlacing patterns, illustrated iconography and fluid prayer passages using a limited colour palette and presents viewers with his personal interpretation of spiritual guidance in our contemporary context. Similarly inspired by historical Hajj certificates and maps, Doa Bugis and Sara Al Abdali's prints (cat. 49) reinterpret these spiritual artefacts in a contemporary fashion. Continuing on the theme of navigation and guidance, Bayan Barboud creates a three-dimensional calligraphic installation of a *qibla* using sound, light and calligraphy (cat. 54).

The Holy Qur'an represents the divine word first transmitted through recitation before being inscribed 300 years later into *masahif* (codexes). This spoken word, therefore, goes to the core of Islamic spirituality and culture. A reverence for both recitation and the written word has always permeated Islamic culture and worship practices. The auditory aspect of prayer that delineates a spiritual boundary and experience is explored in Sara Alharbali's work *Revelation Spectrogram of Surah al-'Alaq (The Clot)* (cat. 61). This surah is presented as a visual mapping of its recitation's sound waves, which conjure a "language" that can be felt and understood as universal.

The notion of sound and repetition as a means for prayer and meditation is also reflected in Faig Ahmed's installation *The Alif and Rhythm* (cat. 75), which consists of an oversized 999-bead *misbah* (rosary), a large manuscript-style book of repeated *alifs*, and a video. It is a performative work whereby viewers are confronted in total darkness with a space of meditation, where the artist performs his flipping of the pages of the book in a steady rhythm (mirroring the rhythm of the letters on the pages), thus capturing the cosmic breath of the universe. Prayer also features in the representation of places of worship in Nada Debs's *Tajawuz* (Transcendence)

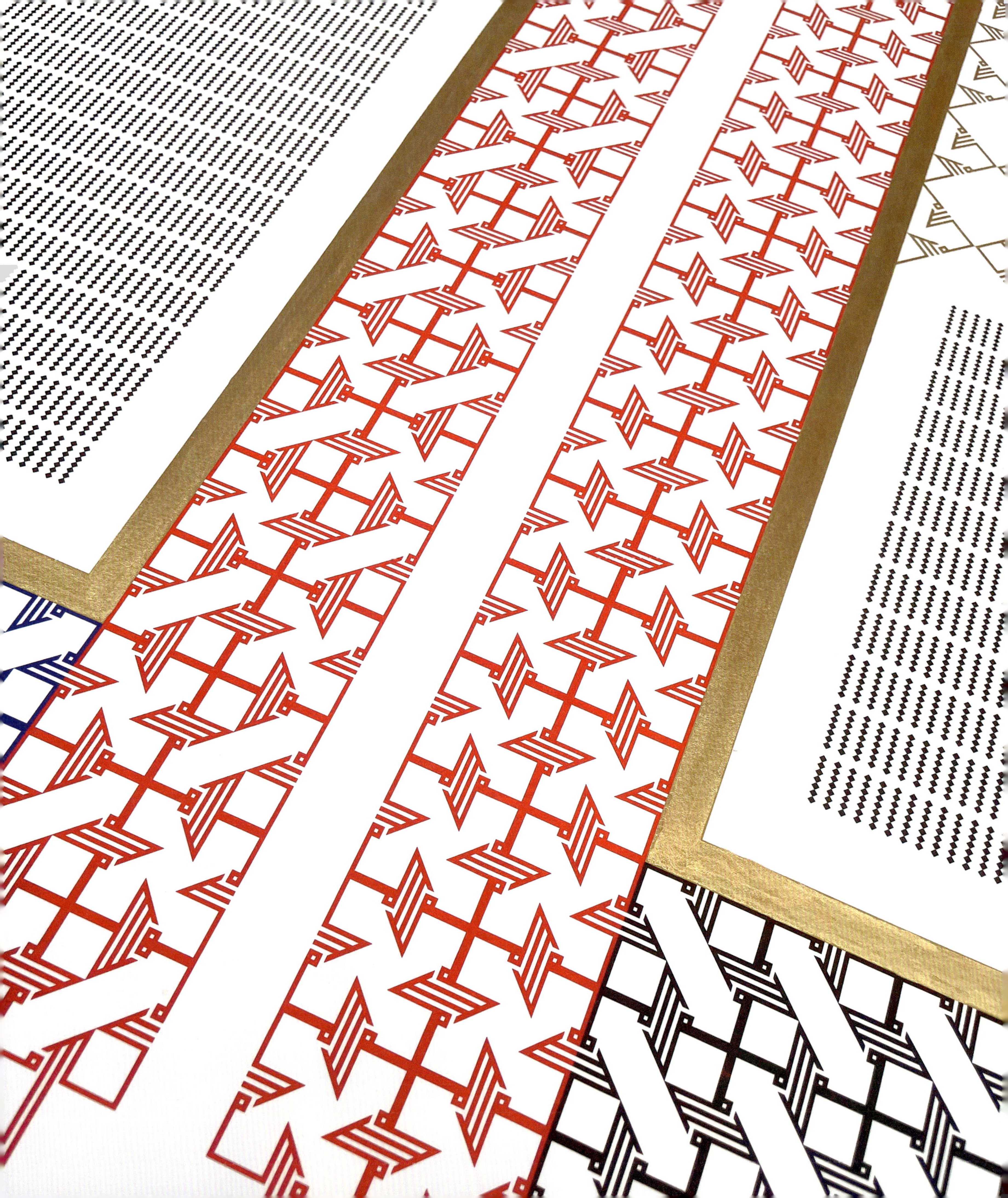

Noor Saab
The Voyage of a Word on a Spread, 2022
(detail of cat. 21)

prayer mat (cat. 63). Repetition and rhythm are reflected in the universal symbolism of spiritual spaces across religions, with arches symbolizing the dome of the heavens. The designer transformed the personal prayer space of a human-sized carpet into a one-and-a-half dimensional design (a relief weaving technique) that visualizes the experience of transcendence through prayer. The surface of the textile thus becomes a space with a stair-like gateway into another dimension.

Delineating personal spaces of meditation is also explored in the work of Hala Kaiksow. Her textile installation, *Al-Thureya* (cat. 77), addresses the spiritual experience of looking into the space within oneself. The repetitive act of hand-weaving is in itself a form of meditation through natural materials. The designer explores notions of origin and roots, lineage and motherhood as a space within which life begins. She reflects on her personal experience and connects it to larger shared universal stories of women, inscribing a personal narrative in the form of upside-down hanging vegetal roots embroidered with personal texts.

POETIC INSPIRATIONS AND JOURNEYS

Poetry holds an elevated position as an art form in Arab and Islamic cultures. Its oral tradition is mythical, having fired up the imagination of many artists and calligraphers over the centuries. The musical rhythms, the layered meanings, and the play on words inherent in poetry are some of the characteristics that have inspired the works in this exhibition.

In Yazid Kheloufi's sculpture *Naffas* (cat. 84), the "breath" of the universe is invoked. It speaks of the human breath as not only the essential respiration of the body but also that of the soul, conveying the poetics of the Arabic language whereby words that sound similar also have conceptual connections: for example, *al-nafas* (breath) sounds like *al-nafs* (self or soul). The piece employs a calligraphic style often used for engraving in stone and is designed like an epitaph on a tombstone. Poetry is more directly approached in Farah Behbehani's artist book, *The Conference of the Birds* (cat. 85). The artist explores Farid al-Din Attar's poem by the same name in which each of the birds represents a different human type, and much of the poem consists of stories told by their leader in answer to their objections or questions about a journey towards spiritual enlightenment. The artist created a calligraphic reading of the poem, drawing each bird in *jaly diwani* using their name in Arabic combined with a verse from the poem that captures the essence of each bird. The book turns the text into visual poetry, which goes beyond the linguistic dimension and adds a visual allegory that reflects the artist's personal interpretation.

Poetry in jewellery design is rather uncommon, but Azza Fahmy's work is a beautiful exception (cat. 90). Her installation displays her personal journey as jewellery designer, using Arabic calligraphy to inscribe her work with poetry that adorns and protects the body and inspires the soul. She is renowned for extracting symbols and forms from diverse sources to create pieces of jewellery that document and present the region's cultural and visual heritage to the world. She finds inspiration in history, the built environment, music, and above all, poetry. In her designs, she transforms the spiritual (poetry and calligraphy) into pieces of refined craftsmanship with a lot of soul.

To conclude, whether inscribed, woven, embroidered, drawn, painted, printed, or sculpted, the scripts and letterforms in this exhibition reveal subtle and thought-provoking interpretations and reflections on spiritual dimensions in contemporary art and design. These artistic works bring forth age-old values that remain of relevance and that uphold individuals in persevering and finding peace and meaning in their everyday strife. Art and design can offer a space for us to find our inner peace and sense of protection in a tumultuous and often overwhelming world.

[1] S. H. Nasr, *Islamic Art and Spirituality* (Albany: SUNY Press, 1987), p. 18.

Poet and Writer

Letters Embracing One Another in the Mirror of Self

Dr. Issa Makhlouf

IN THE STUDIO OF KHODEIR EL-BORSAIDY

Darkness falls. We are headed towards the heart of historical Cairo, on Al-Mu'izz Street in the al-Jamaliya District, towards the studio of Egyptian calligrapher Khodeir El-Borsaidy. A neighbourhood of mosques, monuments, markets and cafés, where a continuous flow of people of all nationalities mingle day and night. In front of the Hussein Mosque, the elaborate lighting casts its rays on the charming façades and the magnificent architecture, both aimed at lifting the viewer above this earth, towards heaven. Following a long walk, we turn down a narrow and almost dark alleyway. We have reached our destination. Above the lintel, there is a sign with words written in *thuluth* script: "The Khodeir El-Borsaidy Museum" – a private museum named after its owner, containing thousands of calligraphy works; a melting pot of one man's different styles of composition and insight into this man's artistic vision.

Khodeir El-Borsaidy was born in 1942 in Port Said, where he began his artistic career at a very young age. His early canvases were walls, streets, asphalt roads. At the time, he used to imitate the style of two calligraphers who wrote nationalist slogans against the corrupt rule and the British occupation, for instance: "Death to those who cooperate with the colonizer!", "Down with the occupation!", "Long live free Egypt!". For colours, he dipped into the paint used as camouflage on windowsills against air raids. He was five years old. He had not joined the school yet. He did not know how to read or write.

Copying lines was for him a drawing exercise. Then, little by little, the child calligrapher moved away from copying and imitating to become a professional. He learnt at the hands of great calligraphers such as Muhammad Husni, Muhammad Abdul-Qadir and Sayyid Ibrahim. He earned a diploma in Arabic calligraphy and then specialized in gilding. He was appointed professor of calligraphy in Port Said, Cairo and Tanta and held exhibitions in Egypt and elsewhere across East and West. He founded the Egyptian Society of Arabic Calligraphers, the first union of Arabic calligraphers ever to be created in Egypt and the Arab world. This man from Port Said approached letters first with his eyes, then, over time, burning with passion for them, he let them become part of his subconscious. As his knowledge and skill deepened, he began to apprehend letters differently, as if he wanted to unveil them and reveal their inner identity by displaying their beauty and hidden energy through the art of calligraphy.

The works of El-Borsaidy can be admired in public spaces, especially in Cairo: he drew names of road signs, mosques, streets, cafés and shops. They could also be admired during his long tenure as the head of the Egyptian Television Arabic Calligraphy Department, a time during which he gained recognition for his specific technique, where he often mixed drawing and calligraphy. During these 28 long years, he achieved one of his main objectives: to present a programme that taught the rules of Arabic calligraphy and to introduce viewers to its beauty. He published a number of books on his art and gave lectures in Arabic calligraphy schools across Egyptian cities such as Cairo and Alexandria.

Despite working with other Arabic scripts whose technique he had fully mastered, his favourite one remains the *thuluth*. To him, it is the "Master of all Scripts" because it takes long years of practice and experience in order to master its rules and technique. Furthermore, this style adapts itself to the calligrapher's psychological state of mind as he is absorbed in his work; in some cases, if the artist's work is suddenly interrupted, even for one day, the effects can be seen on the script. Calligrapher Al-Hafez Uthman says about that: "If I were to be presented with all the work I had done all week, my artistic sensitivity would tell me which piece I did on a Saturday: my lines flow less on a Saturday compared to the rest of the week because I take a break from calligraphy on Fridays". Does this statement apply to most calligraphers? "Yes", says El-Borsaidy before adding: "There is an organic relationship between me and the script. It is my world, my language. It is where I reside. Sometimes, while I am working on calligraphy, I spend long hours during which I forget everything around me. It is as if a mysterious power lifted me towards a feeling of serenity. It is quite difficult for me to return. When I come to and see what I have done, I myself am surprised by what I see". There is no boasting in these words but rather a fascination with the manifestations of calligraphy, regardless of their author or style, modern or classical. For El-Borsaidy, calligraphy itself is a means of attaining the unattainable. It is a path to wonder. We saw him in his studio, marvelling at his own work as if seeing it with us for the very first time.

In calligraphy, one can marvel at both the content of the words and the artistic formation of letters. For instance: "light upon light" is a radiating sentence in itself, yet it shines even more through calligraphy as the latter, by celebrating these words, illuminates them even more. This expression may be composed of a few letters; one glimpse is sufficient for the eye to remember the entire verse. The same applies to a beautiful poem or a meaningful proverb. Here, calligraphy is to words what weaving is to the cloth or what performance is to music or opera, where an aria shines even more brightly when it is performed to perfection. As such, calligraphy can be considered a form of spiritual architecture. El-Borsaidy talks with fascination about letters and shaping them through calligraphy so as to make lines match every letter and word, taking into account the spirit of the sentence itself. He tells us how he approaches words and how he seeks to draw the best shape through which a letter is able to express itself. He says: "'Abd al-Basit 'Abd al-Samad can recite a surah in one breath, and I have written the Beautiful Names of Allah in one breath too". It is an experience where everything is possible and where the purpose is, among others, to reach the highest degree of beauty. After all, wasn't the saying: "Good calligraphy makes truth clearer" attributed to 'Ali bin Abi Taleb?

What drew him to the *thuluth* script, and why is he so partial to it? "The high degree of fluidity and the solidity of the composition. It translates into new forms, each with its own characteristics, such as the *thuluth al-jaly* (the royal *thuluth*), the *thuluth muhaqqaq* (the woven *thuluth*) and the *thuluth al-zakhrafi* (the ornamental *thuluth*), the *thuluth* influenced by different types of drawing, and the *thuluth al-mutanazir* (the symmetrical *thuluth*). The *thuluth* script requires great precision and leaves no room for error: its harmony can easily be broken should the calligrapher have not mastered it". He adds: "In general, calligraphers focus on the *thuluth* and come to it at the last stage of their calligraphy studies. Even then, sometimes they cannot master it. By contrast, I started with it, loved it, and worked with it, and I have my own innovative way of using it". El-Borsaidy concludes by saying: "How simple this script looks once work is done, and yet how difficult it is to master". Such is the *thuluth* script, with its strong and elegant posture and its hauteur that knows neither beginning nor end.

In the early days of his journey into the art of calligraphy, Khodeir El-Borsaidy focused on calligraphy compositions using a classical style. He then gradually opened up to new experiments. He had always aspired to move Arabic calligraphy away from being a functional means of recording information towards becoming a creative, intellectual and artistic space with its own rules and principles. He wanted to have innovative methods for calligraphic composition, including what he called "interlanguage communicative writing", where Arabic and Latin characters simultaneously overlap, and the final product can be read from right to left and left to right. He showed us two examples of that, where he had calligraphed the name of God "Allah" and the sentence "Muhammad is the prophet of God". In some of his works, he had mixed different types of Arabic scripts into one painting. In others, the composition could be read both horizontally and vertically. All these works are to be viewed first holistically, as an integrated unit, then by focusing on each letter individually, examining the connection between letters and observing the integration of every letter into the full harmony of the artistic work. He showed us drawings made with calligraphic lines: human bodies, living organisms, animals, trees and flowers; they almost looked like graphic designs. In these pieces, which can be considered writing through drawing, letters emerge from their abstract meanings and move towards another horizon. In El-Borsaidy's work, letters are at the centre of the painting because he sees them as its main element, unlike graphic designers who treat letters as merely a component of their work.

El-Borsaidy works with letters and builds his own relationship with them without resorting to modern technologies or computers. "Computers are the language of the age", he says, "but when they type a letter, they cast it into a rigid mould. There are those who resort to computers in order to complete a painting. I don't. I don't make use of modern technologies in my work as a calligrapher. I believe Arabic calligraphy is a living being; once a computer enters the equation, the soul departs – *Praise be to the one who taught by the pen!* Computers type a straight automatic *alif*, as if drawn with a ruler. When we enlarge the letter dozens of times, we can see it's rigid and lifeless, whereas if we enlarge a letter I have drawn myself, the letter might look upright, yet my heart beats and flutters within".

This describes El-Borsaidy's relationship with letters: to him, each one has its secrets and its distinct personality. Without a deep awareness of every letter's specificity, a thorough understanding of their characteristics and a strong sensitivity so as to grasp their personalities, he would not have been able to shape and use them in various calligraphy styles. Letters have a presence and a role in Arab culture. They have perspective and a voice. They are present in Qur'anic sciences, exegesis and linguistics. They appear outwardly still and yet hide endless inner movement. When a creative mind approaches them, whether it be a calligrapher, an artist or a poet, he awakens their soul and brings their hidden energy to the surface. "Arabic letters are like architecture; they have corners, entrances and direction", says El-Borsaidy. "Each letter has a particular structure, which means you need to handle it differently. Regardless of the script, one does not write the *alif* like the *ba'* or any other letter. A calligrapher's strength lies in his ability to fashion letters creating a harmony that reaches its apex upon achieving artistic unity within diversity".

Once El-Borsaidy mastered and perfected his craft, he did not restrict himself to the acknowledged calligraphy rules of the day. His obsession with renewal and modernization prompted him to design scripts bearing his signature, including the "El-Borsaidy script". Some critics and Arabic calligraphy purists wondered how was it possible for a master calligrapher, who had dedicated his life to classical calligraphy, to experience such a change of heart. When asked about that, El-Borsaidy always answers by asking in return: "Weren't great Arabic calligraphers, such as Yaqut al-Musta'simi, innovators in calligraphy? And didn't they bring in significant additions that became classics over time?"

Indeed, the development of Arabic calligraphy is part of a general evolution. The rules of calligraphy were not always a fixed constant. Calligraphy was not born the way it reached us. According to El-Borsaidy, this form of art went through many stages: first, the primitive script, which then evolved with the apparition of diacritical points and the use of ornamentation and embellishment. At that point, calligraphy had gradually evolved and adopted the artistic shapes we come to know today. What we designate today as calligraphy is the sum total of all changes to the Arabic script throughout its history. To El-Borsaidy, this means that the gates of innovation are open to those who feel the need to cross them and who want to use calligraphy in other artistic contexts within modern art, architecture or decoration.

Ibn Muqla, considered the "engineer of Arabic calligraphy" and believed to be the father of the *thuluth* script, designed letters and adjusted scripts according to the aesthetic criteria of the time, thus laying the foundation for subsequent developments. He was followed by Ibn al-Bawwab, who took another progressive step into the art of calligraphy and achieved a major qualitative leap. Abu al-'Ala' al-Ma'arri referred to the beauty of his script in his poem *Overjoyed by the Light of the Glorious Most High*, where a verse said: "A half-moon shone like the letter *nun* wonderfully drawn by Ibn Hilal (Ibn al-Bawwab)".

El-Borsaidy does not regard calligraphy as an immutable heritage. He believes that, as predecessors innovated, successors must do the same rather than freeze and force this form of art to remain at a standstill, while it is in the nature of art to always look towards a horizon without end. Art is always in motion and covers a wide array of styles. Could that make him lose his personal touch? El-Borsaidy says his style permeates everything he has done from the beginning until this day. Neither the spirit nor the deep essence of his calligraphy has changed. Rather, it has gained more strength through its constant departures and journeys into the unknown. He also stresses that Arabic calligraphy is not a monolith. Its existence is not dependent on past achievements belonging exclusively inside museums. It is a living being in constant movement, morphing into different shapes over time; it has the ability to keep up with changes across the world. How could it not be so when "Arabic calligraphy can embrace these changes and carry the seeds of continuous openness and renewal"?

El-Borsaidy calls for calligraphers to come out of their isolation like a butterfly emerging from its cocoon into the wider world. Let them firmly rely on their roots and heritage while opening up to contemporary changes, to current artistic and calligraphic experiments, to different cultures and their achievements; and let them dialogue with them. Modern calligraphy is rooted into its classical foundations while aspiring to the infinite so as to project a new vision. This is the compulsive nature of art, which knows no immobility but rather listens to, and interacts with, changes and innovations over time.

Western artists did not turn a blind eye to the discovery of photography in the nineteenth century. It was a major tool for documentation and preservation and left its mark on the arts in general, even before it became a form of art at the hand of creative photographers, with dedicated exhibitions and photography sections inside museums across the world. Photography artists were also aware of scientific discoveries and great technological innovations that competed with poetry itself. The Hubble telescope allowed us to see the birth and death of stars. It offered us a better view into deep space. It prompted major developments in astrophysics. All of this did not take place on another planet. It was reality, and left a profound effect on various fields, including philosophy, literature and art.

"I find myself in calligraphy", says El-Borsaidy, adding: "When I practice calligraphy, I feel neither the passing of time nor the weight of reality. I feel united with the words I have written, as if in another world". These words remind me of François Cheng, a writer and member of the Académie française. He is also a calligrapher who enjoys a special relationship with his art. He believes calligraphy to be at the centre of his life, especially the one he feasted his eyes upon in China, his native country. In his book *The Soul Becomes a Sign: A Painting in the Chinese Ink of the Spirit*, Cheng says: "My father left me no furniture or jewellery, but sticks of ink. To me, these represent a family treasure more valuable than gold. Every morning, I practice calligraphy in order to quieten myself, free myself from anxiety and enter the dance of life. This daily exercise has become indispensable to me, like an inner prayer. Every day, you have to start from scratch and plunge within, looking for truth and beauty". Isn't this what ordinary calligraphers feel, as do other artists in every time and place?

Shaping letters is, in itself, a gate towards visual and spiritual aesthetics. If not, what else could have prompted artists to use letters in their works and make them an integral part of their paintings? What brought Western artists to seek inspiration in Arabic letters, like the Swiss-German painter-designer Paul Klee who said, "Art does not reproduce the visible, rather, it makes visible"? The aesthetic and spiritual dimensions of Arabic calligraphy can therefore be felt, even among those who have no knowledge of the Arabic language but wish to draw near this form of art and its secret. As the work of many artists and writers throughout the ages can testify, it attracts an eager eye in search for beauty. Arabic calligraphy began to garner attention during the Renaissance with great masters such as Michelangelo and well into modern times with artists like Picasso. German poet and writer Goethe, who lived between the eighteenth and nineteenth centuries, said: "Perhaps no language creates such harmony between word, spirit and script as does Arabic. It is a strange harmony in the shadow of one body". In modern times, the voice of Japanese calligrapher Honda Kouichi, who also practises Arabic calligraphy, combining the quality of pure Japanese art with the harmony of Arabic characters, gives us an insight: "The shapes of letters, all letters, look natural and well balanced. The proportions are breathtaking. Arabic calligraphy possesses a kind of musical rhythm, almost like a melody . . . We feel something towards it, even if we fail to grasp the meaning of the words". A thousand years earlier, Abu Hayyan al-Tawhidi, an encyclopaedic philosopher who also worked as a paper maker and who, during part of his life, copied books and manuscripts, compared the art of calligraphy to music. His writings include an *Epistle about the Science of Writing*, which shows a wide knowledge of scripts and script types. It is one of the unique monuments of the Arabic language.

During the eighteenth century, the West turned its eye towards the East when it discovered the tales of *A Thousand and One Nights*, translated first into French by the Orientalist Antoine Galland and then into other European languages. While it had a later impact on art and literature, it planted into the Western mind an imaginary picture of the Orient. However, over the nineteenth and early twentieth centuries, thanks to travellers, writers and artists, the region was no longer shrouded in mystery. They had seen Islamic architecture with their own eyes. They had laid their eyes on calligraphy as an ornament and an essential component of architecture and viewed it as a form of art. Some were influenced by Arabesque art, also known as Arabic ornamentation, which comprises linear patterns and geometric shapes that combine opposites, sum up the fundamental rhythm of an artistic work, often evoke elements of nature (flowers, fruits and leaves) and merge the purest forms of nature and the most complex forms of the human soul. Arabesque – a component of the art heritage in many civilizations, most notably the Islamic one – is drawn on various supports: gold, copper, wood, mother-of-pearl, ivory. It was used in furniture, decoration, architecture and latticework (*mashrabiyya*). One who was mesmerized by it was none other than French poet Charles Baudelaire, who summarized his opinion by saying that Arabesque designs were the most spiritual of all. There are some who view Arabesque as a pure abstract idea that travelled from the world of fine arts into the realm of poetry by going beyond its ornamental decorative function and into the essential meaning of things.

Where architects approach letters using this same perspective and see the Arabic scripts' intrinsic geometrical dimension, calligraphers, for their part, take this dimension into consideration by distributing letters on a given surface, adopting horizontal and vertical measures and proportions, interlacing round and straight, pointed and jagged letters, curved semi-vowels and long letters stretching above and below the line, to compose a harmonious symphony. El-Borsaidy did not shirk away from using circles, squares and rectangles in his work through extension, rotation and overlap. Geometry, here, is a stand-alone state where letters blur until they become a single unit.

Across the museums of the world, inside wings dedicated to Islamic art, we can see how calligraphy espouses the geometric architecture of a given piece, whether it be a painting or a piece of porcelain, wood, ivory, glass or metal. Through the use of calligraphy, the artist's vision and aesthetic values materialize. El-Borsaidy assimilated calligraphy since his childhood, learnt with master calligraphers, and absorbed the calligraphy scripts disseminated across the large open-air museum of Cairo. He was a student of a classical school who sought to find new pathways. He did what many artists do when they go to museums across the world; we have been told that, at the Louvre, for example, artists come to replicate the works of great artists and then, once they are ready to fly, they return to their studios and unleash all their potential in search of their own distinctive style.

El-Borsaidy pays special attention to the design of a painting, its size, its colours and the style of its letters. "The larger the canvas, the more precision I need for its elements to fit together and form a comprehensive whole", he says. A master calligrapher in the classical school of *thuluth*, his scripts take a different direction in a painting that screams modernity and innovation. Words take shape inside the calligrapher himself before they find their way into the light. Calligraphy becomes a journey into the heart of words. Hidden behind letter edges, meanings cast a hidden glance at us as they absorb the beauty. On the canvas, there are words a calligrapher repeats endlessly, like a litany, and that travel to decorate mosques' walls in Samarkand and Bukhara. We ask El-Borsaidy why he lives in Cairo, a city of mosques etched with geometric designs and calligraphic motives: "How much has this affected your artistic career, and are your local and international heritages a key reference in your experience as a calligrapher, knowing that you have drawn calligraphy works inside mosques?" He says that he continues to study the styles and techniques of this artistic heritage up to the present day because it has incredible potential, and no calligrapher can call himself a calligrapher unless he studies tirelessly and deepens his knowledge.

El-Borsaidy practises calligraphy daily. His feet firmly planted in the present, he casts an eye on the past and looks towards the future, seeking to discover the place of calligraphy in the Arab world today. He who has devoted time and effort to teach it seeks today a way to have it taught in schools. He fears this art may fade away and disappear as new generations lose interest in it. It is "one of the main components of our Arab culture". He calls for its preservation as an important aspect of the Arab-Islamic artistic heritage. In addition, teaching calligraphy helps develop students' artistic taste, particularly among those interested in this form of art. It helps them see works of calligraphy through the eye of an expert and develop a taste for beauty while using sound criteria as a reference.

Inside Khodeir El-Borsaidy's studio, we are in a world where words and letters merge, where religious and civil texts find a common place and all interact for the sake of art. As such, his studio is part of the surrounding urban fabric and heritage. It is his permanent museum, where his classical works, in all their splendour, hang next to innovative modern works. An entire life lived through words and letters thrives within these walls. It has taken on new dimensions that reflect his own world and his inner experiences, as well as the path he has chosen. Here, the calligrapher works and lives, his works scattered around him or hanging on walls, a mirror of his artistic and spiritual life. As our eyes linger on them, we hear the pulse of these intertwined letters, where writing becomes existence and a journey in time and space.

Khodeir El-Borsaidy
He and the 99 Names of God,
2014
Ink on paper
Written in *jaly thuluth* and *diwani* scripts
81 × 60 cm
Courtesy of Khodeir El-Borsaidy

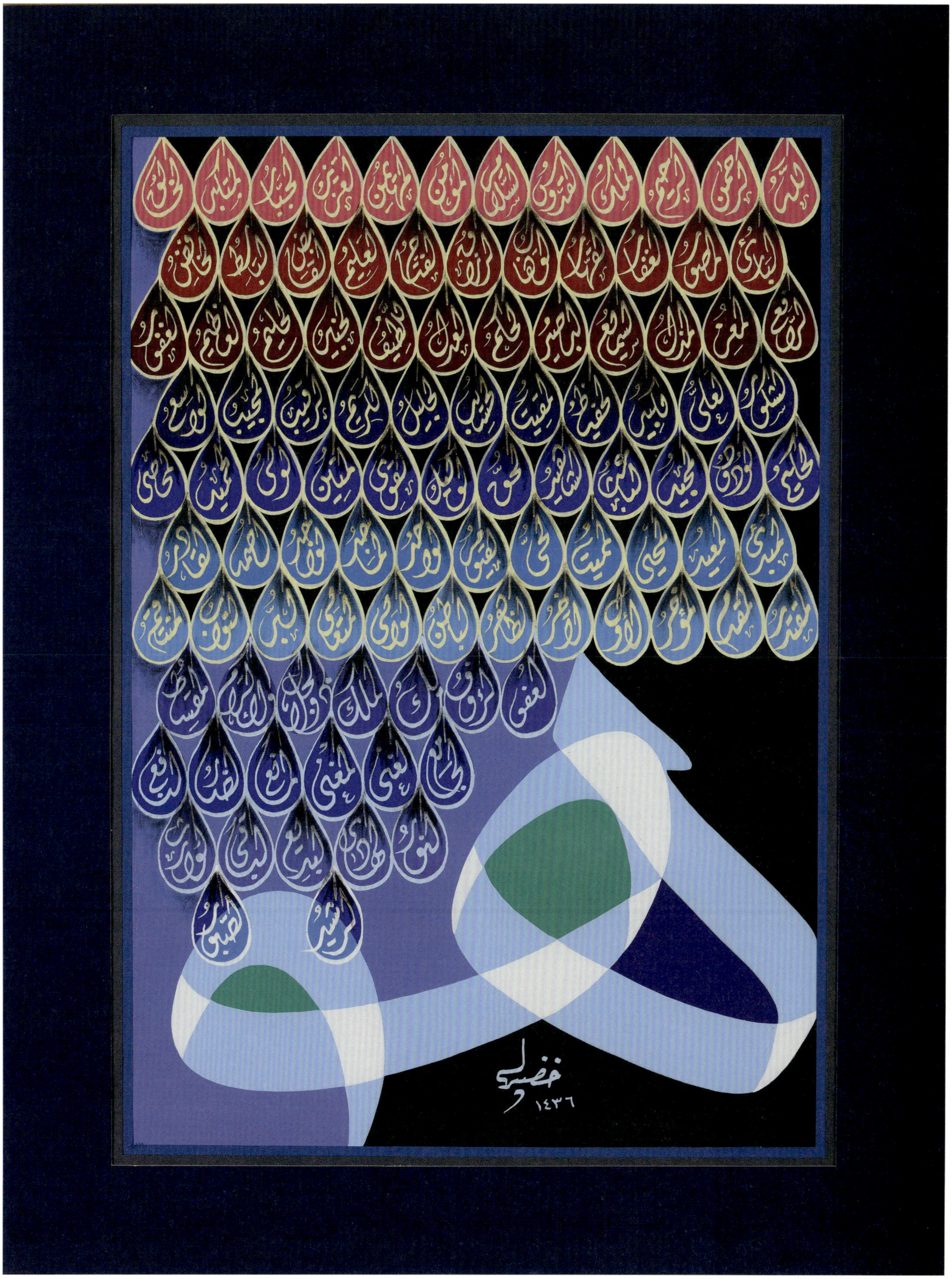

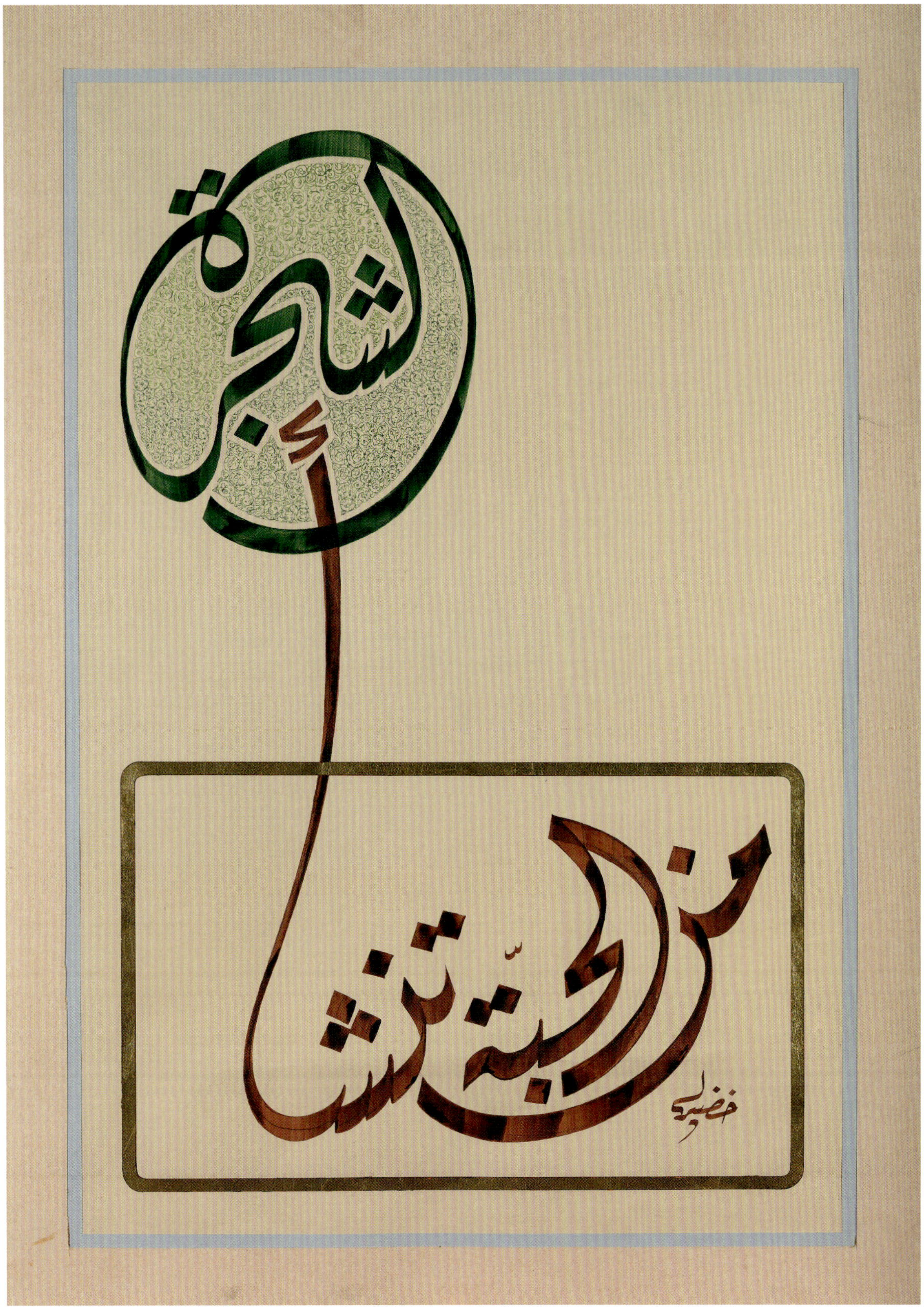

Khodeir El-Borsaidy
A Tree Grows from a Seed, 1979
Coloured ink on paper
Written in *diwani* script
100 × 70 cm
Courtesy of Khodeir El-Borsaidy

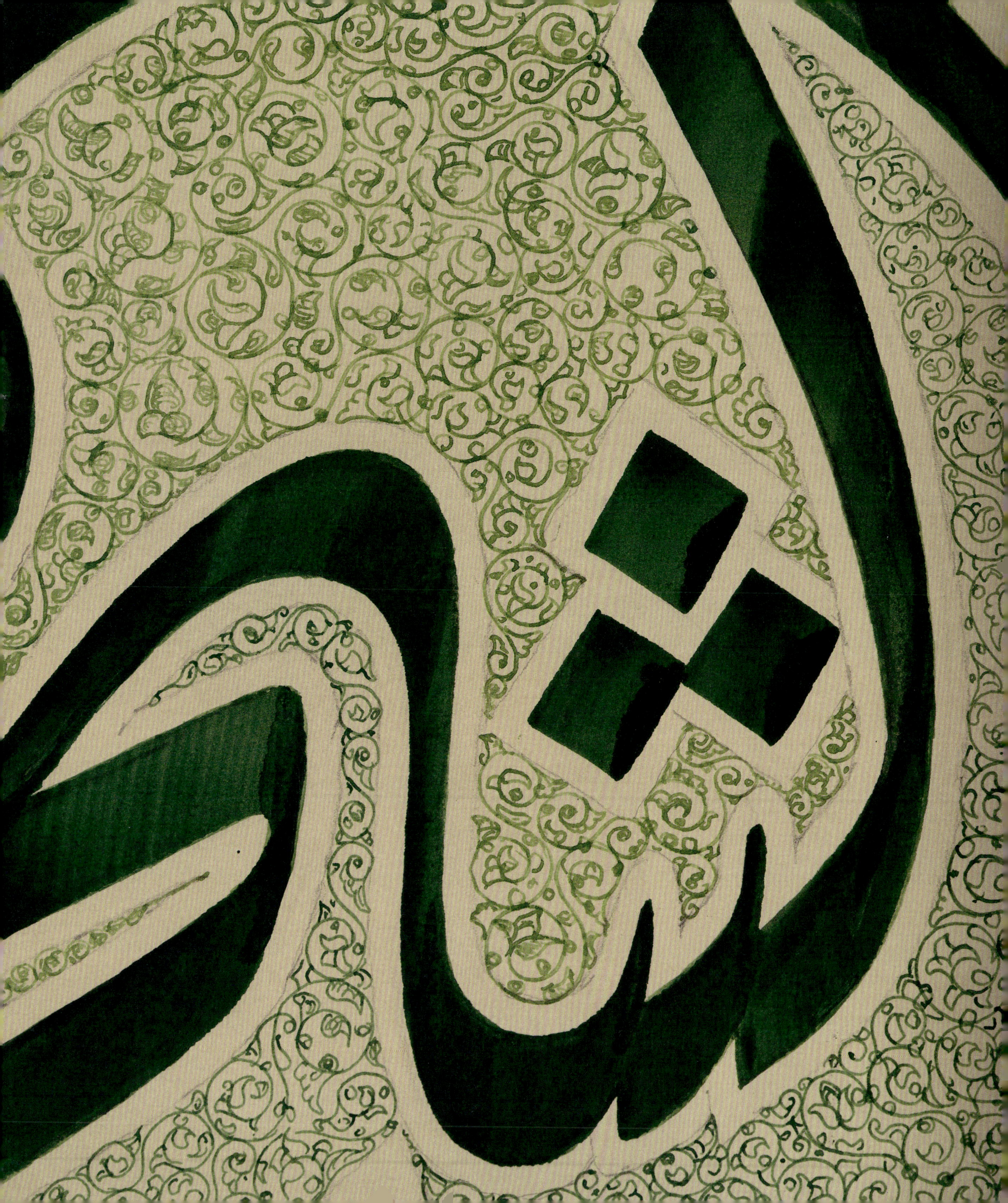

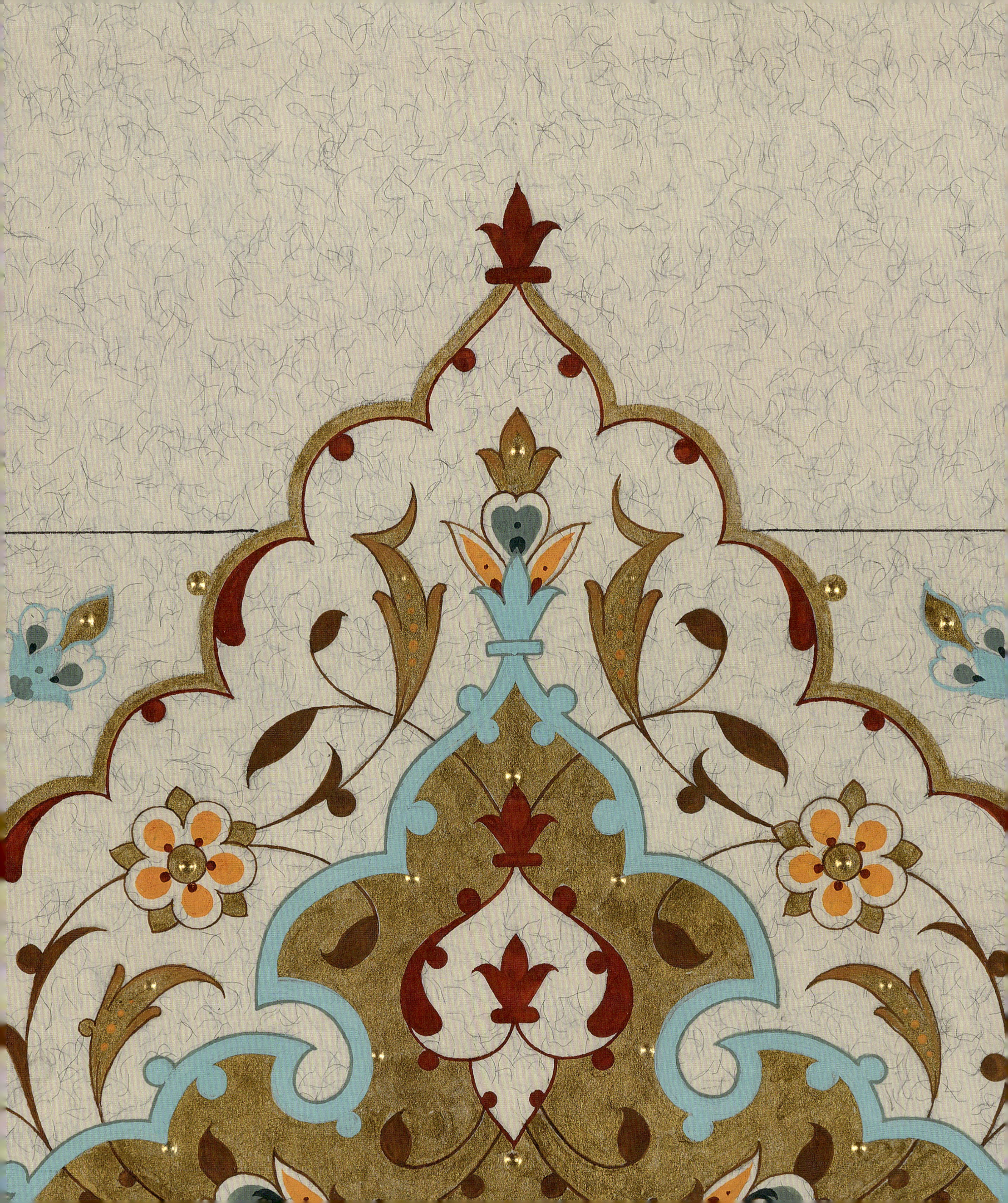

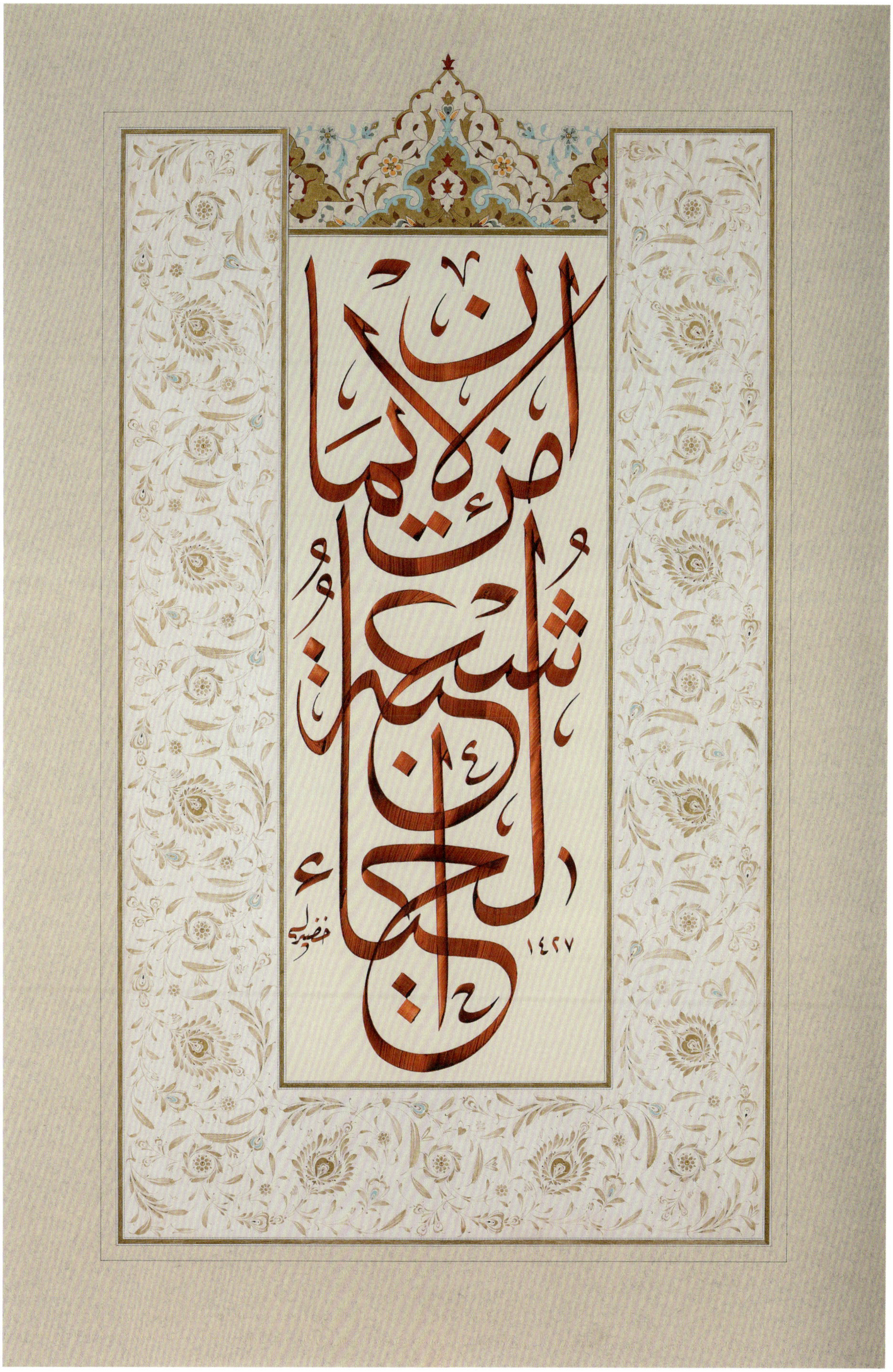

Khodeir El-Borsaidy
Modesty is a Branch of Faith, 2006

Ink on paper
Written in *jaly thuluth* script
87 × 57 cm
Courtesy of Khodeir El-Borsaidy

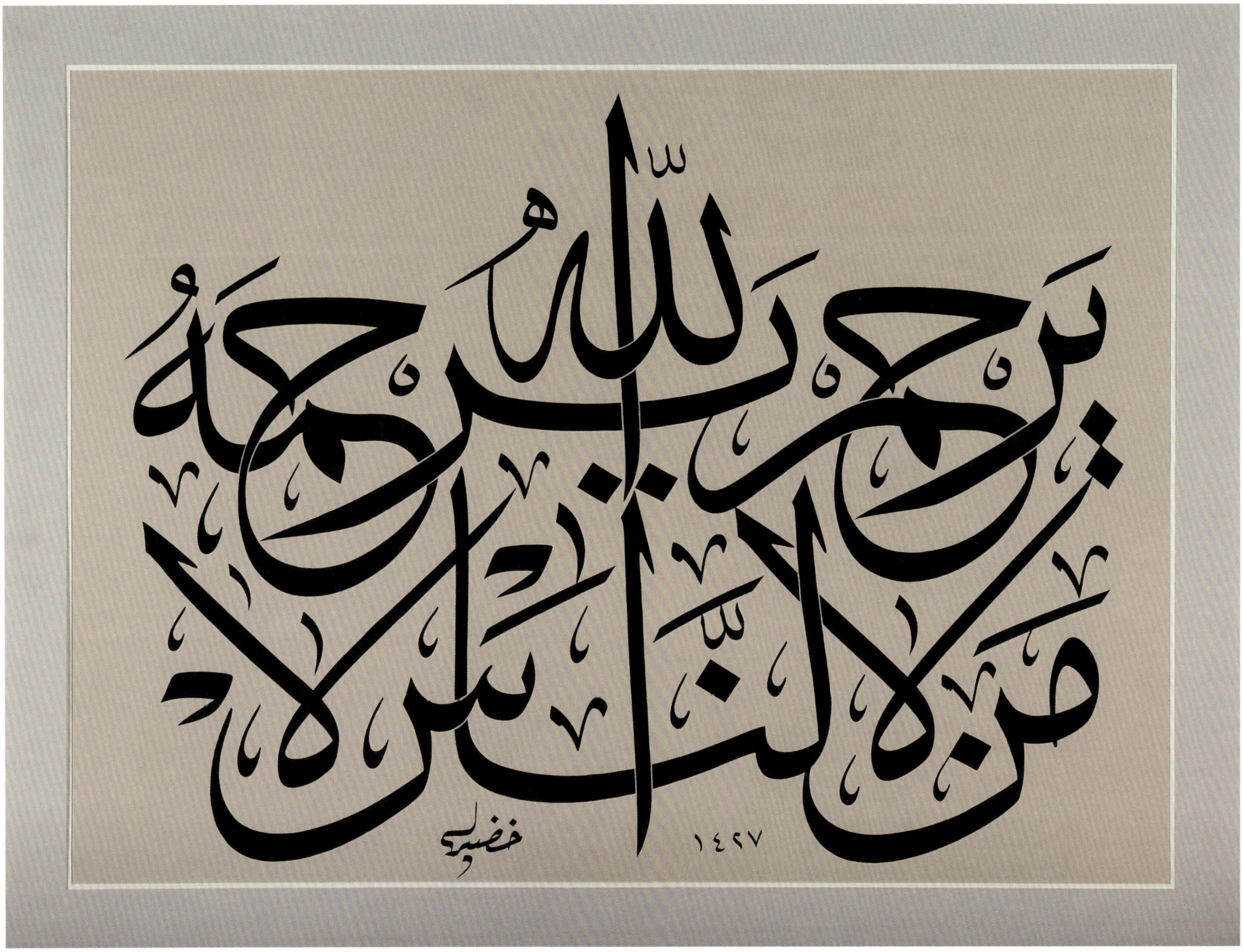

Khodeir El-Borsaidy
He Who Does Not Show Mercy to People, Allah Will Not Show Mercy to Him, 2006

Ink on paper
Written in *jaly thuluth* script
81.2 × 105 cm
Courtesy of Khodeir El-Borsaidy

Khodeir El-Borsaidy
Who Loves Beauty Sees the Light, 2008

Ink on paper
Written in *jaly thuluth* script
89 × 57 cm
Courtesy of Khodeir El-Borsaidy

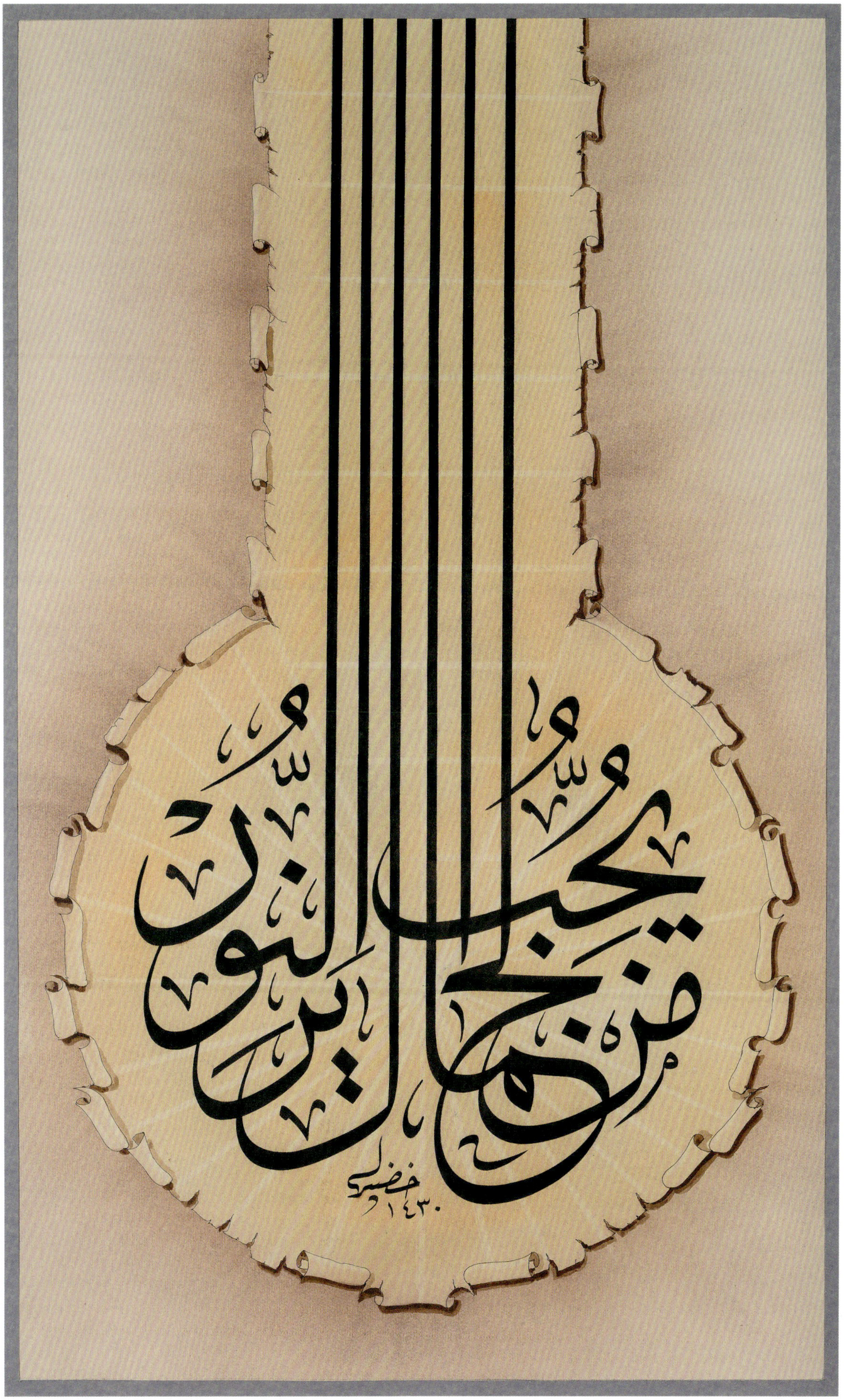

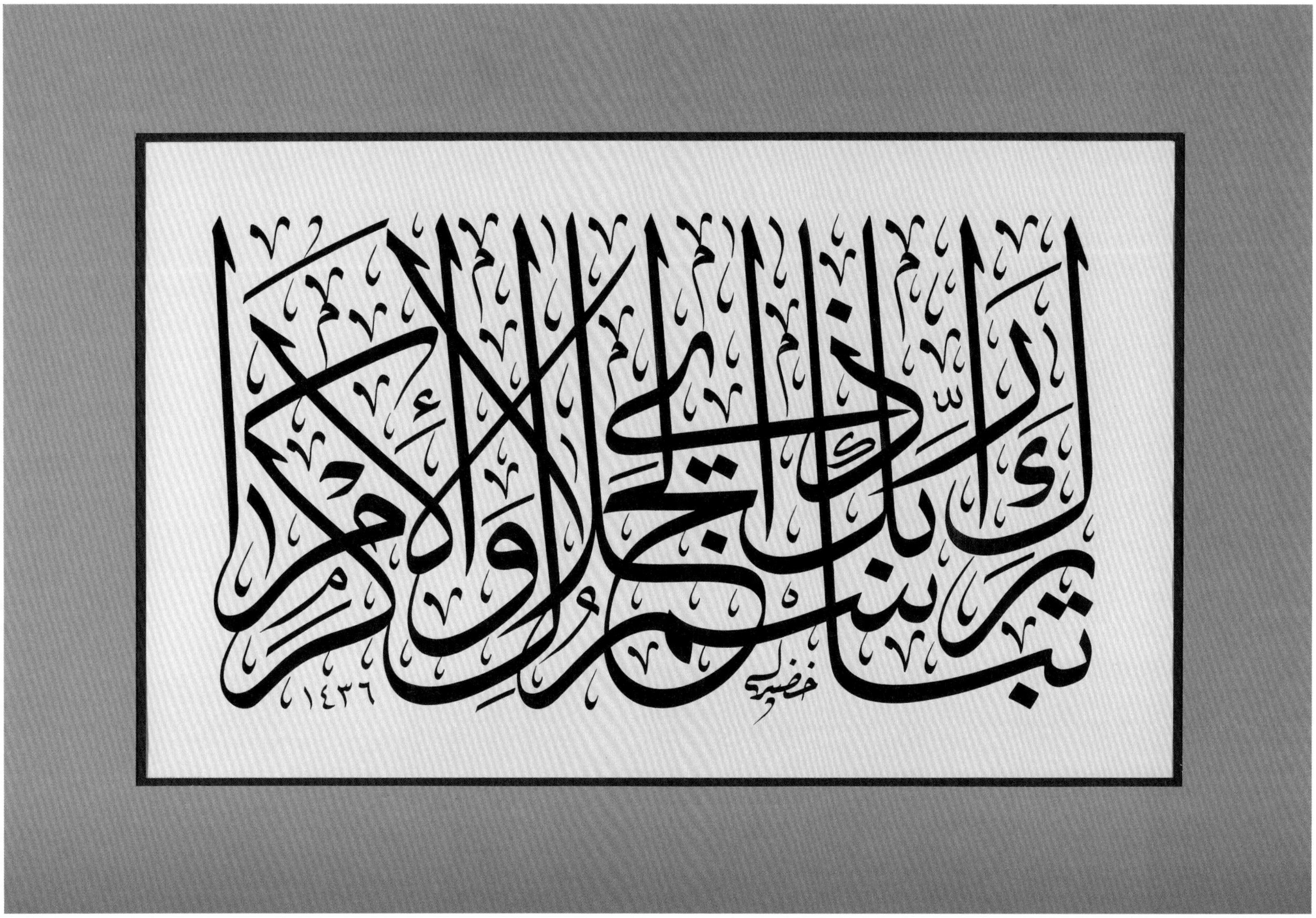

Khodeir El-Borsaidy
Blessed Be the Name of Your Lord of Majesty and Honour, 2014
Ink on paper
Written in *jaly thuluth* script
57 × 89 cm
Courtesy of Khodeir El-Borsaidy

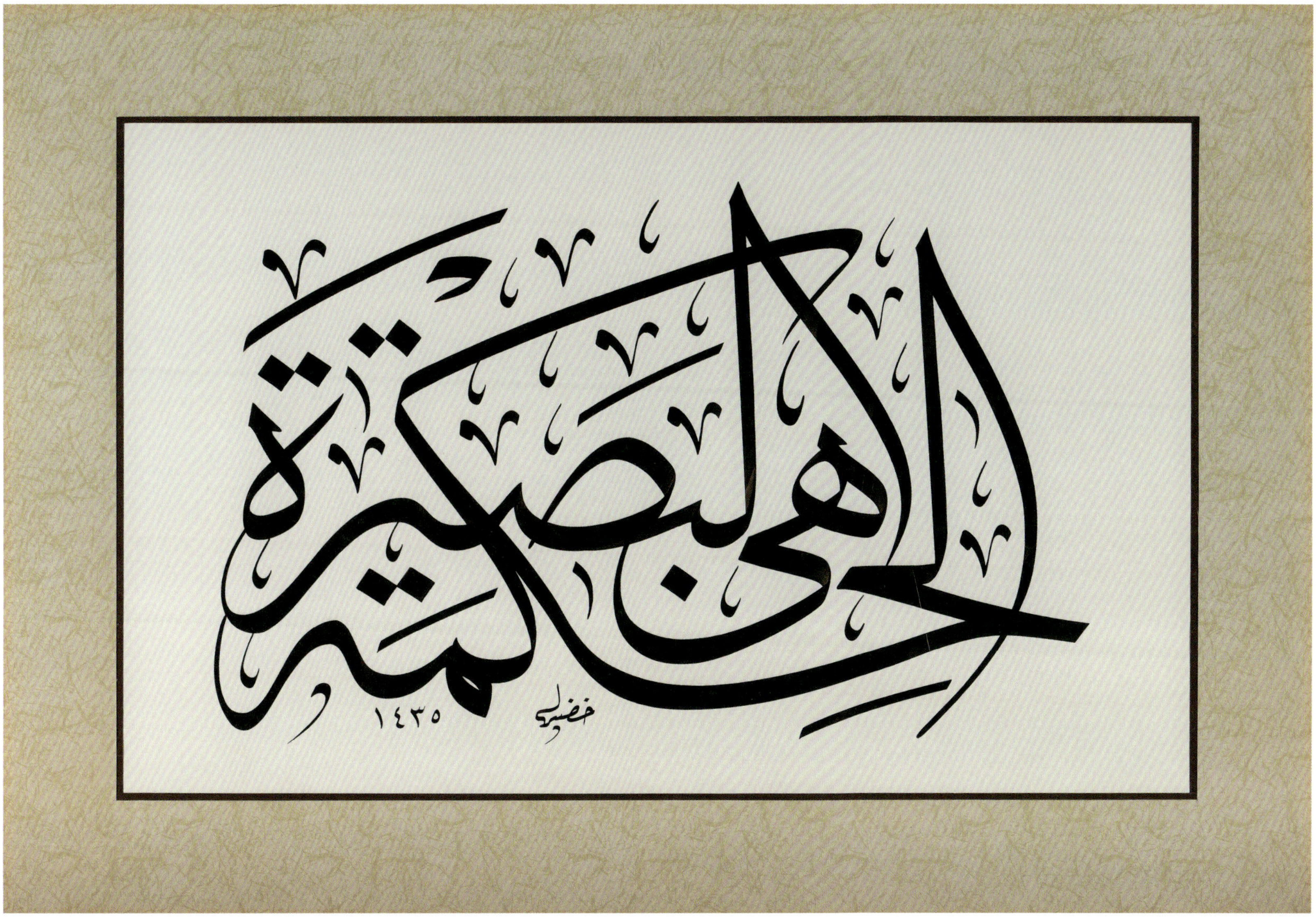

Khodeir El-Borsaidy

Wisdom is Insight, 2013

Ink on paper
Written in *jaly thuluth* script
70 × 100 cm
Courtesy of Khodeir El-Borsaidy

Regent Professor of Art History and Coordinator,
Contemporary Arab and Muslim Cultural Studies Initiative
(CAMCSI), University of North Texas

Performing Modernity through the Arabic Letter: Textual Abstract Formations

Dr. Nada Shabout

The Arabic letter has come to serve artists as a performative site of being, becoming and belonging in the evolution of modern art in the Arab world. The emphasis on the Arabic letter as a dominant visual element in modern art around the middle of the twentieth century is predicated on the specific purpose and meaning it projected, which seemingly centred on issues of identity and embodied several discourses that have been at the core of the formation of modern art and its critique in the Arab world. On an epistemic level, the letter worked as both a unifier and signifier of Arab identity, implying a national pan-Arab art product, or a national Arab art phenomenon that distinguished itself from calligraphy despite engaging it in many instances. On the one hand, it negotiated a new secular consciousness and the means of re-evaluating the relationship between self and other; on the other, it allowed for a perceived historical continuity.

In the last two decades, I have studied the letter's employment in various contexts that all revolve around its usefulness as a malleable and palpable decolonizing sign capable of indexing modernity across the Arab region – as form, as mediation to abstraction, as an identity marker for national consciousness and Arabism that in many incidents necessarily connect to the region's Islamic heritage as well. It is these qualities, along with the letters' abilities of merging and intersecting, that have acquired a specific prominence for modern Arab artists.

What the Arabic letters inherently offered is a unique means of abstraction, a particularly significant textual abstraction that could intrinsically and visually carry their sameness in difference.[1] Abstraction presented Arab modernists with a local understanding of modernism that was grounded in their visual heritage and consequently offered space for resistance; in most cases, the Arabic letter would make its appearance as part of that strategy. As such, the use of the letter is arguably based on two principles: negotiating the letter as a plastic element grounded in modernism and constructing a modern work of art engaged in its cultural particularity. Subsequently, through Arab national imagination, the Arabic letter has been liberated from both its sacredness, as perceived through Islamic calligraphy, and its connectedness as a written script.

Hurufiyya (from the Arabic *hurouf*, plural for *harf*, letter/letters) was advanced as a new category for experiments with the Arabic letter in modern art in the twentieth century.[2] However, the diverse uses of the letter led to a series of debates about terminology and art historical genealogies. Consequently, the term *hurufiyya* became highly contested while it gained popularity among modernists. It was specifically rejected by a number of scholars and artists, who found it reductive and vulgar. On the other hand, the Calligraphic School of Art (*al-Madrassa al-Khattiya Fil-Fann*) was proposed by artist and art historian Wijdan Al-Hashemi to express a perceived continuation with Islamic calligraphy. More recently, calligraphic abstraction has been introduced and preferred by art historians Salah Hassan and Iftikhar Dadi. While an initial proponent of the term *hurufiyya*, I now prefer the term "modern textual abstraction", particularly for works that distance themselves from calligraphy as a recognizable style. Nevertheless, this preference does not negate the specific instances of calligraphic abstractions.

TO BECOME MODERN

The understanding of modernism in the Arab world has been dominated by the repressive discourse of identity. It is true that throughout most of the twentieth-century identity – religious (Islamic), political and cultural

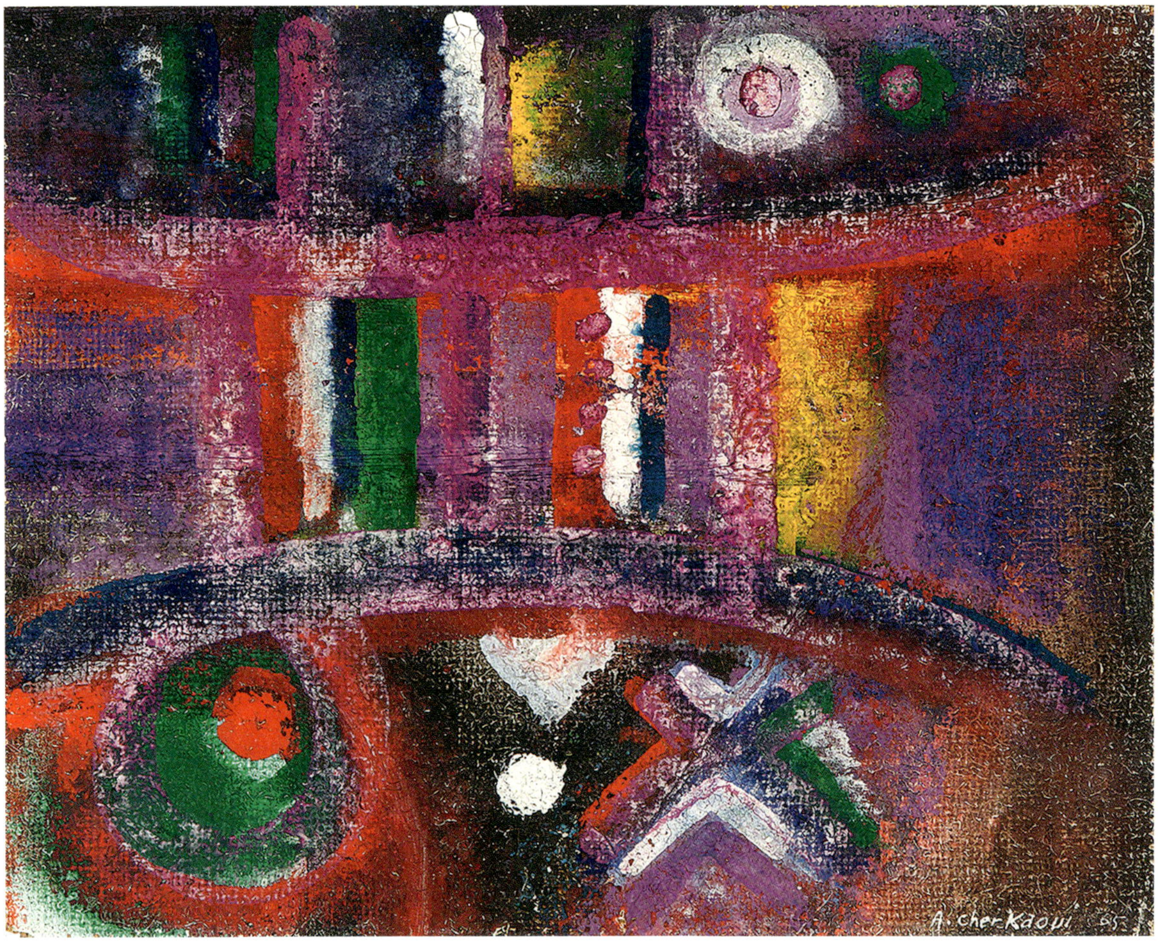

Ahmed Cherkaoui
Les Miroirs rouges, 1965
Oil on jute boards
53 × 58 cm
Courtesy of the Barjeel Art Foundation, Sharjah

Farid Belkahia
Composition, Prague, 1962
Mixed media on panel
76 × 65 cm
Courtesy of the Barjeel Art Foundation, Sharjah

(Arab), and regional (specific country) – was a main objective in the nations' post-colonial efforts to claim their past and future, including through the visual. Identity, to a large part, remains a vital element for various reasons. These different identities were and are always present, but their priorities shifted and continue to shift based on political demands and specific necessities of the time. Moreover, geographically, the Arab countries of Maghreb had to grapple with being part of the African continent. In the height of Arabism, with Egypt in the lead and the centre of the discourse, the African identity gained importance as a new block of political alliance.

Artists specifically explored ways of deciphering and expressing the polyvalence of these identities and their shifts. Their work explored and challenged preconceived notions as formulated by the increased dominance of political alliances during the period of the Cold War. The Arabic letter, which had appeared sporadically in earlier work, would specifically act as a unifying Arab cultural element in the region's multivalent visual expressions. Despite plausibility that visual negotiations of the Arabic letter in modern art can be seen as an acknowledgement of a shared Islamic past, during this period it specifically signalled the understanding of a new political and cultural necessity. It became a point of intersection and connection based on cultural unity, not racial or ethnic reductions. Arabism, within its period formulation, is understood here as a cultural unifier in the broad sense, allowing for difference and accepting ethnic multiplicity.

Research on the pre-modern period and its evolution through to modernism is still in its infancy, allowing for the persistence of the simplistic narrative of the Arab artists' sudden confrontation with modernism through colonialism, orientalists, and scholarships to Europe. In the absence of contrary evidence, I am arguing that artists of the new Arab world partook in a period of belonging to a wider international context where

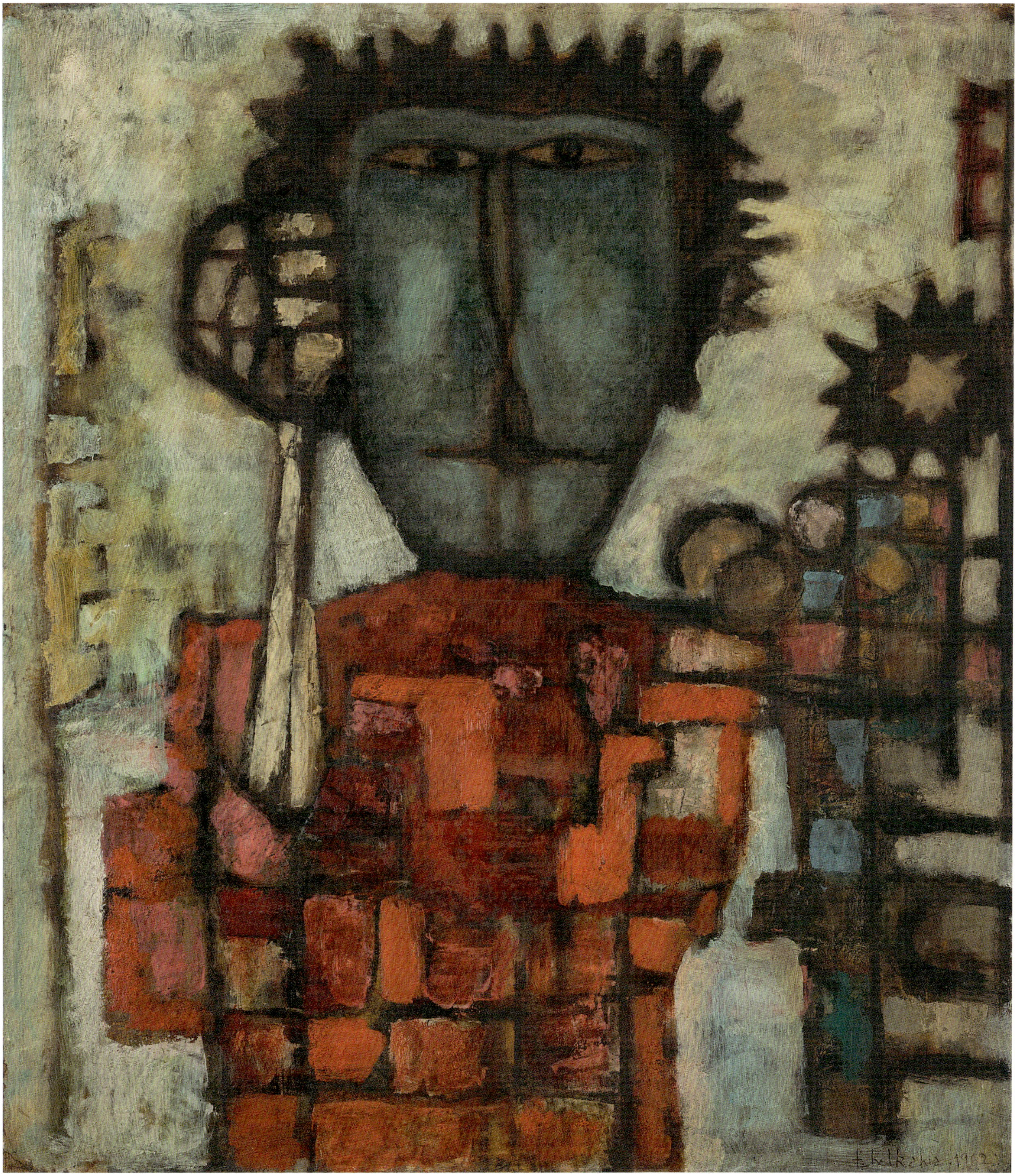

they in fact did not feel as less but rather as equal contributors. Simply stated, they too, as is the case with any student today at different academies around the world, were learning from a teacher and would distil their own individual style through different interactions. For many Arab artists, this is where the Arabic letter would offer many possibilities for individuality through a shared heritage. Significantly, and despite engaging with Western modernism and its various concepts that infiltrated Arab thought during the mid-twentieth century, and while political Arabism called for a form of centrality, modern art as negotiated in the Arab world veered away from the exclusivity and binarism created by Western modernism. Modernism in the Arab world did not deny the past but on the contrary, endeavoured to reconnect with its wide and varied history. It was conceived within a global vision of inclusivity.

Saving a couple of exceptions, modern art movements dominated the Arab world during the 1950s and mainly flourished in the post-colonial era of independence. Artists and movements of the 1950s and 1960s in the Arab world were mostly local and isolated; however, as Pan-Arabism swept the region and climaxed, their work became more interactive. The 1970s was a decade of combined efforts and shared goals through cultural meetings and joint exhibits. Collectively, they explored spaces for defining the role of the arts in constructing a unified Arab culture based on perceived commonalities. To this end, the Union of Arab Plastic Artists was established following the first meeting of Arab artists held in Damascus in 1971. The Union organized its first conference in 1973 in Baghdad and the first Arab Biennale was decided in Baghdad the following year.[3] In response, modern art took on a nationalist role and became grounded in nation-building. The new generation of established artists perceived art as part of the whole notion of knowledge. They changed the course of the aesthetic debate, which had been concerned with the content/interpretation level only to focus on the unity between content and form, with styles evolving from socio-cultural realities. The local negotiation of modern art became an essential part of the search for a national visual identity.

INVOKING THE ARABIC LETTER: *ISTILHAM*

Early examples of negotiating the Arabic letter in modern art are credited in two individual isolated efforts. Both Iraqi artists, Madiha Umar (1908–2005) and Jamil Hamoudi (1924–2003) charged their experiments with the Arabic letter with the awareness of being different while studying art outside of Iraq.

Umar became interested in the graphic possibilities of the Arabic letter and its abstractness as a form while investigating Islamic calligraphy as an art student at the Corcoran School of Art in the United States (1952 and 1959). She exhibited twenty-two paintings at the Georgetown Public Library in Washington, DC in 1949 and published a written declaration titled "Arabic Calligraphy: An Element of Inspiration in Abstract Art". For Umar, calligraphy, with its roots in Islamic heritage and the pride of the region, was an artistic development that valued the Arabic letter for its sacred connection to the Qur'an. Liberating the letter from calligraphic rules detached it from the sacred and allowed it to be seen for its plastic qualities, yet retaining its ornamental values as exemplified in the arabesque constructed through text.[4] She was thus able to recognize the letter's plasticity, which first and foremost transformed it into a line of mediation.

Hamoudi was a champion of modernism who promoted new ideas and styles through his magazine *Al-Fikr al-Hadith* (Modern Thoughts) in the 1940s. While in Baghdad, Surrealism was an obvious interest in his work. While in Paris on a scholarship, he turned to the Arabic letter as a form of self-expression and identity preservation. In time, his Surrealist approach led to *kufi*-Cubist formulations of Arabic letters. In 1971, Hamoudi explained the reasons for introducing Arabic letters into his work: "the artist's objective can be summed up as the return to authenticity in expression and the subjection of artistic form to cultural bases with specific ethnic standards".[5]

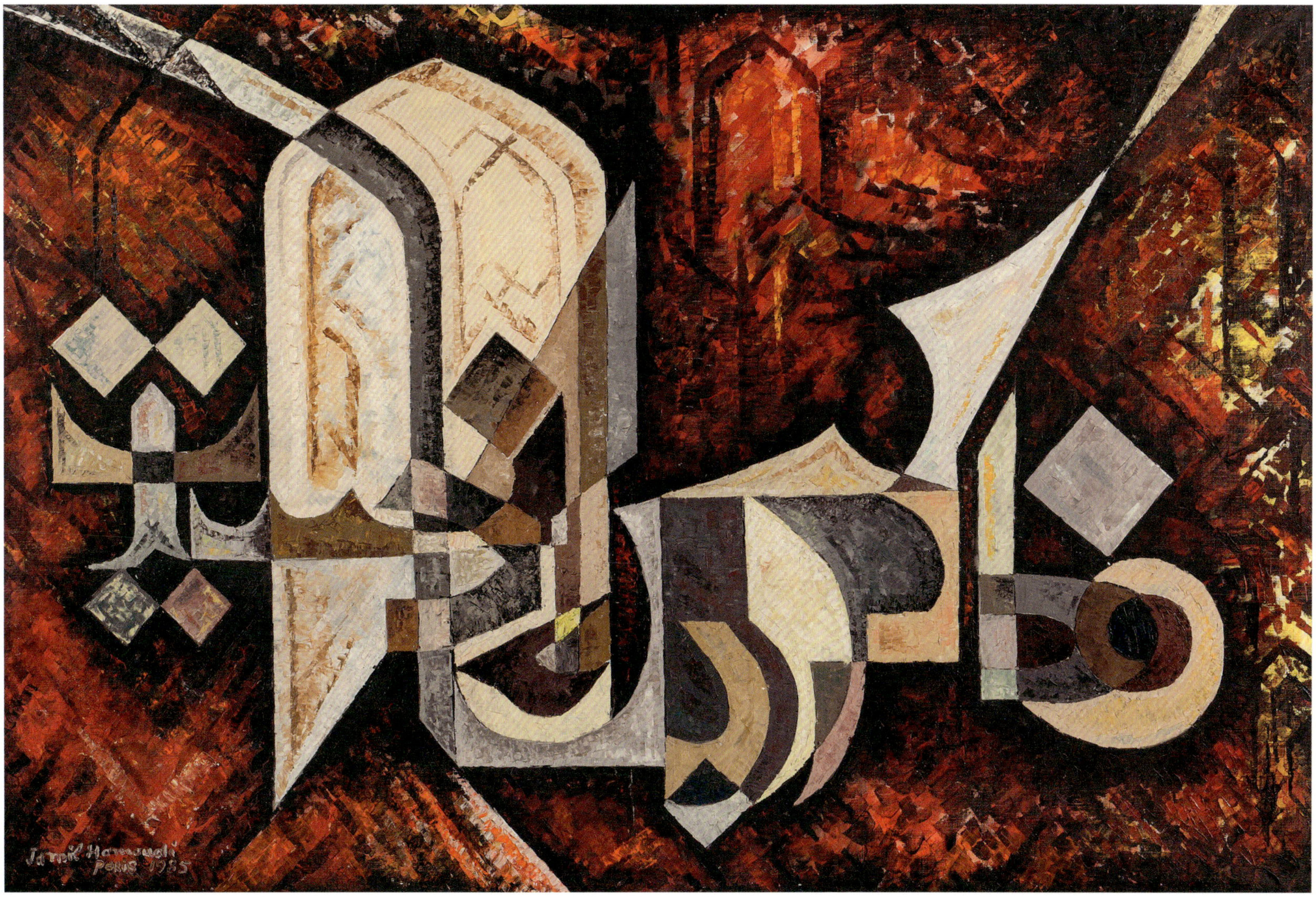

Jamil Hamoudi
If Ever Forgetful Mention Allah,
1985
Oil on canvas
87 × 129 cm
Courtesy of the Barjeel Art Foundation, Sharjah

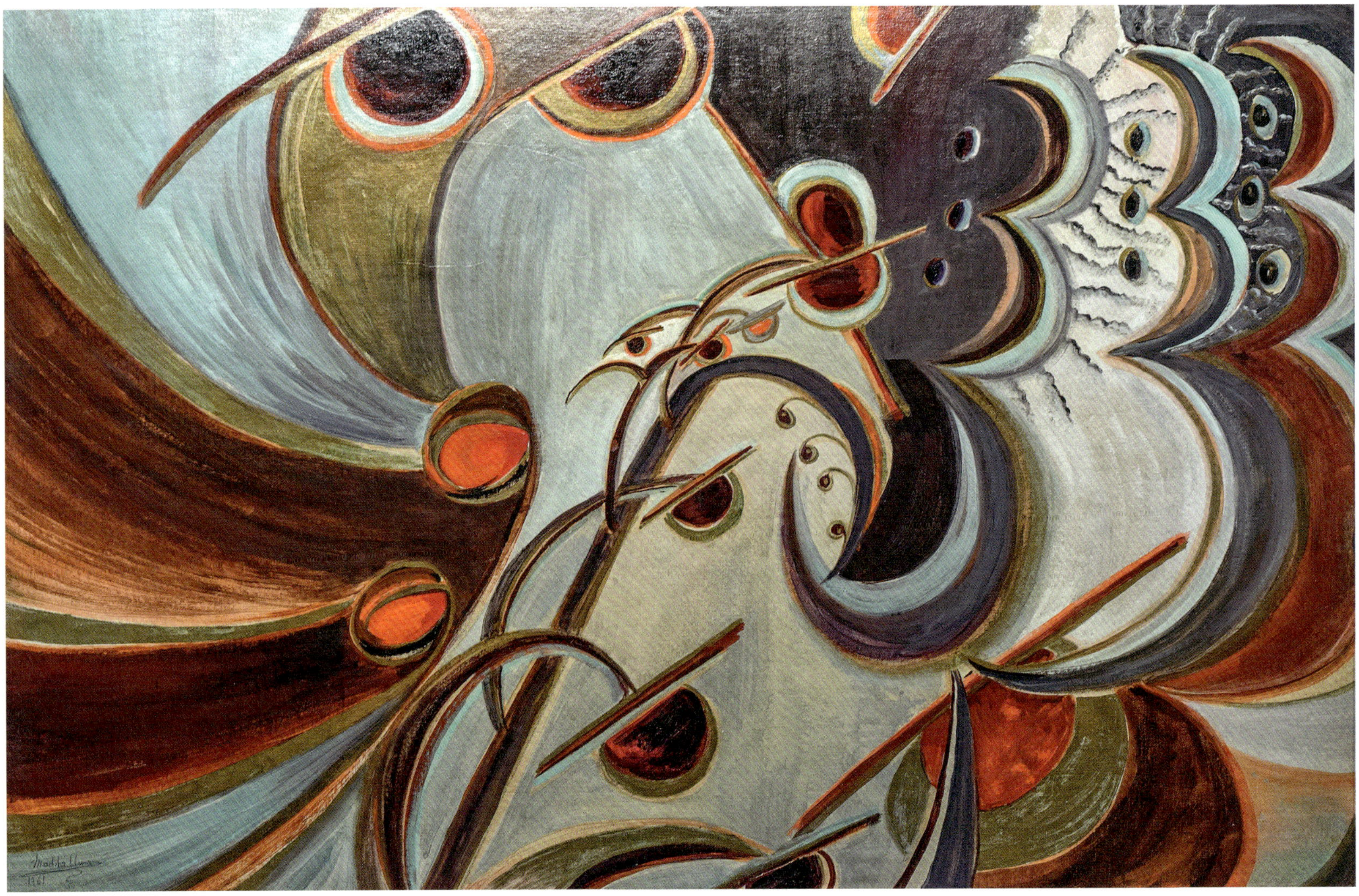

Madiha Umar
The Eyes of Night, 1961
Oil on canvas
60 × 90 cm
Courtesy of the Barjeel Art Foundation, Sharjah

Both Umar and Hamoudi's experiments invoked the notion of *istilham*, which would be coined by the Baghdad Group for Modern Art in 1951 as the site of negotiating Iraqi modernism. The verb *istilham* is derived from the word *ilham*: inspiration; instinct, which in turn is derived from the root *ihm*: to inspire; to pray. For Iraqi modernists, it became a conscious process-oriented performative act embroiled with agency, as it advocated mediation between what already existed to inform a becoming that would extend into the future. It thus equally embodied acts of deconstruction and unpacking in order to perform pointed constructions that would necessarily carry personal significance.

In the group's manifesto, the notion of *istilham al-turath* was explicated as a methodology to negotiate new art forms in their search for identity through *turath* (Arabic for heritage and tradition). Artists Shakir Hassan Al Said and Jewad Selim, co-founders of the group, drew from Mesopotamian iconography, from the thirteenth-century manuscript *Maqamat al-Hariri*, with its paintings by Yahya ibn Mahmud al-Wasiti, and from aspects of Baghdadi folk life. *Istilham* facilitated their move away from representation.

In Al Said's earlier works, text remained relational to a narrative, although equally merged in the flow of the line; but after his 1966 "Contemplative Art Manifesto", he rapidly abandoned the narrative.[6] Contemplative art, as he explained it, was an abstract description of past existence and the bonds between people and their world. In his transition to abstraction, the Arabic letter was his enabler. His research into Islamic philosophy and thought resulted in a fascination with the line and its relationship to the surface, where he saw the letter as a dynamic line.

In 1971 Al Said took *istilham* further to what he called *istilham al-harf*: a specific exploration into the Arabic letter to find that spiritual continuity where the letter carries the collective memory of local characteristics. This led him to establish the One Dimension Group (al-Bu'd al-Wahid) and, two years later, to publish the treatise of the same name, in which he framed the concept's technical and philosophical scope.

Umar and Hamoudi were both part of the group and contributors to the booklet *Al-Bu'd al-Wahid* that was published on the occasion of the One Dimension Group's second exhibition. Along with works by the contributors, Al Said also published a number of artworks that engaged letters, such as a Sumerian tablet as the oldest example, different Qur'anic pages, a Chinese scroll, as well as works by contemporary American and European artists and one by the Iranian artist Hossein Zendaroudi, thus contextualizing its trajectory. What is significant about these inclusions is that Al Said was not thinking only locally. In fact, he saw the letter as an entry into a primordial pre-civilizational being; as a form of basic globalization.

The group did not last long but further experiments were carried out by its members. Notable among these is artist Dia al-Azzawi, who participated in the first group meeting but then found its direction disagreeable to his line of thought. Most interesting are Azzawi's experiments with the narrative and the epic, away from direct dependency and specifically through poetry.

Azzawi's explorations would lead further – specifically, to a re-examination of the very concept of the book in relation to Arab cultures. He produced a number of sculptural books engaging poetry that were meant to be consumed on a visual level instead of being read. Projects such as these initiated a trend among Iraqi artists in the 1990s of what became known as *dafatir* (artist's books). *Dafatir* opened up a space for Iraqi artists to negotiate and document issues of invasion and economic sanctions under very difficult circumstances.[7]

DECOLONIZING MODERNISM

In the Arab world, the 1950s were charged with post-war defiance and resistance. Consequently, artists looked to their local traditions and systems of signs and symbols as means for evoking collective memories, and accordingly combat colonial policies with their imposed foreign languages and cultures. Moroccan artist Ahmed Cherkaoui (1934–1967) initiated a study of native motifs including Berber tattoos, rugs and jewellery. His work of bright and contrasting colours explored these motifs as signs and abstract shapes, juxtaposed at times in accordance to traditional Islamic techniques. Farid Belkahia (1934–2014), as the director of the École des Beaux-Arts in Casablanca (1962–1974), initiated a programme of localizing art studies by introducing students to the local heritage. He replaced the old models of Greek statues and still life paintings with Moroccan artefacts, and added teaching Arabic/Islamic calligraphy in the school's curriculum. Known as The Casablanca School, a group that included Belkahia, Mohammed Melehi and Cherkaoui broke away from academic teaching and naive painting and taught their students the history of local crafts in order to reconcile the past with the present.[8]

In these struggles, the Arabic letter represented an obvious and excellent vehicle for mediation between their various concerns. As Arabic text and Islamic calligraphy provided for centuries the means for political and visual unity and mediation between the sacred and the profane (between the desired afterlife and transient life), so did the Arabic letter in the modern age. With its connection to Islam through the Qur'an, the Arabic language was above ethnicity and nationality. It remained so during the modern age and played a political and spiritual role. Thus, one of the most prominent constants connecting the past with the present and the future, capable of bridging "tradition and modernity", has been the Arabic language; and visually, the Arabic text.

Rooted in its connection as a cultural signifier, in North Africa the Arabic text carried an added significance as a forbidden language during occupation. The Old Khartoum School, established in the mid-1950s by a group of Sudanese painters and sculptors, aimed at consciously steering away from Western influences, concepts and methods through looking into their own heritage. Their understanding of heritage included African cultural traditions, Islamic visual tradition, and local customs. They also explored forming modern indigenous concepts for representing their new constructions of heritage. The graphic values of Arabic calligraphy introduced to them through calligraphy classes taught at the School of Design in Khartoum offered them possibilities.

Artist Osman Waqialla (1925–2007) formulated new visual dimensions for "calligraphy" through his articulation of the letters in space as living entities. Art historian Salah Hassan argues that Waqialla's "pioneering experimentation with classical Arabic calligraphy led to the rise of a distinct style within postwar Sudanese art".[9] Trained in classical calligraphy, Waqialla engaged text from the Qur'an in spontaneous and abstract manners. Nevertheless, he remained more faithful to the integrity of the text when articulating verses from the Qur'an than he did with poetry.

Along with his younger colleagues Ibrahim El-Salahi (b. 1930) and Ahmad Shibrain (1931–2017), he would not only revolutionize the curricula of the Khartoum School but influence the very development of modernism in Sudan and beyond. Just like the various other experiments around the Arab world, theirs was rooted in its specific locality and its search for a national culture. Hassan argues that "Totalizing terms such as 'Sudanese culture', 'Sudanese identity', 'Sudanese literature', and 'Sudanese art' became central to critical discourse, underlying, it was hoped, a new social, literary, and artistic consciousness that was to come".[10] They were invested in the principles promoted by the literary movement Jungle and Desert School (Madrasat al-Ghaba wa al-Sahra'), which gathered together poets, novelists and critics who strived to modernize literature while constructing its new Sudanese identity.

Less structured than Waqialla, Shibrain's work engaged the potentiality of the Arabic letter as abstracted plastic within a more "Africanized Sudanese" framework. Through his use of earthy colours and manipulation of text, he veered away from the traditional expression of calligraphy. While not abandoning Islamic themes in general,

Shakir Hassan Al Said
Untitled (Grey), 1963
Oil and plaster on board
66.5 × 56.5 cm
Courtesy of the Barjeel Art Foundation, Sharjah

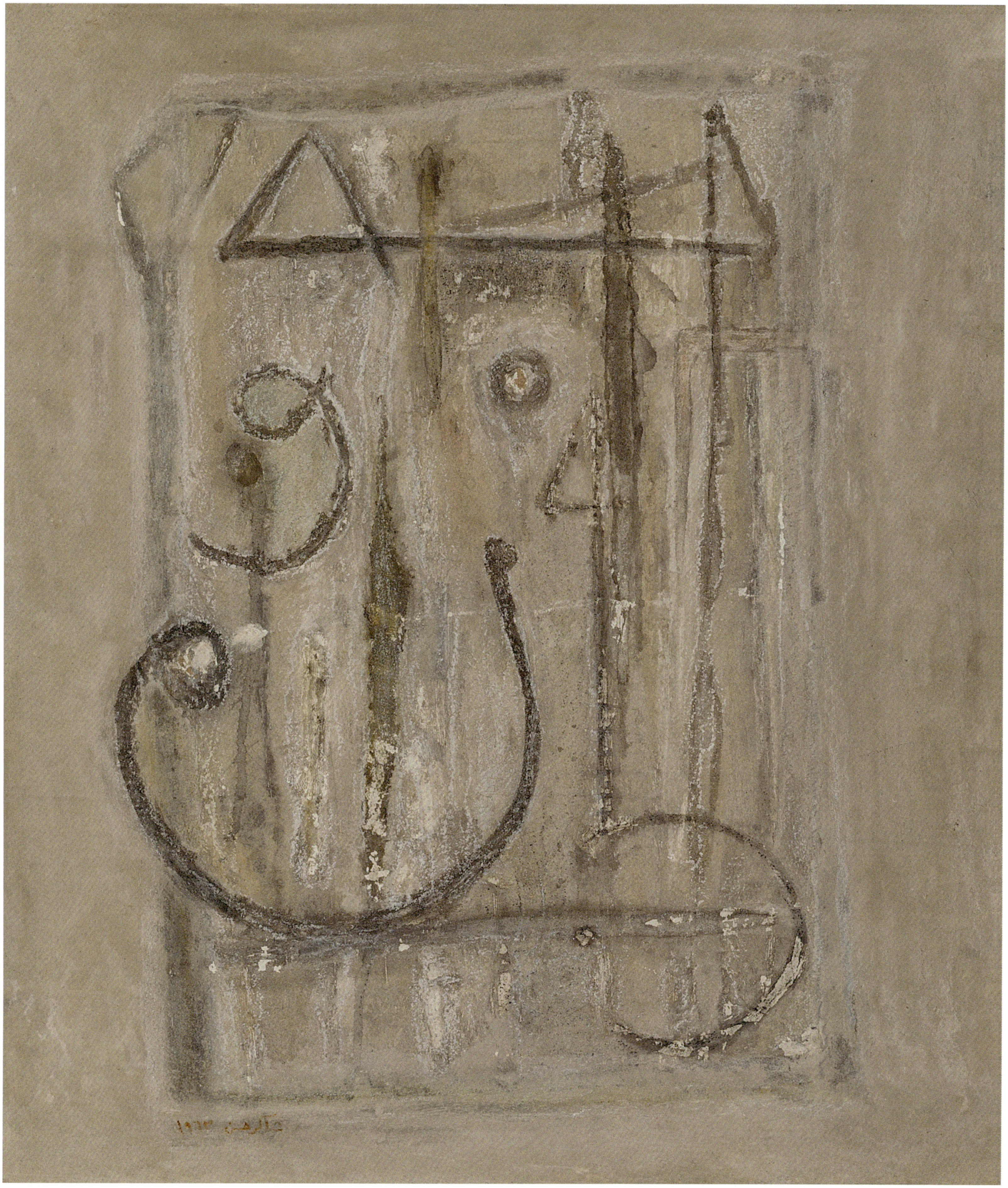

he nevertheless further deconstructed and distanced their Islamic past. El-Salahi's engagements with cultural synthesis and layering would present complex and nuanced transnational constructions that were to resonate through the Arab world and the African continent.

The work of the Algerian Rachid Koraichi (b. 1947) is another example. Koraichi draws on his personal understanding of Sufism, which he experienced within his family environment, the local ancient Berber heritage, the Islamic past, as well as modern Arab history and political struggles. While in exile, Koraichi transformed the various elements from his culture into symbols of protest and contestation. His forms conjure up their aesthetic qualities and mystical properties but at the same time create new meaning through this juxtaposition of old and new. At times, Koraichi invokes colour symbolism as an added element of connection and continuity, such as his use of indigo in reference to its significance and value to cultures across Africa, Asia, the Middle East and Europe, where it was traded across the Silk Road. While it is not necessarily legible in Koraichi's work, the Arabic text (or fragments of it) is indeed central in his visual constructions. Moreover, references to Arab poets and poetry certainly evoke a Pan-Arab sentiment.

Equally, Egyptian artist Omar El-Nagdi (1931–2019), who experimented in different styles and media, found the Arabic letter to be a meeting ground for his various interests, including music. El-Nagdi was a member of the Liberal Artists group headed by Taha Hussein, and later formed the Egyptian Mosaics Group in 1964. On similar transnational/translocal lines, he experimented with different linkages from historical Egyptian civilizations that necessarily included Pharaonic, Islamic, Coptic, and multiple connections.

Thus, the potentiality of the Arabic letter would come to serve El-Nagdi's purposes of bridging and connecting in the 1960s, while studying in Venice. In his iconic work, he composed abstract rhythmic repetitions that expressed both the letters' spirituality and plastic qualities as well as their musicality. The rhythm of the design is what dictates the transformation and choreography of letters into signs. Order, harmony and balance necessarily reflect the aesthetics of contemplation and spirituality within its geometrical or organic compositions.

A DISCOURSE OF MULTITUDES

The articulation of the Arabic letter in modern art served artists of the Arab world during the twentieth century as part of a more complex discourse of signs that drew on a collective and historical memory of difference, which often disrupted and subverted the rhetoric of separation. Its prominence in this imaginative and constructed discourse alluded to an emphasis on shared cultural overlaps and intersections while reinforcing a specific local identity. Formally manipulating the Arabic letter as an art element was a direct mediation between national identity and heritage and modern art.

Nevertheless, the individual experiments of the 1940s and 1950s morphed into a veritable trend beginning in the 1960s. Representations of the Arabic letter in modern art gave artists comfort and confidence that came from the immediate perception of a marked cultural (and at times political) identity for the work. Thus this trend attracted an increasing number of artists around the Arab world and gained momentum during the 1970s and 1980s, turning into a phenomenon in which almost every artist across al-Mashriq and al-Maghrib al-Arabi experimented at one time or another with the letter. However, it never became a unified movement or school of style, despite several efforts. While its naming remains contested, as discussed earlier, it does necessarily allow for a differentiation between calligraphy as a specific style of art, with its own rules and traditions, and the abstract ways Arabic text is deconstructed in modern art.

This distinction is significant in constructing spaces of knowledge and meaning that these works carry. It also differentiates between a modern calligrapher and a painter, although they clearly conflate at times. A modern calligrapher is a person who manipulates the text within an established tradition of calligraphy that should be allowed to continue in innovative ways and not be folded within "modern art" in its Western etymology. Artists in their own right, modern calligraphers reference the tradition of calligraphy at least on the visual level, if not following altogether its specific rules.

But what is more important than observing the above distinction is the problem of grouping innovative experiments together with the repetitiveness, decorativeness and simplicity of others. In the first instance, the letter is part of a more complex work, where perhaps it was a necessary but transitional methodology, and many later abandoned it. In the second instance, the letter constitutes the work, like in the later Islamic revival experiments by artists such as Shibrain. These works are largely conditioned by the market and generally well received, because they share a closer relationship with traditional religious calligraphy. Nevertheless, a new trend is spreading among contemporary artists, who find spiritual connections with the Islamic age and are using the Arabic letter in new experiments. While these new formulations are no longer connected to the modern notion of *hurufiyya*, they are instigating a re-evaluation of the modern trend.

[1] See N. Shabout, "Mediating Abstraction through the Arabic Letter", in *Taking Shape: Abstraction from The Arab World*, eds. S. Takesh and L. Gumpert, exh. cat., Grey Art Gallery, New York University, New York, 2020 (Munich: Hirmer Publishers, 2020), pp. 41–49.

[2] See C. Dagher, *Al-Hurufiyah al-Arabiyah: Fann wa Hawiyah* (Beirut: Sharikat al-Matbuaat Lil Tawzi' wa al-Nashir, 1990); in English, C. Dagher, *Arabic Hurufiyya: Art and Identity* (Milan: Skira, 2017).

[3] See N. Shabout, "Transregional Solidarity: The Arab Biennial in Retrospect", in #5 *Refractions of Socialist Solidarity*, Mezosfera's fifth thematic issue, ed. E. Szakács, May 2018. The magazine was published in conjunction with the Budapest presentation of the three-channel film *Two Meetings and a Funeral*, http://mezosfera.org/transregional-solidarity/.

[4] M. Umar, "Arabic Calligraphy: An Inspiring Element in Abstract Art (1949–50)", in *Modern Art in the Arab World: Primary Documents*, eds. A. Lenssen, S. Rogers and N. Shabout (Durham NC: Duke University Press, 2018), p. 141.

[5] J. Hamoudi, "About the Letter . . . A Response (1973)", ibid., p. 362.

[6] S. Hassan Al Said, "Contemplative Art Manifesto (1966)", ibid., p. 252.

[7] See N. Shabout, "*Dafatir*: Testimonies of Forgotten Times", in *Theater of Operations: The Gulf Wars 1991–2011*, exh. cat., MoMA PS1, New York, 2019–20 (New York: MoMA PS1, 2019).

[8] The group also boycotted exhibition halls run by foreign embassies and instead exhibited their work in public squares where popular crafts and performers were on display.

[9] S. M. Hassan, "When Identity becomes 'Form': Calligraphic Abstraction and Sudanese Modernism", in *Taking Shape*, p. 61.

[10] Ibid., p. 62.

Poet and Critic

Words beneath the Throne

Mohammed Al Harz

No longer will

looks proceed
alone, unarmed.

No longer will

lips cease
to scream
in the face
of the storm
and its remains.

No longer will

life near broken staircases
conceal from the blind
the virtue of rising.

Because mimics and gestures
will not suffice,
why not then,
have everyone climb down their trees
every day after midday:
reed heads dipped in mud
on the banks,

rivers leaping into their arms
like fish.
Fingers alone protected by the blaze of inspiration
and the glint of the written word.

As you lie here, buried in this earth,
kicking death like a retired footballer,
one hand on the edge of the grave,
like a letter fleeing from Ibn Muqla's shrine,
the other slowly
drawing out memories
so as not to awaken the dead,
as if withdrawing an ancient stone inscription
hidden by a calligrapher in the apple of his eye.

But slumbering sorcerers
inside your body thought:
the blood may have cut its holiday short
and returned without warning,
and the abyss wasn't faithful
when it smuggled out prisoners
guilty of penning the names of God
on forbidden amber stones,
and drawing angels
on wine glasses.

Upon hearing water burbling in the bones,
they thought
the lake of your days had grown weary
of staring into the deep,

so the valleys and fields overflowed
with words of light.

Awakening after their last slumber
they decided to cross.
Beneath the shadows of the bridge,
they surrendered incantations to the body
and poured saffron water
over its head.

All that was left was the name.
Seeking the Lord's forgiveness, they tore it from their flesh, like an arrow from a wound.

No longer will they rest in your body,
you who have been dipped in the ink of the world.

Once more shall the birds rest on your hand,
while even their still siblings,
painted on walls
or silken fabrics
shall flap their wings.

The light shall follow you
as you cast away dust from the first stone.
Then the angels who seek its blessings every night
shall take notice of the deception:

When the stranger returns home
after a long absence,
his stray secrets

shall fall from his clothes,
and passers-by will mistake them
for pens made from the trees of paradise.

Your reflection in polished mirrors
shall be like buried treasures, places where oxygen was forcibly drawn,
a deserted cave on whose walls a carving cries out to its shadow.
But that which you have failed to see in your blindness,
by discernment you shall perceive.
Your breath shall be your guide; your compass, the winds;
and they shall erase the misunderstanding between you and the desert stones.
You give them meaning and they give you the treasure trove of time.

Words illuminate your night like the stars, guiding many an eye,
and many a soul longing for the unseen.
Under their light in the long, dreary nights, scrolls are spread, hands reach out, and
souls are dipped into the hollows of the writing reeds.
You merely need but make a noise, and your words shall awaken beneath the throne,
and the world shall shine resplendently with the truth.

Your heirs
generation after generation
allowed their lives to linger in the gardens of saints.
Like an acrobat, they walked the tight rope between two poles: Inspiration and Pen,
as though walking on a knife's edge.
And then, beyond the Tree of Knowledge,
In horror they stared: the book in the hands of the angel,
an illusion toying with language.

Your heirs

are poets

too.

Their tongues are riddles of speech; their tremors, a lover's messengers; their prayer, a desire
to reach the shape of a full stop, though there is no laying anchor on this journey;
and their disobedience, a lightning flash "snatched away from sight", yet dwelling in those
eyes that have lost sight.
With the breaths of gazelles, they walk. With the eyes of hawks, they see,
lost in wonder at the feel of the stars.
When they fall under their gaze, when they lift up their eyes: an abyss of light, they are.

As people closed their books, so was earth folded up from its edges.
They placed them in a large saddlebag on their mounts, their eyes fixed upon eternity.
Yet, here you are, undecided about a destination.
Will you proceed, as you were determined to at the moment of resurrection,
to reveal the secret of secrets in the presence of the Divine?
Or will you go back to whence you came,
leaving your limbs hanging on a clothesline
for their secrets to be dried out by the heat of the sun?!

You are the blind for whom glimpses provide no relief.
When will you realize that the hour of resurrection has not yet come for your words,
and that the echo of their voice remains stuck in the throat of Time?!

LIGHT

Light gives life to the Earth; and at the heart of this Creation, human beings capture another form of light that, at their innermost core, brings them knowledge, wisdom, faith. This intangible light, which is first conveyed in the spoken word, has subsequently been transposed in writing for over six thousand years. More than any other, the civilization of Islam has endowed writing with a dimension that goes well beyond the mere transmission of ideas, knowledge and narrations. The calligraphic layout of the letter, the word and the sentence truly embody the life energy and the rhythm of human thought. Arabic calligraphy, whose aesthetic is based on harmony and balance, guides the mind of whoever reads and contemplates it towards the elusive, the awe-inspiring. In works of classical calligraphy, this incorporeal light is embellished with the colours and golds of illumination, as are, on occasion, the diacritical marks. On supports other than parchment and paper, the incarnation of this inner light is based on a luminosity that is specific to the material on which the calligraphy – be it verses from the Qur'an, good wishes or aphorisms – is deployed. Both the craftsmen of old and contemporary designers know how to create wonder with the mastery of the effects inherent in the material they work with. This light, opalescent (porcelain), translucent (glass) or emerging from openwork (wood and metal) transcends the meaning of what can be read on the pieces they have fashioned.

CAT. 1

Sara Ouhaddou

An-Nur, 2022

Coloured glass and wood frame
Diameter 150 cm
Commissioned by the Ministry of Culture, Saudi Arabia
inv. CA 2022.4

An-Nur is part of a long-term project to revive the dying art of stained glass in Morocco. In her quest to reconnect with past know-how and rewrite the movement of exchanges between North Africa and the Middle East, Ouhaddou conducted workshops across the country using different materials and techniques (ceramic, weaving, embroidery and glass), studying the history of the Moroccan people through traditional objects and finding new narratives to empower local stories.
This circular stained-glass artwork combines an original antique handmade glass artefact, which dates back to the eleventh century and comes from what was known at the time as the Great Syria, with Moorish glass from Spain, coloured glass from India and industrial glass from China. A reference to the surah *an-Nur*, this stained-glass disc contains a poem calligraphed in an intricate abstract alphabet born out of Islamic geometric shapes. As it captures the glow, glass becomes the material embodiment of light.

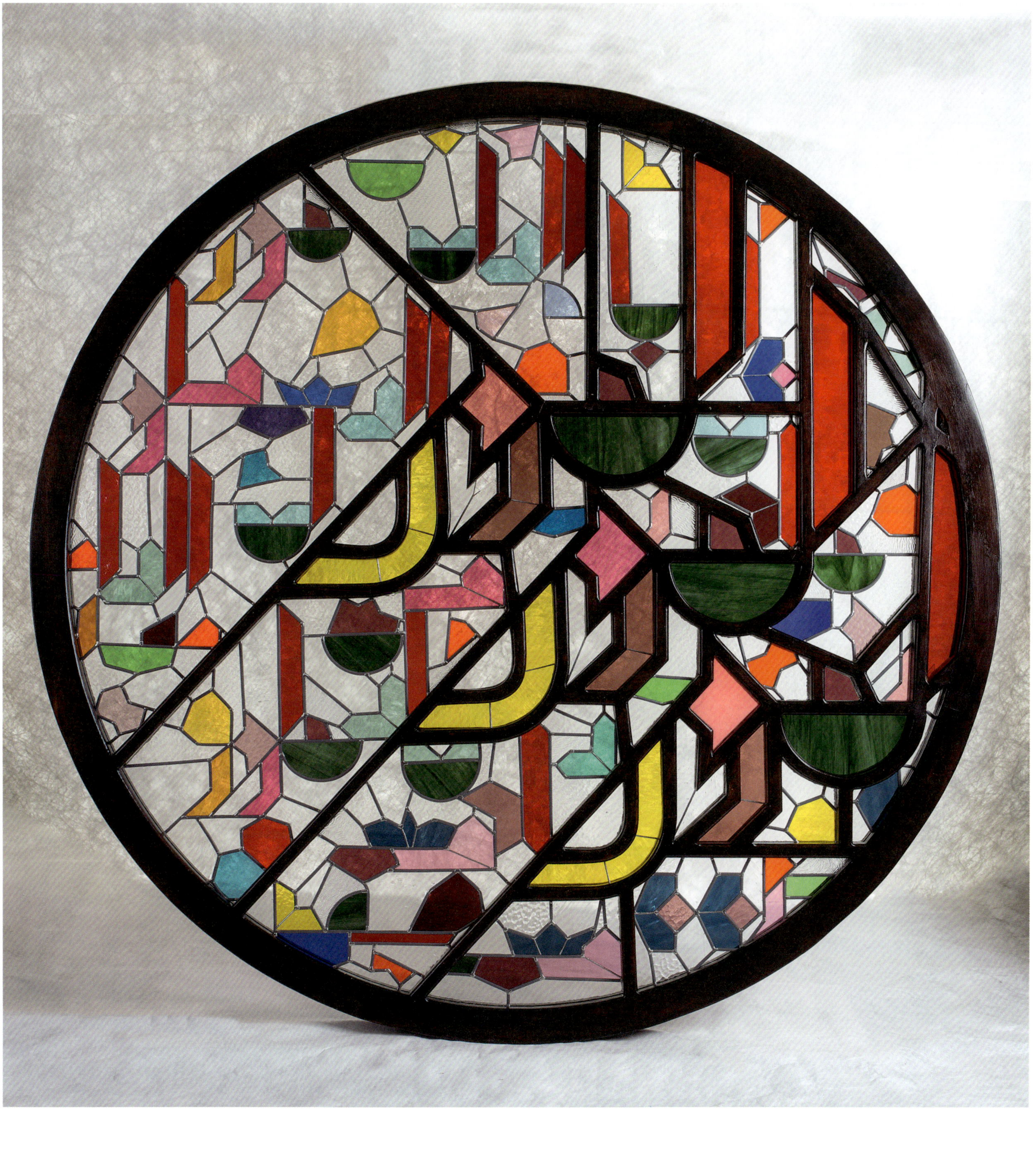

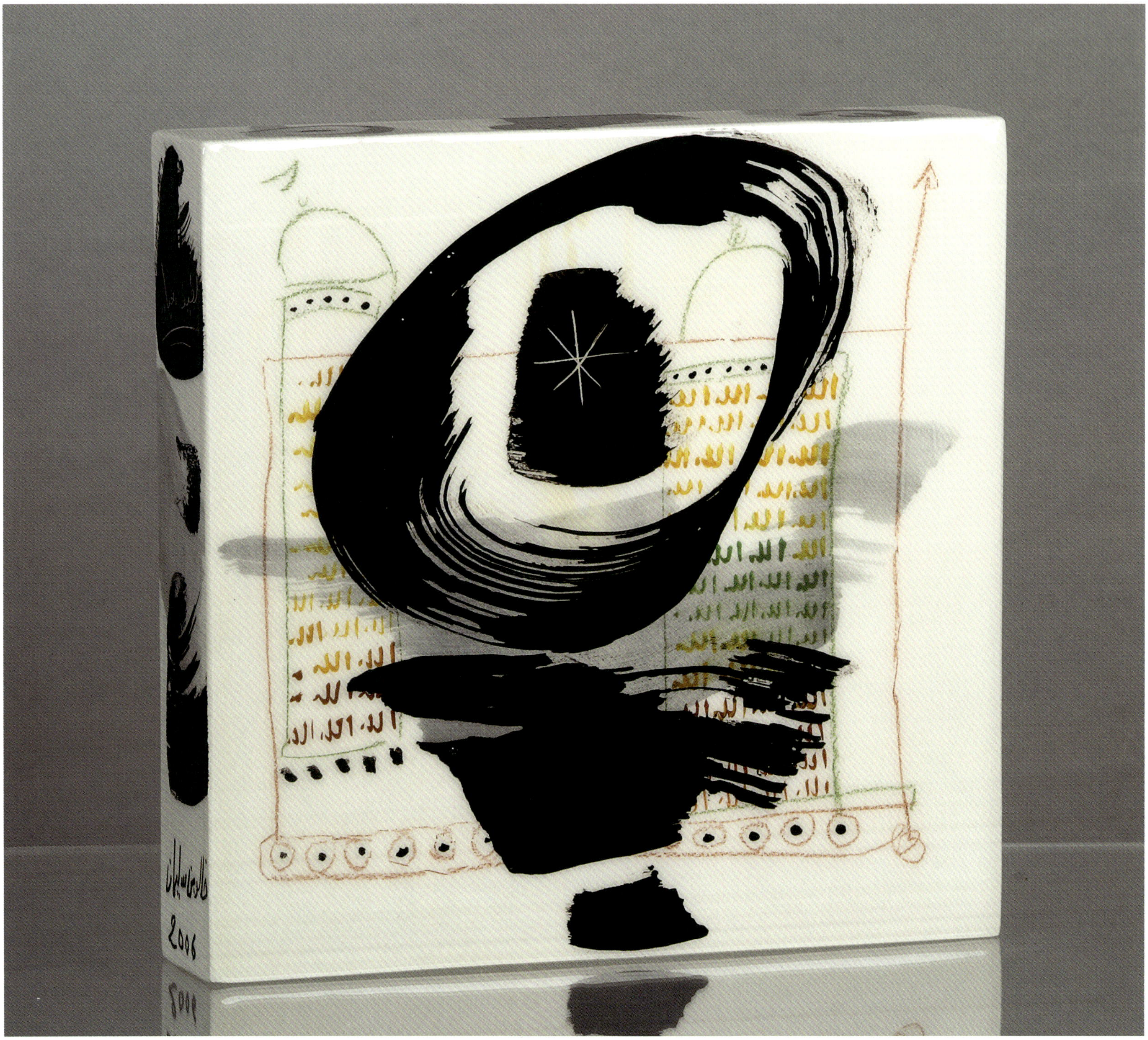

CAT. 2

Khaled Ben Slimane
***Howa 1*, 2006**

Glazed ceramic
25 × 25 cm
Courtesy of Elmarsa Gallery, United Arab Emirates, Dubai

Inscription-like concentric circles invoking *Howa* (Him) recall the endless whirl of the *Sema* dance practised by Al Rumi's followers to the rhythm of drums and *ney*. The artist manifests a preference for simple geometric forms and the flowing texture of the brush rather than the firm control of the traditional Arabic *qalam* (pen), a result of the influence of his training under Japanese master potters and calligraphers.

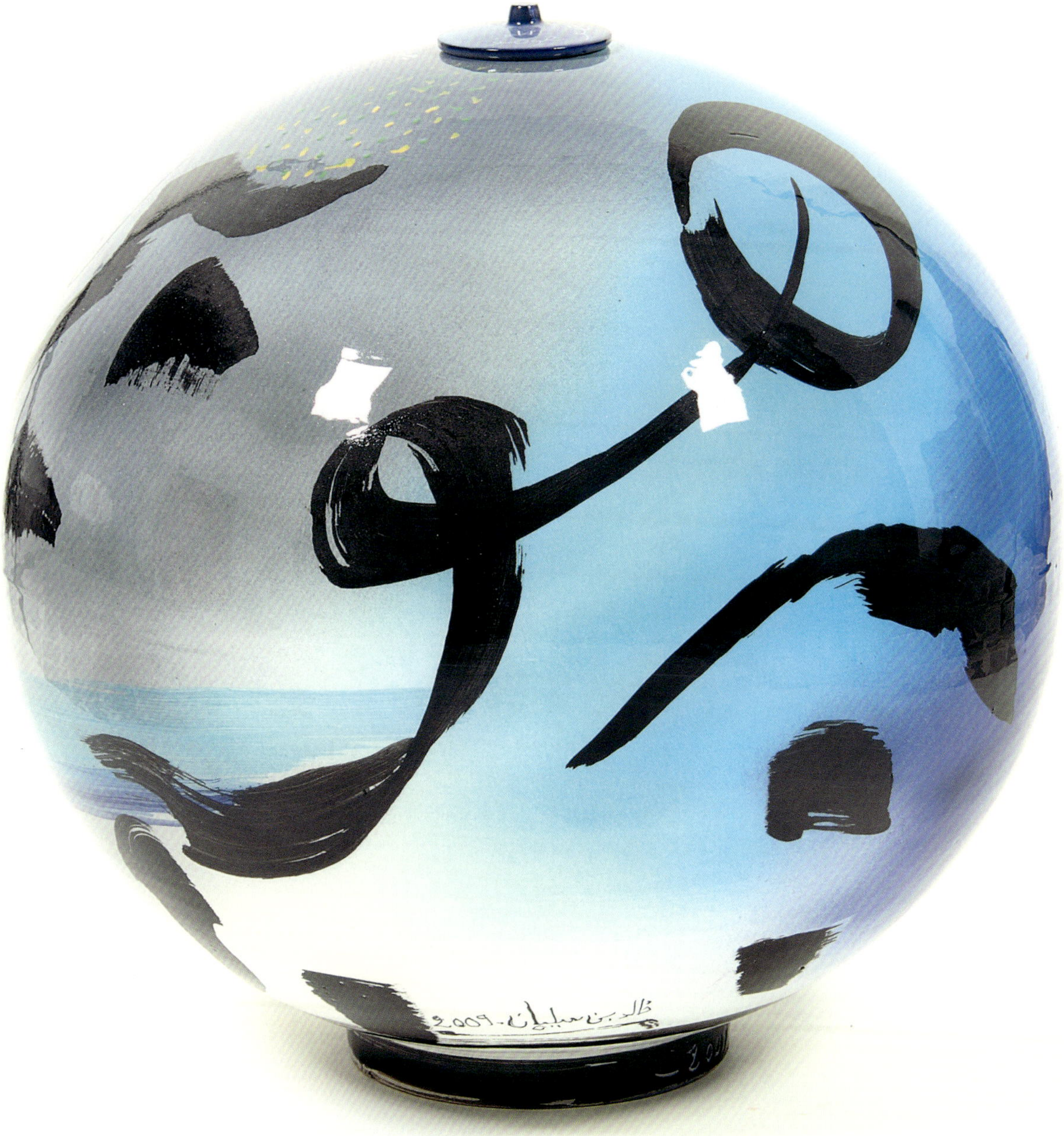

CAT. 3

Khaled Ben Slimane
Ceramic Ball, 2009

Glazed ceramic
50 × 52 cm
Courtesy of Elmarsa Gallery, United Arab Emirates, Dubai

A meaningful and meditative gesture is embodied into this glazed ceramic. The *Ceramic Ball*, with its circular shape, evokes the turning of the potter's wheel. This dynamic artwork suggests many sources, such as humanism and Zen philosophy, betraying a modern sensitivity tempered with a compelling appreciation for tradition.

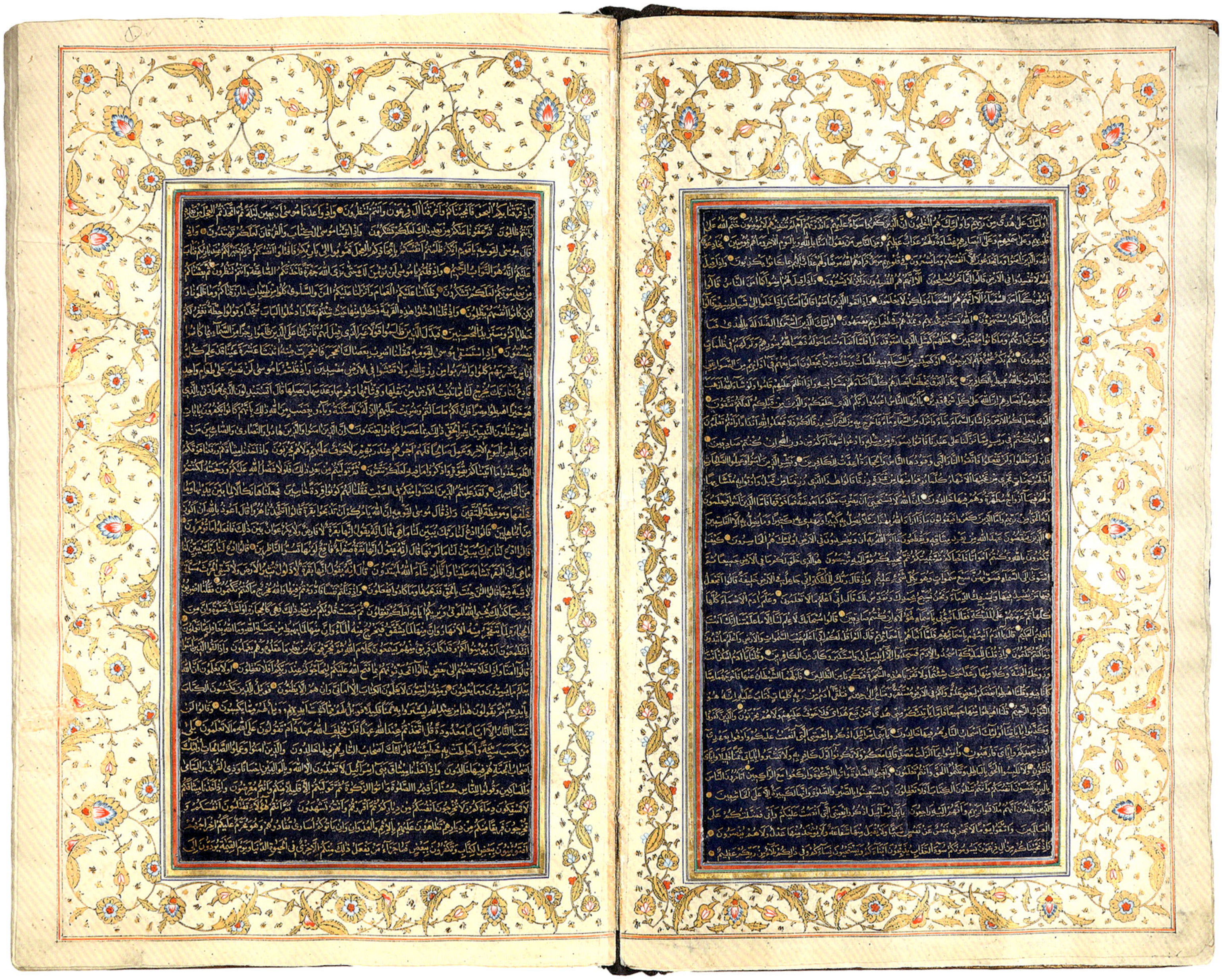

CAT. 4

The Holy Qur'an

Persia, thirteenth–fourteenth century AH / late nineteenth–early twentieth century AD

Ink and gold on paper
Written in *naskh* script
31 × 19 cm (closed)
Collection of the Ministry of Culture, Saudi Arabia
inv. IA 2021.20

Manuscript on blue paper, 64 leaves plus 2 flyleaves, each folio with 33 lines to the page of elegant gold *naskh* script, gold verse roundels, surah headings as clouds on a blue hatched ground, text panels within gold and polychrome rules, the opening bifolio with a gold and polychrome illuminated floral headpiece, the blue-ink heading in cloud reserved against hatched ground, the margins with gold and polychrome scrolling floral vines. Lacquer binding decorated with flowers and birds.

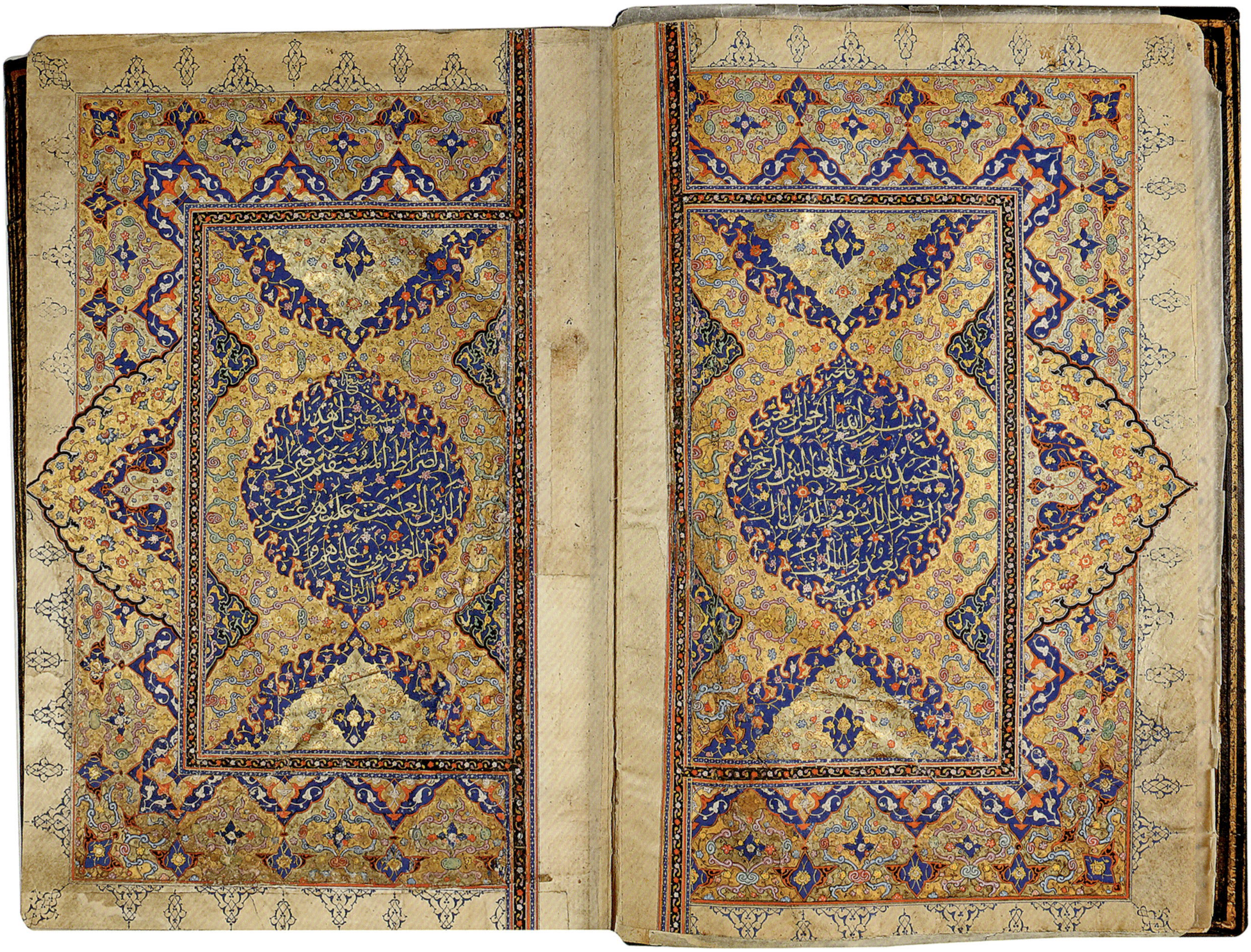

CAT. 5

The Holy Qur'an

Persia, tenth century AH / sixteenth century AD

Copied by 'Ala'-al-din Muhammad Al-Tabrizi
Ink and gold on paper
Written in *naskh* script
33.5 × 22 cm (closed)
Collection of the Ministry of Culture, Saudi Arabia
inv. IA 2021.19

Manuscript on buff paper, 356 pages plus 2 flyleaves, with 12 lines to the page, written in black *naskh* script, verses separated by gold and polychrome pointed floral roundels, surah headings in white cursive script against gold ground within cusped cartouches on illuminated panels, some including words written in *naskh* script within clouds on reserved ground, margins ruled in colours and gold.

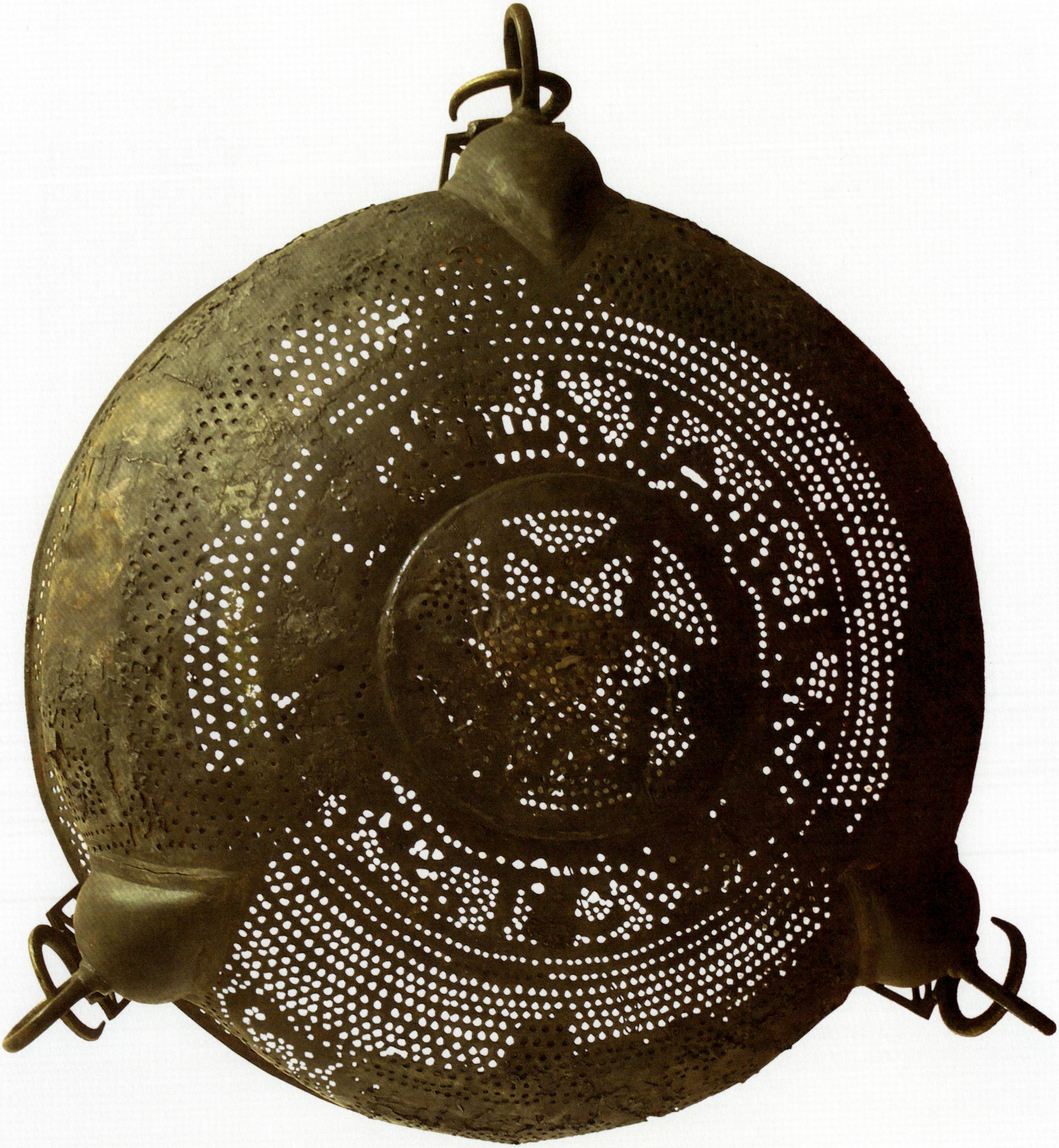

CAT. 6

Lantern, Great Mosque of Kairouan, Tunisia

424–443 AH / 1032–51 AD

Cast by Muhammad bin Ali al-Qaysi
Al-Saffar for Al-Mu'izz bin Badis
Cast and bronze
Written in *kufi* script
118 × 51.5 cm
Collection of the Raqqada Museum
of Civilization and Islamic Arts, Kairouan
inv. 1-13-06-14

This lantern, made of cast and openwork bronze, consists of a bronze hook attached to a hemispherical cap that gives rise to three openwork chains decorated with geometric and stylized floral motifs. These chains suspend a large, hammered brass basin in the shape of a circular vase, riddled with luminous dots obtained by drilling. At the bottom is a six-pointed star surrounded by three inscriptions in *kufi* script: two proclaiming "Praise to God . . . and blessing, happiness, felicity, success, prosperity, salvation and glory to its possessor" and the other mentioning the names of the artist and the patron of the lantern: "the work of Muhammad son of Ali al-Qaysi Al-Saffar (the coppersmith) for Al-Mu'izz".

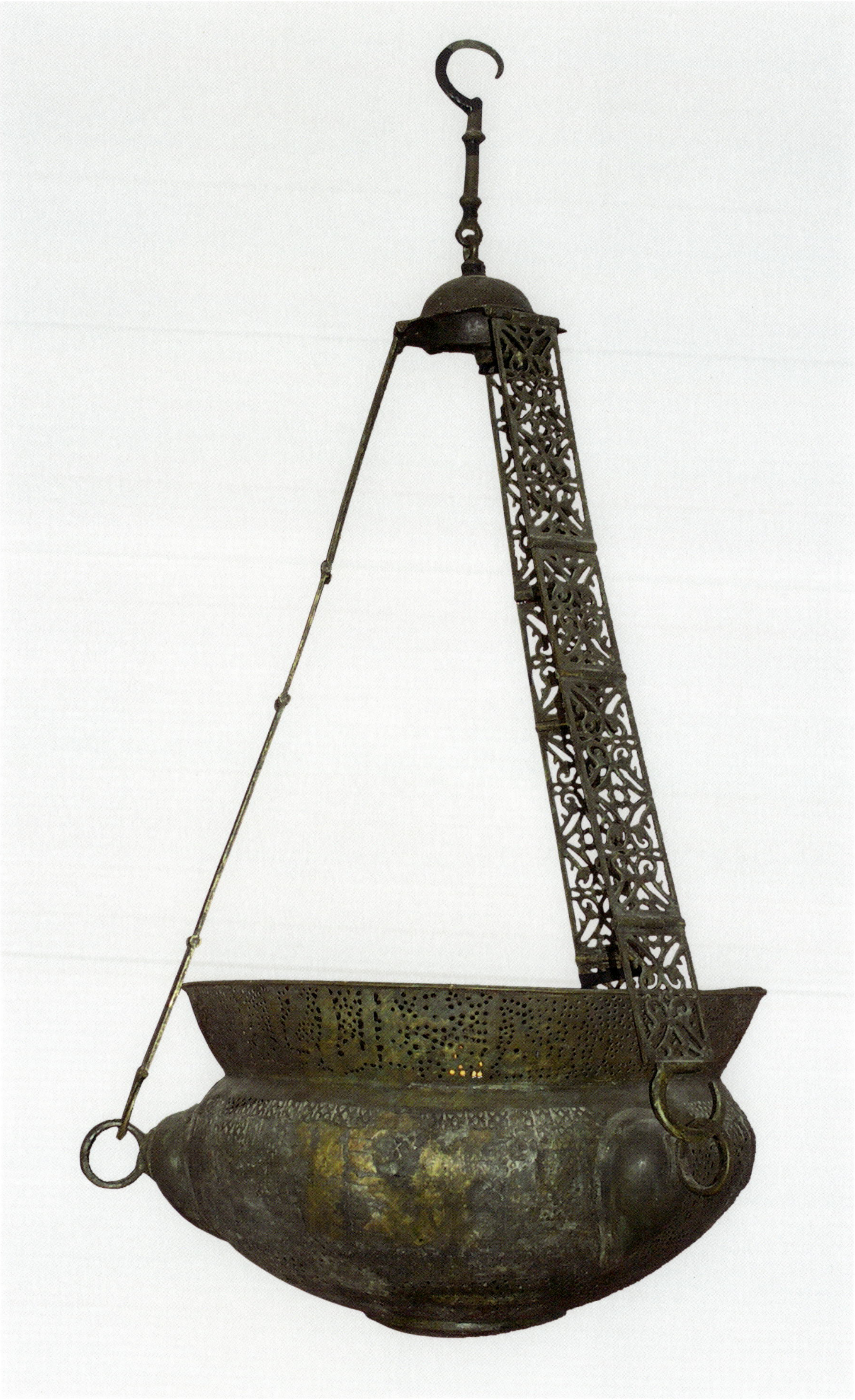

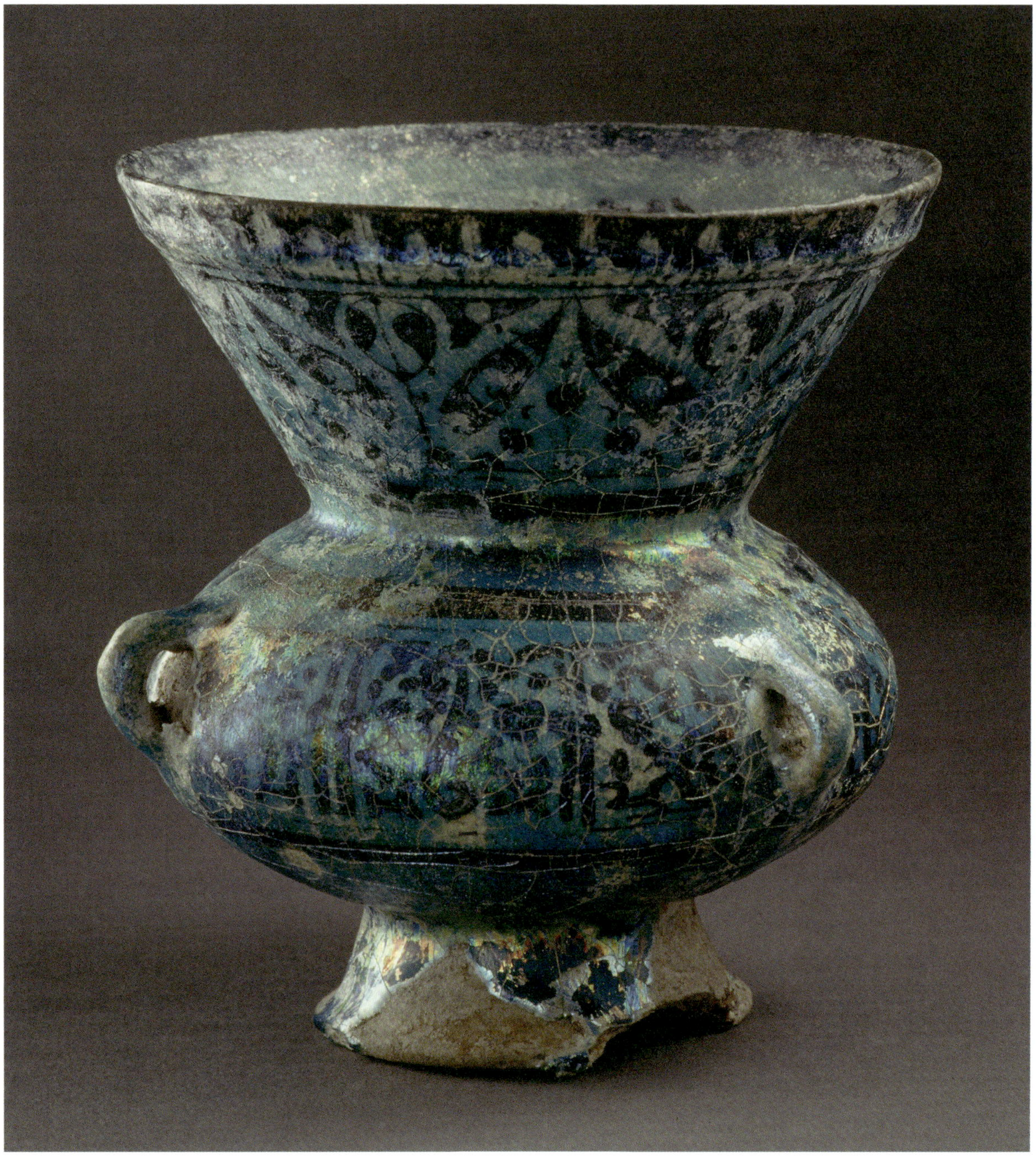

CAT. 7

Mosque lamp

Raqqa, Syria, first half of the seventh century AH / first half of the thirteenth century AD (Ayyubid Period)

Frit body, floral and epigraphic decoration painted in black under a turquoise glaze
Written in *kufi* script
16 × 14.6 cm
Collection of the Museum of the Institut du Monde Arabe
inv. AI 94-32

This so-called "Mosque lamp" with a globular body, a long, flared neck and a low folded foot is quite rare in earthenware; this shape will be common in enamel and gilded glassware or in pierced metal ware during the Mamluk Period. Four suspension loops are attached to its body and a *kufi* inscription records part of surah *an-Nur* (verse 24).

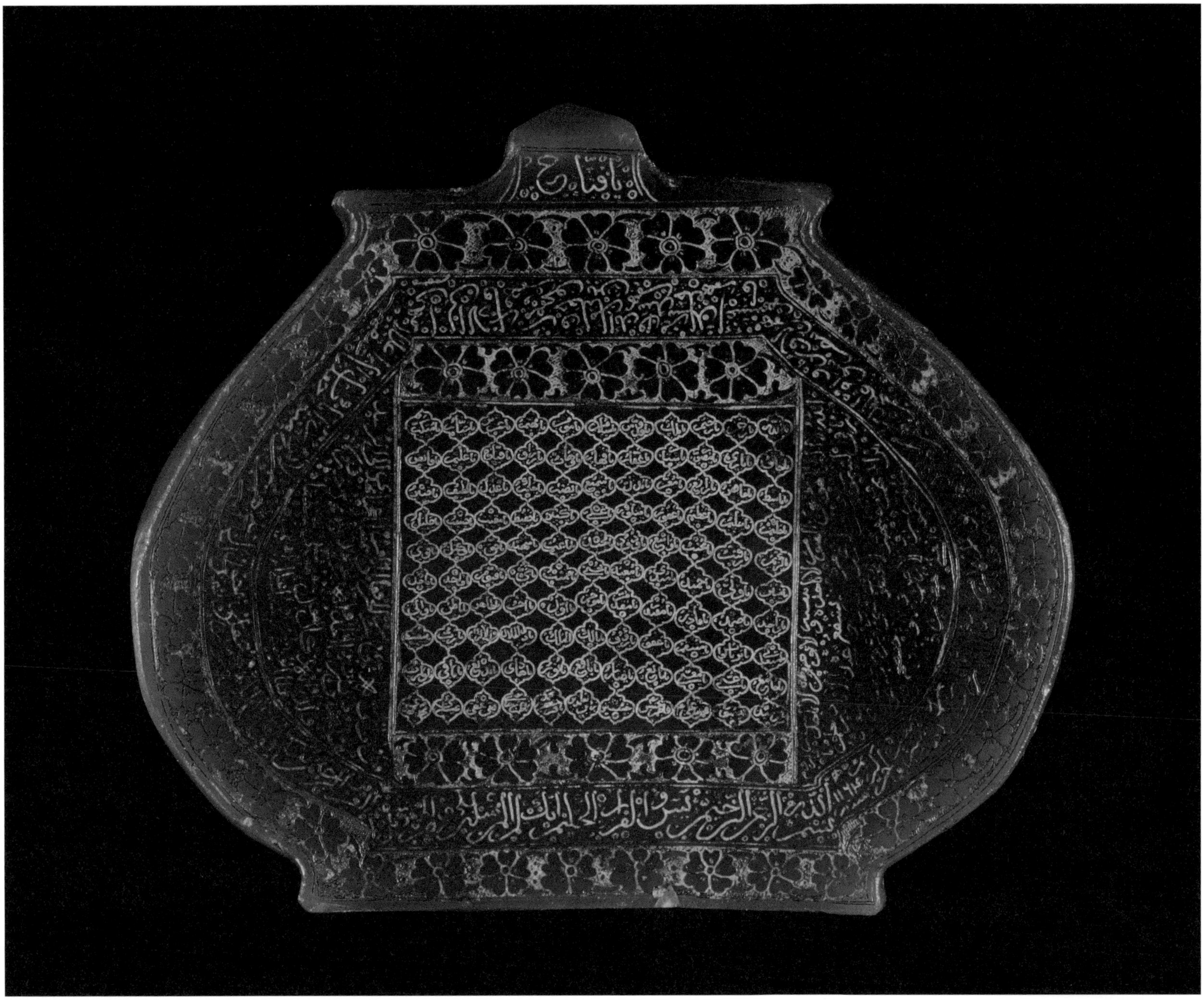

CAT. 8

Agate pendant inscribed with 99 names of God

India, 1164 AH / 1750–51 AD

Grey agate, polished and engraved
6.7 × 7.8 × 1 cm
Collection of the Museum of the Institut du Monde Arabe
inv. AI 87-26

A square shape flanked on its upper and lower parts by a six-petal rosette frieze enumerates the 99 names of God, each one inscribed in a multi-lobed cartouche. To the right, verse 225 of surah *al-Baqarah* is engraved and to the left, some verses of surah *al-Djinn* (1–4). Around the gemstone, a *thuluth* inscription includes surah *Ya-sin* verses (1–11). Pierced on the top, the agate was used as a pendant and bears the *ya fattah* inscription. It is considered as a scientific object with respect to special fabrication rules.

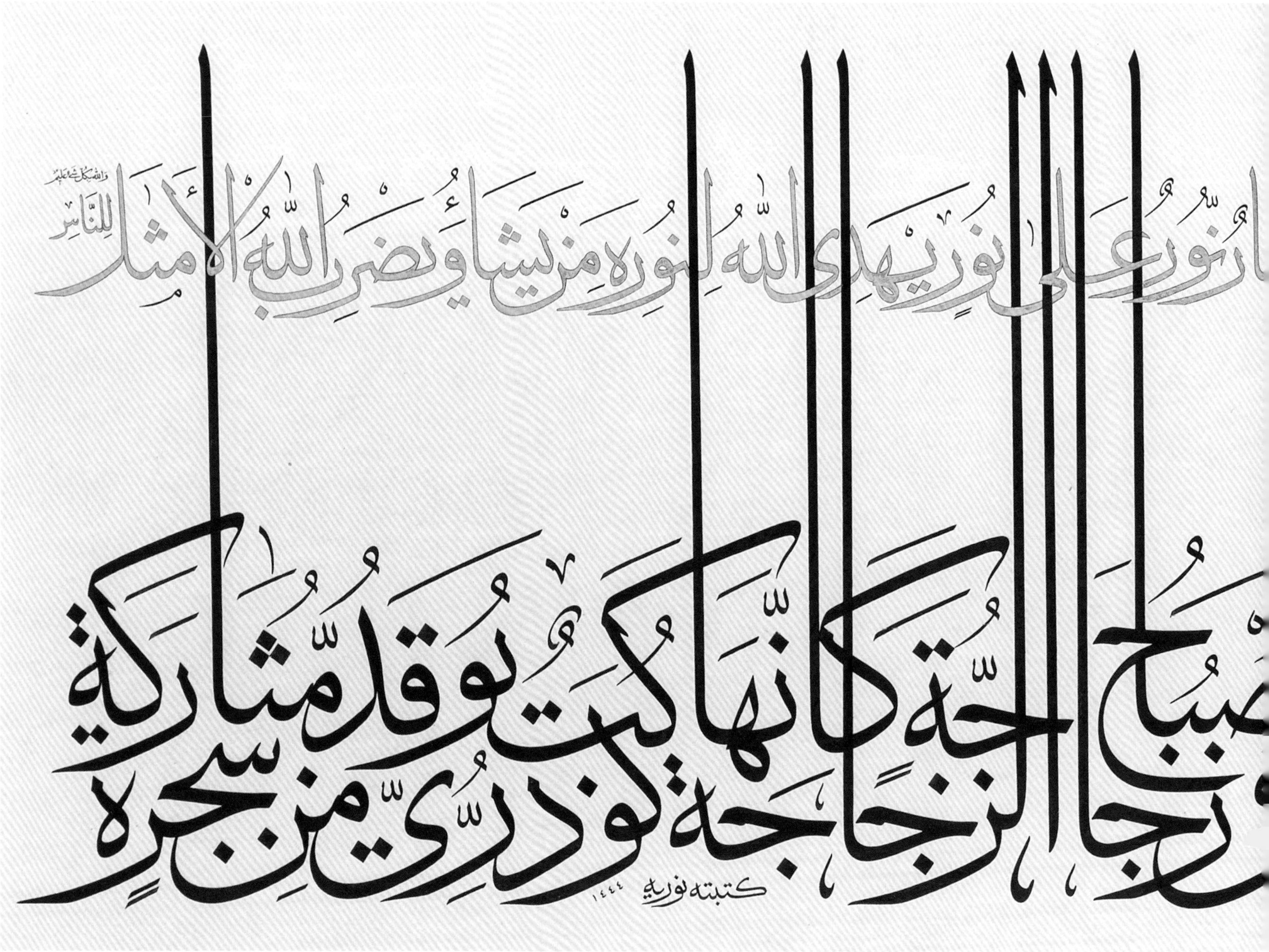

CAT. 9

Nuria García Masip
***Surah an-Nur, verse 35*, 2022**

Ink and gold on paper
Written in *muhaqqaq* script
48 × 120 cm
Commissioned by the Ministry of Culture, Saudi Arabia
inv. IA 2022.14

Surah *an-Nur* is one of the most renowned surahs of the Holy Qur'an. *An-Nur* (light) is an attribute of Allah and the image of a lamp lodged inside the niche stands as a symbol of light in believers' heart. Written in *muhaqqaq* script with two different-sized *qalams* (reed pens) in what is known in classical calligraphy as the "mother-and-child" layout, it symbolizes the Divine Light manifested onto the human plane.

The Name of God is in the lower right section of the frame and the second part of the verse, containing the words "light upon light", is in the upper section of the frame; they are both written in gold. The larger composition in black ink, with the long vertical ascenders of *alif* and *lam*, rises upwards, symbolizing the verticality of the spiritual journey, ascending towards the Divine Light.

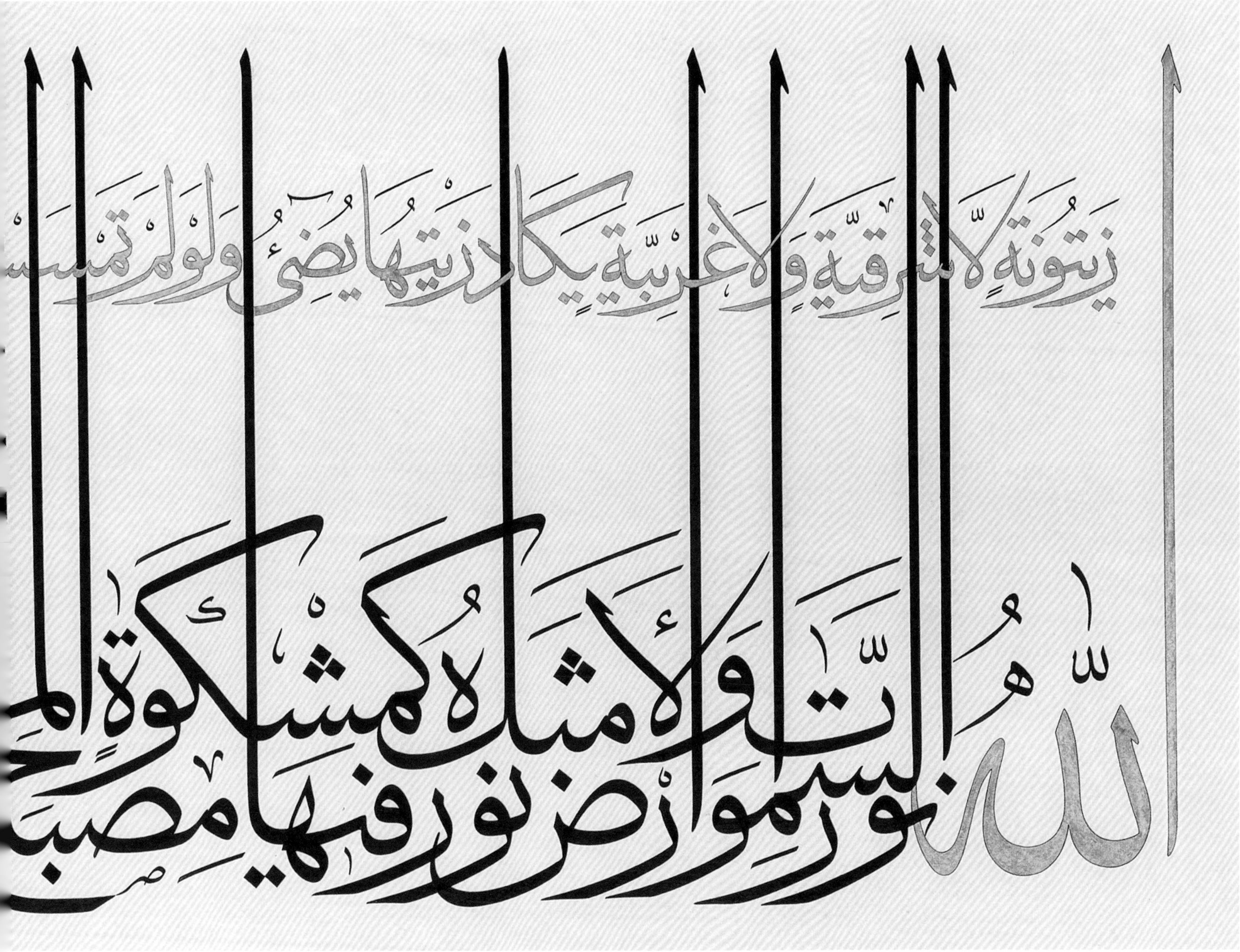
الله نور السموات والأرض مثل نوره كمشكوة فيها مصباح الم
زيتونة لا شرقية ولا غربية يكاد زيتها يضيء ولو لم تمس

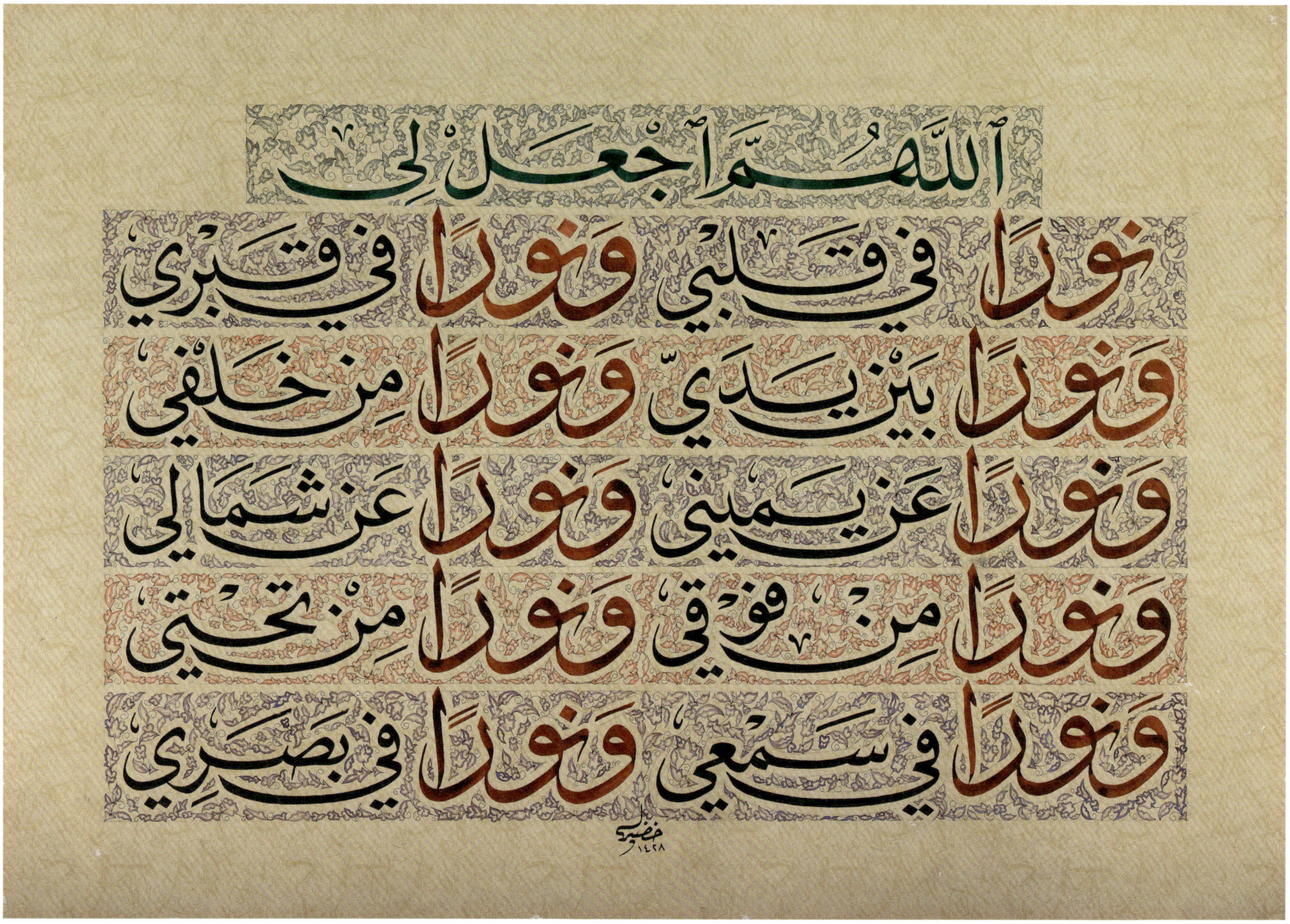

CAT. 10

Khodeir El-Borsaidy
Invocation of Prayers, 2007

Ink on paper
Written in *thuluth* and *naskh* scripts
77 × 107 cm
Collection of the Ministry of Culture, Saudi Arabia
inv. IA 2022.13.1

A *du'a'* (prayer of supplication) written in *naskh* and *thuluth* scripts on the symbolism of *nur* (light). The latter word, appearing repetitively in ruby red colour, imparts light and warmth to the whole canvas. The rest of the *du'a'* is written in large clear *naskh* script for easier reading. With ornamentation finishings in bright colours. The influence of Sayyed Abdel Kader's "al Hajj Zayed" can be detected in the concept of this composition.

The texts read (from the hadith of Abdullah bin 'Abbas): "O Allah, place light in my heart, light in my tongue, light in my sight, light in my hearing, light on my right, light on my left, light above me, light below me, light in front of me, and light behind me, and place a light in my soul for me, and increase the light for me".

CAT. 11

Mohamad Gaber

Hilyah, 2022

Chinese ink, gold and colour on paper
70 × 35 cm
Commissioned by the Ministry of Culture, Saudi Arabia
inv. IA 2022.11

This is a classical *Hilyah* – literally, ornament – written on hand-polished paper with Japanese ink in *thuluth* and *naskh* scripts, enriched with colours and decorated with gold. It presents the merits of the Prophet (PBUH), as *Hilyahs* are also a symbolic expression of his physical and moral qualities.

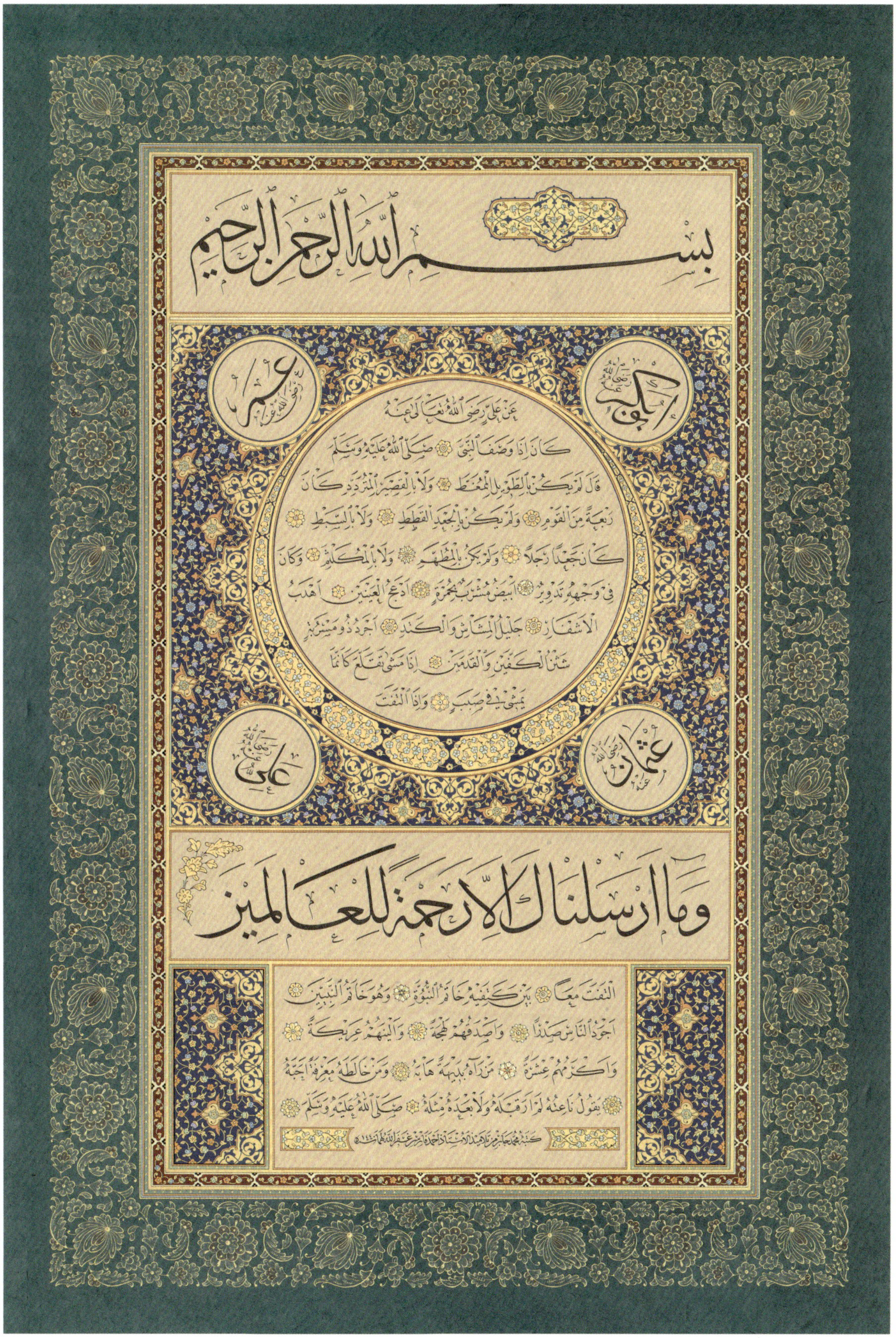

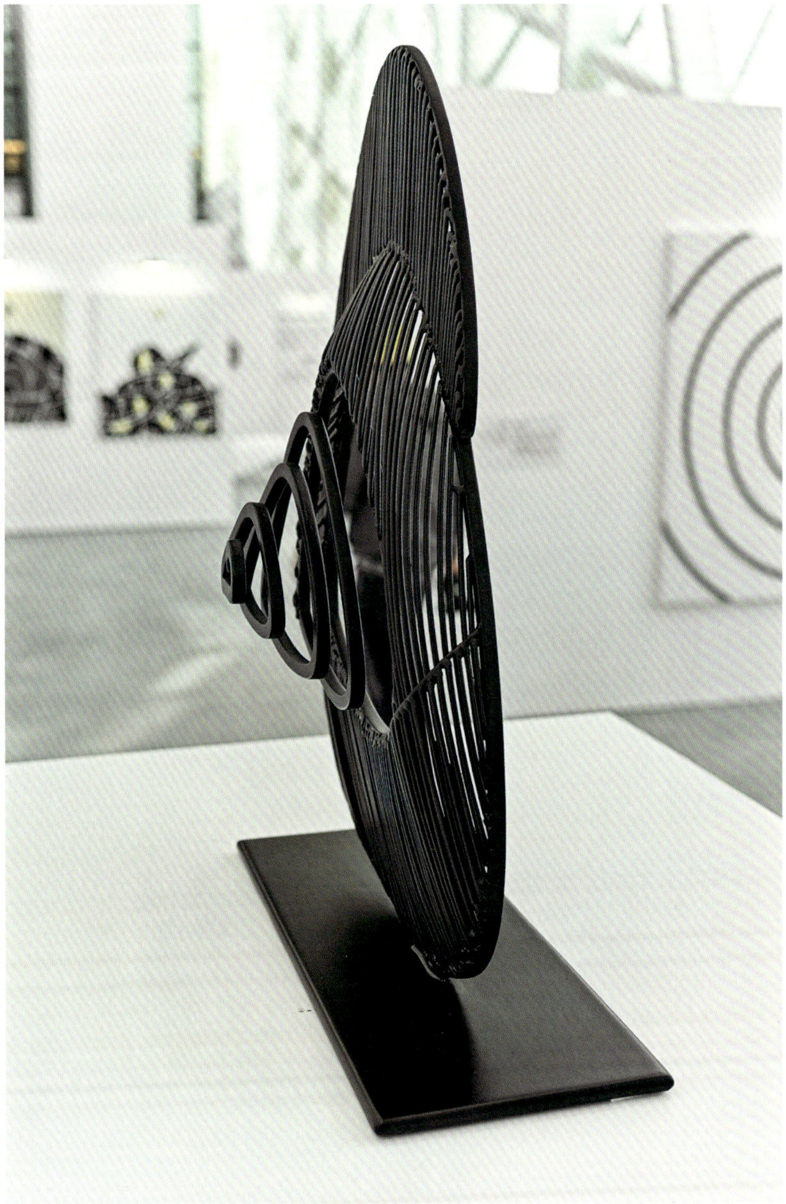

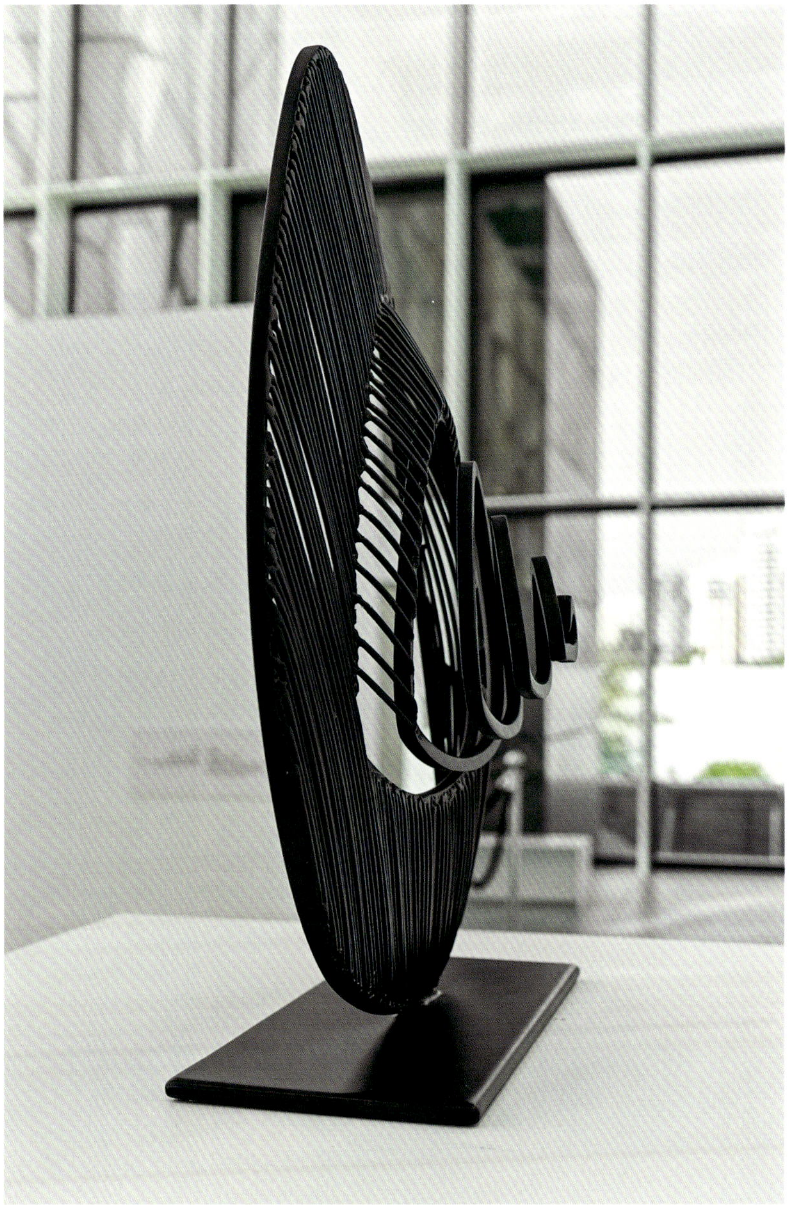

CAT. 12

Jassim Miraj Al-Failakawi
A Pen Creak, 2018

Iron
72 × 31 × 12 cm
Courtesy of Jassim Miraj Al-Failakawi

When a quill is about to run out of ink, we can hear it grating, and this grating produced by the quill is a cry of help to its holder to resupply it with ink from the inkwell. On this basis, Jassim Miraj wanted to create a visible expression of the musical notes that the movement of the quill makes. There are scripts where, at the beginning of the letter, the ink decreases as it descends to the corner and then becomes darker as the following movement starts. Then it gets alternately lighter and darker depending on the movement of the hand. Then the quill embarks on the five orbits of the two letters that are the embodiment of the stand-alone *ha'* and the medial *ha'*, somehow echoing a mother carrying a baby inside her womb as they display closeness and harmony. Presented in the modern wing of the exhibition, this variation on the letter *ha'* explores the relation between this letter and nature as appearing in the verse, "If all the trees on earth were pens, and the sea [were] ink with seven [more] seas to replenish it, the words of God would not be exhausted, for God is Almighty and Wise", conceptualizing through a line the link between the physical world and the Invisible.

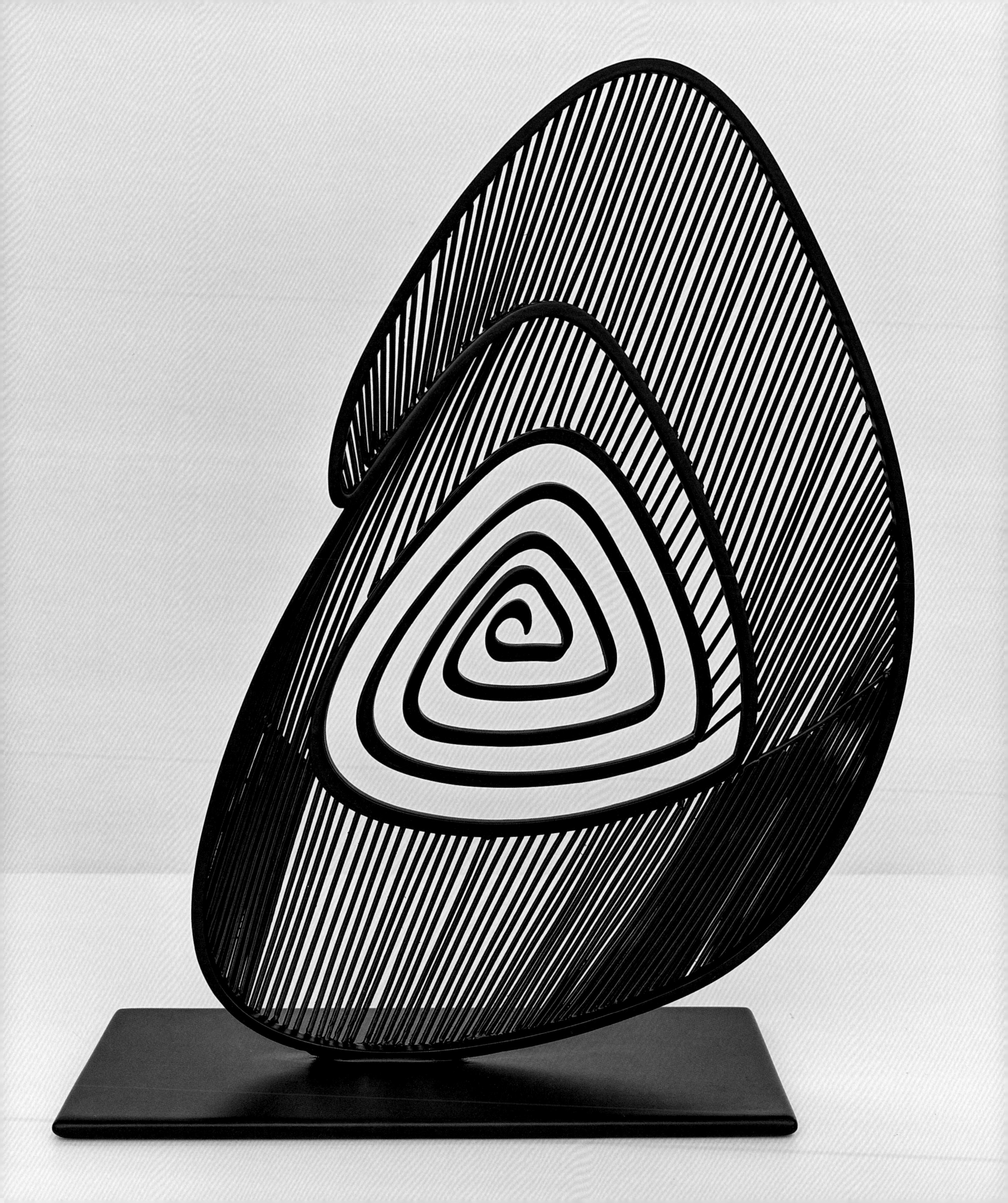

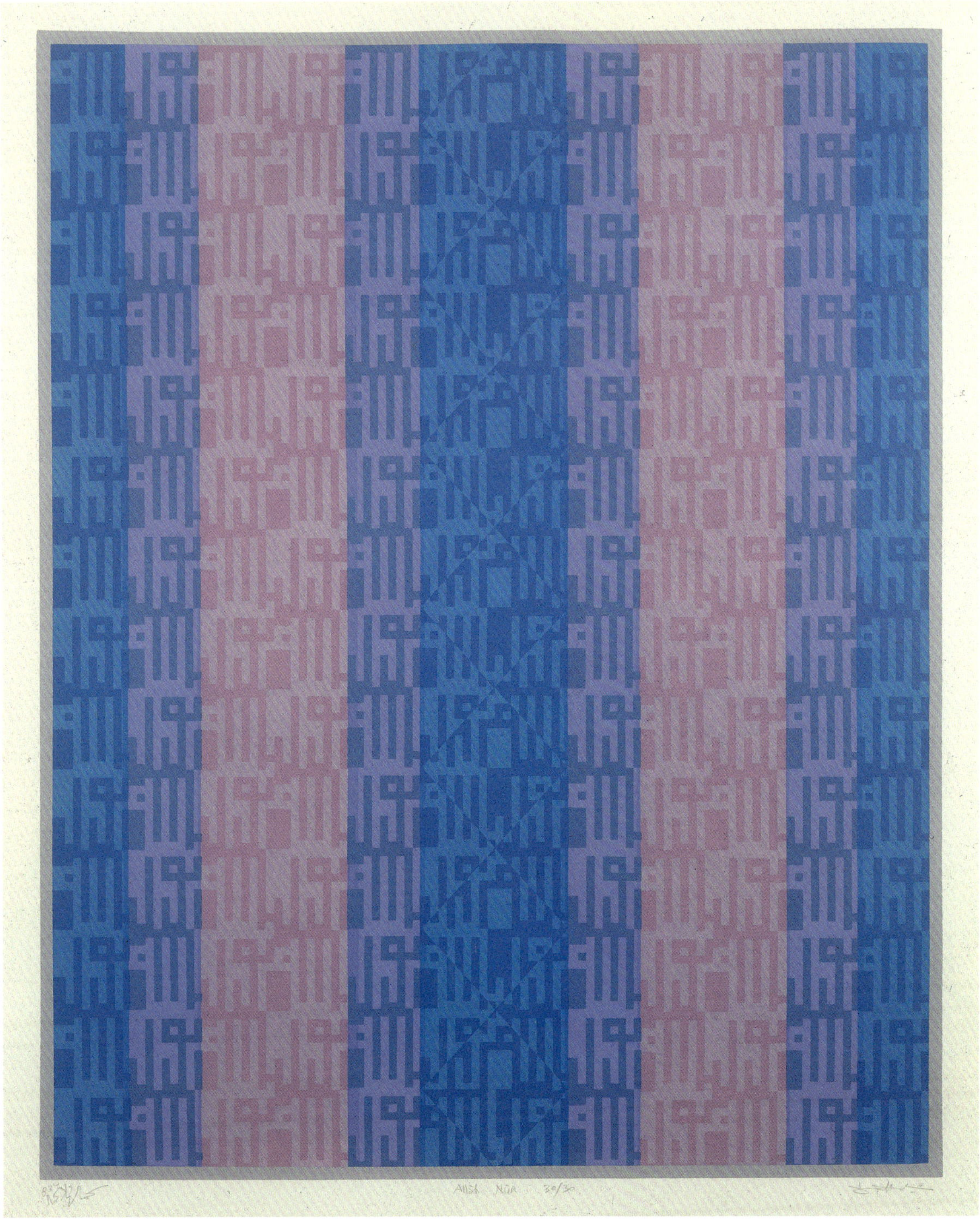

CAT. 13

Kamal Boullata

Allah Nur, 1983

Silkscreen print, 30/30, signed in the lower right-hand corner
Inspired by square *kufi* script
91.8 × 73.8 cm
Collection of the Museum of the Institut du Monde Arabe
inv. AC 86-67

The artist uses characters derived from square *kufi* script, with exclusively right angles as used in architecture during the first centuries of Islam. Relief is given to this composition through the three shades of blue, pink and purple, accentuated in the middle by a cut-out in seven diamonds. The artist states he was committed to creating a symbiosis between linguistic meaning and plastic expression. Here the colour brings to the words a materiality comparable to that of the sound resulting from these pronounced words.

CAT. 14

Susan Hefuna

Ihna, 2009

Ink and painted wood (*mashrabiyya*)
160 × 160 cm
Collection of the Ministry of Culture, Saudi Arabia
inv. CA 2022.13

For as far as she could remember, Susan Hefuna has always been attracted to abstract structures, and more specifically, those minute elements in science and biology – molecules and DNA chains or modules – that build up the larger fabric of life. As a child, she couldn't help but notice similarities between the shapes of the *mashrabiyya* (old lattice wood decorative screens in old Cairo architecture) and molecular structures, especially in the joints where lines meet, cross and then continue their way.
She has been creating her iconic large-scale wooden *mashrabiyya* screens since 2004, interweaving words and sentences into their structure. In her work, language and pattern fuse to become one.

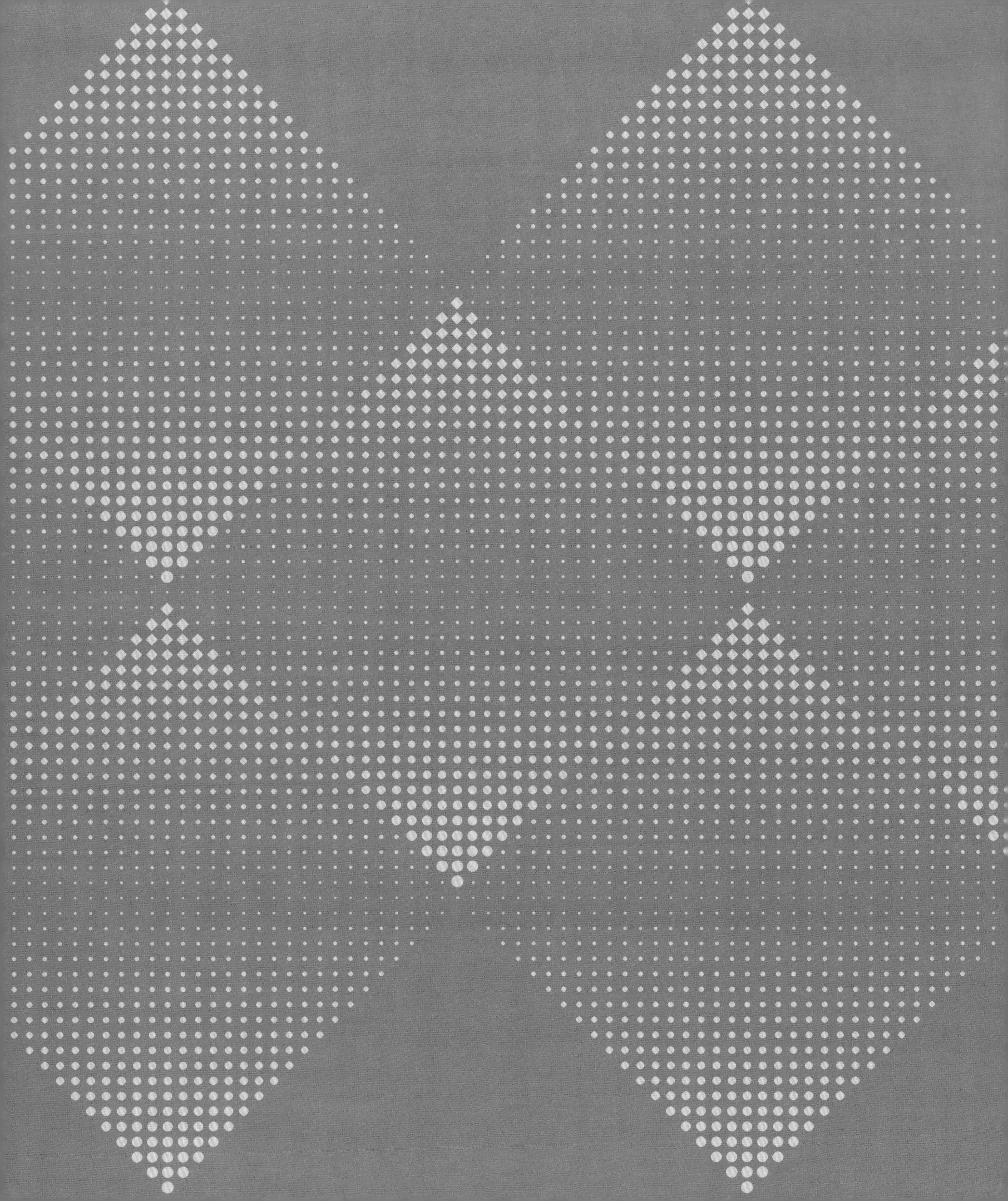

LETTER

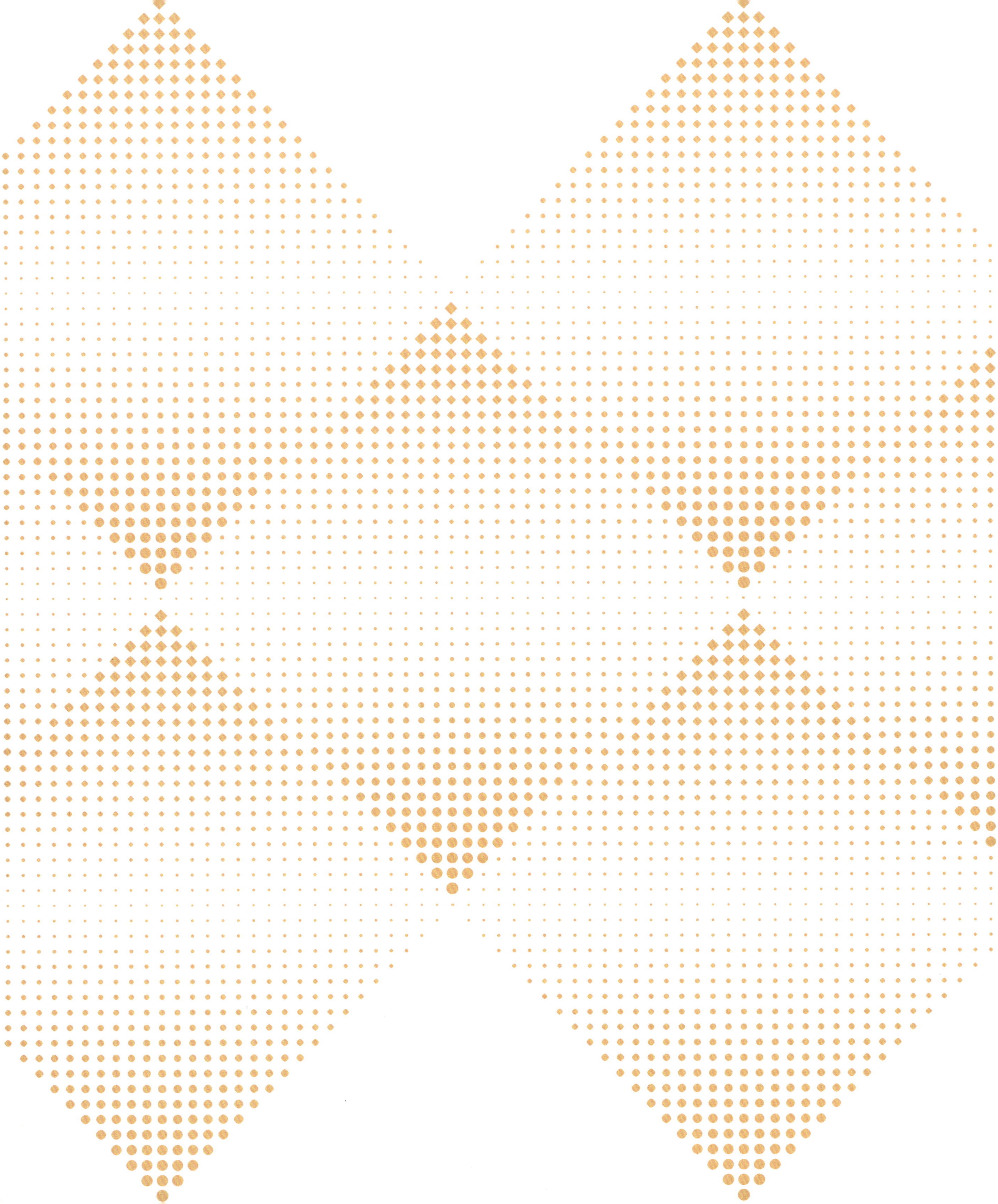

All calligraphy seduces with its apparent simplicity, whether in the geometric design of the *kufi* script characters or in the fluidity of the six classic styles (*al-aqlam al-sitta*) of cursive script. However, this simplicity is the result of a long apprenticeship and then of daily practice: the calligrapher must always study and deepen his knowledge. Mastery of the artists' hand gestures remains inseparable from their state of mind when they are at work.

The master calligrapher respects the proportion and harmony defined by the conventions of *al-khatt al-mansub*, as codified by Ibn Muqla in the third century AH / tenth century AD. The letter is drawn in a circle whose diameter is defined by the height of the letter *alif*. The height of the letter is itself established by the number of *nuqta*, that is, the rhombic dot created by the pressure of the tip of a reed that has been dipped in ink. This number differs according to the classical scripts – *thuluth*, *naskh*, *muhaqqaq*, *rayhani*, *tawqi'*, *riqa'* – as well as for later styles.

However, the pursuit of formal perfection cannot be an end in itself; the master calligraphers accompany it with a deep inner quest, which is indispensable for the transmission and sharing of the beauty, energy and meaning of their art.

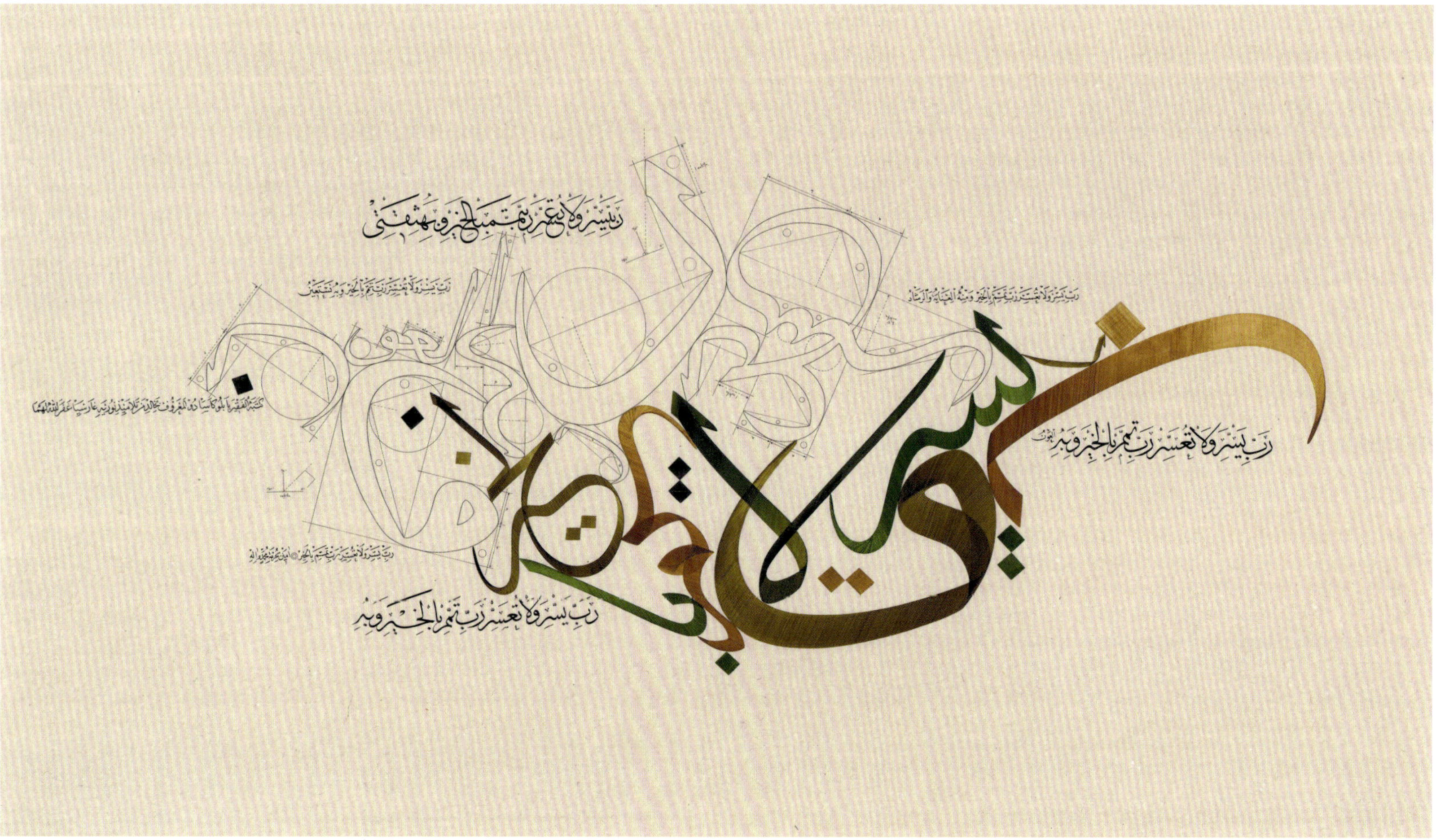

CAT. 15

Pablo Casado
Rabbi Yassir, 2022

Ink on cardboard
50 × 105 cm
Written in *jaly thuluth* script
Commissioned by the Ministry of Culture, Saudi Arabia
inv. IA 2022.3

Based on the *Rabbi Yassir*, an invocation asking God to make things easier, this conceptual contemporary work follows the line traced by all apprentice calligraphers during the early years of their training. The composition is a study of that line as it sinews across letters, words and proportions, following traditional canons. It showcases variations of the same line written by different calligraphers throughout the centuries.

CAT. 16

Ahmed Fares Rezq
Ibn Muqla Theory, 2010

Ink and gold on hand-made sized paper
Written in *jaly thuluth*, *rayhani* and *riqa'* scripts
82 × 56 cm
Collection of the Ministry of Culture, Saudi Arabia
inv. IA 2010.36

Long before Leonardo da Vinci's *Vitruvian Man* (1491 AD), Ibn Muqla (272–328 AH / 886–939 AD) had already written in one of his letters (whose original was lost) of the Golden Ratio, called at the time "the theory of the circle", applied to Arabic letters. Surviving copies present it as follows: if the *alif*, a vertical line, falls within a circle where its top and bottom become the diameter, then proportionally, the *ba'*, a horizontal line with two curved ends, ought to have the same diameter as the *alif*, only horizontally. To achieve proportional harmony, all the other letters of the Arabic alphabet should find their place within that circle. The Safa brothers, contemporaries of Ibn Muqla, also referred to this theory in their correspondence, mentioning the Golden Ratio by name. In older calligraphy manuals, the unit of measurement for pens used to be the hair: a pen would be "24 hair wide". Contour lines were marked by dots with a diameter made of as many as six or seven dots, depending on the type of script. All letters ought to fit geometrically inside the *alif* and its circle. It is the same principle Da Vinci applied to ideal human body proportions: the unit of measurement being the palm width, a hand is therefore the equivalent of four fingers, a foot is four hands, and an arm six hands. Where Westerners chose to explore the human body proportions, Muslims perfected letters. In this piece, the artist presents examples of Arabic letters inserted within their circle, surrounded with sayings and explanations about the Golden Ratio.

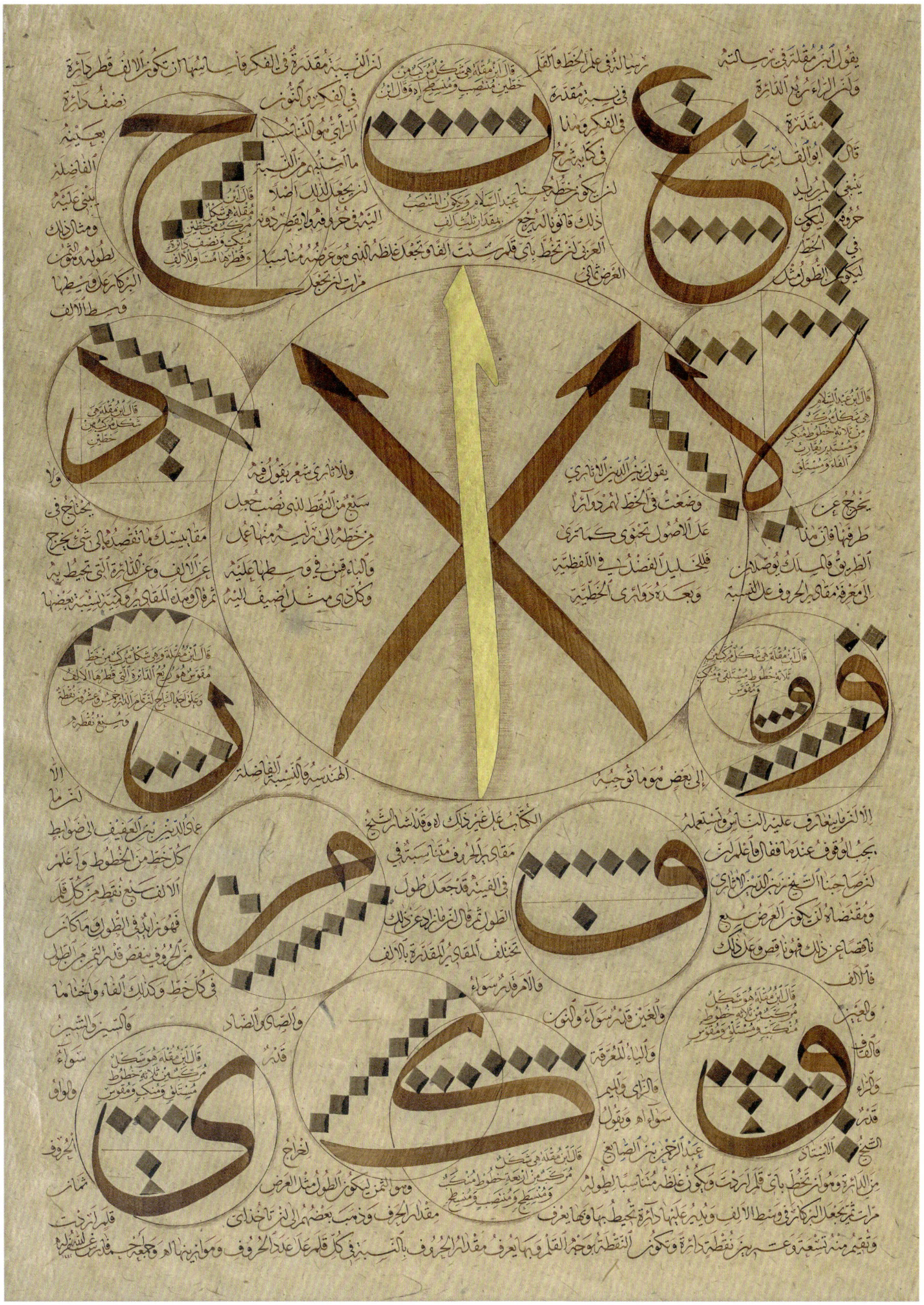

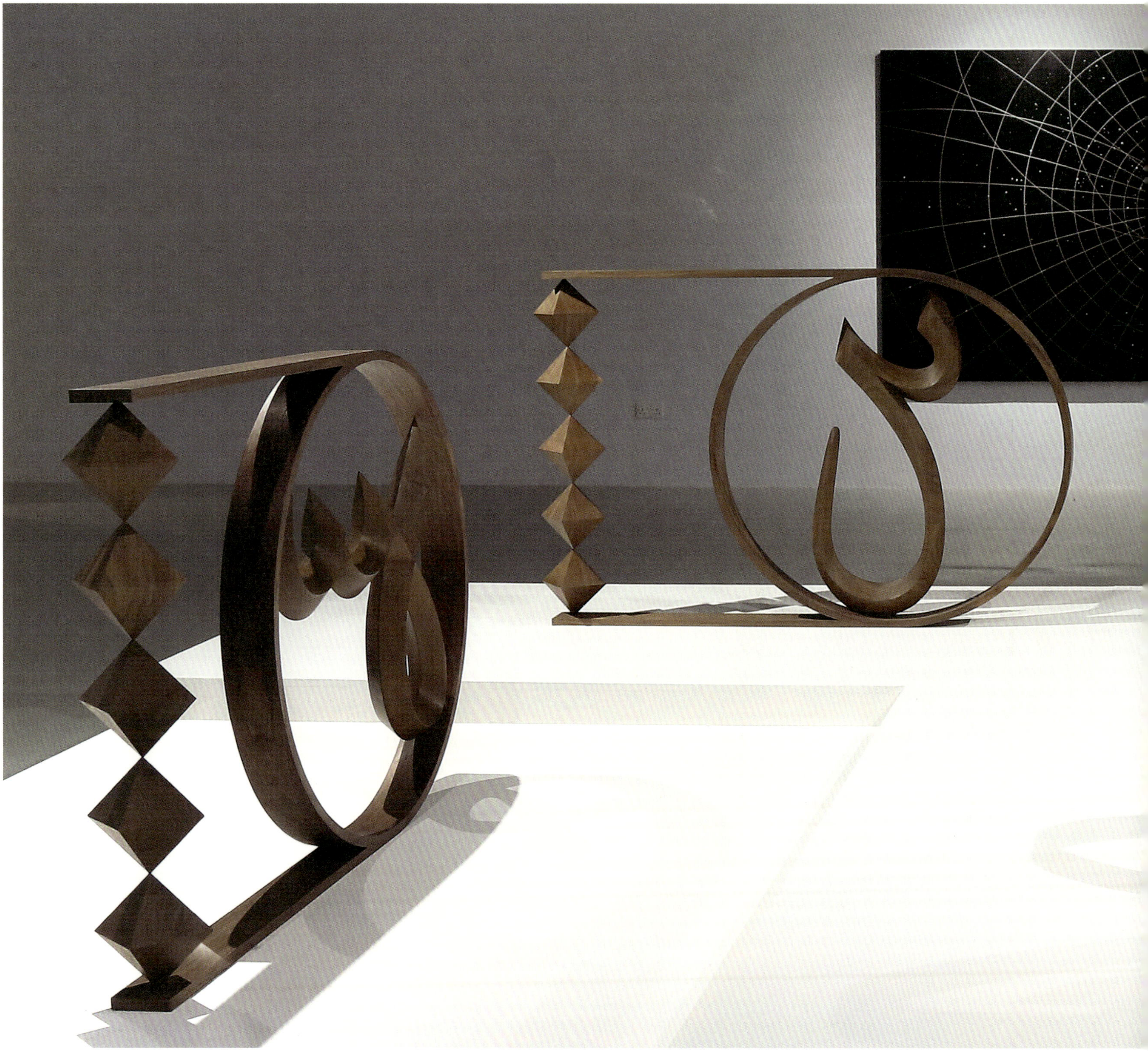

CAT. 17

Timo Nasseri
The Unknown Letters, 2015–17

Nutwood
120 × 14 × 20 cm each
Collection of the Ministry of Culture, Saudi Arabia
inv. CA 2022.11

Representing the "Unknown Letters", these four wooden sculptures were born out of Timo Nasseri's drawings inspired by the life of Ibn Muqla (272–328 AH / 886–939 AD), the famous Baghdadi calligrapher who, in 323 AH / 935 AD, attempted to add four letters to the Arabic alphabet. His innovation was lost and his letters never added to the alphabet; however, his system of proportionality is still in use today. Eager to recover this lost heritage, Nasseri delved intensely into Arabic script and alphabet, paying particular attention to form and aesthetics. Indeed, wondering whether Ibn Muqla might have glimpsed his letters in the stars, he lifted his eyes to the night sky and searched for constellations whose bright spots might have served as inspiration, and whose shape might embody the curves of Ibn Muqla's lost letters in the Baghdad sky of over a thousand years ago. The result was a number of ink drawings that compose a "Mind Map", which served as inspiration for the wooden structures displayed.

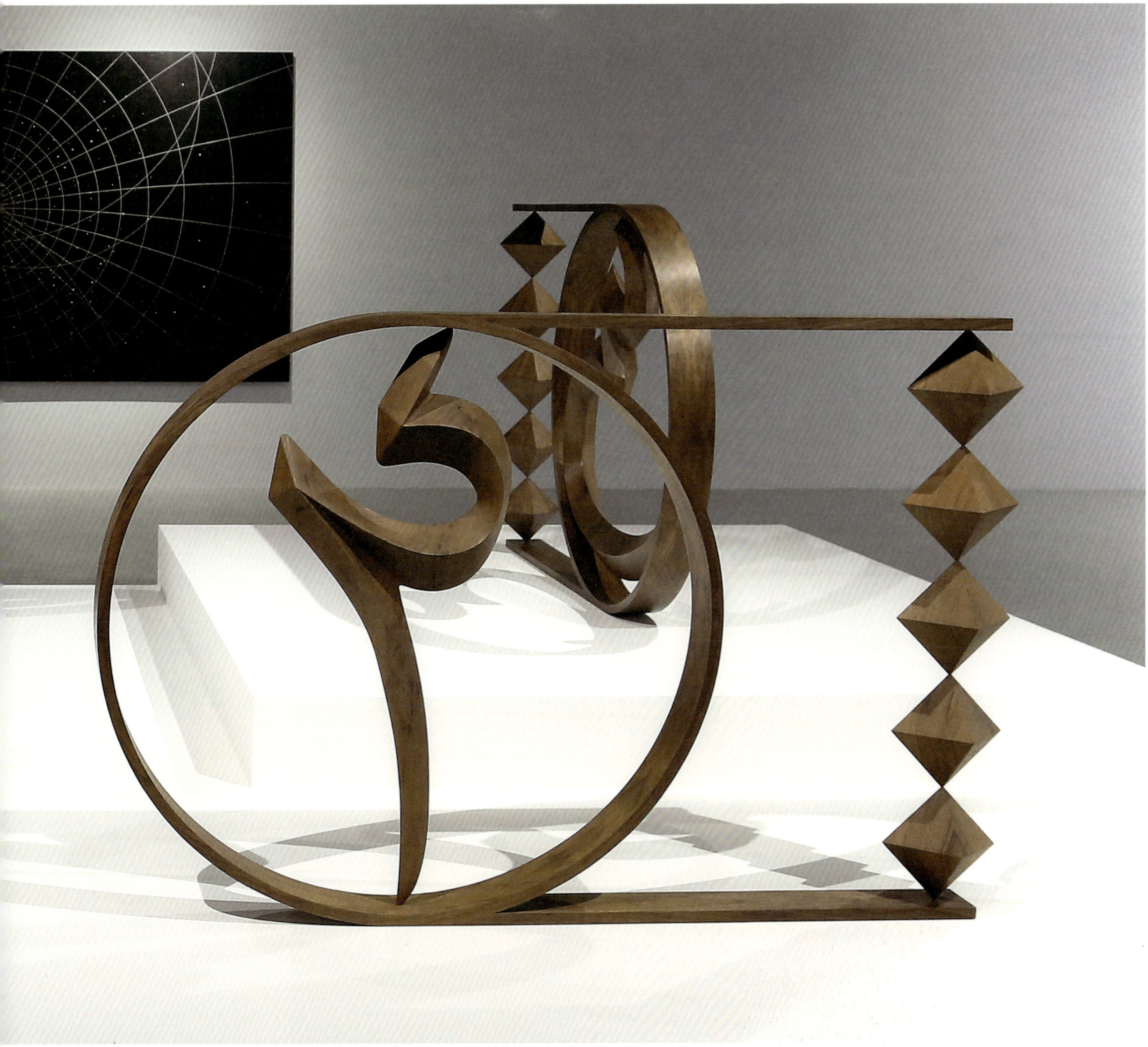

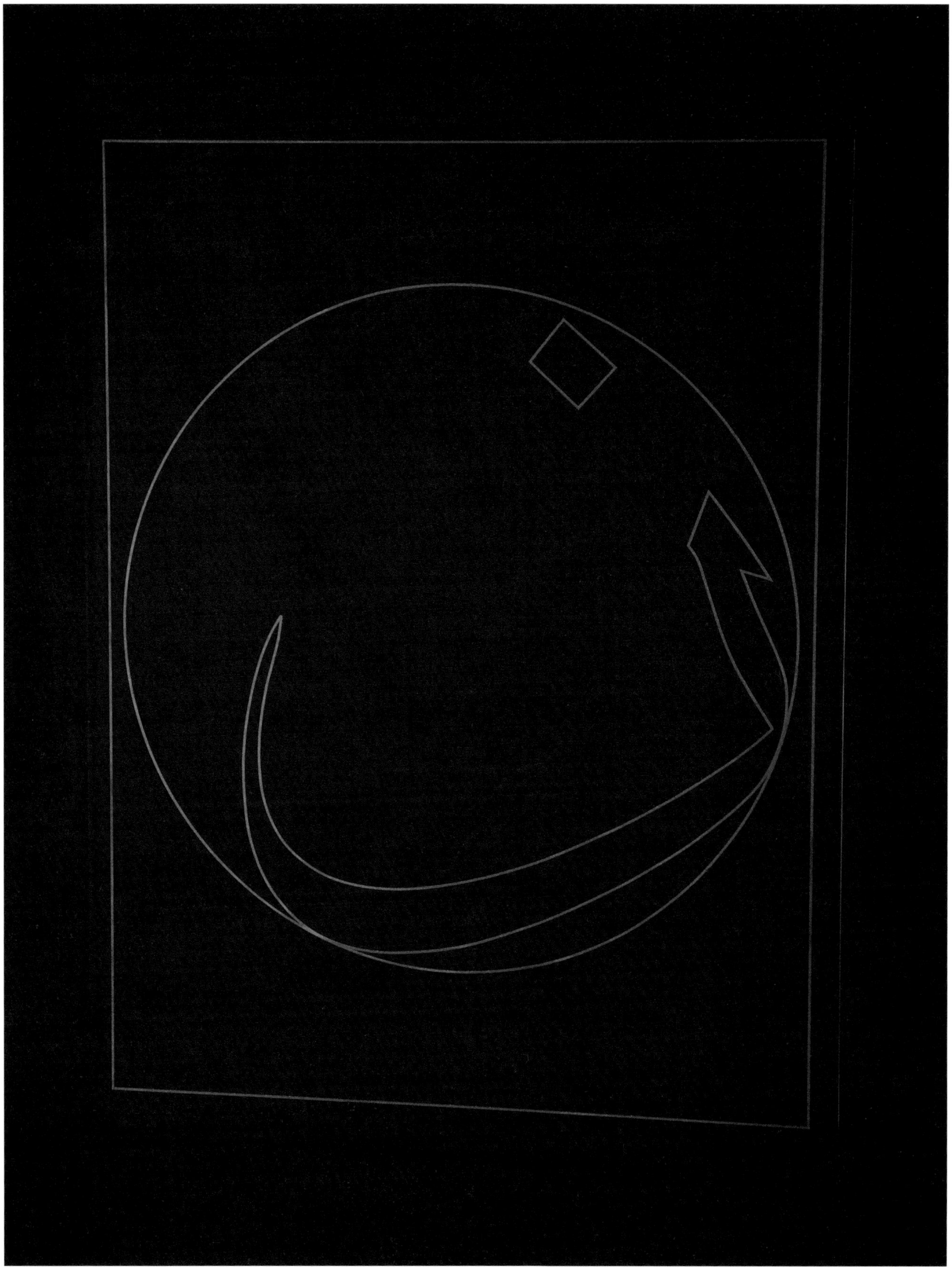

CAT. 18

Lama Abdulrahman

Noon, 2022

3 glass panels
85 × 60 cm each
Commissioned by the Ministry of Culture, Saudi Arabia
inv. CA 2022.7

Construction is at the heart of Islamic geometry and Islamic biomorphic art. Specific ratios marked by dots are instrumental in drawing Arabic letters according to precise proportions and measurements, and *thuluth* calligraphy is no exception. On this glass panel, the artist derived the *thuluth* letter ratios using circles and lines instead of dots, thus creating an original construction for the letter *nun* (ن). The use of geometric forms combined with calligraphy reflects a new way of communicating. The originality of this abstract artwork is that it illustrates the illusion of reality while at the same time evoking a message through geometry and calligraphy.

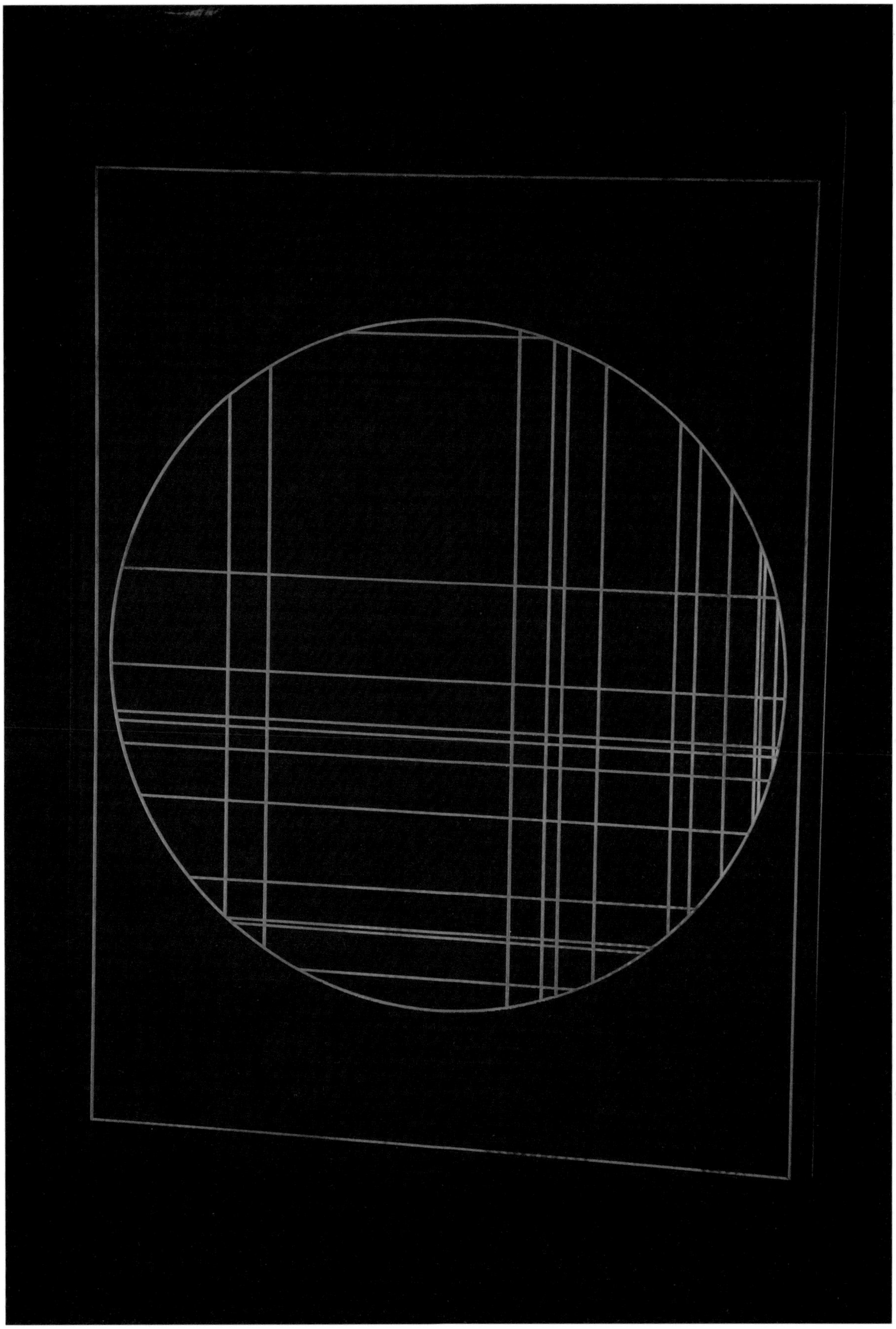

CAT. 19

Lara Assouad

Companions of the Road, 2022

3 silkscreens and 3 objects
100 × 70 cm each silkscreen
20 × 20 cm each object
Commissioned by the Ministry of Culture, Saudi Arabia
inv. CA 2022.3

These three prints on silk showcasing structured drawings are the expression of letters we carry with and within us. They are a reminder of values we wish to embody and live by, of loved ones we hold dear and remember as we go through our life journeys. Assouad calls them *Companions of the Road* as she explores the different forms in which these letters are expressed.

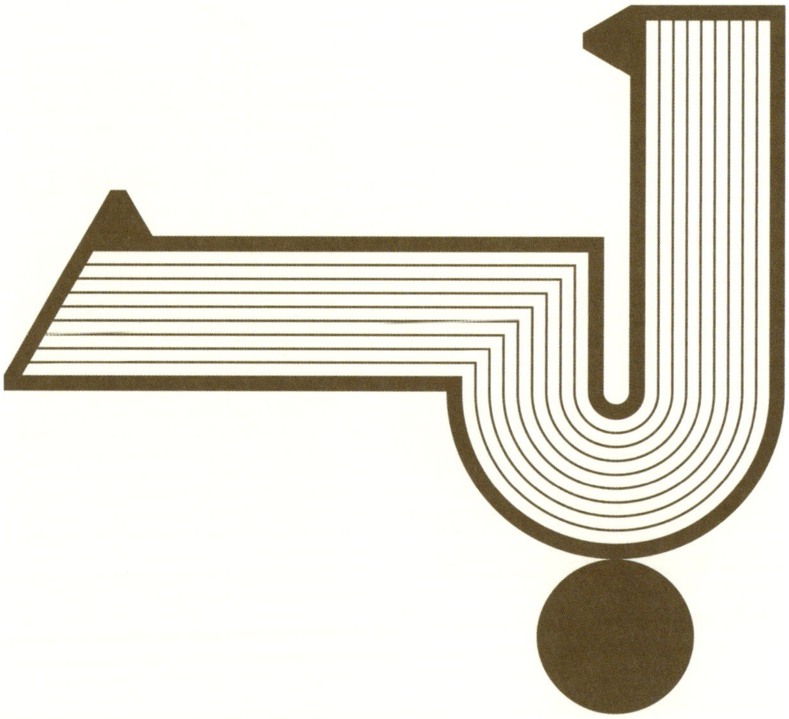

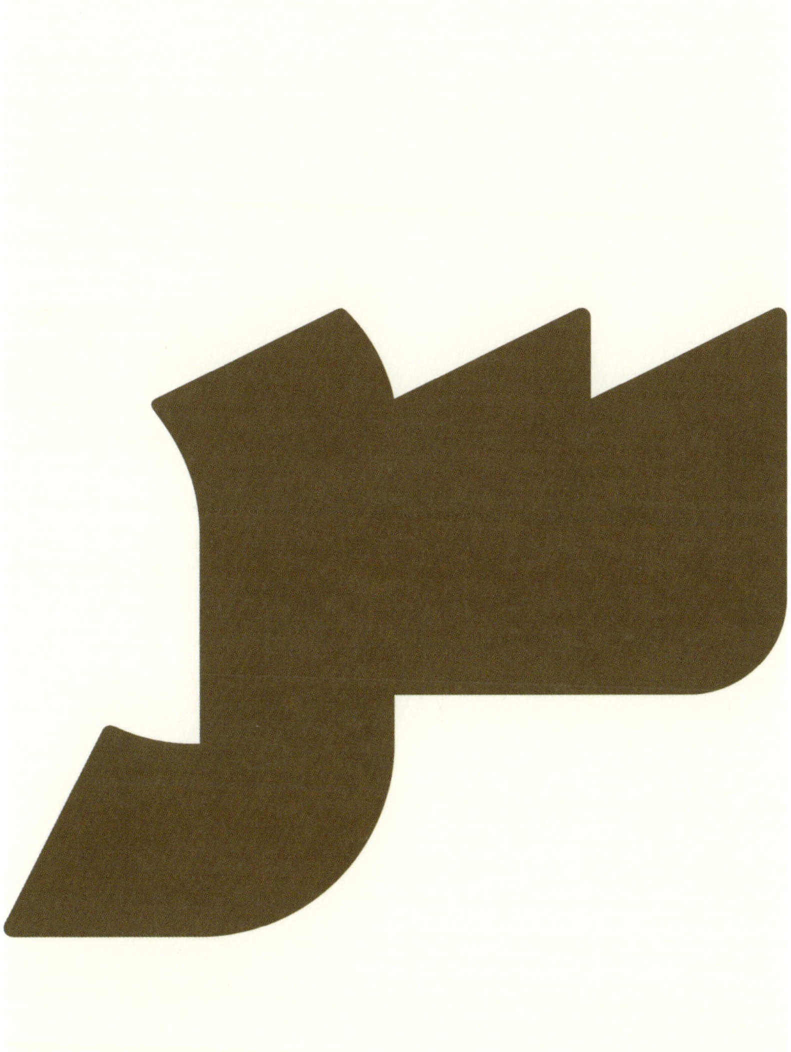

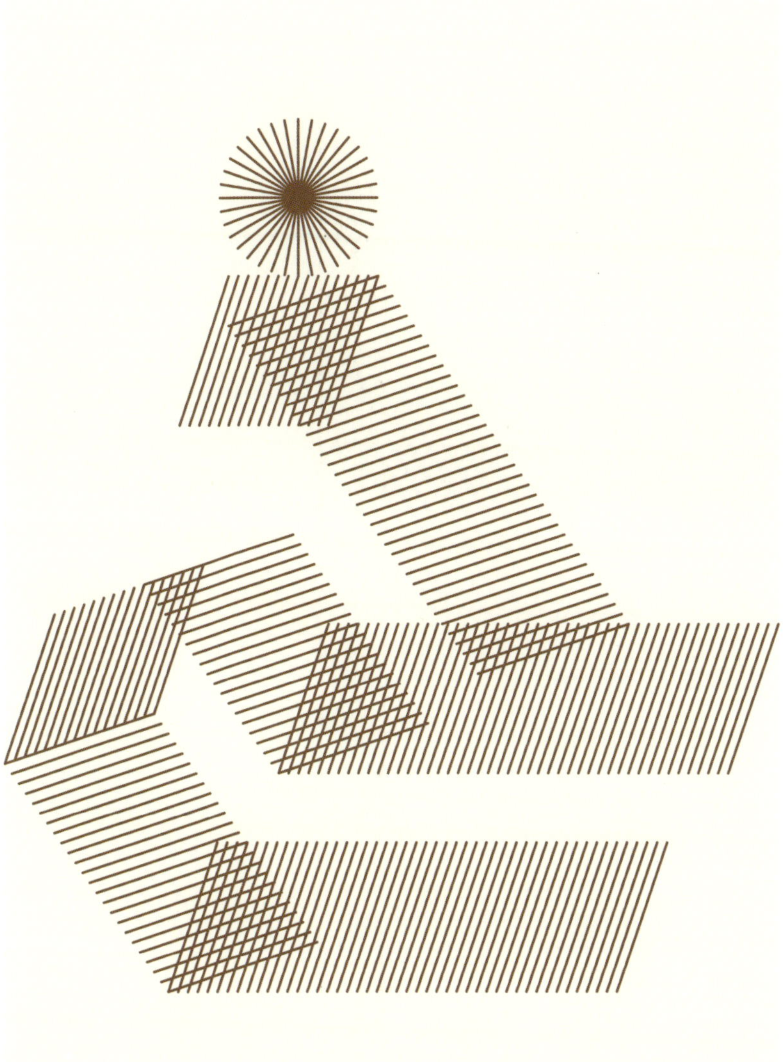

CAT. 20

Samir Sayegh

Noon, 2009

Acrylic and gold leaf on canvas
100 × 100 cm
Collection of the Ministry of Culture,
Saudi Arabia
inv. CA 2022.1

Through the formal elements of line and space, Arabic letters and words are abstracted into dynamic geometric compositions that often cover the entire surface of the support. A disciple of both modern art and geometric minimalism, driven by a deep interest in the formal power of letters, Sayegh bridges in his work two artistic traditions.

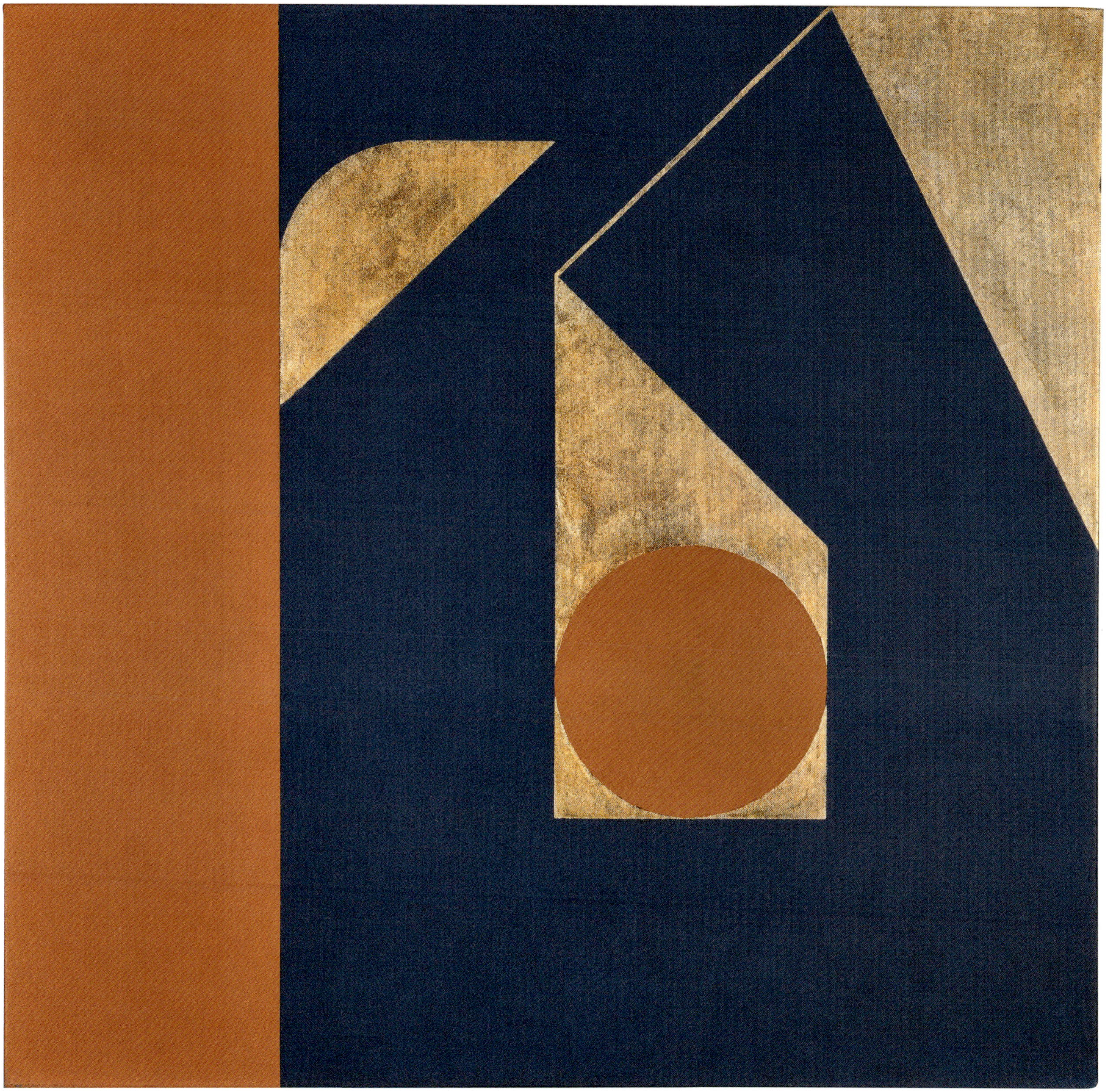

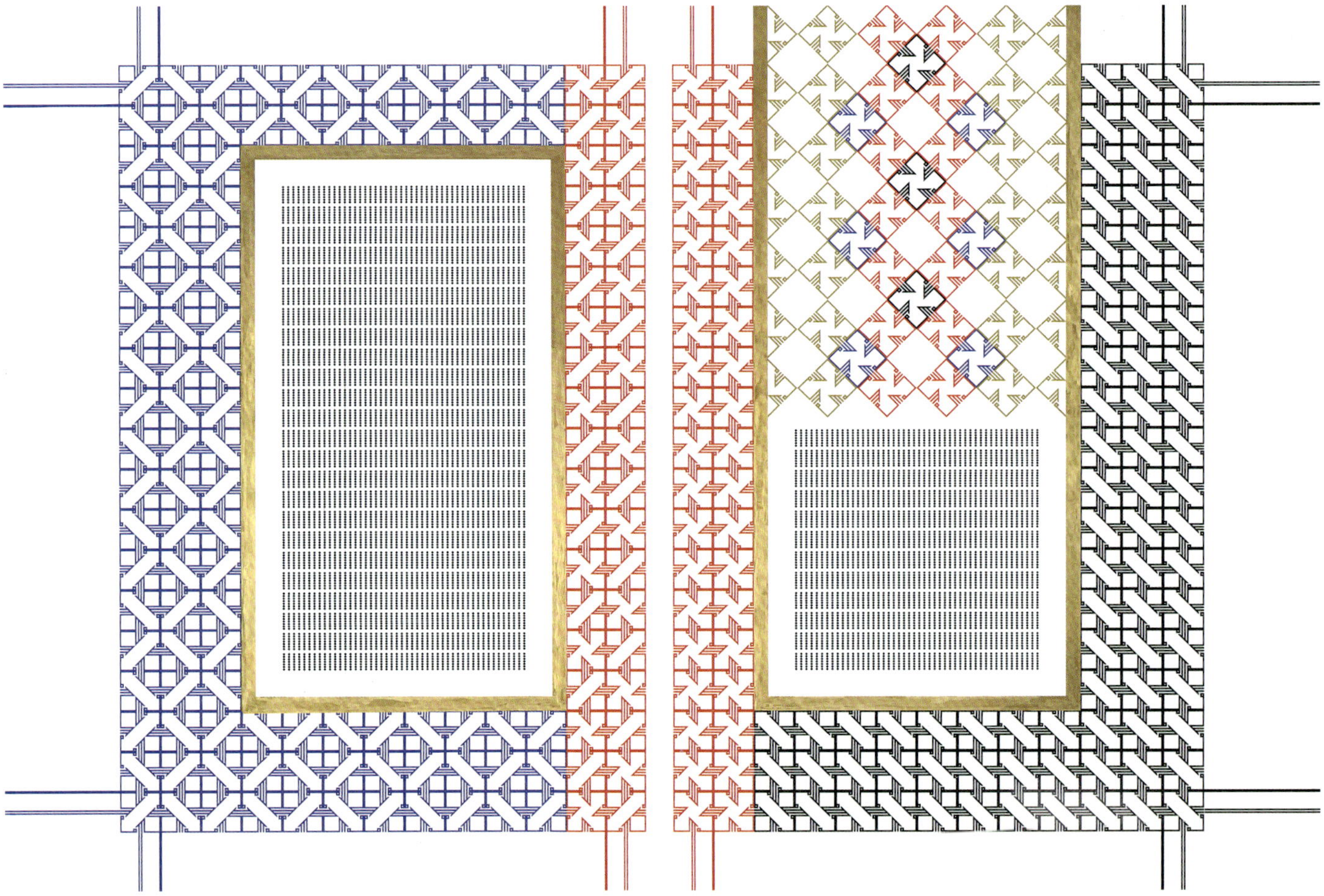

CAT. 21

Noor Saab
The Voyage of a Word on a Spread, 2022

3 silkscreens, colours and metallic ink
65 × 95 cm each
Commissioned by the Ministry of Culture, Saudi Arabia
inv. CA 2022.6

The words *khatt*, *qalam* and *baraka* explore a new approach towards apprehending manuscripts, pushing the boundaries of form and structure over function and focusing on abstracting the aesthetic value, where calligraphic patterns take precedence over intelligible words and text and become inextricable from the mesmerizing arabesque patterns and geometric composition of the page. Onlookers' feelings are guided into the fascinating world of a manuscript, invited to interact exclusively with the aesthetic rather than the literal, linguistic meaning of words. This experience also carries with it a spiritual dimension, more abstract but just as intense and absorbing. Each of the three components is built around a single calligraphic module and manipulated to produce various calligraphic patterns, which are brought to life using colour and illumination. The choice of the words *khatt*, *qalam* and *baraka* invites us to consider the basic elements of what makes a manuscript, be it secular or holy: where *khatt* addresses the medium of writing and the writing itself, *qalam* brings forth the act of "communicating" through reading or speech, and finally, *baraka* celebrates the blessing inherent in humans' ability to pass on knowledge and build on it for posterity through manuscripts.

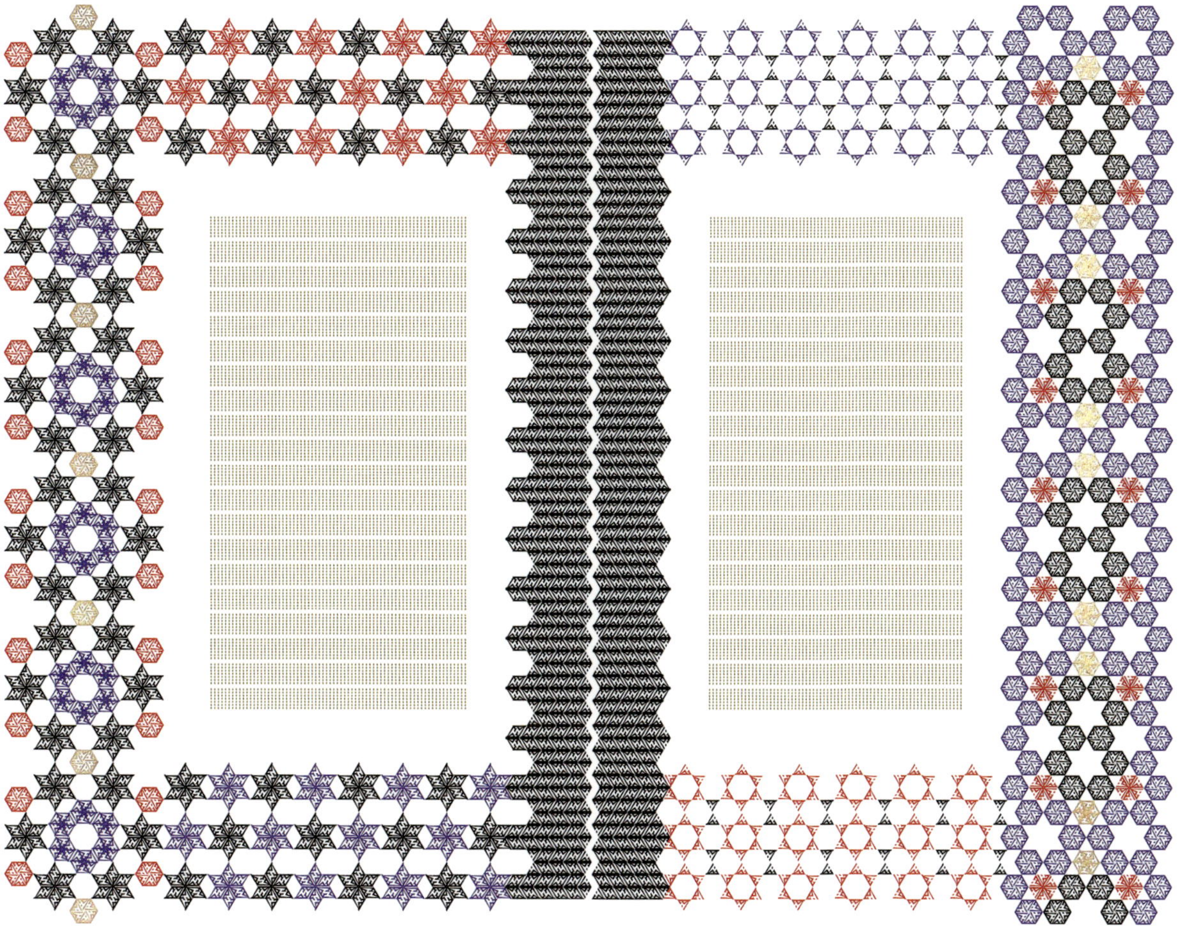

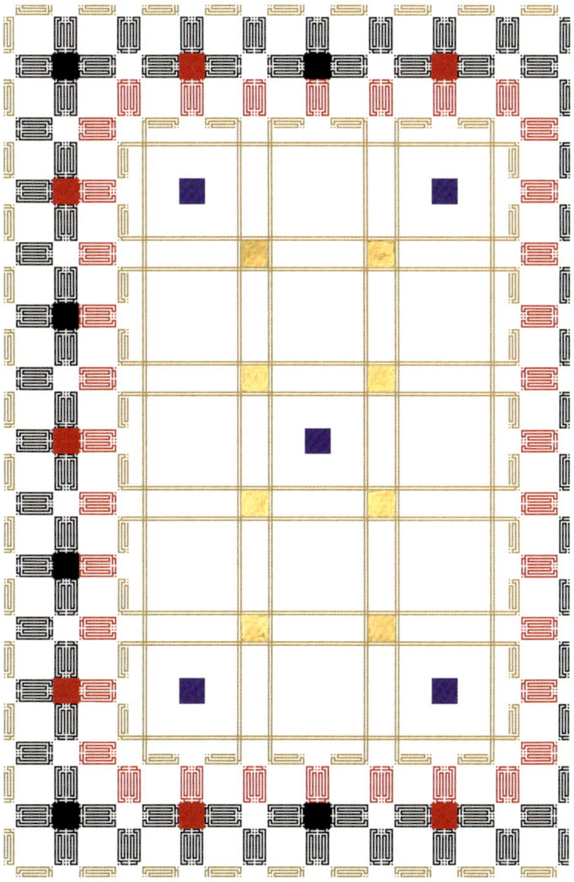

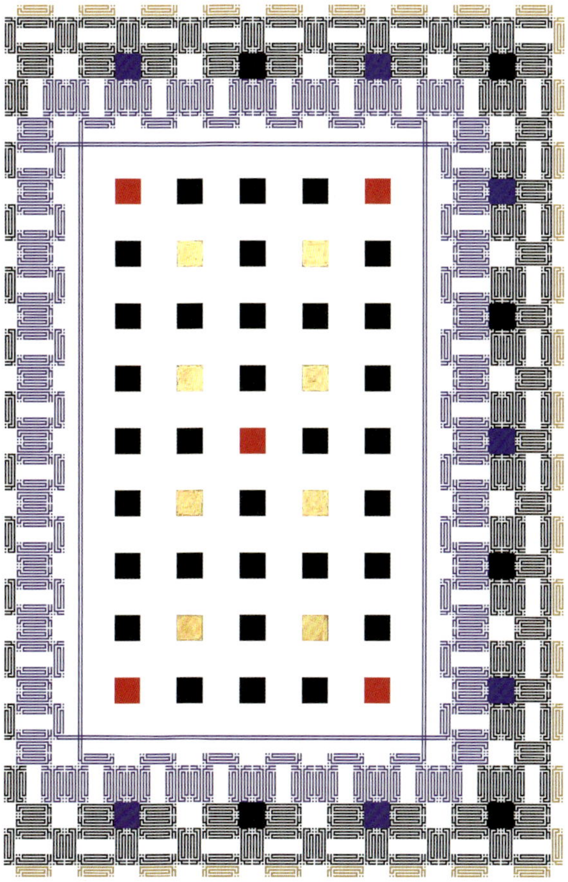

CAT. 22

Obaid Al Nofaey

And You Are Truly a Man of Outstanding Character, 2022

Surah *al-Qalam*, verse 4
Ink on paper
Written in *jaly thuluth* script
100 × 70 cm
Commissioned by the Ministry of Culture, Saudi Arabia
inv. IA 2022.5

Calligrapher Obaid Al Nofaey composed the verse using a basic classical structure in a clear *thuluth* script set so as to resemble the shape of a drop of water. His aim is to represent the purity and clarity of the character of the Prophet (PBUH) and point to the pure spring from which his nobility flows. The verse was written in golden colour to show the great value of the prophetic virtues that are praised in the Holy Qur'an.

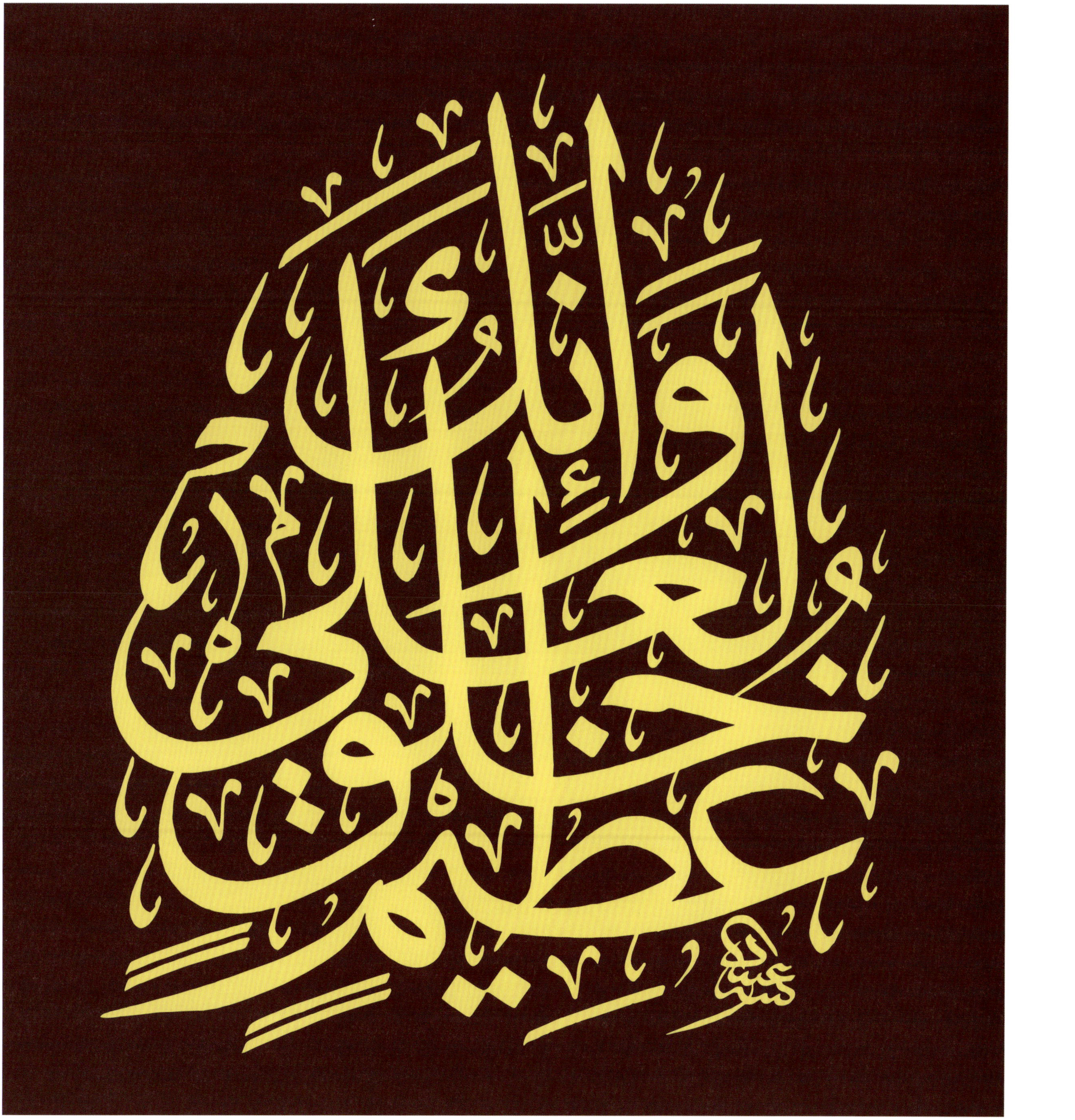
وإنك لعلى خلق عظيم

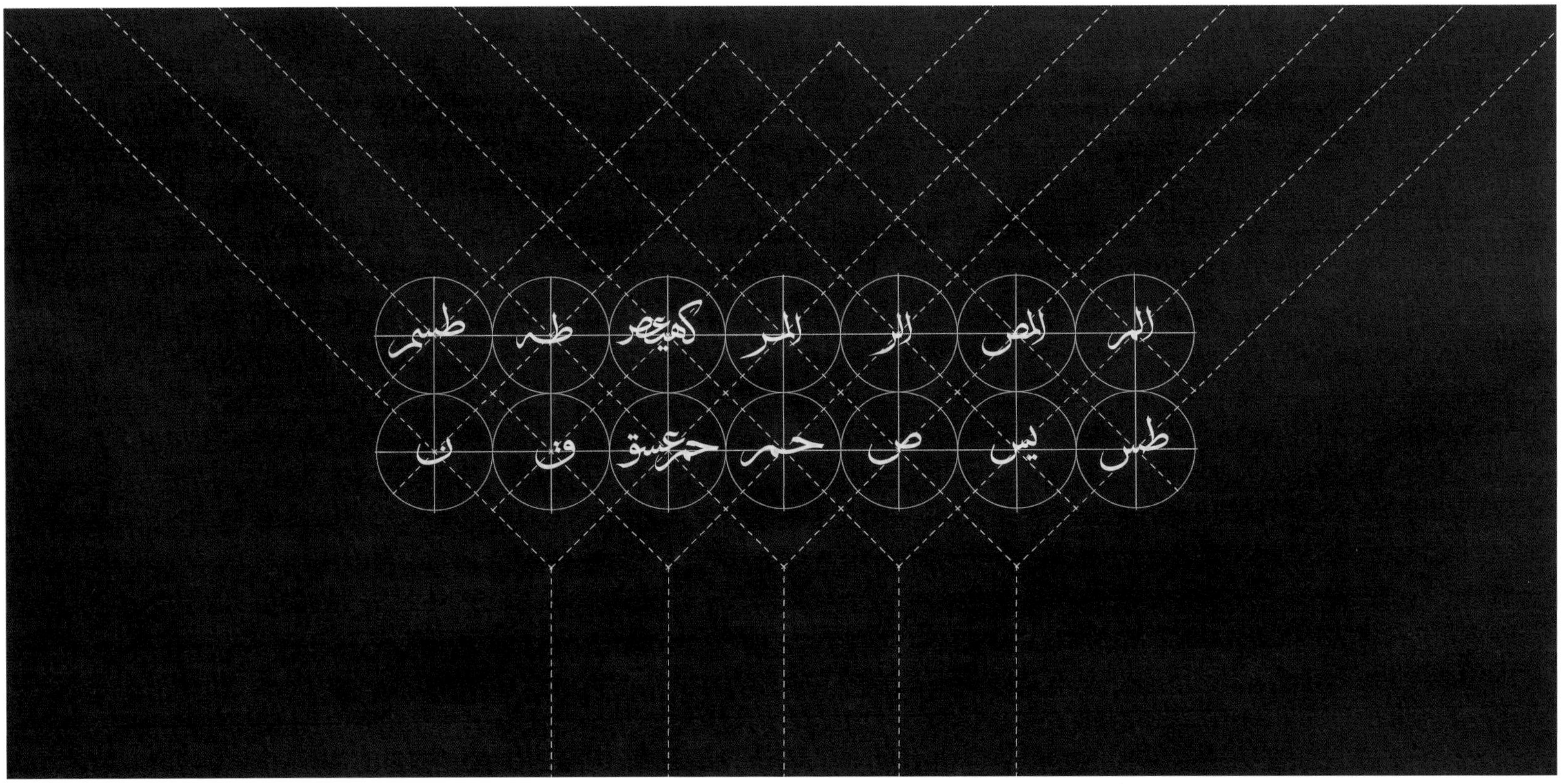

CAT. 23

Abdelrahman Elshahed

Wise Text, 2022

2 lightboxes, ink on paper
Written in *ijaza* and *jaly thuluth* scripts
60 × 120 cm each
Commissioned by the Ministry of Culture, Saudi Arabia
inv. CA 2022.8

This ink on paper takes us into the realm of the *al-Muqatta'ah* (abbreviated) letters. These detached, independent letters, considered to be a divine miracle of the Holy Qur'an, can be found at the beginning of 29 surahs. Scholars hold no less than forty theories about them: some believe them to be chapter titles, others see them as undecipherable mysteries of the Divine.

When combined, after eliminating duplicates, and arranged chronologically according to the revelation of the Qur'an (from *Iqraa* to *al-Fat'h*, from *al-Fatiha* to *an-Nas*), the following sentence appears: "A Wise Text that Holds an Absolute Secret" (*Nas Hakeem Laho Sir Qati'a*).

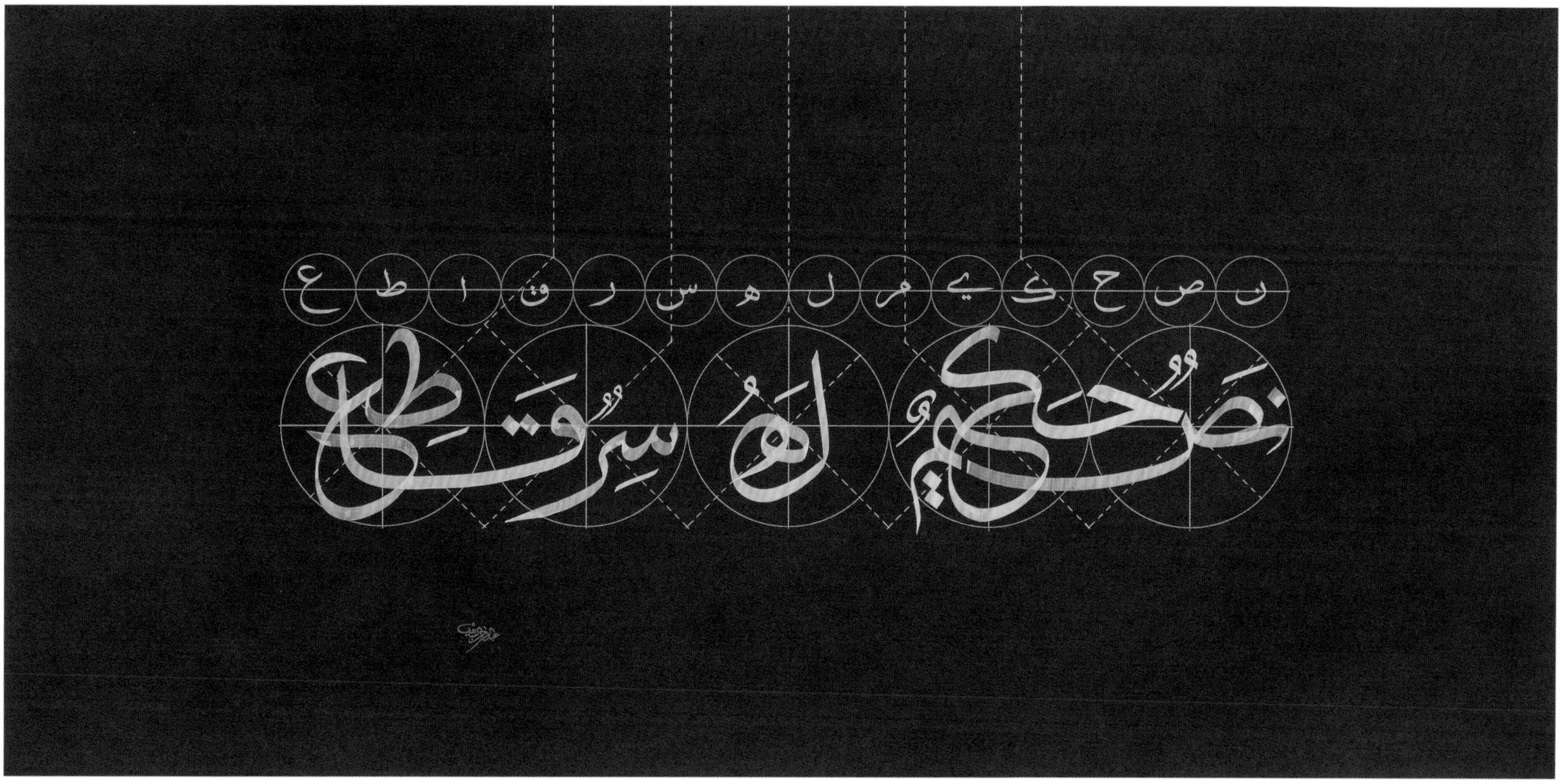

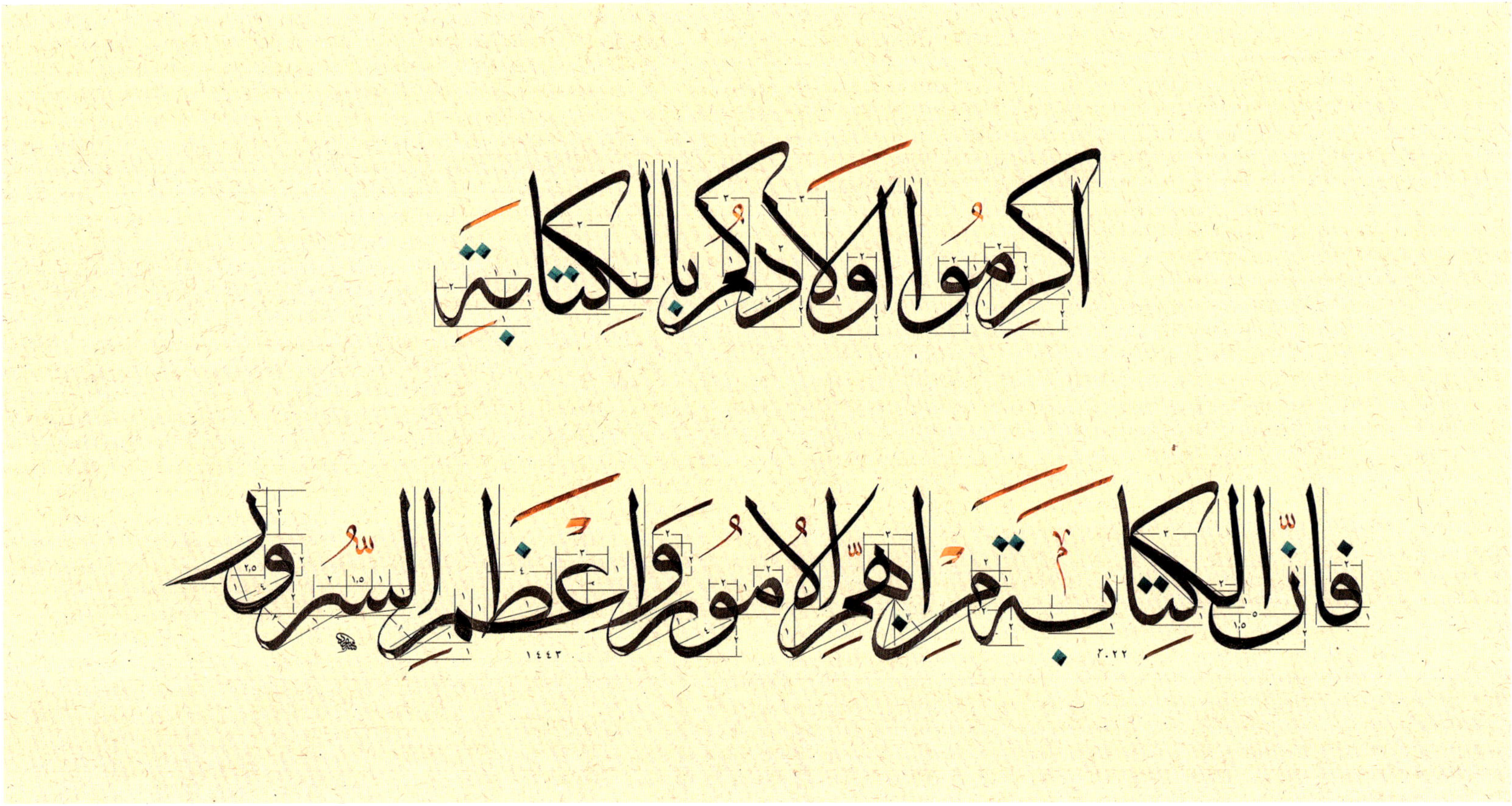

CAT. 24

Majid Alyousef
A Glimpse of the Beginnings, 2022

Ink on paper
Written in *thuluth* script
70 × 100 cm
Commissioned by the Ministry of Culture, Saudi Arabia
inv. IA 2022.4

This ink drawing on paper illustrates the quote "gift your children with writing, for in writing lies the reading of things and the greatest joy". The style and presentation are classical *thuluth* in linear composition, deliberately made to look like a calligraphy lesson where the ratios and measurements of letters and syllables are marked through several dots, according to the traditional learning method. The piece looks raw and unfinished: in certain places, the viewer can see touch-ups, small corrections and improvements. This is precisely the process calligraphers must undergo before producing a finished artwork; by making it obvious in this work, Majid Alyousef brings us closer to the type of involvement and discipline calligraphy entails. This is a sort of snapshot from a calligrapher's journey.

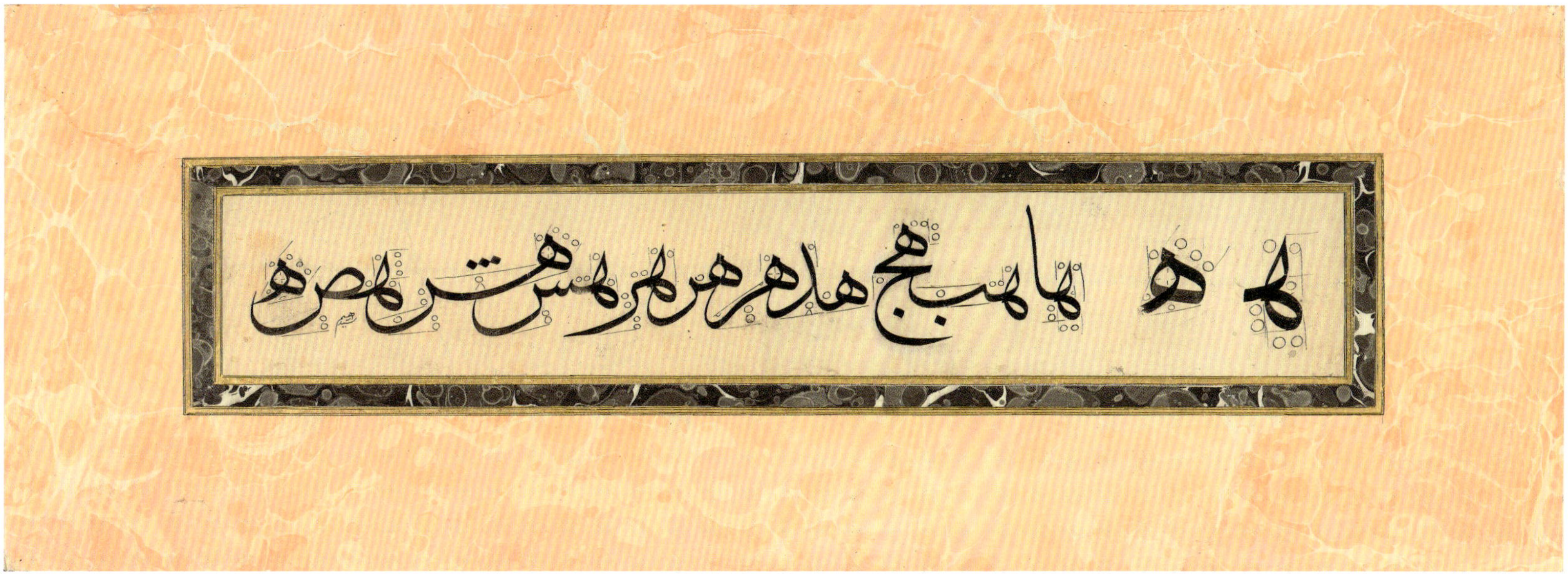

CAT. 25

Sayyid Ibrahim
Ha'a, 1943
Ink on paper
Written in *thuluth* script
20 × 56 cm
Collection of the Ministry of Culture, Saudi Arabia
inv. IA 2022.15.1

A model of the Arabic letter *ha'a* drawn by Sayyid Ibrahim for his textbook of Arabic calligraphy, which was printed in the 1940s. In this illustration, he presented the various forms of the letter *ha'a* in *thuluth* script, both the stand-alone and the initial forms – or, to use the technical terms, the "eye of the cat" and the "ear of the Persians". The illustration is decorated with two different types of cloud, which give it a distinctive aesthetic dimension.

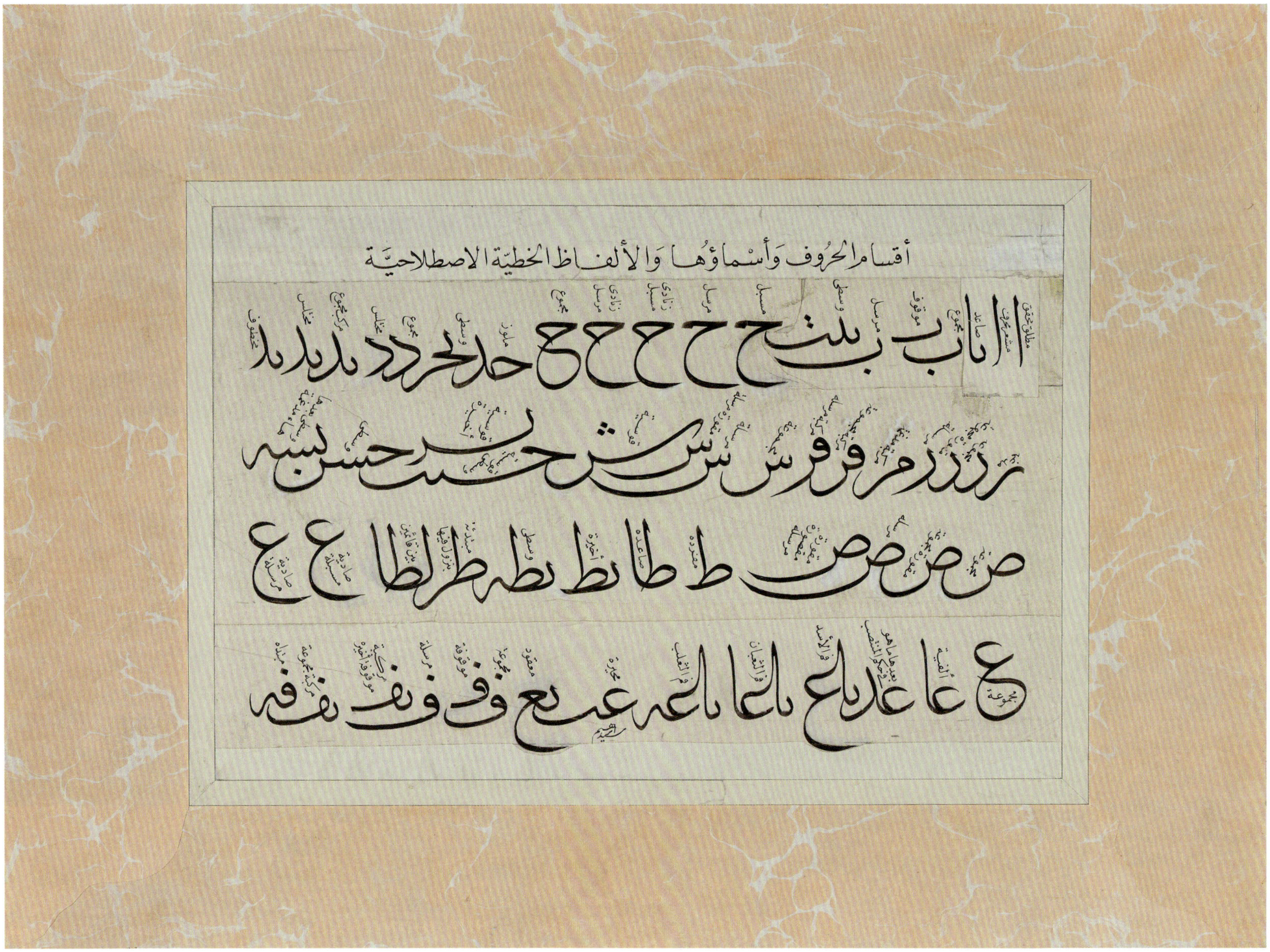

CAT. 26–27

Sayyid Ibrahim
Parts of the letters, their names and their calligraphic terms, 1963
Ink on paper
Written in *thuluth* script
40 × 50 cm each
Collection of the Ministry of Culture, Saudi Arabia
inv. IA 2022.15.2/3

Sayyid Ibrahim wrote the names of the letters in *thuluth* script. In every set of letters, there are the stand-alone and the medial versions. These terms were the result of years of research in the traditional calligraphy books and reflect two aspects: the first is the development of an understanding of Arabic calligraphy from the Abbasid age to the present; the second is the conscious reading by Sayyid Ibrahim of the Arabic calligraphic heritage from ancient manuscripts and books. The chart followed the pattern of the Arabic calligraphy teaching book that Ibrahim had printed in the 1940s. The first part of the chart begins with the letter *alif* and ends with the letter *fa'*; the second begins with the letter *qaf* and completes the alphabet up to the letter *ya*.

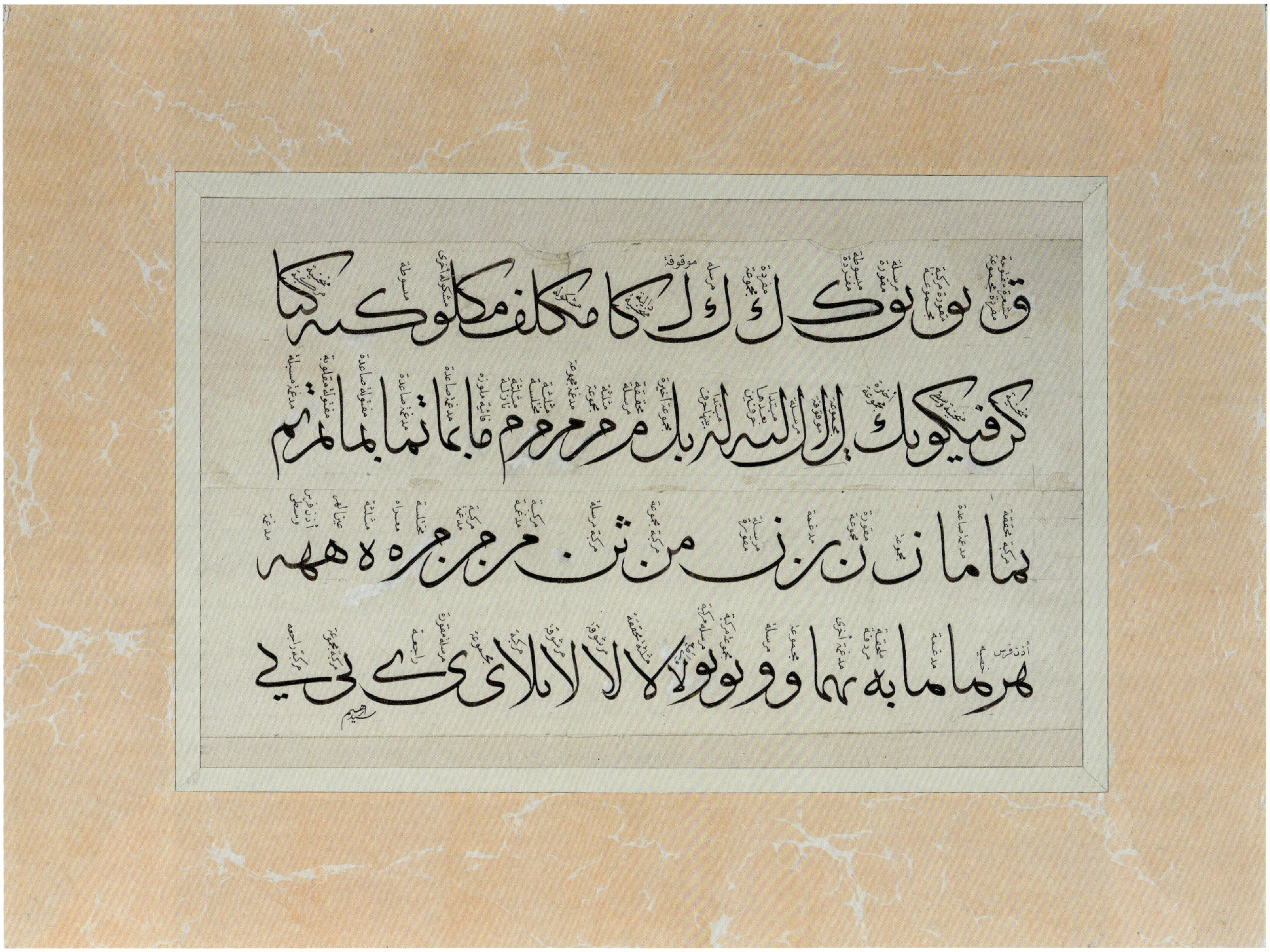

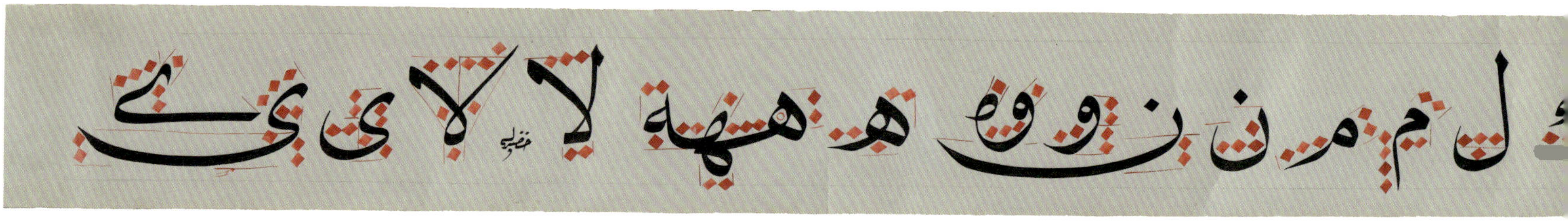

CAT. 28

Khodeir El-Borsaidy

Mashq, 1970

Ink on paper
Written in *naskh* script
29 × 480 cm
Collection of the Ministry of Culture, Saudi Arabia
inv. IA 2022.13.2

A ribbon of single letters in *naskh* script, each surrounded by marking red dots fitting each letter into its Golden Ratio. These are examples of Khodeir El-Borsaidy's unique artistic sense and teaching method, evidenced by the thick line and the dots, also called scales, for a better understanding of Arabic letter construction.

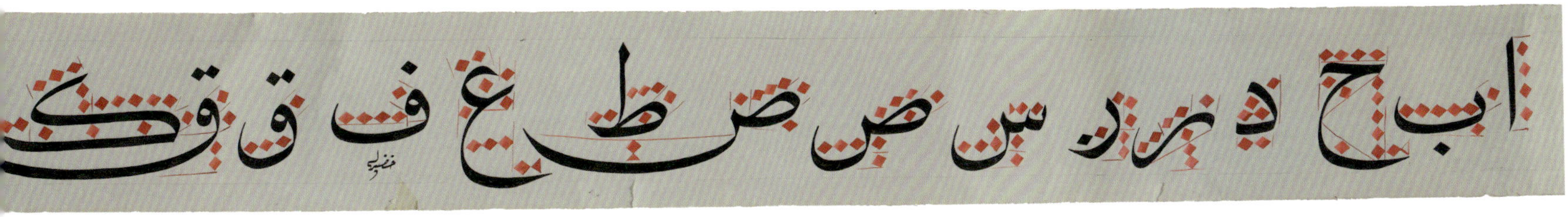

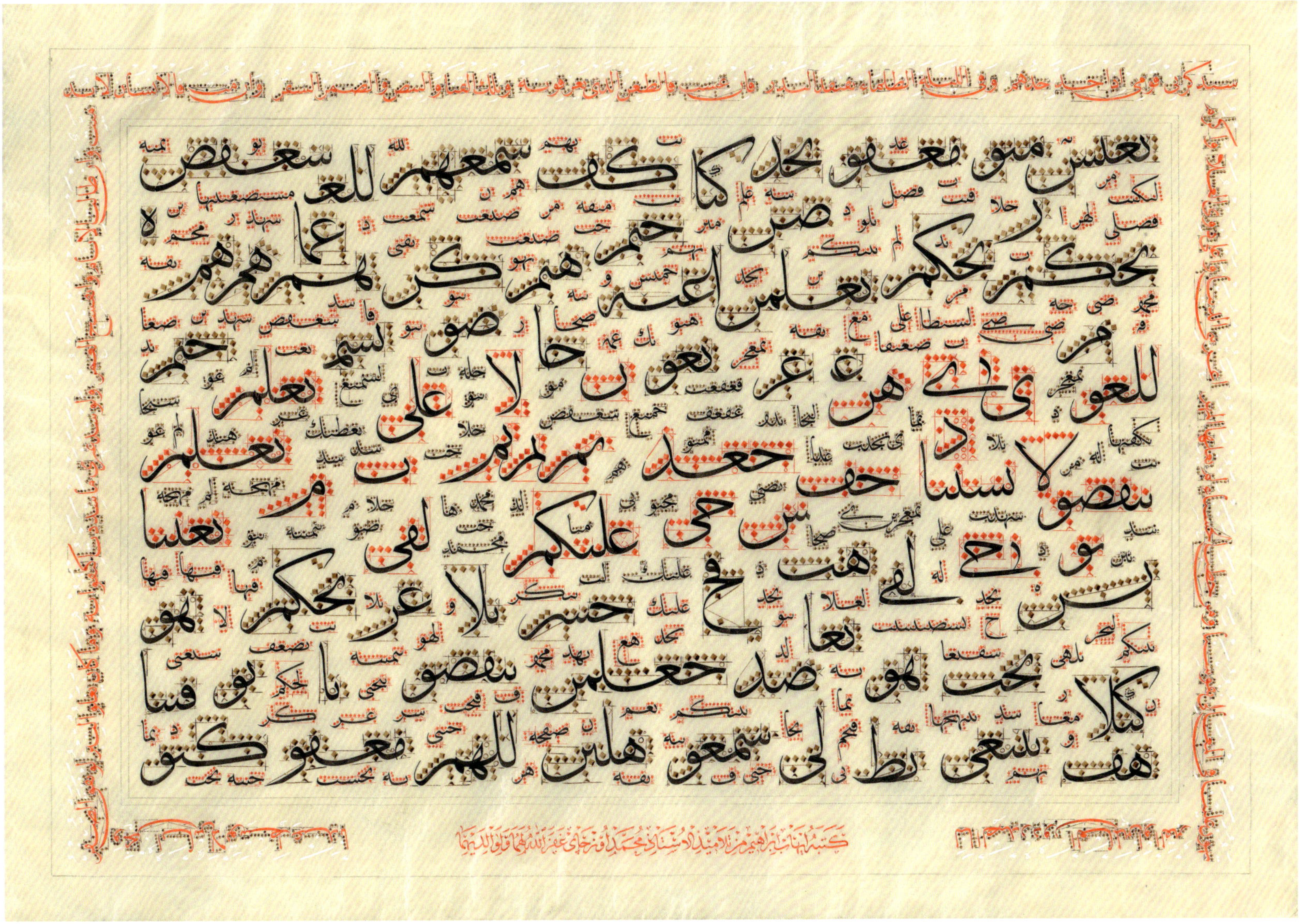

CAT. 29

Ihab Thabet

***Karalama*, 2022**

Ink on paper
Written in *thuluth* and *naskh* scripts
50 × 70 cm
Commissioned by the Ministry of Culture, Saudi Arabia
inv. IA 2022.2

Karalama is a study of dotted characters; dotting is a technique whereby pre-existing dots are set on paper to delineate the shape, size and proportions of letters. Used in the study of calligraphy, it presents the many ways in which one letter can be written. *Karalama* is an exercise that keeps a calligrapher's hand nimble, steady and trained. It consists in spontaneously writing anything that comes to mind: Qur'anic verses, hadith quotes, proverbs, idioms, poetry, unconnected letters, even non-related words. Poorly shaped letters are then re-written multiple times on the same sheet of paper until a satisfying result is reached. When the paper is so full that it is almost black and letters and words overlap, the attempt is called a "Blackening". When letters and words do not overlap, it is called an exercise. Calligraphers may use this technique to seek the ideal proportions, image, vocalization, or shape to build a word or a paragraph. They may choose their best attempt inside this spontaneous composition to use in the final work. These are a good source of inspiration for young calligraphers, as their eyes are trained to the perception of beauty. *Karalama* can be done using any script, although it's mostly done in *thuluth* or *thuluth naskh*. The exercise is generally conducted in black on light paper. Other inks, colours, or paper shades can be used for the sake of aesthetics. This is the second painting by Ihab Thabet after obtaining his *ijazah* (calligraphy certification), and the first he signs jointly with his teacher, the late Mohammed Oujazi.

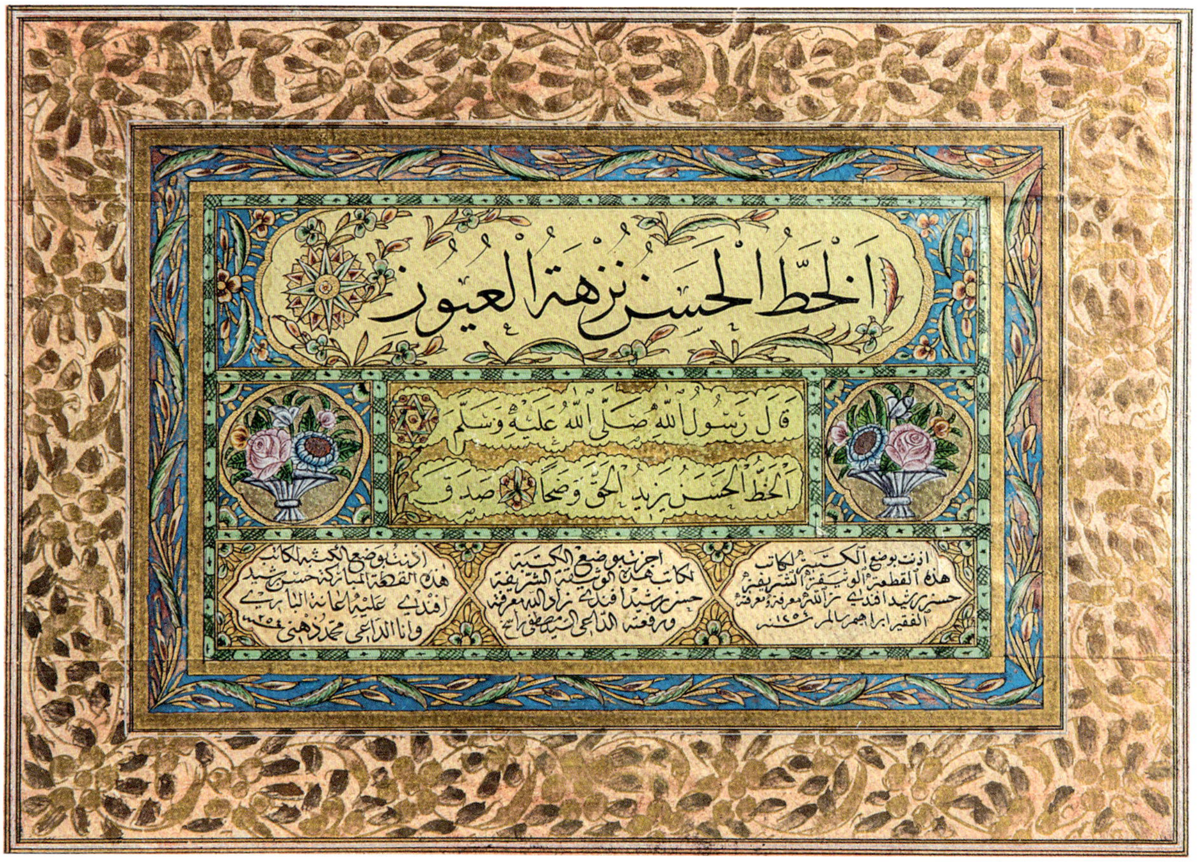

CAT. 30

Illuminated calligrapher's certification (ijazah), 1254 AH / 1838–39 AD (dated twice)

Signed by Husain Rashid Effendi
and witnessed by Ibrahim Salem,
Mustafa Rasekh and Muhammad Zuhni
10 × 17 cm
Collection of the Ministry of Culture,
Saudi Arabia
inv. IA 2020.14

Manuscript on paper laid down on card, text written in one line of *thuluth* script in black ink within a cartouche on a light green ground, above two lines of smaller *naskh* script on the same ground and within gold cloud bands, flanked by stylized floral vases. Below, three cartouches with calligraphers' details, all within a rectangular panel richly decorated with stylized floral motifs and serrated leaves in colours and gold, ruled margins and outer border in colours and gold.

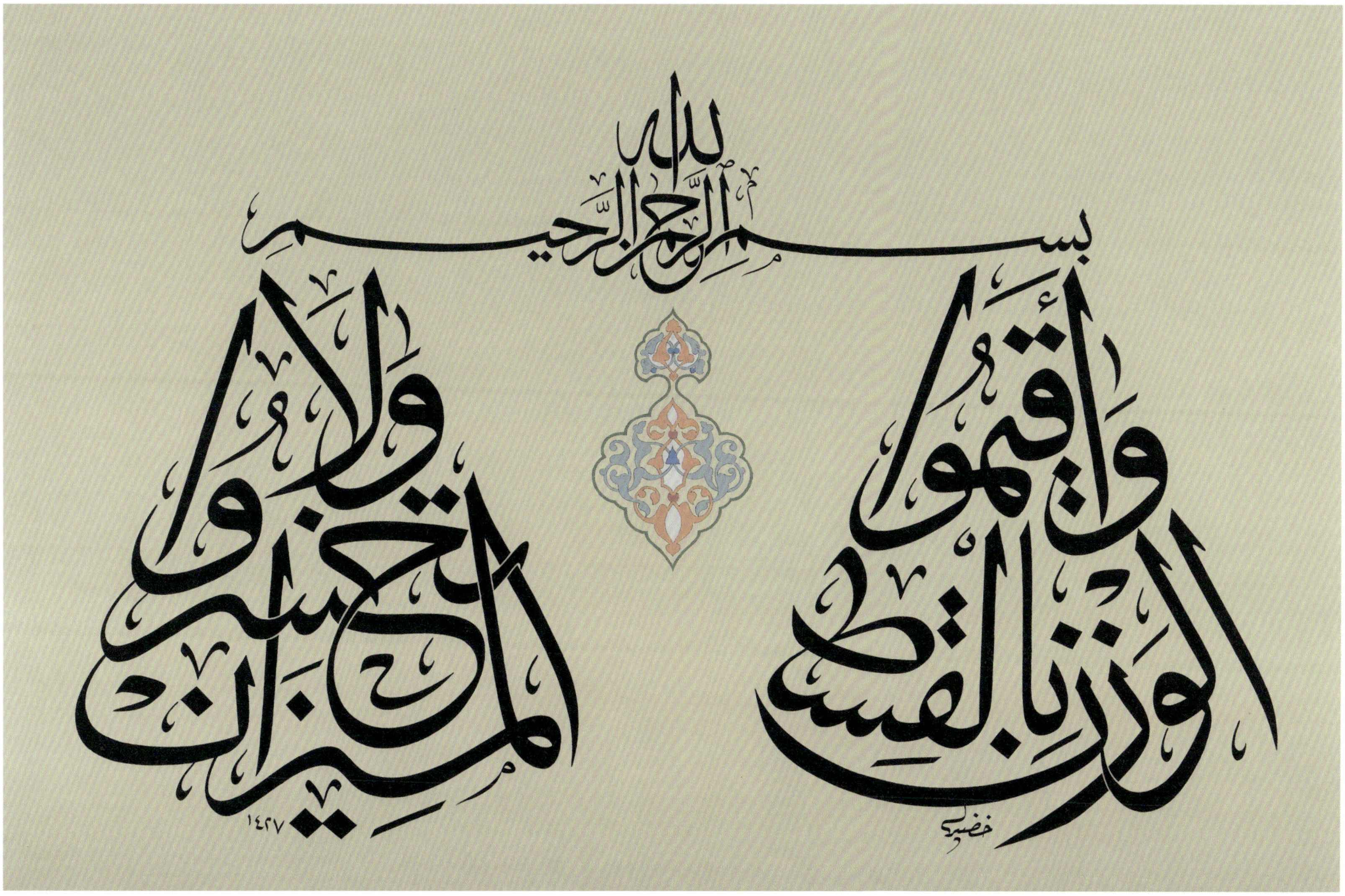

CAT. 31

Khodeir El-Borsaidy
And Establish Weight in Justice and Do Not Make the Balance Deficient, 2006

Ink on paper
Written in *jaly thuluth* script
78 × 116 cm
Collection of the Ministry of Culture, Saudi Arabia
inv. IA 2022.13.3

A graphic composition in *jaly thuluth* script where Khodeir El-Borsaidy stylizes the following Qur'anic verse in a dual pyramidal design to form the two plates of a scale: "And establish weight in justice and do not make the balance deficient" (surah *ar-Rahman*, verse 9), with the *basmala* (In the name of God most Merciful, most Compassionate) stretched between the two plates so as to form the arms of the scale, and the name of God, point of balance of life and the universe, occupying the upper central part of the *basmala*. The Arabic ornamental design placed at the centre is drawn in pale colours so as not to distract from the main components of the composition.

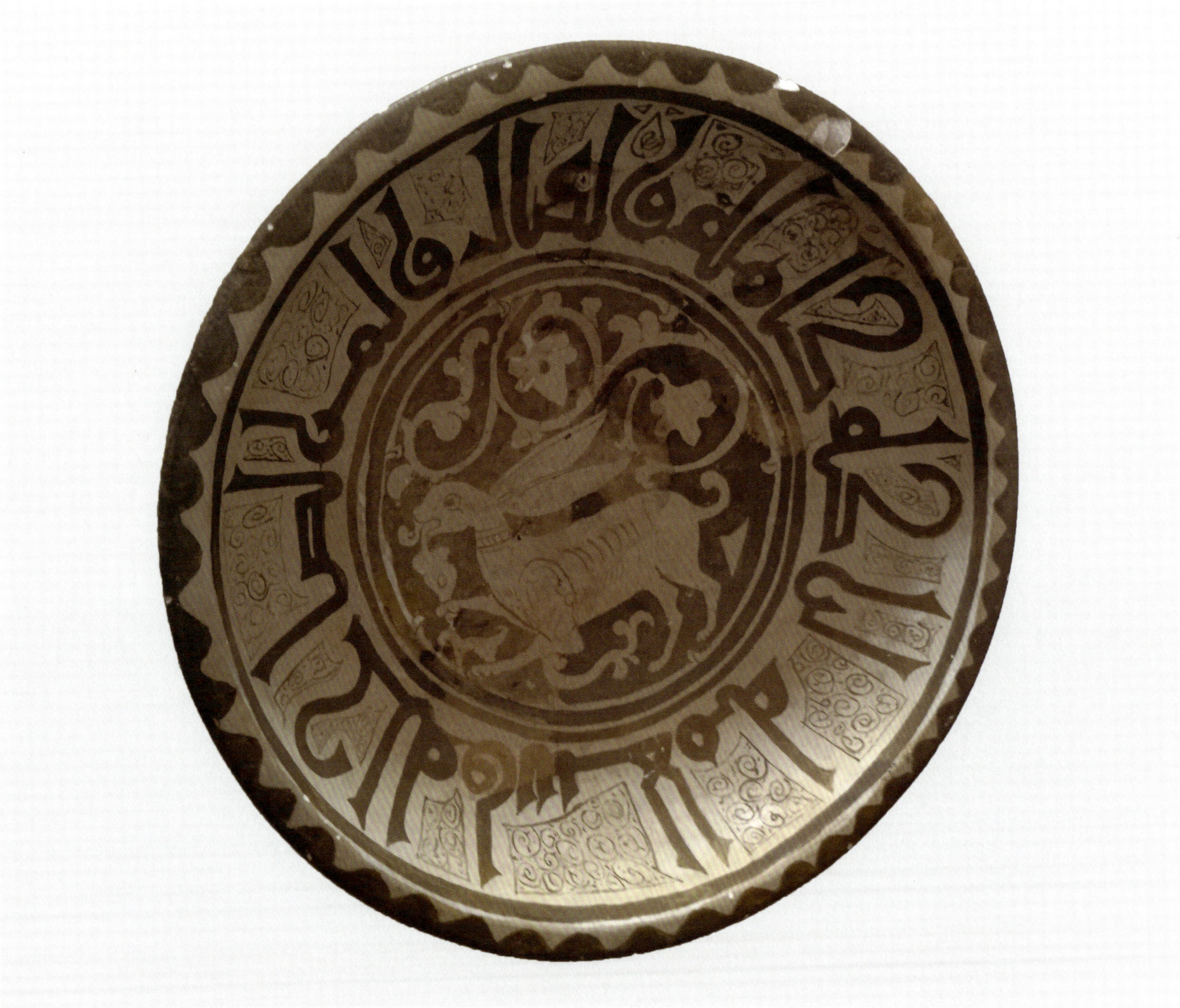

CAT. 32

Bowl inscribed with the word Baraka (Blessing)

Egypt, third–fourth century AH / ninth–tenth century AD

Earthenware, lustre painted on opaque white glaze
Written in *kufi* script
34.5 × 18 × 8.5 cm
Collection of the Raqqada Museum of Civilization and Islamic Arts, Kairouan
inv. D26/D287

Deep cup with lustrous decoration (metallic sheen). In the central medallion a hare is surrounded by foliage and holds a flower in its mouth. Around this medallion, a circular inscription in *kufi* style reads: "Full blessing, success, happiness and health to its owner".

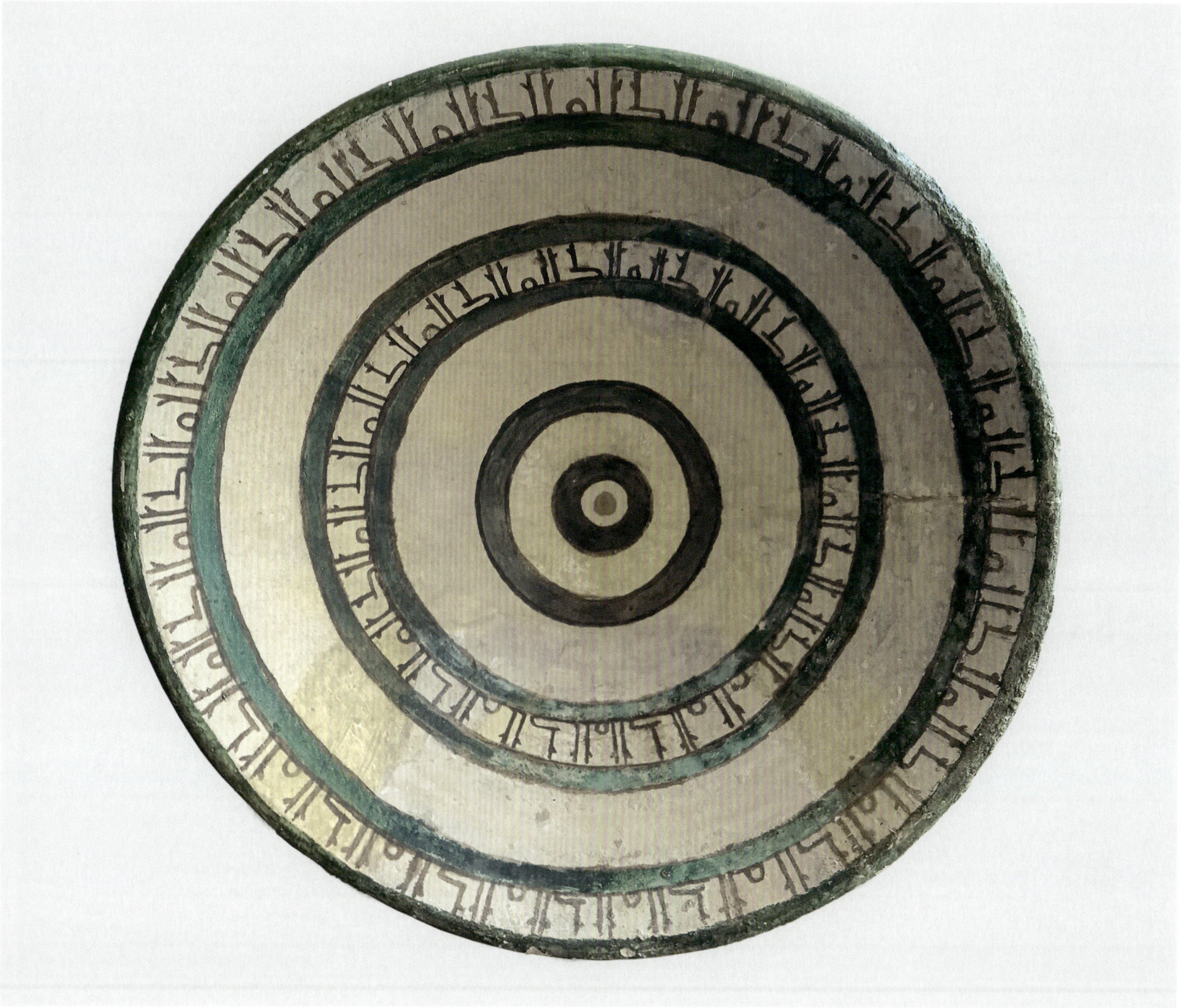

CAT. 33

Bowl inscribed with the word Al-malik (The Sovereign)
third century AH / ninth century AD

Earthenware, white slip with black slip decoration under transparent glaze
Written in *kufi* script
Diameter 31 cm
Collection of the Raqqada Museum of Civilization and Islamic Arts, Kairouan
inv. R2126/767

Bowl decorated with concentric circles and a *kufi* inscription consisting of the word *Al-malik*.

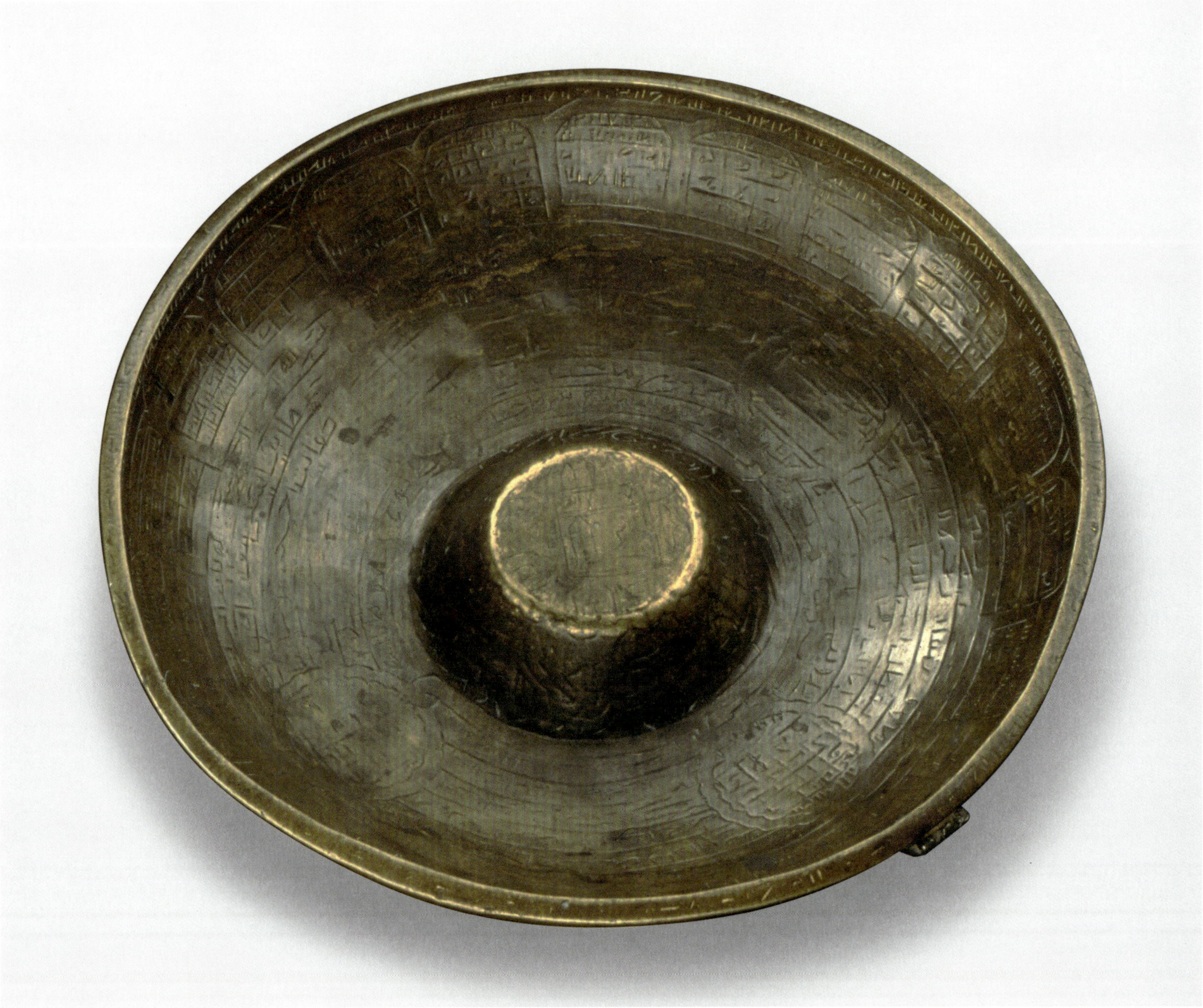

CAT. 34

Medicine bowl

Middle East, tenth century AH / sixteenth century AD

Copper alloy, previously gilded
Diameter 20.5 cm
Collection of the Museum of the Institut du Monde Arabe, Paris
inv. AI 01-07

The Prophet (PBUH) inaugurated an Era of Science and Knowledge. More than 160 Qur'anic verses concern medicine and science. This rounded medicine bowl with a circular foot and averted rim has a central tapering boss depicting the representation of the Kaaba. The inner surface is decorated with engraved Arabic inscriptions in an angular script, relating pious formulas associated with numbers.

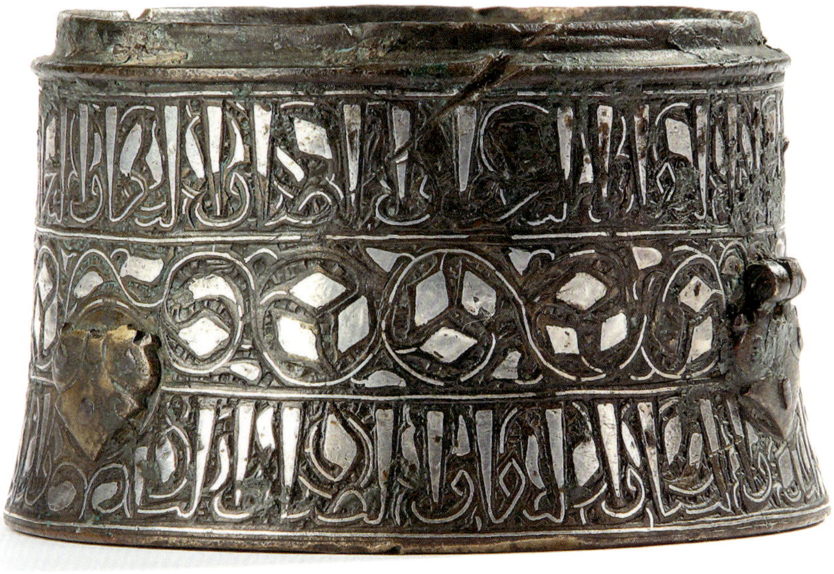

CAT. 35

Inkwell

Khorasan, fifth–sixth century AH / eleventh–twelfth century AD

Bronze inlaid with silver
6 × 9.5 cm
Collection of the Ministry of Culture, Saudi Arabia
inv. IA 2021.32

The inscription on this inkwell reads, "Glory and prosperity and wealth and endurance and generosity".

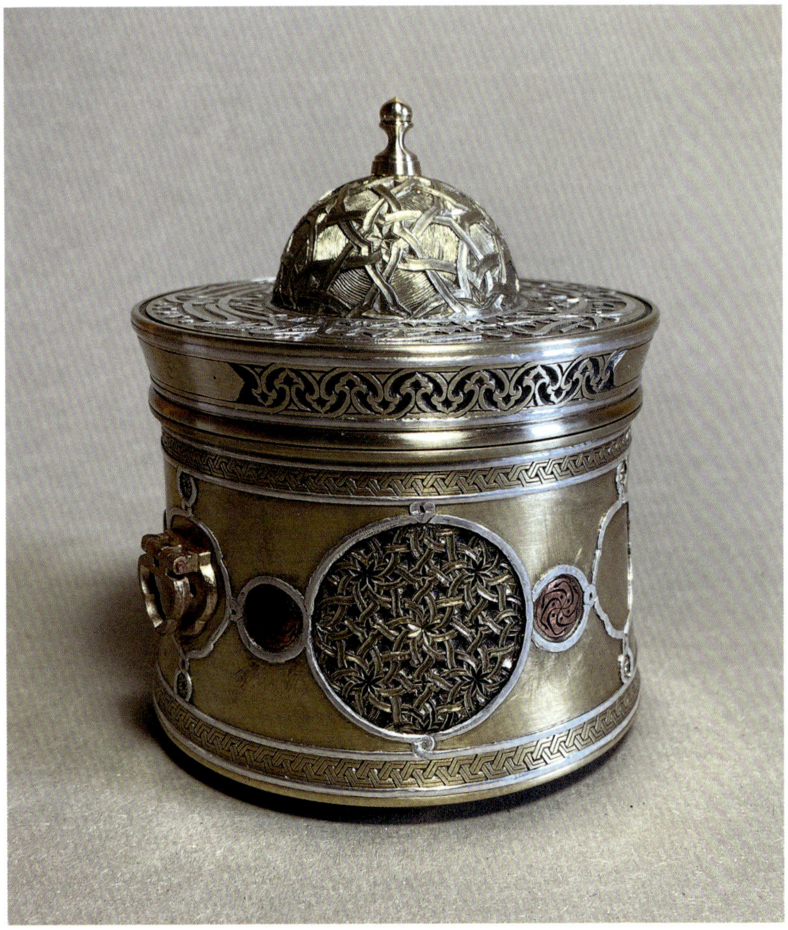

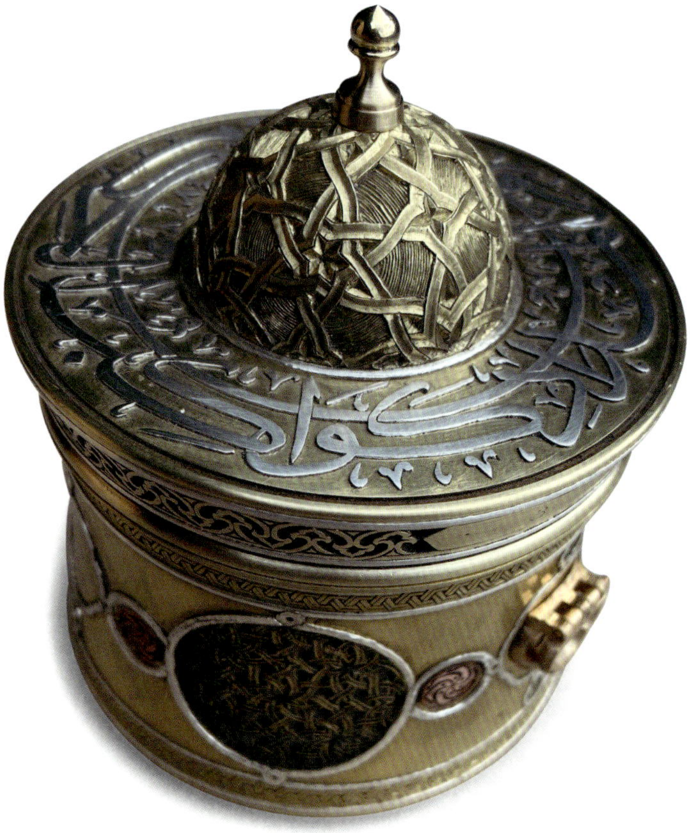

CAT. 36

Ibrahim Batchelder
Inkwell, 2022

Cast bronze
8 × 11 cm
Commissioned by the Ministry of Culture, Saudi Arabia
inv. IA 2022.12

A bronze cylindrical inkwell with ornamental inlaid silver inspired by twelfth- and thirteenth-century specimens from Khorasan. Two horizontal protruding bands, one at the base, the other at the mouth, encircle the vessel. The upper part features a calligraphic inscription in *thuluth* script that reads, "Stars of wisdom in the darkness of ink", a verse attributed to the Abbasid Caliph Al-Ma'mun (r. 198–217 AH / 813–833 AD). An engraved blessing wishes good fortune to the owner. On the body of the inkwell, inlaid silver forms a series of ornamental arabesque motifs.

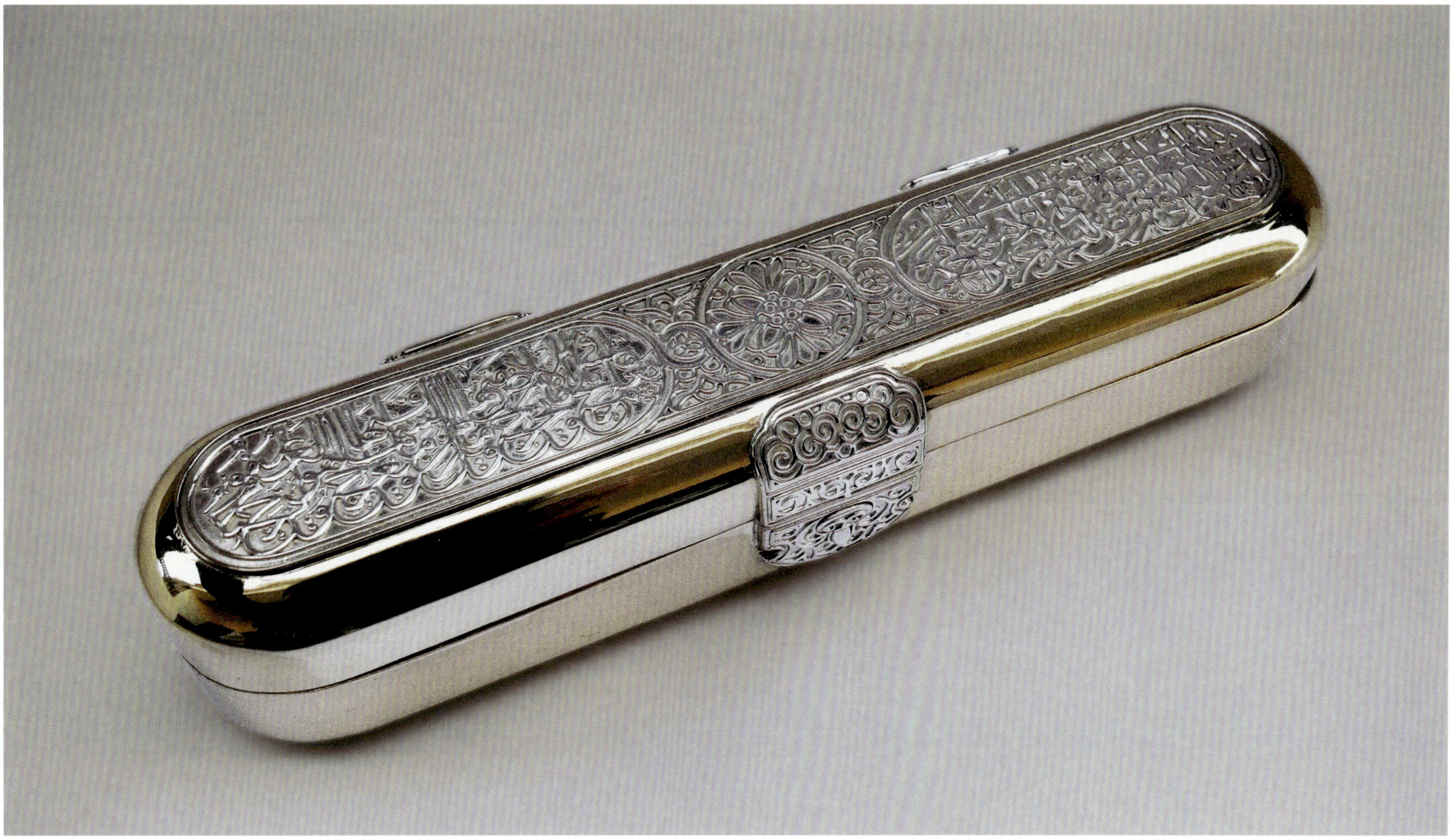

CAT. 37

Randa Fahmy

Nizwani pencil case, 2022

Silver-plated brass and brass
22 × 5 × 4.5 cm
Commissioned by the Ministry of Culture, Saudi Arabia
inv. IA 2022.16

Inspired by a fourteenth-century engraved pen case, currently housed at the National Museum of Oman, this re-interpretation of a rare and traditional piece merges intricate ornament with calligraphy. The top inscription is an original design of two calligraphed Qur'anic verses from surah *Saba*, joined together by a floral pattern. "All praise is for God, to Whom belongs whatever is in the heavens and whatever is on the earth. And praise be to Him in the Hereafter. He is the All-Wise, All-Aware. He knows whatever goes into the earth and whatever comes out of it, and whatever descends from the sky and whatever ascends into it. And He is the Most Merciful, All-Forgiving".

CAT. 38

Inscribed camel shoulder blade
Arabian Peninsula,
thirteenth century AH /
nineteenth century AD

Ink on bone
h. 42.5 cm
Collection of the Ministry of Culture,
Saudi Arabia
inv. IA 2022.23

The fragments of Qur'anic verses inscribed on this camel shoulder blade convey a sense of the victory of patience. These preventive or protective contents are almost omnipresent in this type of texts.

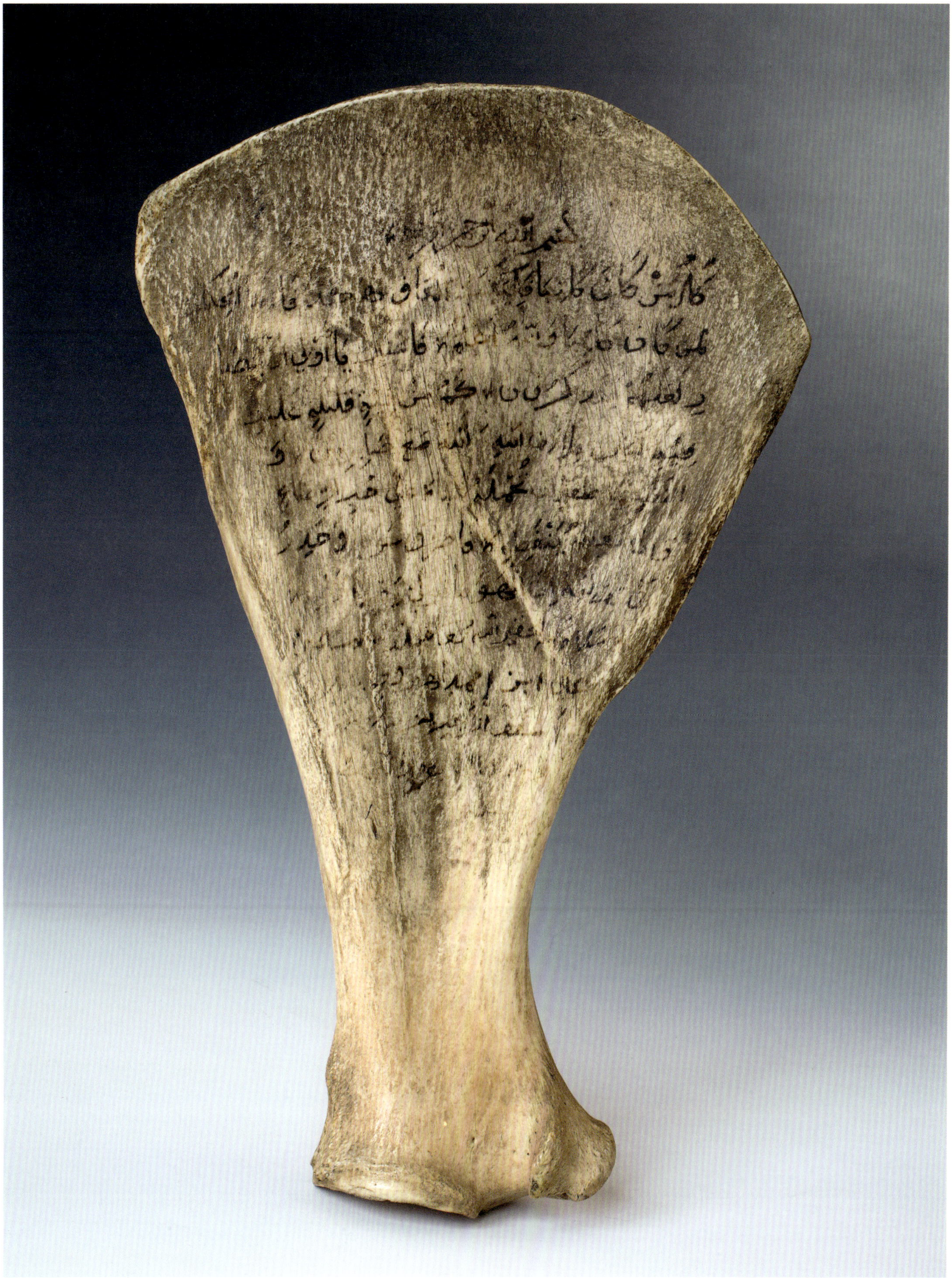

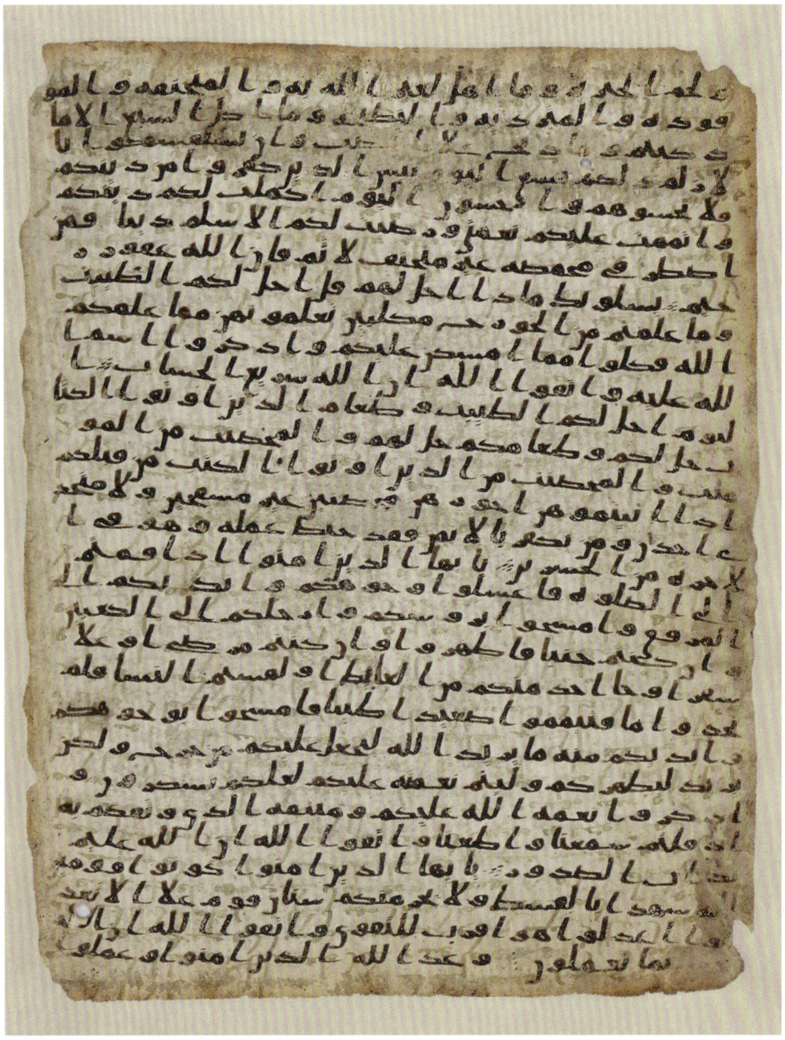

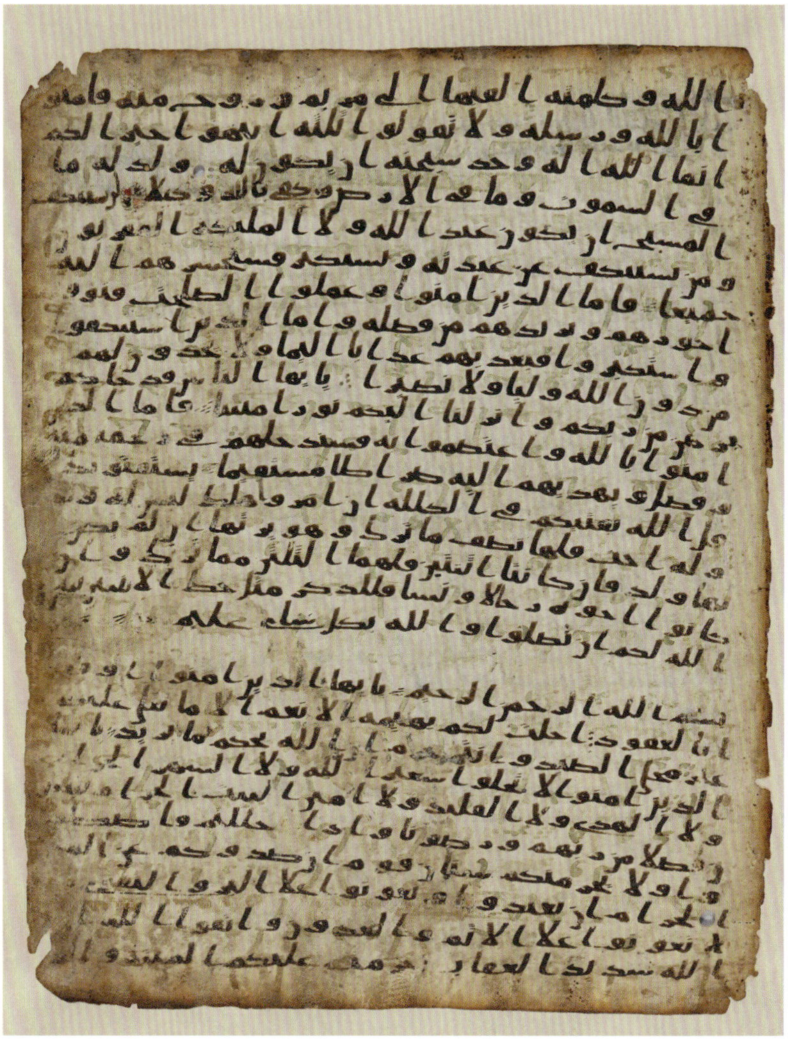

CAT. 39

Folio from the Holy Qur'an

Probably Medina,
mid-first century AH /
mid-seventh century AD

Surah *an-Nisa*, verse 171
Surah *al-Ma'ida*, verses 1–9
Ink on vellum
36.3 × 28 cm
Collection of the Ministry of Culture, Saudi Arabia
inv. IA 2020.39

Manuscript on vellum with slightly worn and torn edges fixed on modern paper lining. Text comprising extracts from surah *an-Nisa* on the recto (28 lines) and surah *al-Ma'ida* (30 lines) on the verso. Barely visible traces of a different erased Qur'anic text from surah *al-Jumu'ah* under the original *hijazi* script, whose verses in sepia are separated by a small medallion in red, green and brown, highlighted with gold.

CAT. 40

Folio from the Holy Qur'an

Persia or Mesopotamia,
c. 750–751 AH / c. 1350 AD

Surah *an-Nisa*, verses 26–29
Ink, colours and gold on paper
Written in *thuluth muhaqqaq* script
40 x 29 cm
Collection of the Ministry of Culture,
Saudi Arabia
inv. IA 2020.50

A single double leaf with five lines to each side, written in large elegant black *thuluth muhaqqaq* script outlined in gold. Gold and blue verse markers outlined in red, with diacritics and vowel points in black, all ruled in red and purple borders.

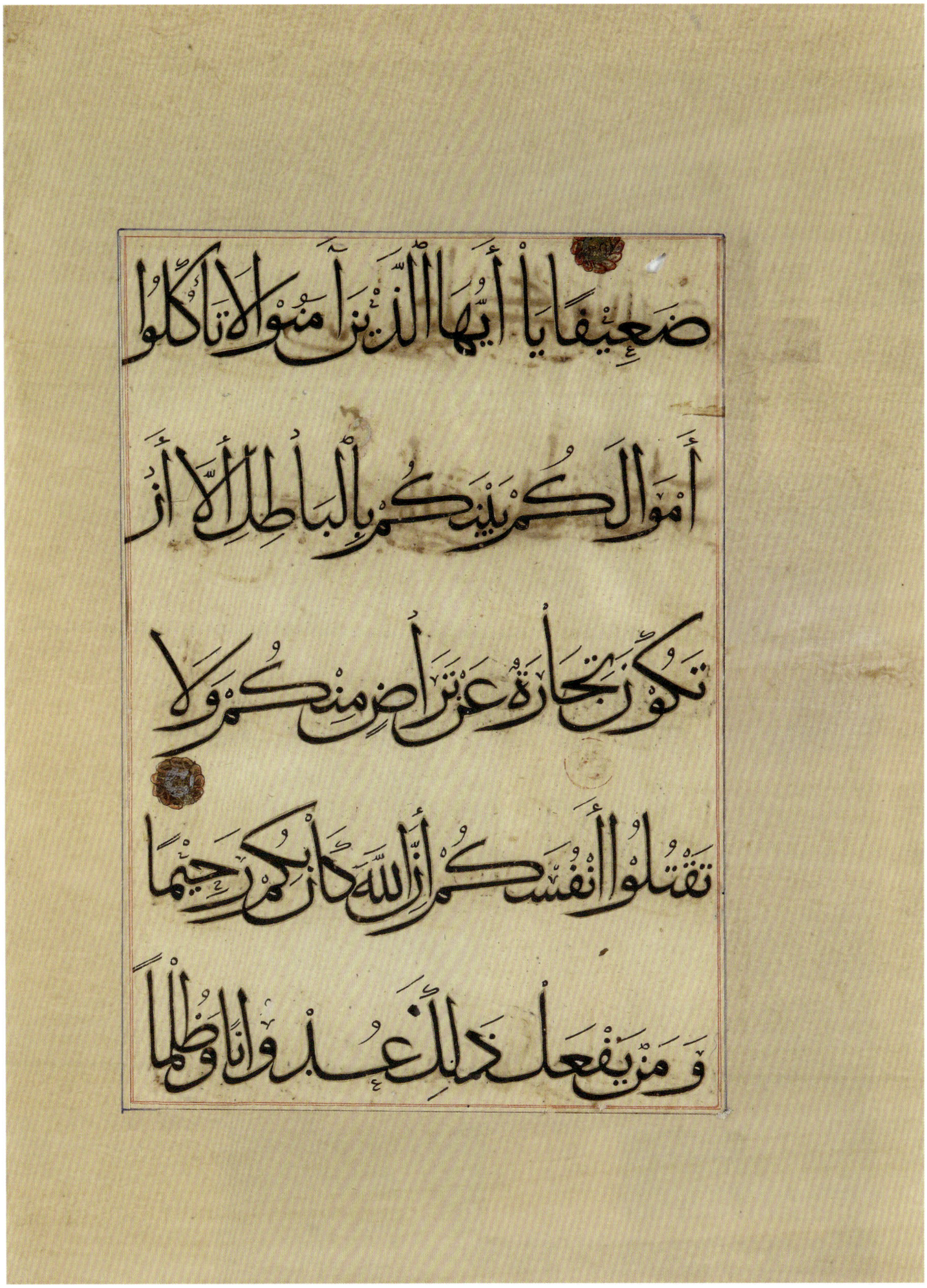

ضعيفا يا أيها الذين آمنوا لا تأكلوا
أموالكم بينكم بالباطل إلا أن
تكون تجارة عن تراض منكم ولا
تقتلوا أنفسكم إن الله كان بكم رحيما
ومن يفعل ذلك عدوانا وظلما

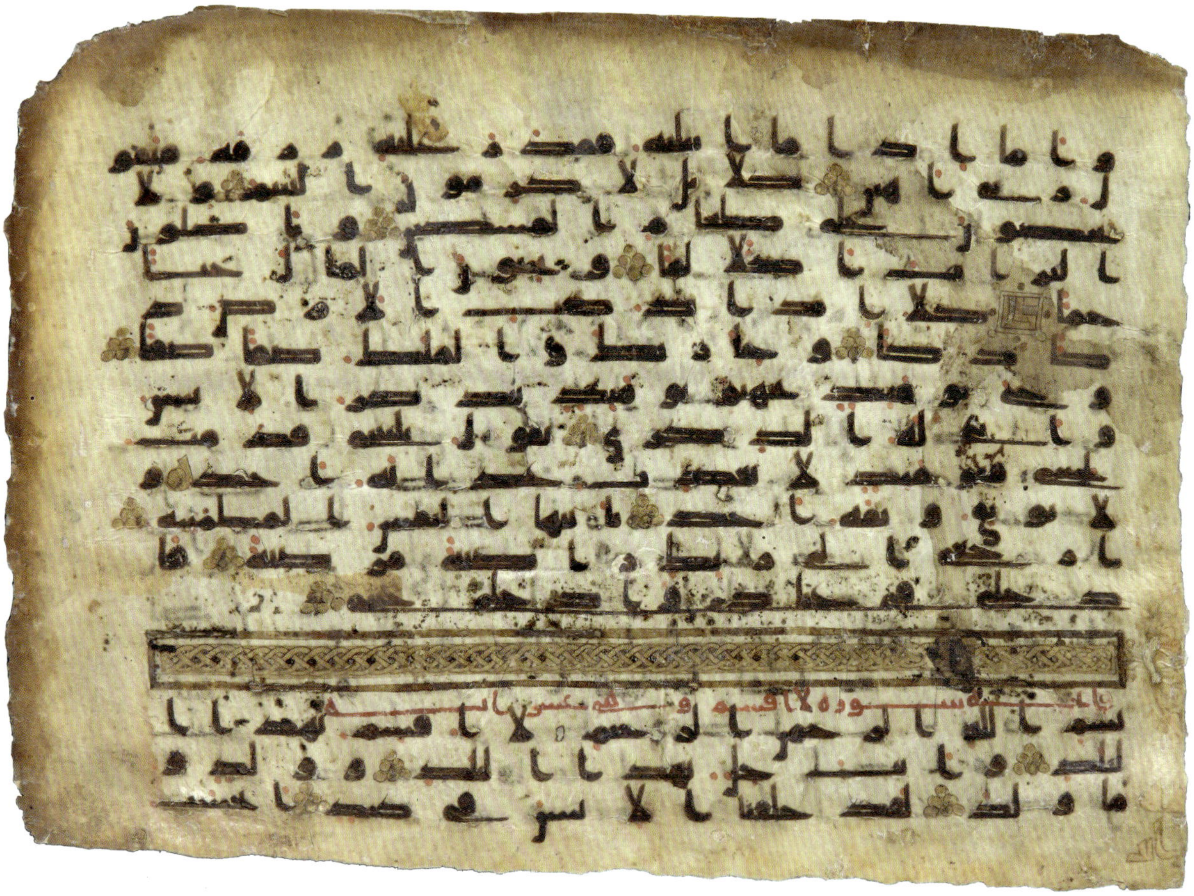

CAT. 41

Folio from the Holy Qur'an

first–second century AH /
seventh–eighth century AD

Surah *al-Ghashiyah*, verses 19–26
Surah *al-Fajr*, verse 90
Surah *al-Balad*, verses 1–6
Ink on paper
Written in *kufi* script
19 × 25 cm
Collection of the Ministry of Culture, Saudi Arabia
inv. IA 2020.49

Written in brown with red diacritical points, this manuscript on vellum in long *kufi* script contains extracts from three Qur'anic surahs whose headings appear in red: *al-Ghashiyah*, *al-Fajr* and *al-Balad*. A triangular motif in gold dots marks the separation between verses. The page is covered with 15 lines and two bands with a braided coil motif.

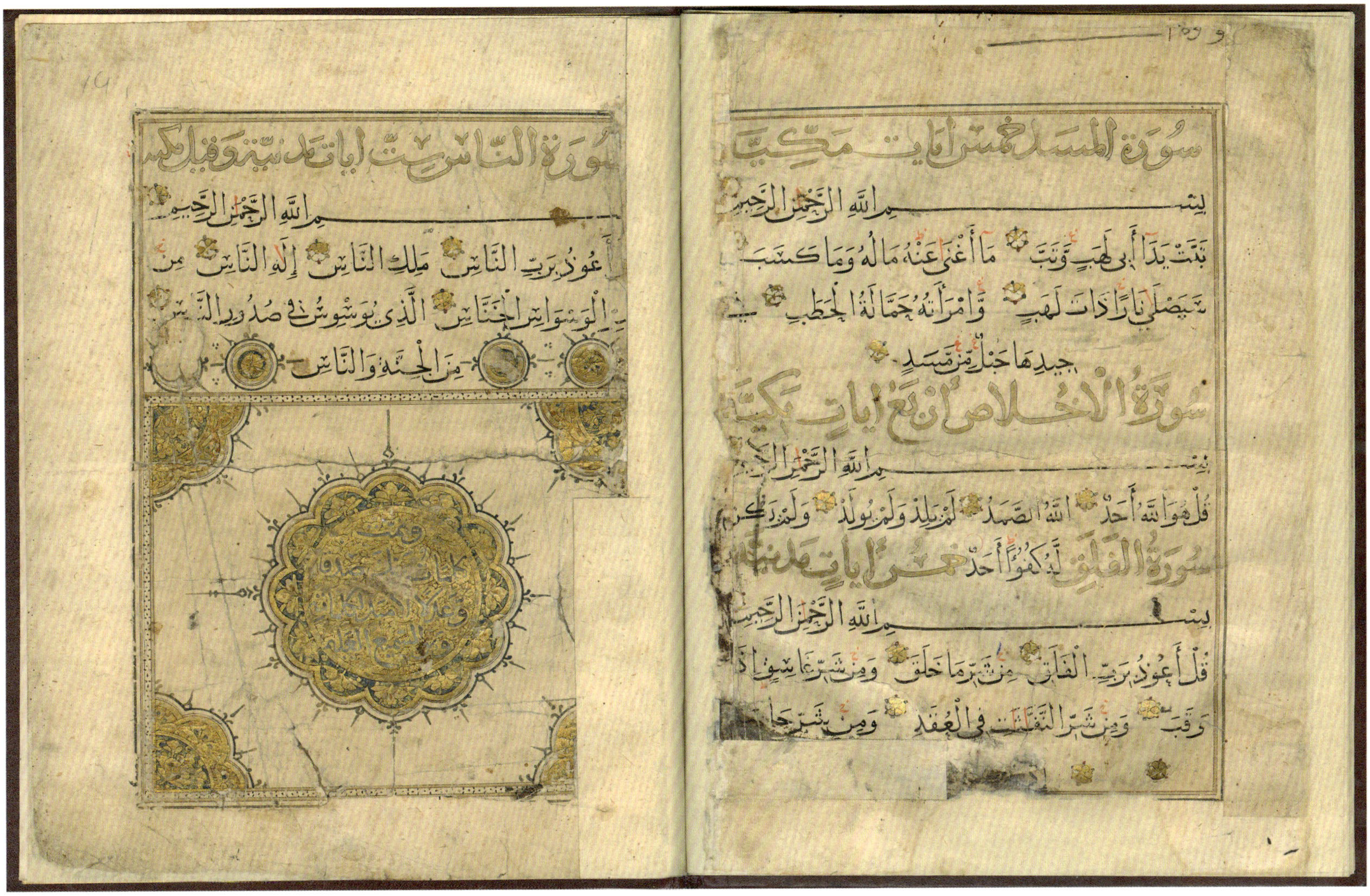

CAT. 42

The Holy Qur'an

Probably Egypt, eighth–ninth century AH / fourteenth–fifteenth century AD

30th *juz'*, from surah *al-Mursalat*, verse 29, to surah *an-Nas*
Ink and gold on paper
Written in *muhaqqaq* script
37.5 × 28 cm (closed)
Collection of the Ministry of Culture, Saudi Arabia
inv. IA 2021.24

Manuscript on paper with small repairs to margins. In black *muhaqqaq* script, with surah headings in gold accentuated with black. 13 lines on each of the 14 folios between two fly leaves, and last folio on card. Text representing the 30th subdivision of the Qur'an (*juz'*). Separation between verses made with multicoloured roundels and end of *juz'* marked with a multicoloured and gilded colophon inside a larger square with spandrel corners. Cover in gilded brown Morocco.

CAT. 43

Haythem Zakaria
Al-Fatiha, 2015/2022

Laminated digital print, algorithm
80 × 200 cm
Collection of the Ministry of Culture, Saudi Arabia
inv. CA 2022.22

Al-Fatiha is a laminated digital print revealing a panoramic landscape made of stipples that, seen up close, unveil thousands of Arabic letters forming the surah *al-Fatiha* through combinatorial writing. The result is achieved thanks to a computer software specifically conceived and developed for this very purpose. This piece transcends the text of a surah through extreme abstraction. The process used takes this print beyond language, to the limits of the intelligible, to the very frontiers of what can be named. In his constant pursuit of shapes and letters, Zakaria reveals in this artwork multiple meanings, where visual art search meets spiritual quest.

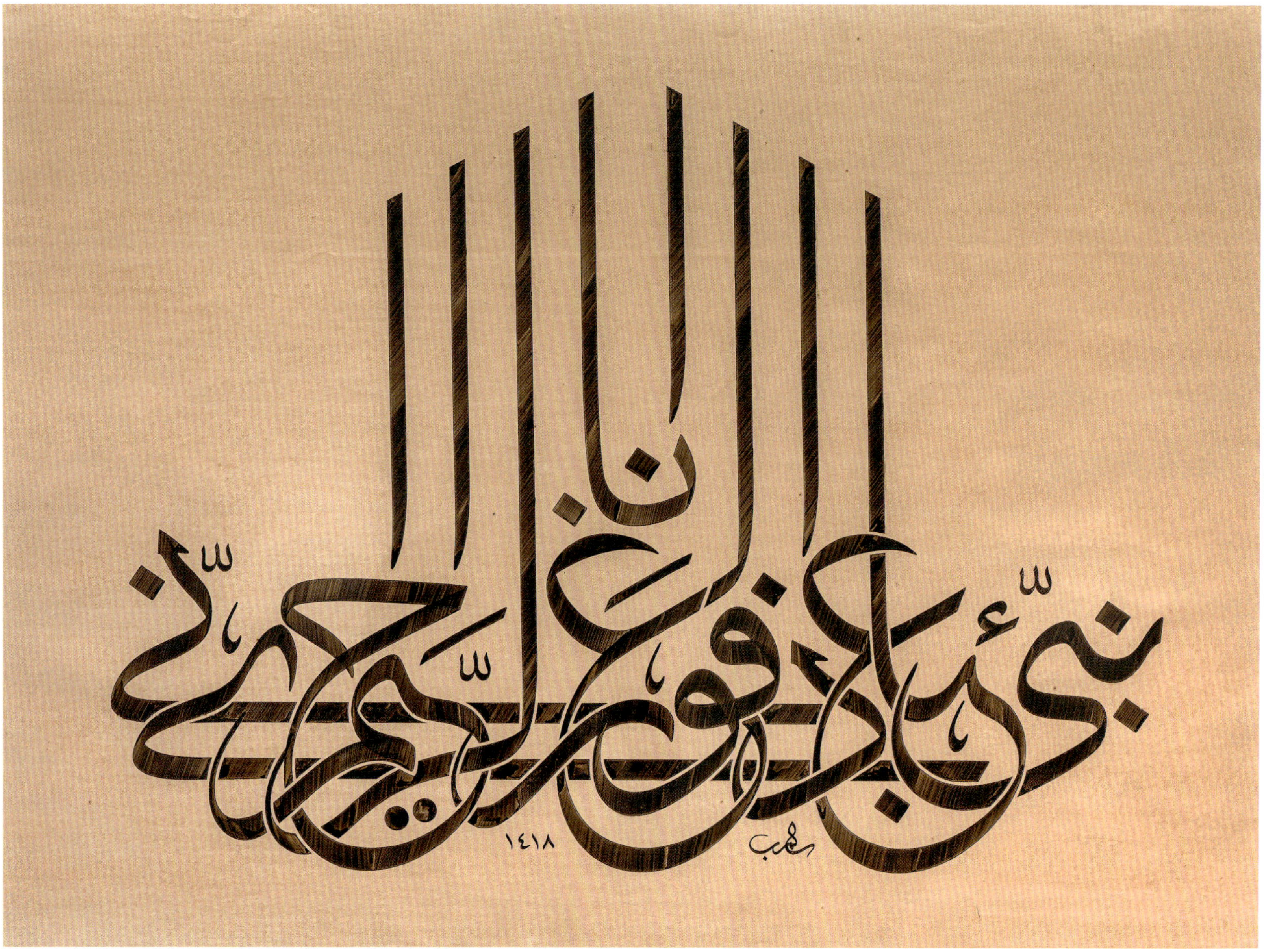

CAT. 44

Mohammad Salem Bajnaid
Inform My Servants, O Prophet, that I Am Truly the All-Forgiving, Most Merciful, 1997
Surah *al-Hijr*, verse 49
Ink on paper
70 × 90 cm
Courtesy of Salem M. Fawzi Bajnaid

The letters *alif* and *lam* written in ink on paper extend to form an impression of one corner of the Kaaba. The other letters are scattered to illustrate the movement of people performing the *Tawaf* (circling the Holy Kaaba seven times in an anti-clockwise direction) in the House of God. The double *alif* in the Divine "I Am" extends beyond the limits of the other elongations to signify the absolute transcendence of God. Only with its presence, the Kaaba forms a structural correspondence with the verses, "As the Kaaba connects the Earth to Al-Bait Al-Ma'mour in heaven, so does repentance connect the repentant with the All-Forgiving". The scene carries a constant flow of spiritual abundance that encapsulates the meanings of forgiveness, faith, righteousness and guidance. The calligrapher conveys all the urgency of his message, showing his ability to manifest the similarity of meanings that attract him towards the Ancient House of God and the beauty and homogeneity of the surah before His eyes.

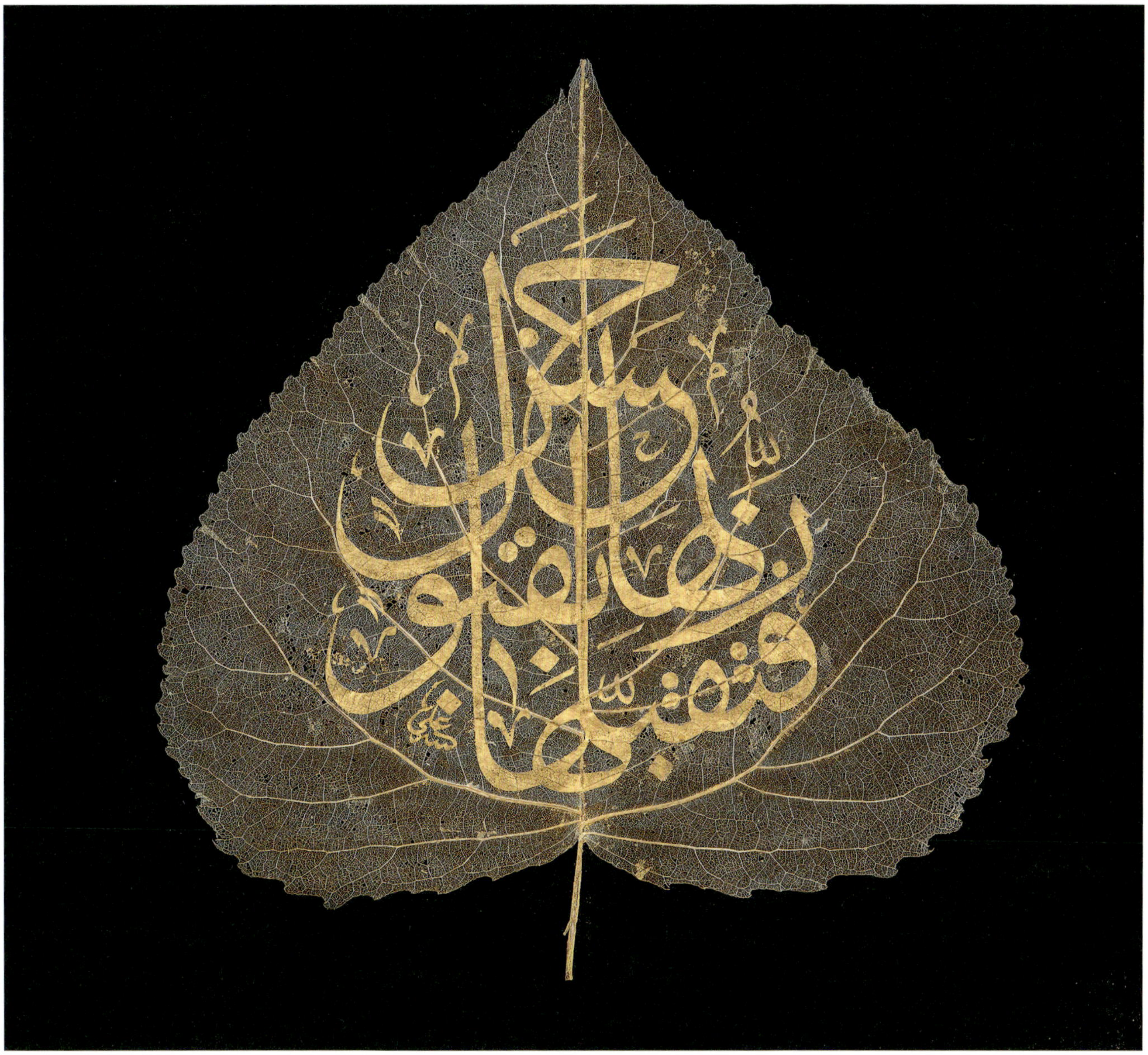

CAT. 45

So, Her Lord Accepted Her Graciously and Blessed Her with a Pleasant Upbringing

thirteenth-fourteenth century AH / nineteenth–twentieth century AD

Surah *al-Imran*, verse 37
Gold on leaf
33.5 × 35.5 cm
Collection of the Ministry of Culture, Saudi Arabia
inv. IA 2020.1

This inscription is written in gold using a dried leaf as a support: an extremely delicate and elaborate technique that developed during the nineteenth century. This composition was originally written by the great calligrapher Mehmed Ali Circili Efendi in 1290 AH / 1873 AD in *jaly thuluth* script. It was later transferred on the leaf with the aid of a stencil made to scale and gilded. The artist aligned the central vein of the leaf with the letter *lam* of the word *fataqabbalaha* and rested the base of the composition on the lower veins extending outwards, creating a beautiful rapport between the writing and the organic matrix of the leaf.

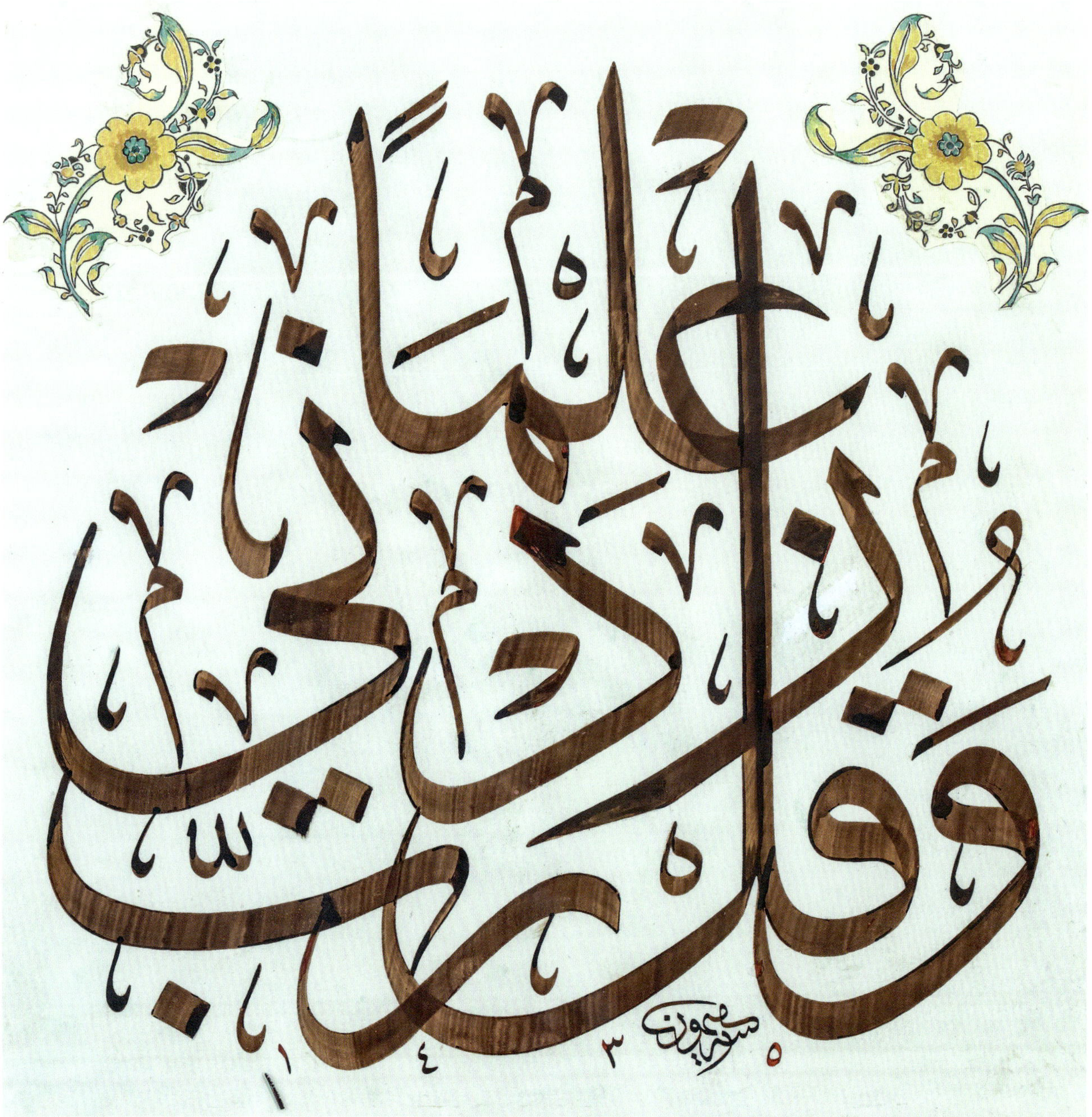

CAT. 46

Nasser Al Maymoun
Exalted Is Allah, the True King! Do Not Rush to Recite a Revelation of the Qur'an O Prophet Before It Is Properly Conveyed to You, and Pray, "My Lord! Increase Me in Knowledge", 2013

Surah *Taha*, verse 114
Ink on paper
65 × 65 cm
Collection of the Ministry of Culture, Saudi Arabia
inv. MOC 2022.1

A reminder of the importance of seeking and acquiring knowledge, this Qur'anic verse, "And pray, 'My Lord! Increase me in knowledge'" (surah *Taha*, verse 114), which is often chosen by calligraphers, sees the Prophet Muhammad (PBUH) addressing a prayer to God to grant him more knowledge. *Thuluth* is a strongly balanced script, filled with unique details. In *jaly thuluth* script, this verse is beautifully and innovatively represented in an ascending composition, linking the rising design to the increase in knowledge required by the content of the verse. The two ornamental elements at the top add further balance both to the eye and to the aesthetics of the written text.

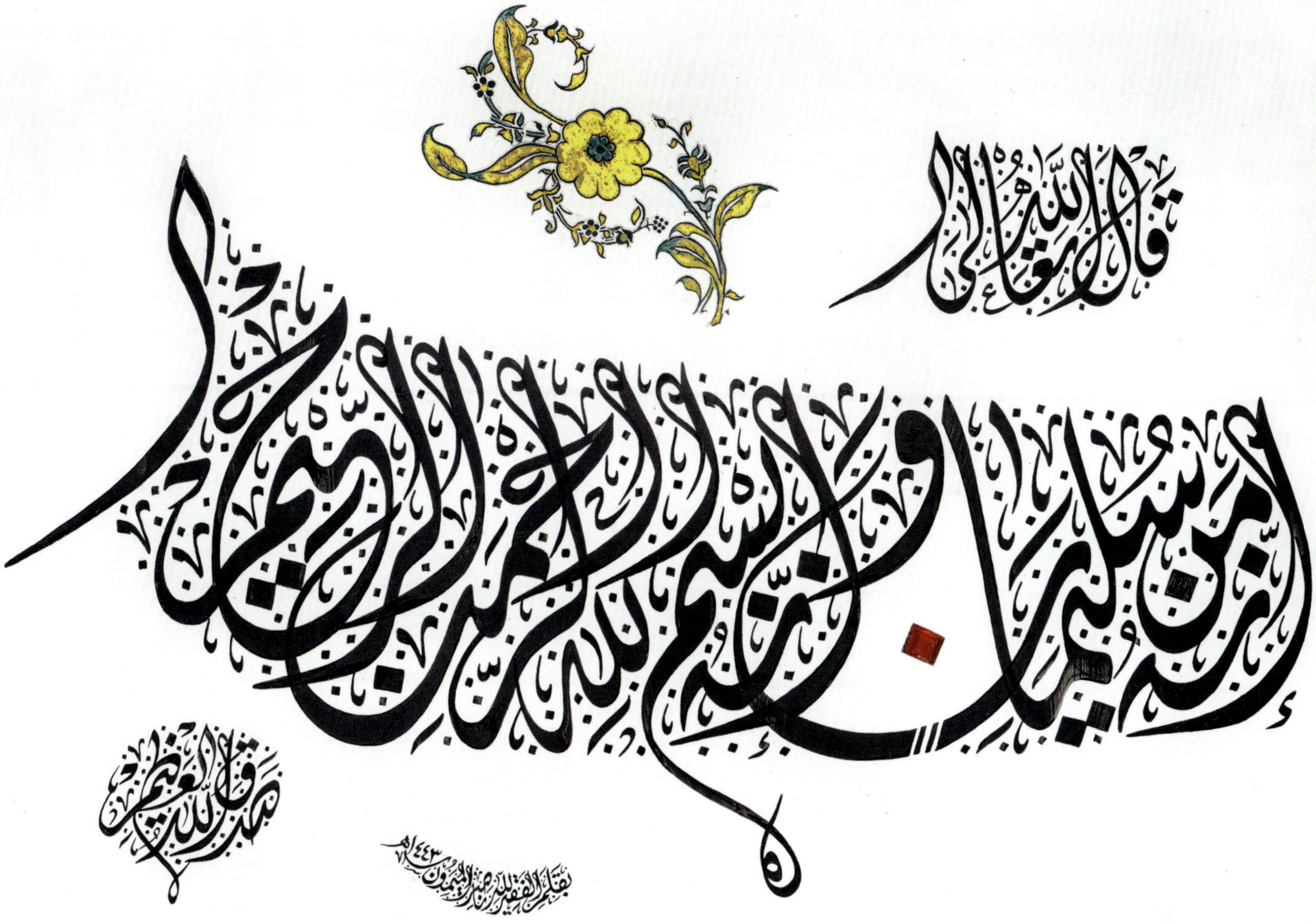

CAT. 47

Nasser Al Maymoun
In the Name of Allah, the Most Merciful, the Most Compassionate. Surely It Is from Sulayman (Solomon) and Surely It Is in the Name of Allah, the All-Merciful, the Ever Merciful, 2021

Surah *an-Naml*, verse 30
Ink on paper
50 × 70 cm
Courtesy of Nasser Al Maymoun

"In the Name of Allah, the All-Merciful, the Ever Merciful'" (surah *an-Naml*, verse 30): this is a verse of blessing used by all Muslims, in imitation of the Prophet (PBUH), to initiate any action. A very short, expressive, beautifully written verse, also used by the Prophet Sulayman (Solomon) when, in a letter carried by the hoopoe bird, he addressed the Queen of Sheba and the inhabitants of Saba' (the story is narrated in its entirety in the surah *an-Naml*). Al Maymoun used a beautifully flowing *jaly diwani* script, ornamented with diacritical points and vocalization signs. A single unique ornamental design is added at the top to further enhance the flow of the written letters.

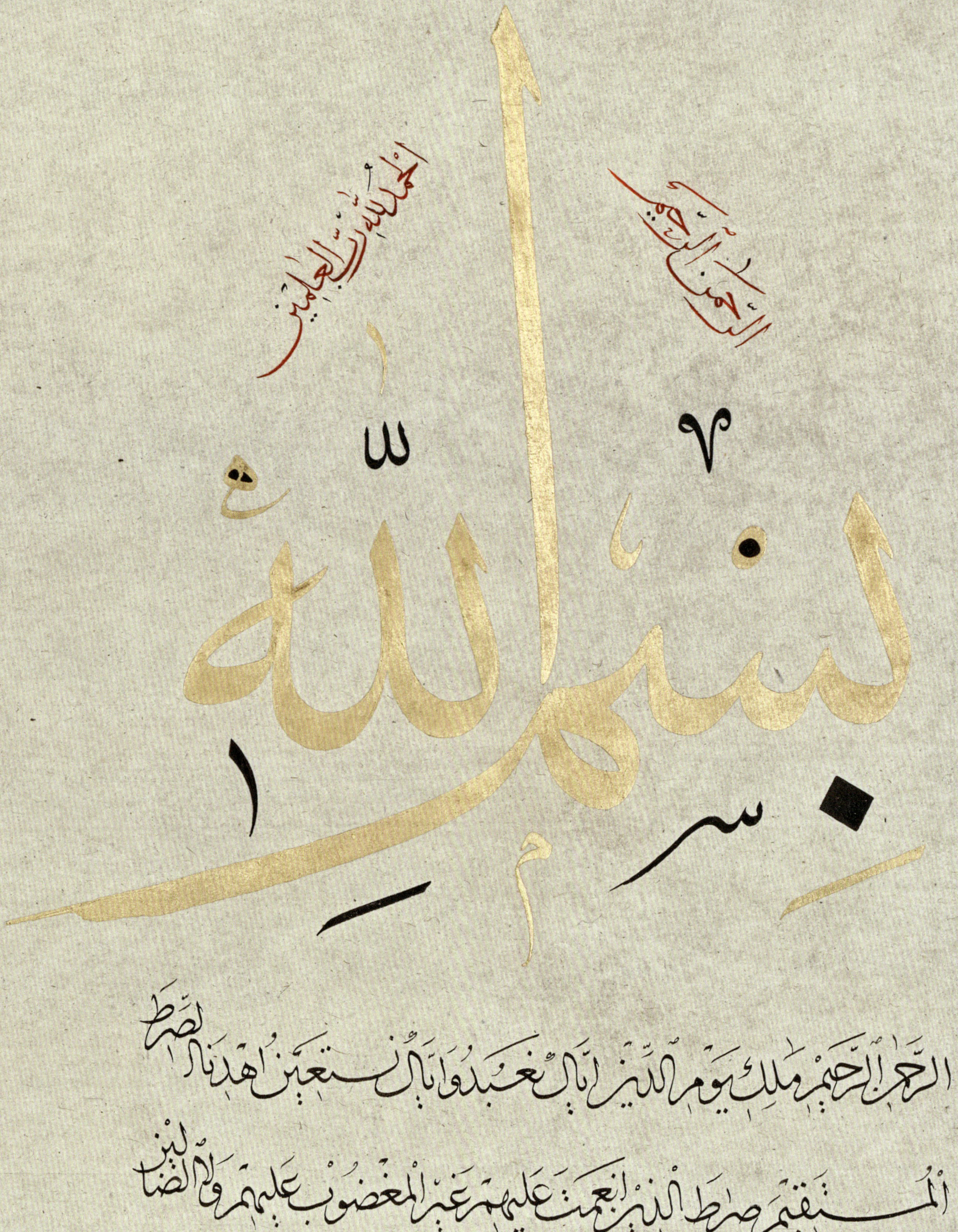

بسم الله
الرحمن الرحيم
الحمد لله رب العالمين
الرحمن الرحيم ملك يوم الدين إياك نعبد وإياك نستعين اهدنا الصراط
المستقيم صراط الذين أنعمت عليهم غير المغضوب عليهم ولا الضالين

CAT. 48

Jassim Miraj Al-Failakawi
Spiritual Journey, 2022

Ink and watercolours on ibru paper
Written in square *kufi*, *muhaqqaq*, *thuluth*, *tawqi'* and *riqa'* scripts
300 × 30 cm
Collection of the Ministry of Culture, Saudi Arabia
inv. IA.2022.17

Before awareness or thought, there was the word: it was at the centre of humans' inner world, at the beginning of civilization. As conveyors of ideas, words grant writing its importance. Thus in the Islamic world, calligraphy became a major art, its system developed and perfected along with literature. An understanding of the letter and its design potential, as well as its acoustic and semantic dimensions, expands the calligrapher's imagination. Each letter carries various impressions within its folds, and its secrets are unveiled using different materials and techniques.

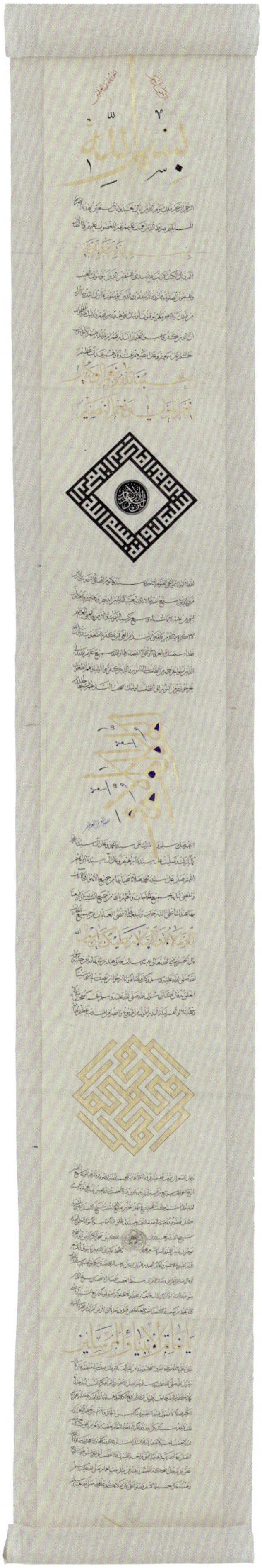

SPACE

The Egyptian calligrapher Khodeir El-Borsaidy, to whom this exhibition pays tribute, links the letters of the Arabic alphabet to the vocabulary of architecture: their lines and angles suggest an entrance or a direction, like wandering around a city or a monument. It is also a way of emphasizing the omnipresence of calligraphy in the Muslim environment. Since the first century AH / seventh century AD, calligraphy has indeed covered buildings, sacred as well as profane, and royal or everyday objects. In the third century AH / tenth century AD, beautiful written script became an art in itself and flourished simultaneously on a wide variety of supports, as well as in formats ranging from the most minuscule to the monumental. Master calligraphers exercised their art and excelled in the realm of the manuscript book. Attached to the court workshops of the sovereigns, as evidenced in archival documents from the fifteenth century, they also provided text panels for creations intended for public spaces: monumental inscriptions were drawn on ceramics or carved in wood, stucco and stone, or even sewn on textiles, the most significant of which are the bands embroidered with Qur'anic verses that adorn the *kiswa*. Calligraphy accompanies everyone in their everyday life; beyond its linguistic value, it takes on a symbolic dimension and gives rise to a feeling of belonging to a civilization that has made it its main cultural marker.

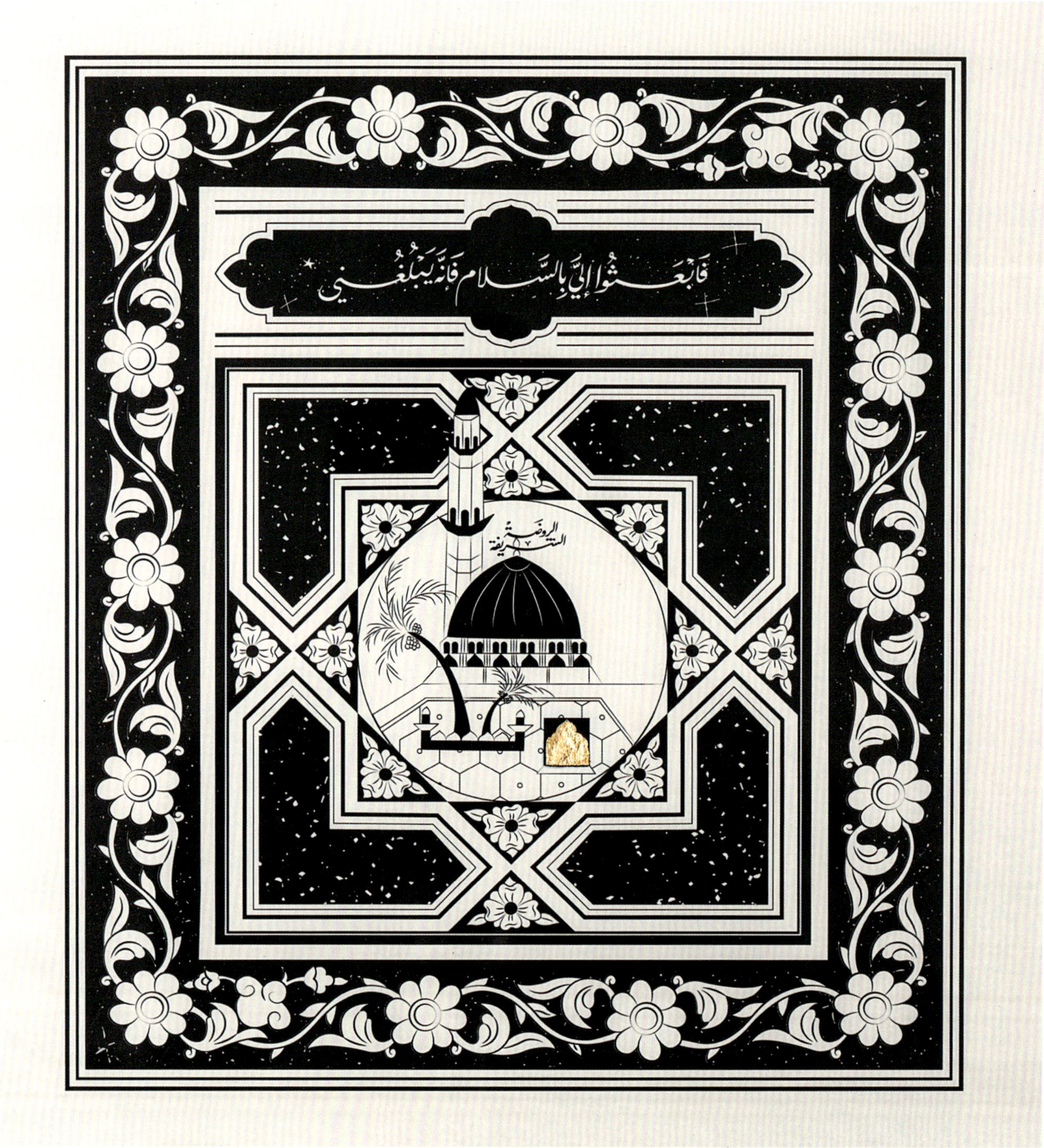

CAT. 49

Doa Bugis and Sara Al Abdali
The Home, the Tomb, 2019

2 silkscreens, 24k gold leaf on organic cotton paper
33 × 30 cm each
Courtesy of Doa Bugis and Sara Al Abdali

Inspired by pilgrimage accounts provided by calligraphers and engravers throughout the Muslim world, the idea of producing pilgrimage testimonies in a contemporary style came as a collaborative work created by the artists Sara Al Abdali and Doa Bugis. These documents are scenes, excerpts and beautiful artistic documentation of all that pilgrims confront during the different stages of their journey. It is an art practised by many pilgrims through painters, who are keen to accompany them on their journeys so that their brushes and their colours may convey what they have discovered, not just with their bodies but also with their hearts. It is strange that the secrets of this journey – however different the details of their various struggles – are shared by all pilgrims who, in their desire to perform the Hajj or the Umrah, have headed for this land throughout the ages. It is in this spirit that the two artists have determined to make a gift of this work to every pilgrim, every devotee, every traveller, and every lover who has undertaken this arduous journey, always optimistic about the final outcome.

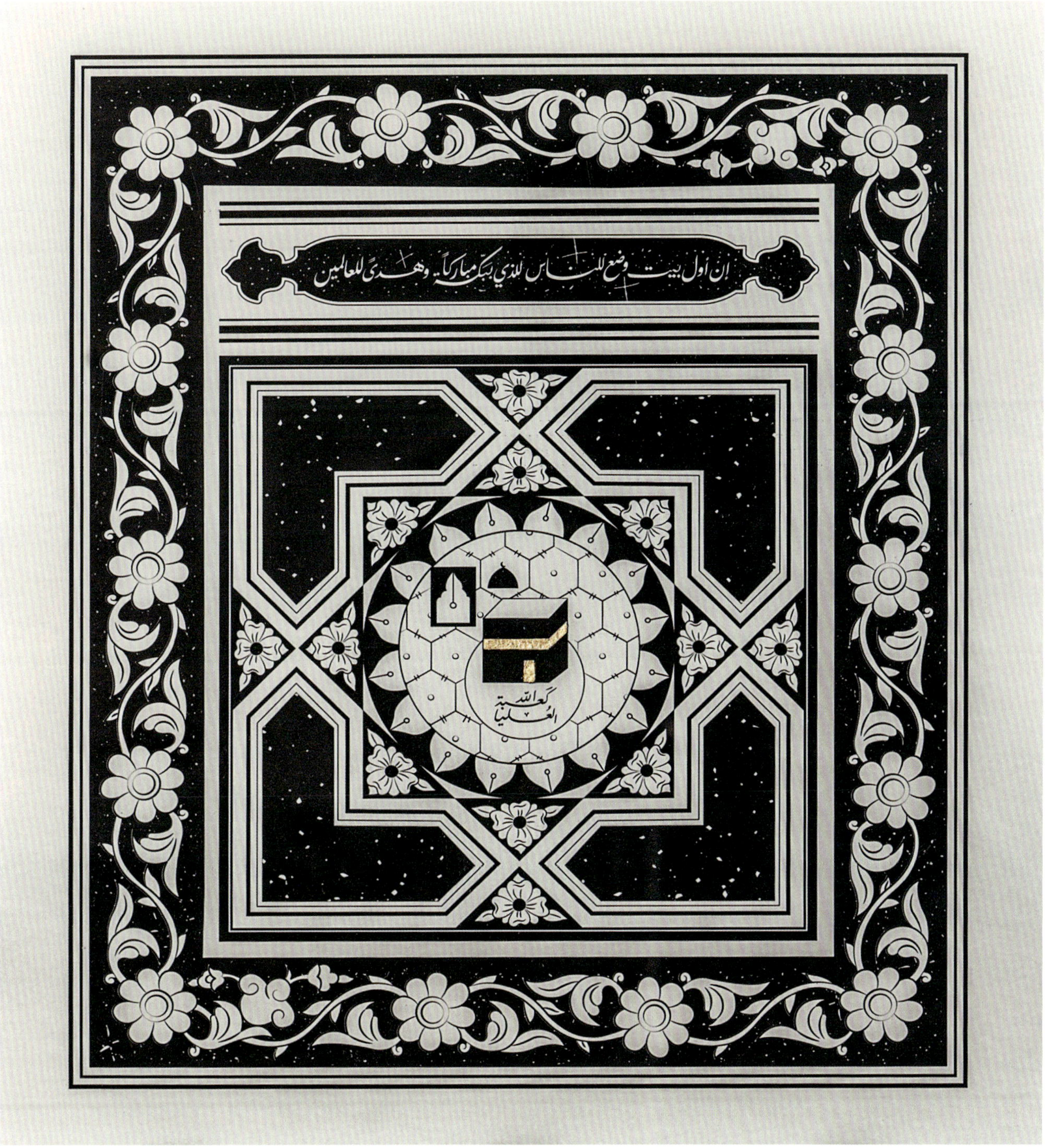
إن أول بيت وضع للناس للذي ببكة مباركاً وهدىً للعالمين
كعبة الله العليا

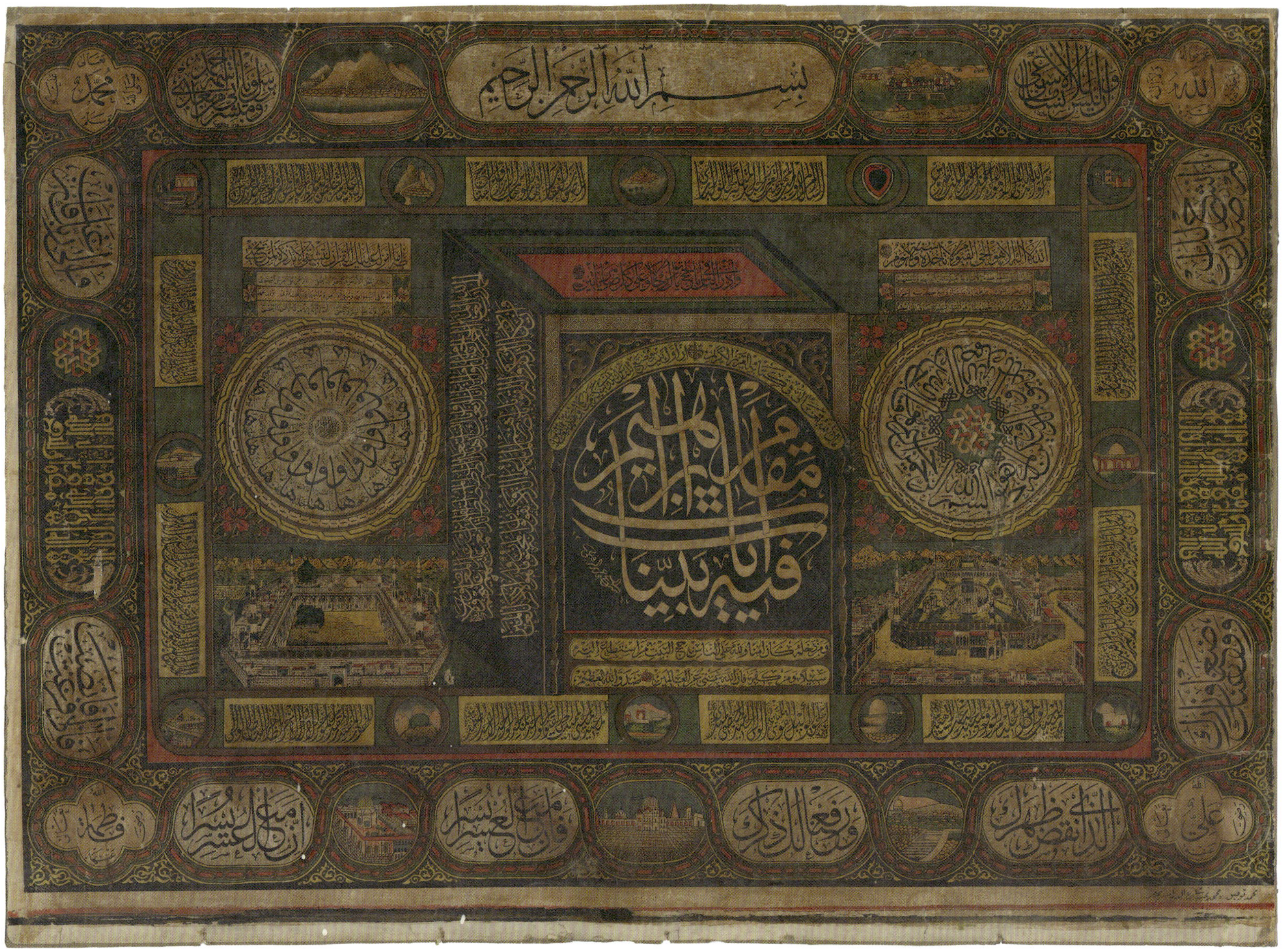

CAT. 50

Hajj certificate

Cairo, Egypt, c. 1338 AH / 1920 AD

Printed by Muhammad Tawfiq
and Muhammad Naguib
49 × 66 cm
Collection of the Ministry of Culture,
Saudi Arabia
inv. PT 2020.71

This Hajj certificate, printed in colours, proves that the owner completed the pilgrimage to Mecca. The Kaaba at the centre is surrounded by 19 vignettes representing both the phases of the pilgrimage and the circular procession of people (*Tawaf*). The vignettes intersect with medallions inscribed with short supplications (*du'a'*) written in *thuluth* script. Flanked on the sides by columns with floral motifs to symbolize the pillars of Islam.

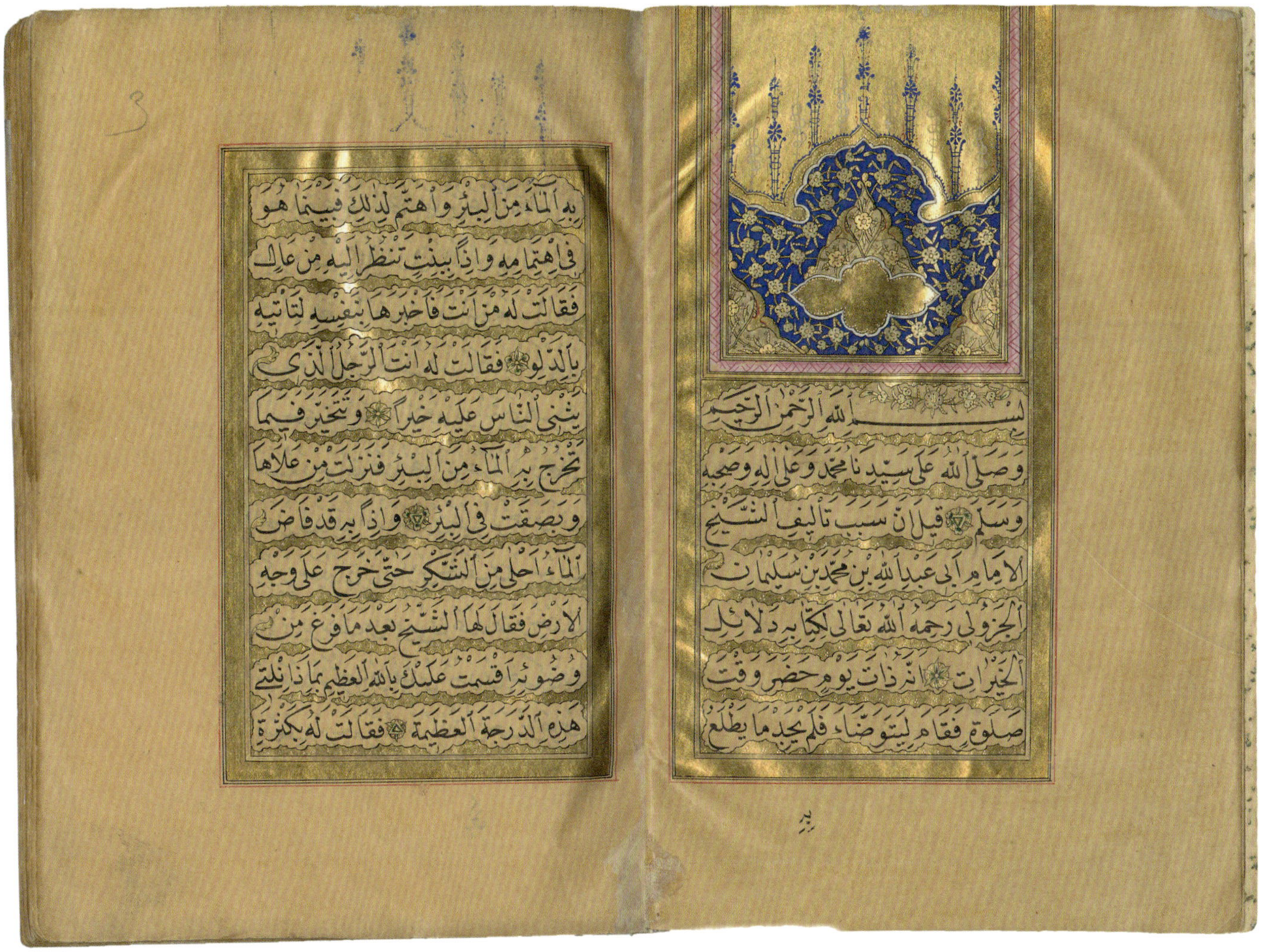

CAT. 51

Dala'il al-Khayrat

1262 AH / 1845 AD

Copied by Hassan Husseini, pupil of Ibrahim Sidqy Effendi
Ink, colours and gold on paper
Written in *naskh* script
15 × 10 cm (closed)
Collection of the Ministry of Culture, Saudi Arabia
inv. IA 2021.26

Illuminated manuscript illustrated by three double frontispieces set in a golden frame, covering the entire folio and representing Mecca and Medina. With 12 lines to each of the 96 folios, in fine black *naskh* script.

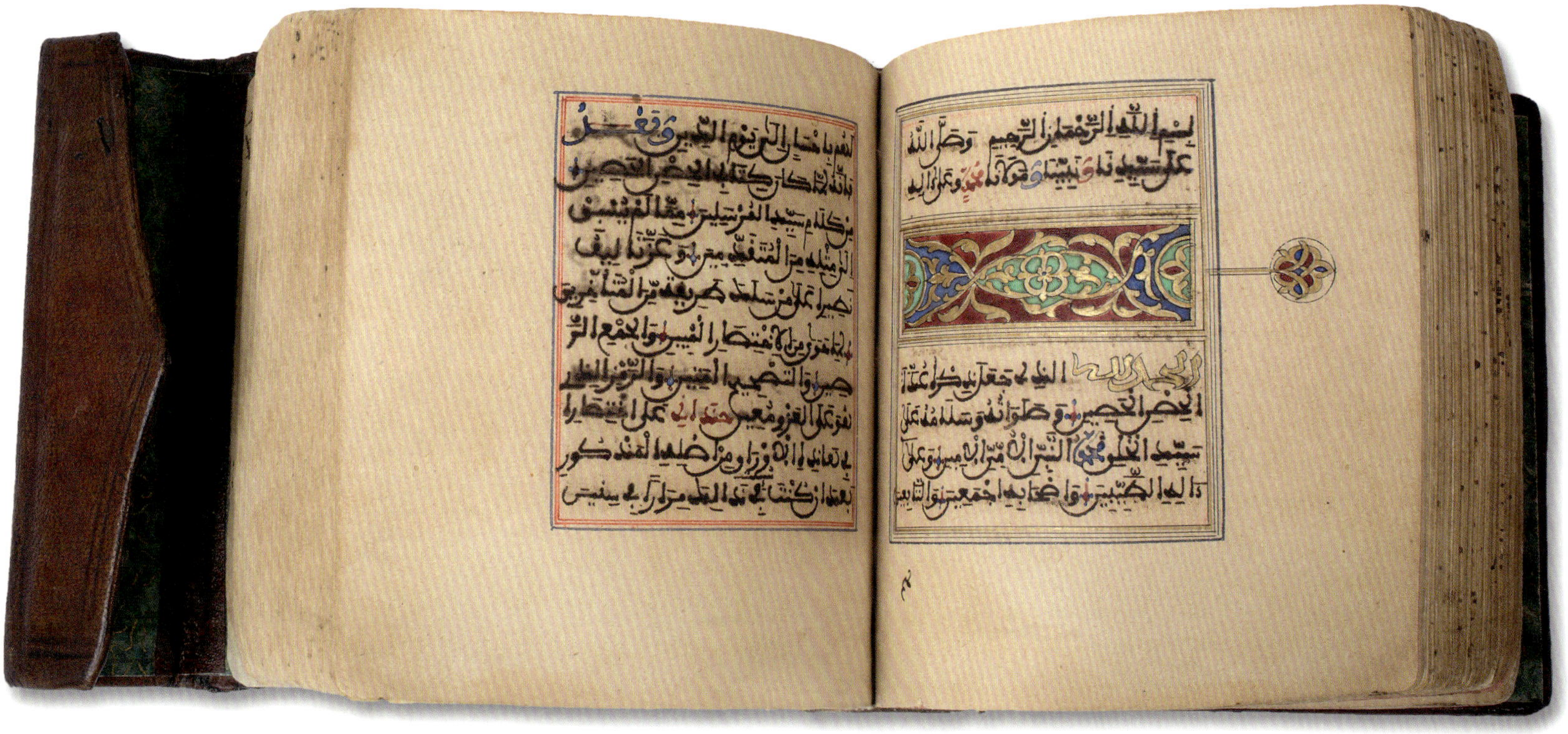

CAT. 52

Dala'il al-Khayrat

Morocco, c. 1215 AH / c. 1800 AD

Ink on paper
Written in *maghribi* script
11.5 × 11 × 3.5 cm (closed)
Collection of the Ministry of Culture, Saudi Arabia
inv. IA 2020.7

One of the famous books among the collections of formulas mentioning the Prophet (PBUH), *Dala'il al-Khayrat* (Guidelines to the Blessings and the Shining of Lights, giving the saying of the blessed prayer over the Prophet, PBUH) was written by the Moroccan religious scholar Abu Abdallah Muhammad ibn Sulayman al-Jazuli (d. 869 AH / 1465 AD).

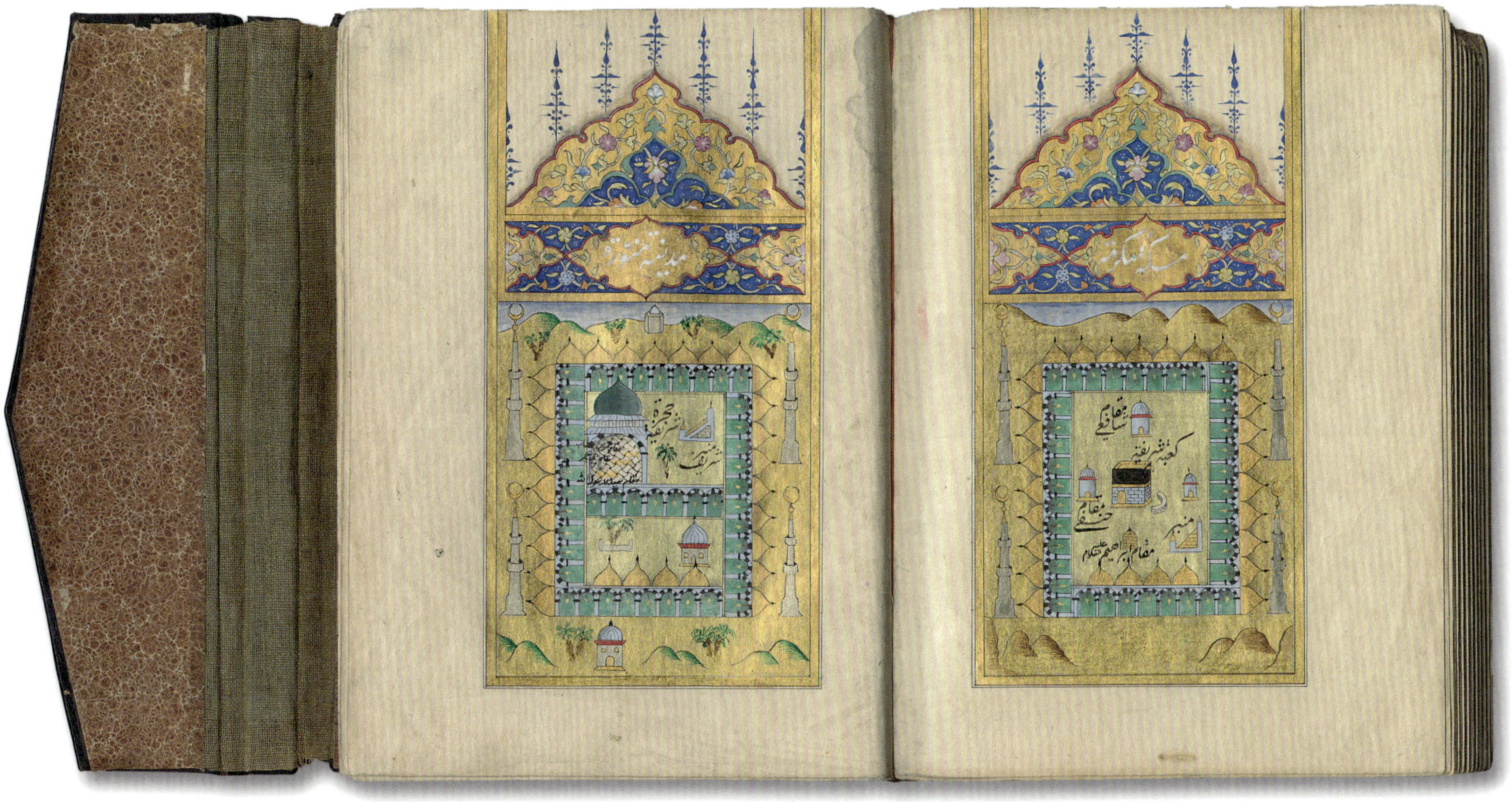

CAT. 53

Manuscript

thirteenth century AH / nineteenth century AD

Ink and gold on paper
19.1 x 14.5 x 2.7 cm (closed)
Collection of the Ministry of Culture, Saudi Arabia
inv. IA 2021.28

This highly illuminated and illustrated manuscript features the holy places: Dome of the Rock in Al-Quds, Mecca Holy Mosque, Mount Arafat.

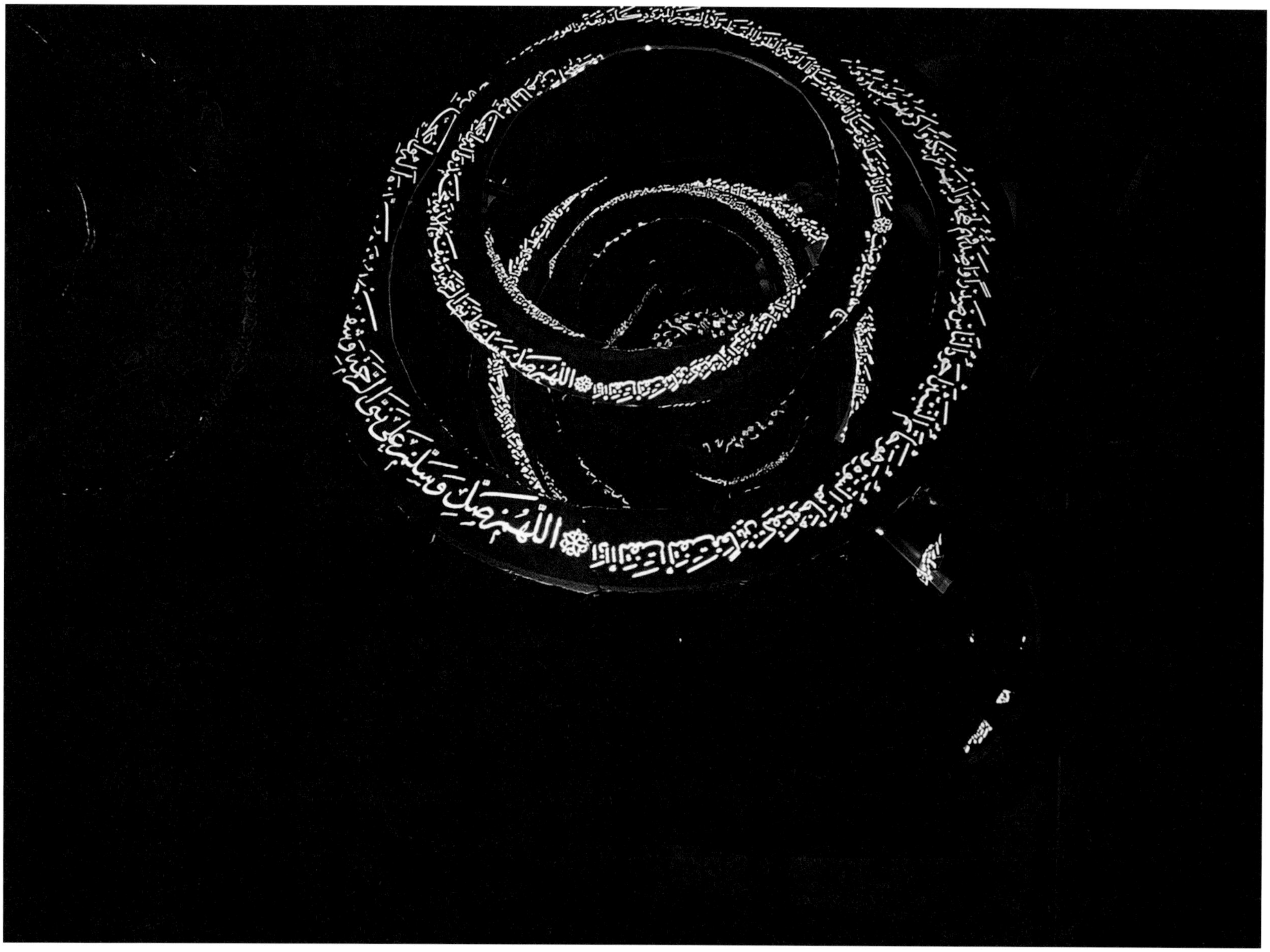

CAT. 54

Bayan Barboud

***Qibla*, 2022**

Installation
450 × 450 cm
Commissioned by the Ministry of Culture, Saudi Arabia

Bayan Barboud sheds light on the principles and the purpose of existence. Her need for concentration, stillness and contemplation grows amidst turmoil, inspiring her to turn to the *qibla* when praying, as God Almighty says: "Hence, from wherever thou mayest come forth, turn thy face [in prayer] toward the Inviolable House of Worship" (surah *al-Baqarah*, verse 150).

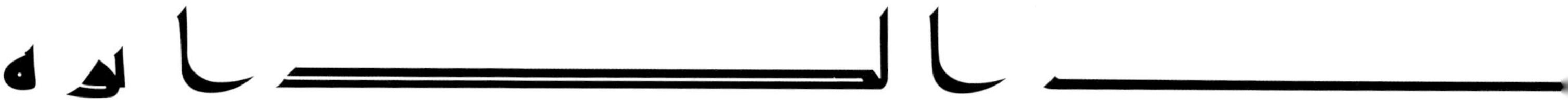

CAT. 55

Nasser Al Salem
What if the Circle Disappeared?, 2016
Silkscreen print
100 × 200 cm
Courtesy of Nasser Al Salem

What if the Circle Disappeared? is a study of the circle and its use throughout the history of calligraphy traditions, as the dot, just like the circle, appeared in the Arabic script around 22 AH / 643 AD. The artist uses a *Mushaf kufi* (old *kufi*) script that pre-dates both the introduction of the "dot" into the alphabet and the traditional Arabic calligraphy system created by Ibn Muqla in the tenth century AD. In this ink on paper, Al Salem wonders about the potential impact of the circle, or absence thereof, using calligraphy to explore social questions. In Arab culture, the circle is the beginning and end of all forms, the origin of countless geometric shapes, and the essential building block in astrolabes before the world was recognized as circular in shape. Written in original *kufi* script, with no dots or circles above or below letters to alter or adapt the pronunciation and meaning of the words, this simple line becomes a means of exploring how something so small has become so fundamental and beneficial for the development of society. As such, it can be read as a commentary on cause and effect leading up to the state of the world today.

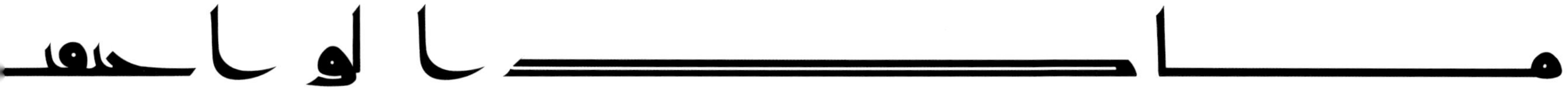

CAT. 56

Sundial and qibla indicator

1247 AH / 1831 AD

Painted wood
10.5 × 16 cm
Collection of the Ministry of Culture,
Saudi Arabia
inv. IA 2021.30

Sundial and *qibla* indicator showing various localities, such as Iraq and others.

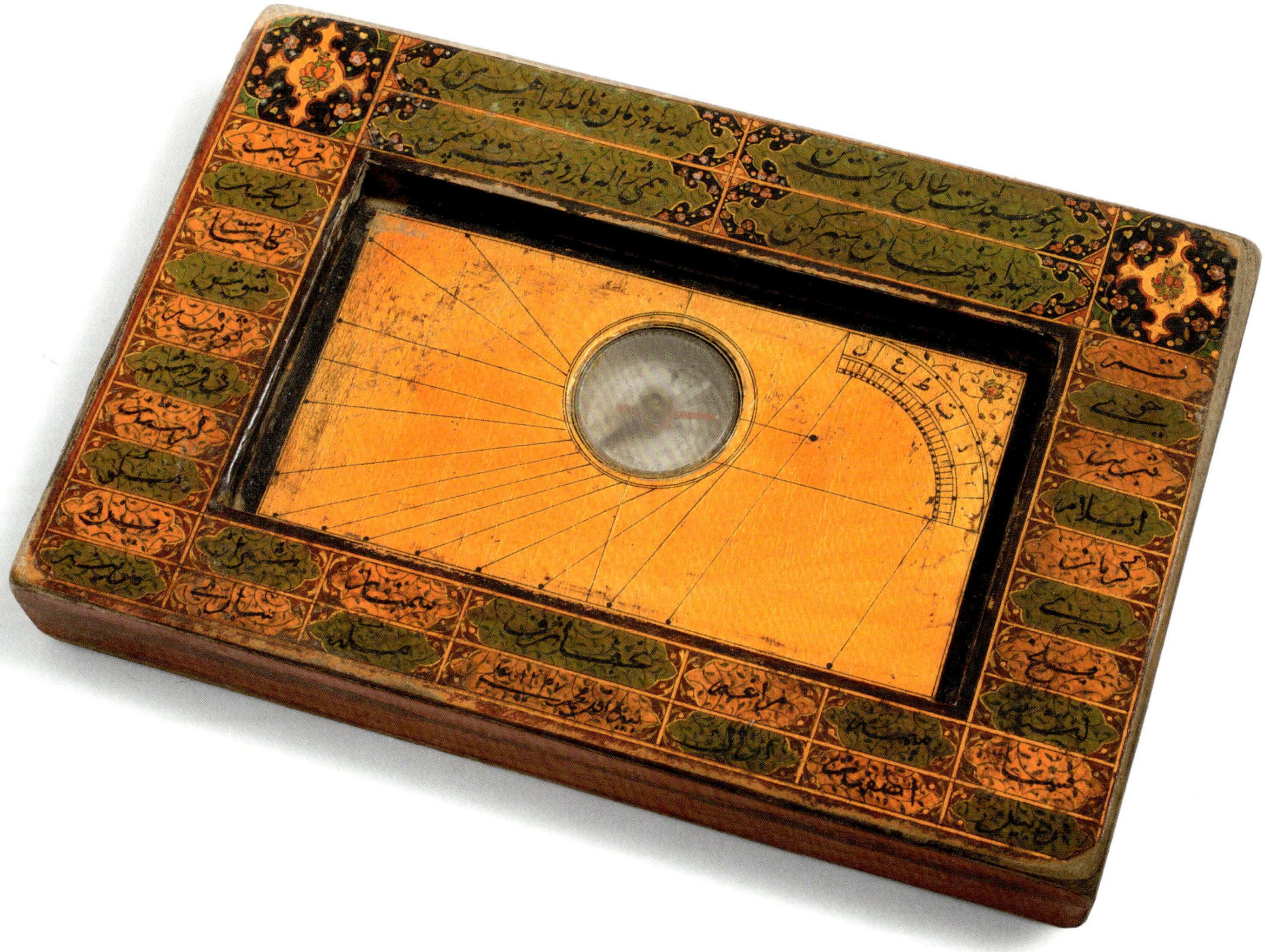

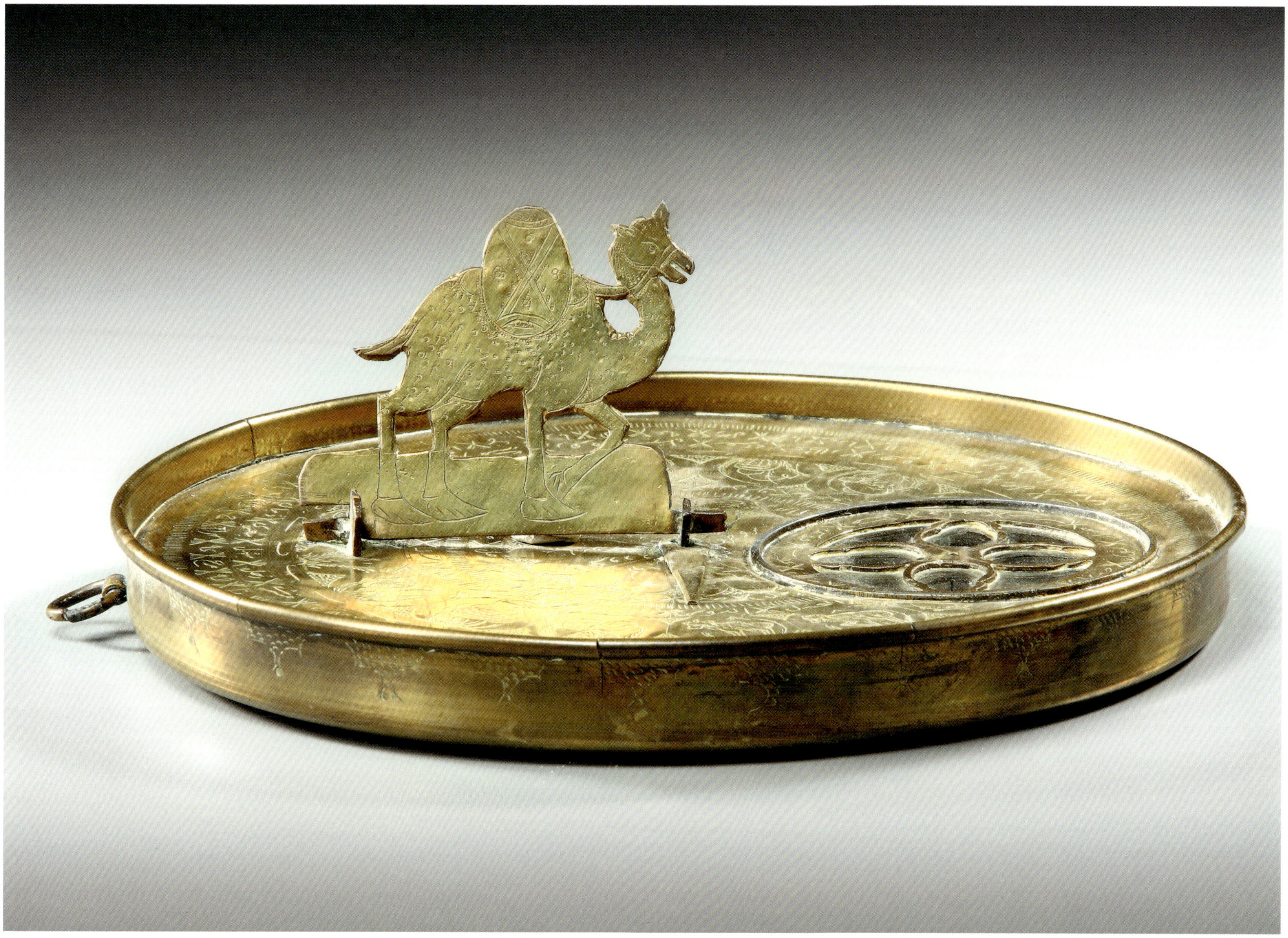

CAT. 57

Qibla indicator

thirteenth century AH / nineteenth century AD

Brass
Diameter 24 cm
Collection of the Ministry of Culture, Saudi Arabia
inv. IA 2022.1

The face of the sundial is engraved with zodiac signs. The folding engraved camel-form gnomon shows the time by the position of its shadow. Various engraved tables appear on the underside and face.

CAT. 58

Sundial and qibla indicator

Egypt or Turkey, 1100 AH / 1688–89 AD

Signed by Muhammad 'Izz Al-Sabbagh
Painted and varnished wood with a chiselled metal and glass compass
Diameter 35 × 17.5 × 6 cm
Collection of the Museum of the Institut du Monde Arabe, Paris
inv. AI 85-05

Semi-circular instrument bearing in its centre two circles separated by a vertical line illustrating the Equator line for all latitudes (*khatt al-istiwa' likull 'ard*). A *mihrab* is depicted in the upper part. To the right, the text explains the operation mode used to determine the *qibla*. To the left, the circle lists 76 cities and regions divided in four sections: North–East, East–South, South–West and West–North. On the edge, the inscription bears the signature of the instrument's maker, Muhammad 'Izz Al-Sabbagh. To reveal the *qibla* direction according to the place where any believer was, the Muslim astronomers devised methods of calculation according to the surah *al-Baqarah*, verse 144: "We see you oft turning your face towards the sky; now we are turning you to the direction that will satisfy you. Turn your face towards the Holy Mosque, and wherever you are, turn your faces towards it in prayer".

CAT. 59

Prayer calendar

1336 AH / 1917–18 AD

Ink on paper
47.5 × 36 cm
Collection of Hasab Allah Bugis, Jeddah

This manuscript of a prayer calendar was conceived and published by the late Hajj Hassan Abdullah al-Buqsi more than a century ago. It is written in the Buginese language (spoken mainly in Sulawesi, Indonesia) using Arabic characters. The manuscript also features a picture indicating the direction of the *qibla*.

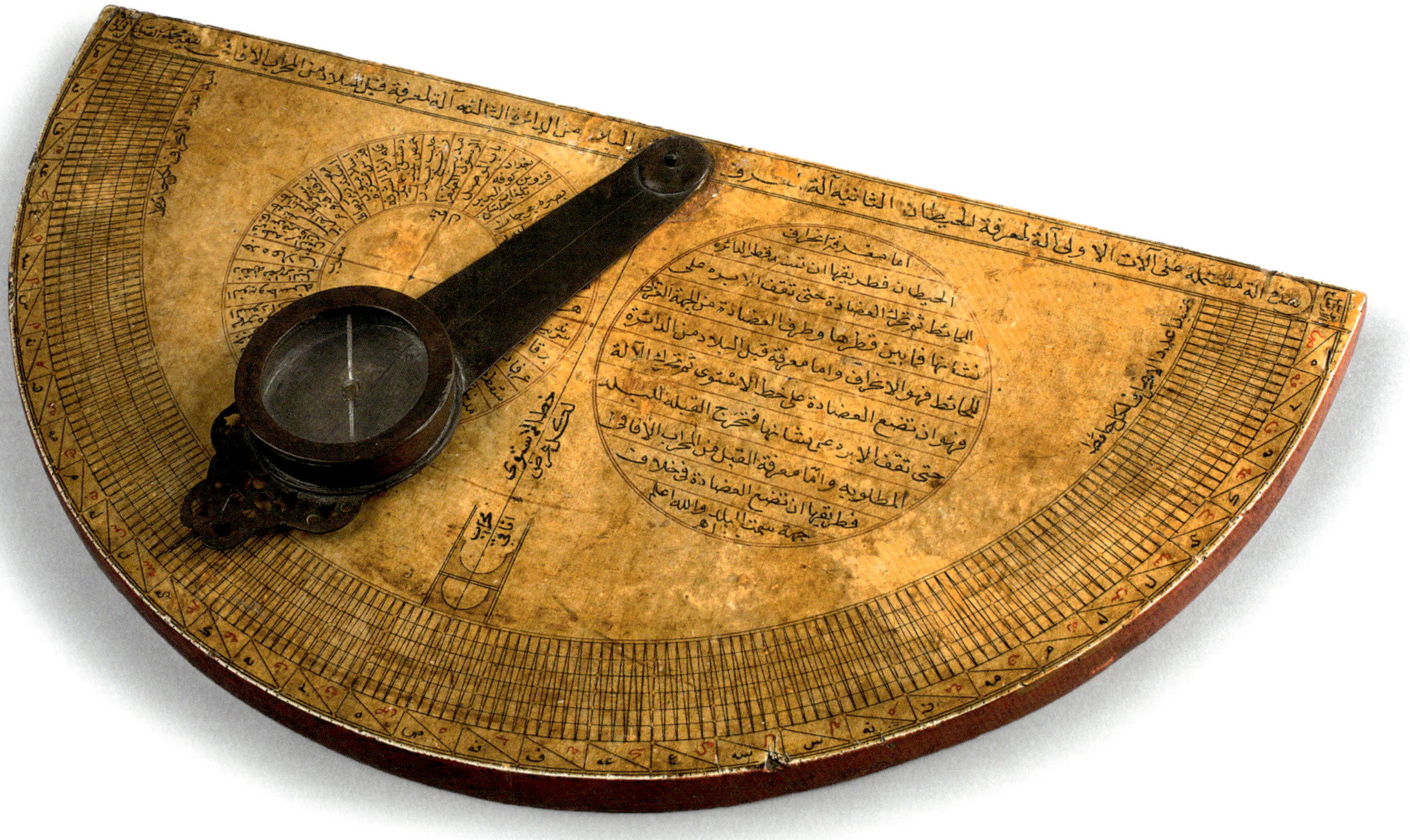

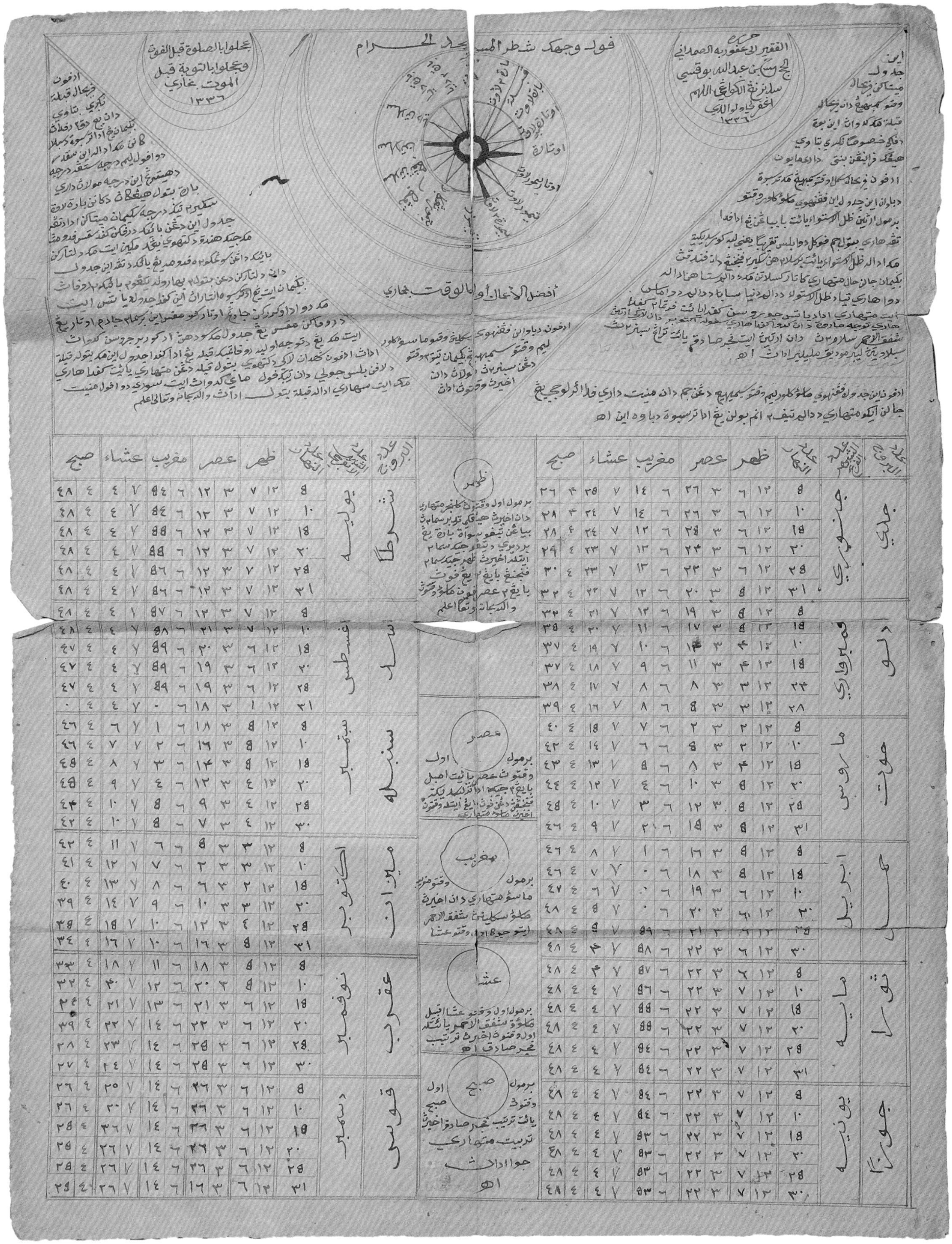

فول وجهك شطر المسجد الحرام
أفضل الأعمال أول الوقت بخاري
صبح
عشاء
مغريب
عصر
ظهر

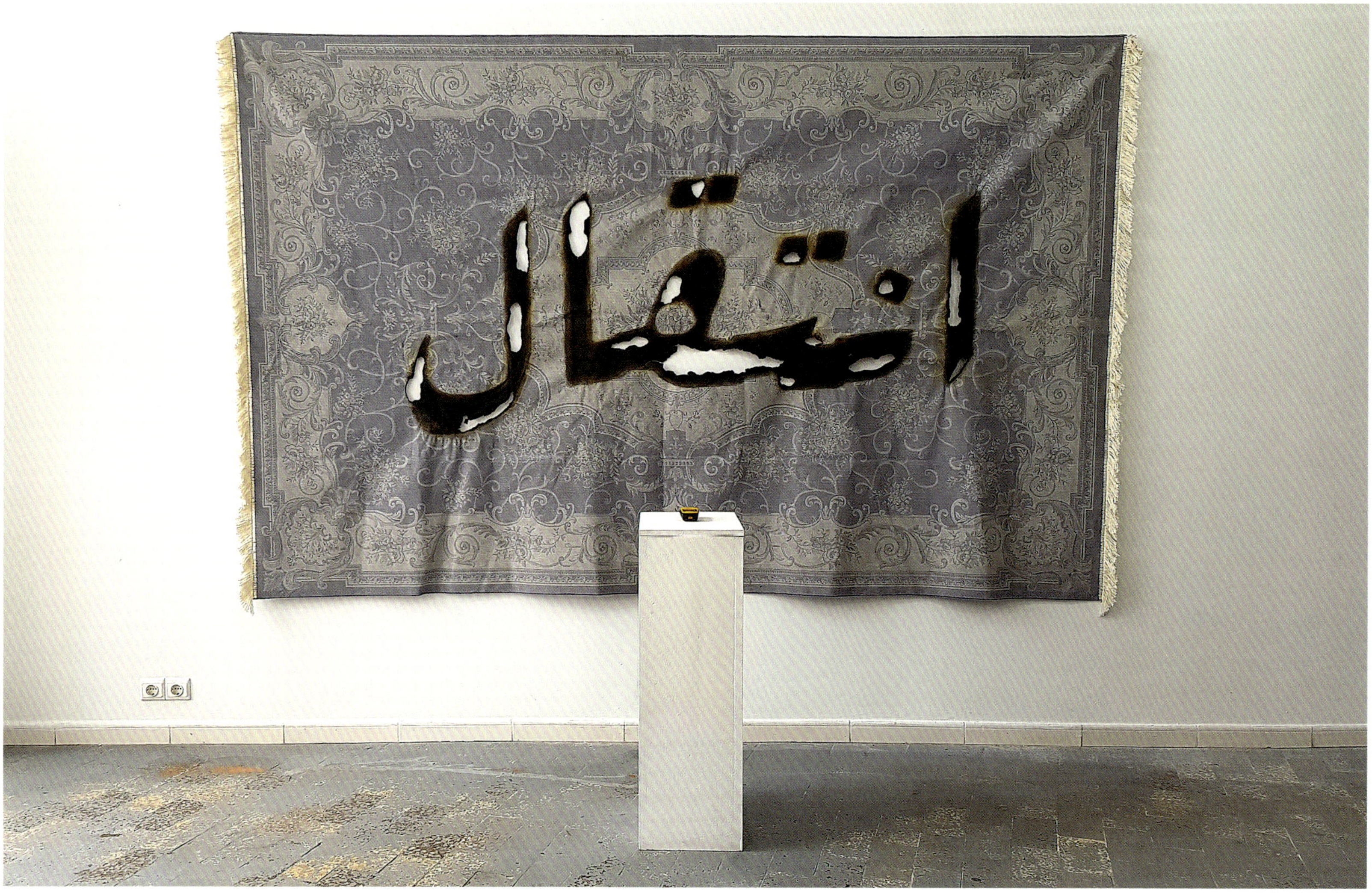

CAT. 60

Sadek Rahim
Mouvement, 2020

Burned carpet and GPS Garmin 73
196 × 306 cm (carpet)
11 × 5.5 × 2.8 cm (GPS)
Collection of the Ministry of Culture, Saudi Arabia
inv. CA 2022.14

The movement of persons from one country to another, the passage from one place to another, the transition from life to death, the end of something, the end of a regime, the death of the feeling of belonging as a result of exile or immigration. . . This is the meaning of *Mouvement* (*Intiqal*). Oran-based artist Sadek Rahim burned this word into the rug – in places straight through the fibre – by dripping refined petroleum made from Algerian crude oil into the synthetic warps and wefts and then setting it on fire. A slim plinth stands in front of the rug with a GPS Garmin 73 device sitting atop. This model is the one most used by *harragas* (burners), people from North Africa who risk their lives attempting to leave their country without any documentation, crossing the Mediterranean in search of economic stability. Rahim's work is thus centred on a word that marks a slip between physical and metaphysical transitions.

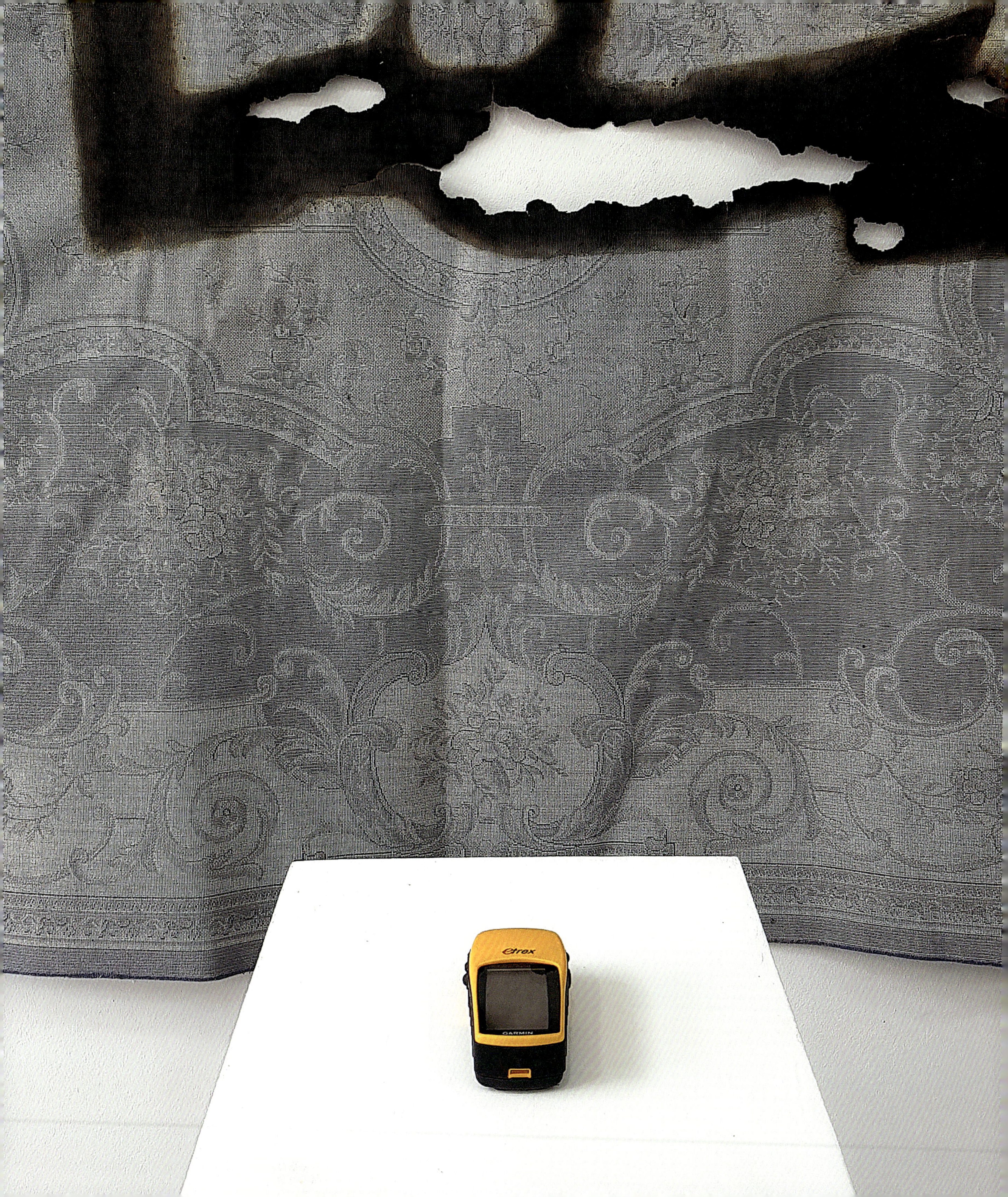
etrex
GARMIN

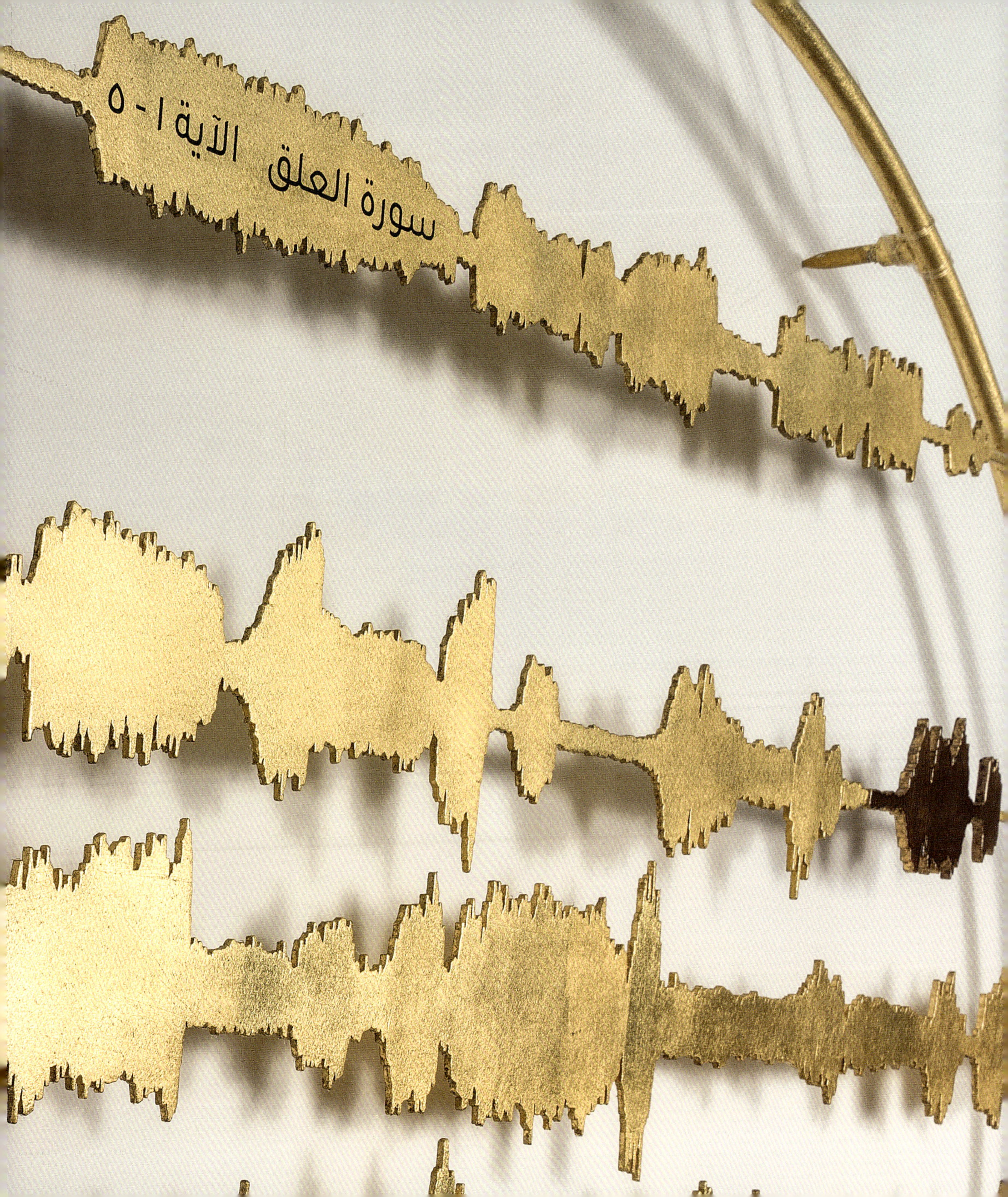
سورة العلق الآية ١ - ٥

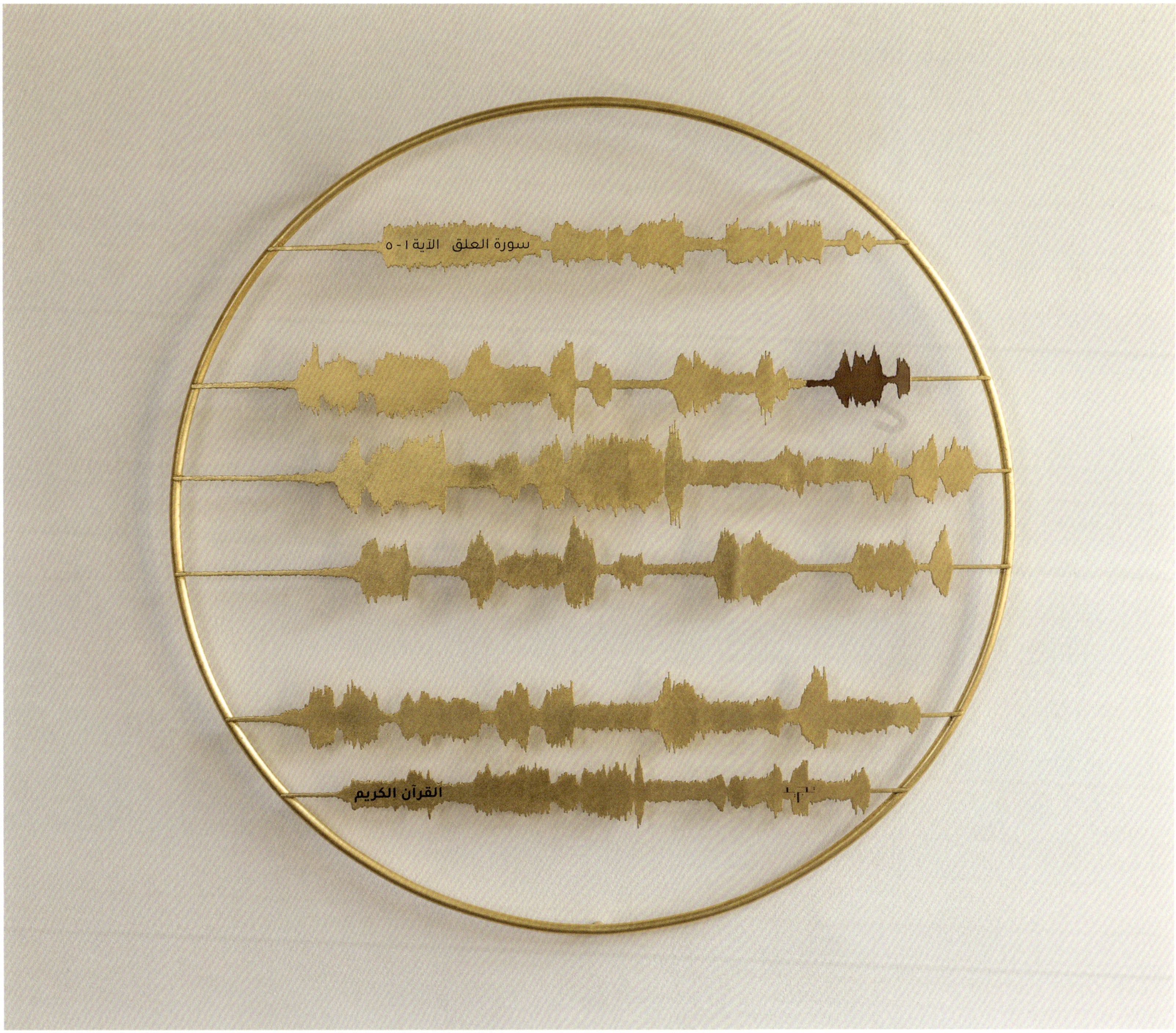

CAT. 61

Sara Alharbali
Revelation Spectrogram of Surah al-ʿAlaq (The Clot), 2022
Steel and gold
Diameter 120 cm
Commissioned by the Ministry of Culture, Saudi Arabia
inv. CA 2022.5

Revelation Spectrogram uses the voice of Abdel Basit Abdel Samad, one of the most prominent reciters of the Qur'an. As the words turn into visual waves, one cannot help but notice the perfection of Qur'anic cantillation where words are perfection, even in their musical form, and sounds and waves produce a healing effect.

CAT. 62

Nabeel Bukhari
The Mihrab of Piety, 2022

Matt fine art (30 grams)
Written in square *kufi* script
125 × 70 cm each
Commissioned by the Ministry of Culture, Saudi Arabia
inv. CA 2022.10

Two rectangular panels bear an inscription in square *kufi* script. As a calligrapher, Nabeel Bukhari believes that his work ought to begin at the *mihrab* (the niche in the wall of the mosque indicating the *qibla*) then turn towards heaven. He expresses his vision on the panel by using a unique, captivating colour combination of brown, black and white.

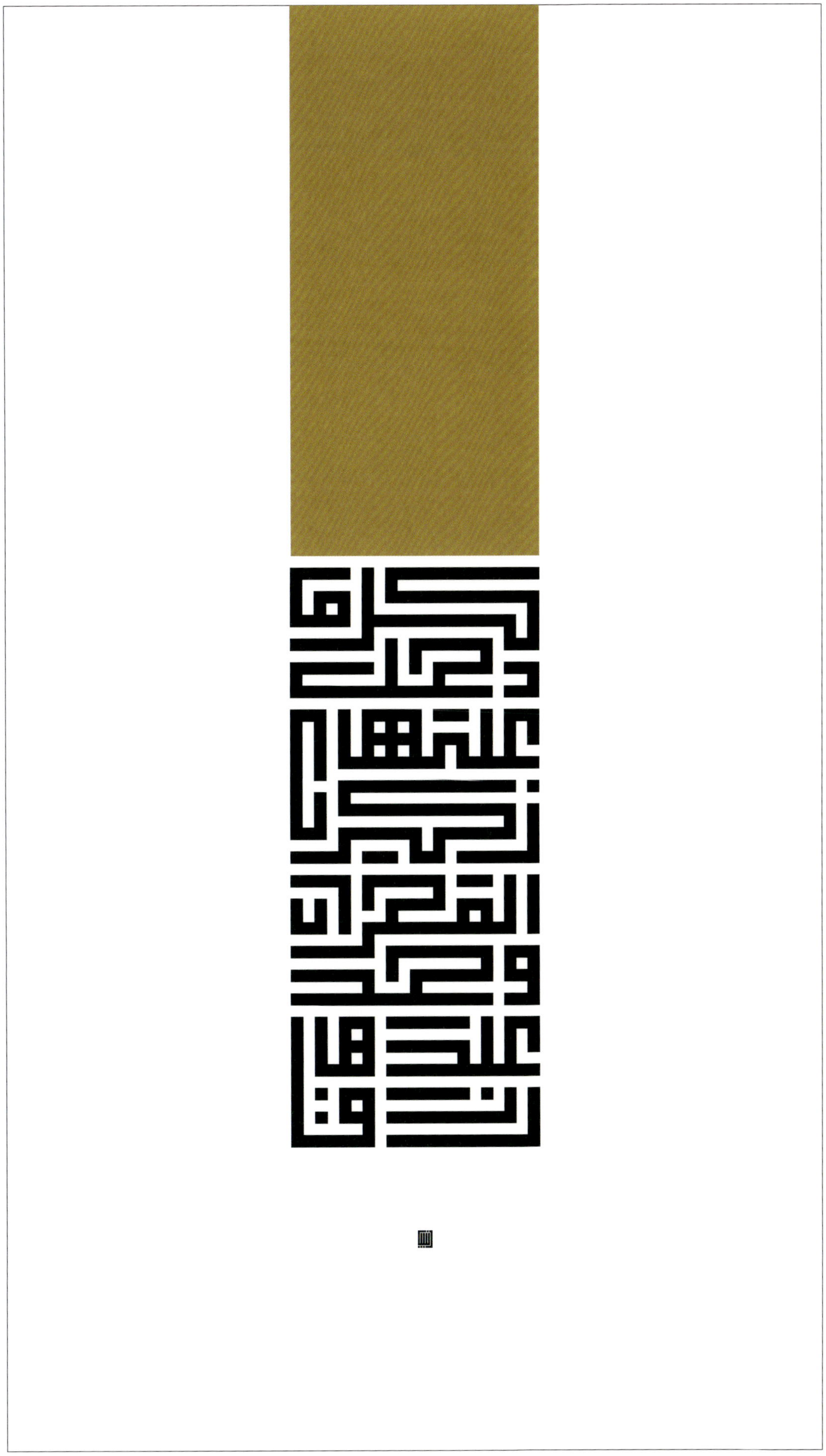

CAT. 63

Nada Debs

Tajawuz, 2022

Hand-woven wool carpet
Written in Nada Debs font
140 × 76 cm
Commissioned by the Ministry of Culture, Saudi Arabia
inv. CA 2022.12

Aptly named *Tajawuz* (Transcendence), this rug is a collaboration between Nada Debs and Zuleya by the Fatima Bint Mohamed Bin Zayed Initiative to support and hire carpet weavers, mostly women, in Afghanistan. Meticulously hand-woven and divinely inspired, this prayer rug reflects the artist's vision of peoples, places, cultures and identities united through faith, prayer and spirituality.

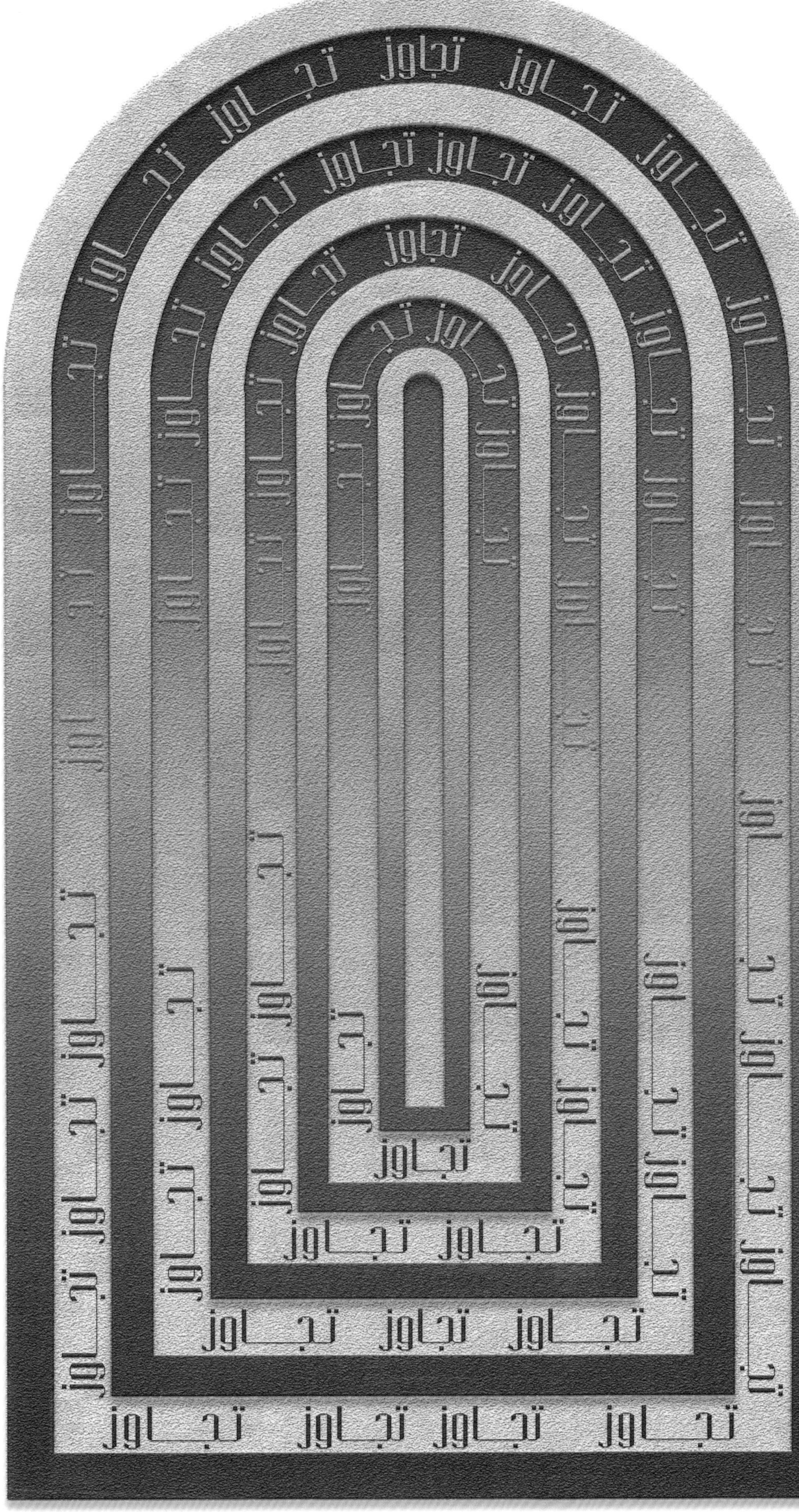
تجاوز

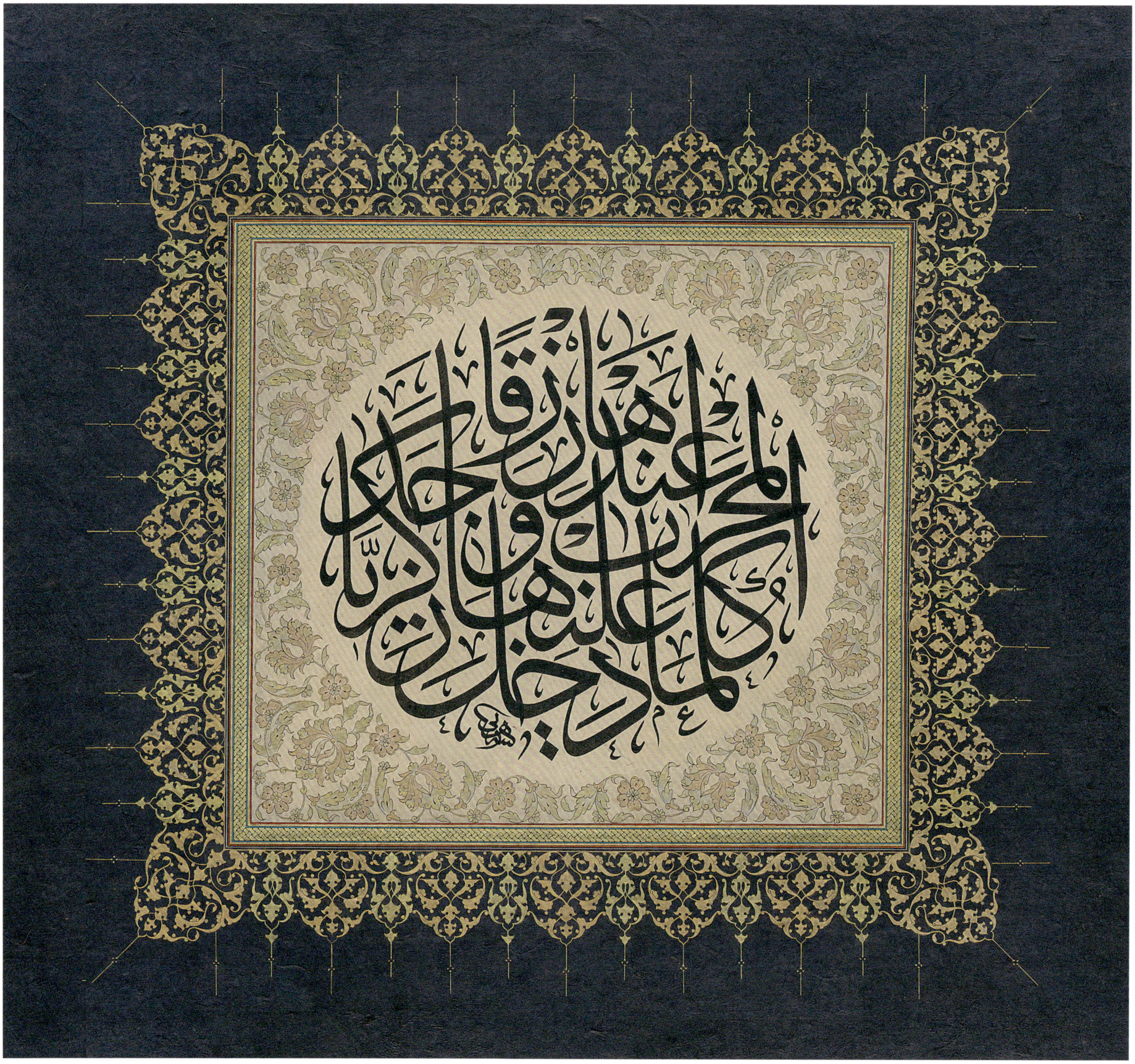

CAT. 64

Hani Al-Tawel
Whenever Zachariah Visited Her in the Sanctuary, He Found Her Supplied with Provisions, 2022

Surah *al-Imran*, verse 37
Arabic natural ink on hand-made sized paper with gold illumination
Written in *jaly thuluth* script
Illuminated by Ustadha Hind Slila
80 × 90 cm
Commissioned by the Ministry of Culture, Saudi Arabia
inv. IA 2022.9

In a central medallion, combining monumentality and rhythm, a sentence appears from verse 37 of surah *al-Imran*: "So her Lord accepted her graciously and blessed her with a pleasant upbringing, entrusting her to the care of Zachariah. Whenever Zachariah visited her in the sanctuary, he found her supplied with provisions. He exclaimed, 'O Mary! Where did this come from?' She replied, 'It is from Allah. Surely Allah provides for whoever He wills without limit'". Inscribed in black ink in the elegant and majestic *jaly thuluth* calligraphy, the inscription, placed within a gilded square border, is illuminated with gold rosettes and petals. The frame is outlined with gilded vine scrolls set on a dark background.

CAT. 65

Amor Jomni
Soliloquy, 2022

Ink and colours on paper
Written in *maghribi* script
75 × 55 cm
Commissioned by the Ministry of Culture, Saudi Arabia
inv. IA 2022.10

Soliloquy presents at its centre verses of a Qur'anic supplication bordered by a purple frieze of inscriptions and letters: written in *maghribi* script, they form a receptacle – that is, the heart of the believer. Above the invocation text, multicoloured calligraphed letters rise in a column from inside that heart towards the sky, indicating the transformation of the prayer into ascending letters directed towards God, surrounded by the verse of response. This is how the artist imagines a silent supplication to God: an internal monologue expressing the emotional reality of the supplicant in his moments of solitude with God.

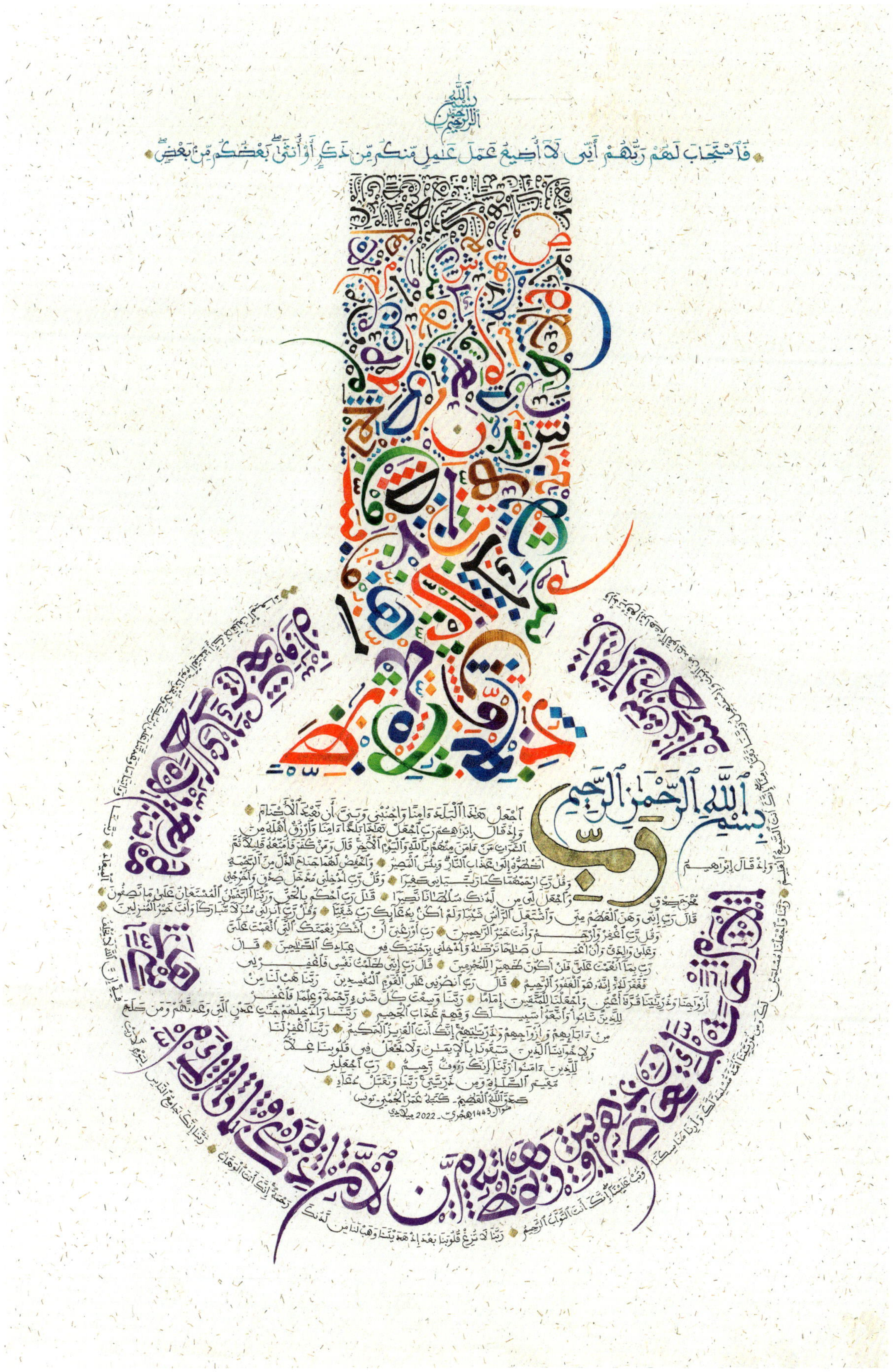

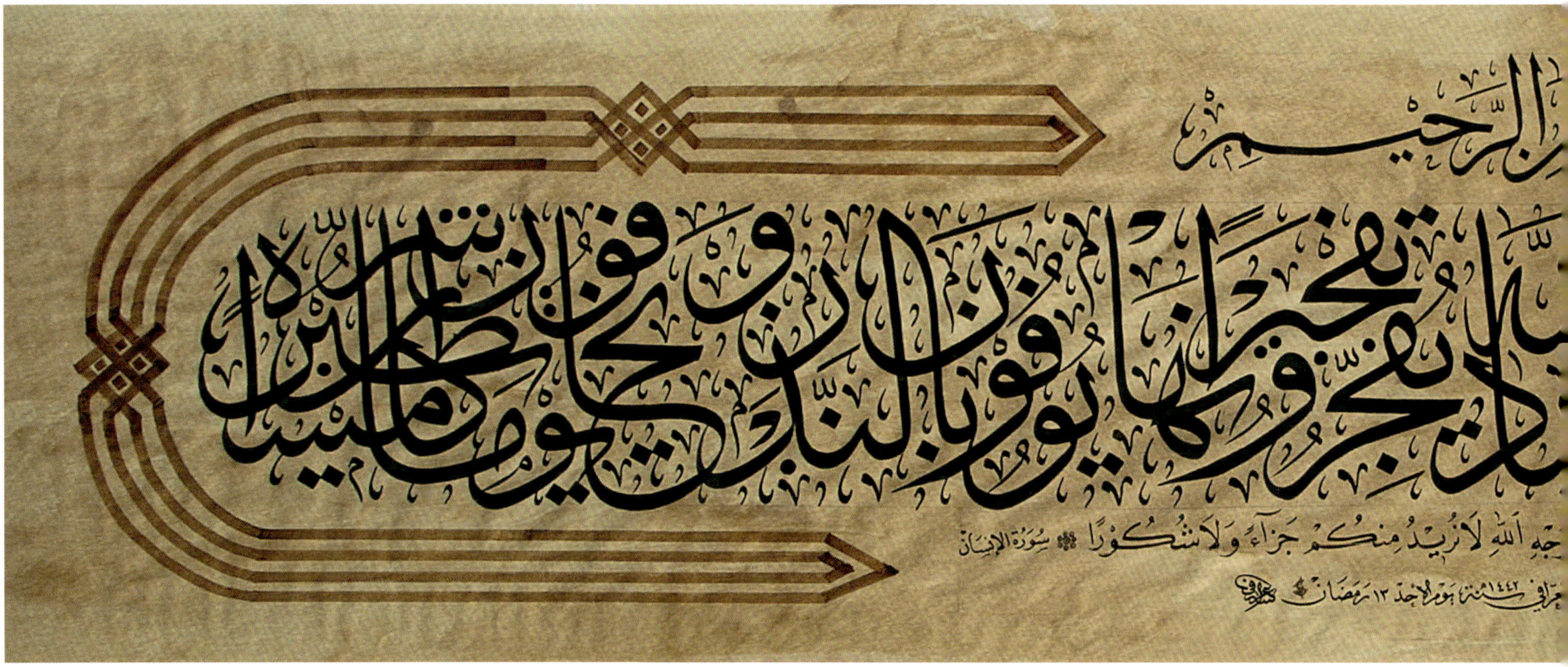

CAT. 66

Ibrahim Al Arafi

***They Are Those Who Fulfill Their Vows and Fear a Day Whose Evil Will Be Widespread*, 2020–21**

Surah *al-Insan*, verse 7
Ink on paper
Written in *thuluth* script
65 × 200 cm
Courtesy of Ibrahim Al Arafi

"Indeed, the virtuous will have a drink of 'pure wine' – flavoured with camphor . . ." (surah *al-Insan*, verses 5–9). These verses tell of the felicity awaiting man in heaven. Inspired by the spirituality intrinsic to the holy month of Ramadan, this black ink on sepia paper set in a golden frame was an exercise in spontaneous writing. In *jaly thuluth* and *naskh* scripts, the text is set inside an oval frieze bearing the first verse of surah *al-Fatiha* ("In the Name of God the Most Merciful, the Most Compassionate") at its upper side and other small-size inscriptions on its lower side. The composition is meant to facilitate reading: as the first word of the verse is located at the bottom inside the frieze and the last one at the top, viewers can read the content while admiring the form and design of letters.

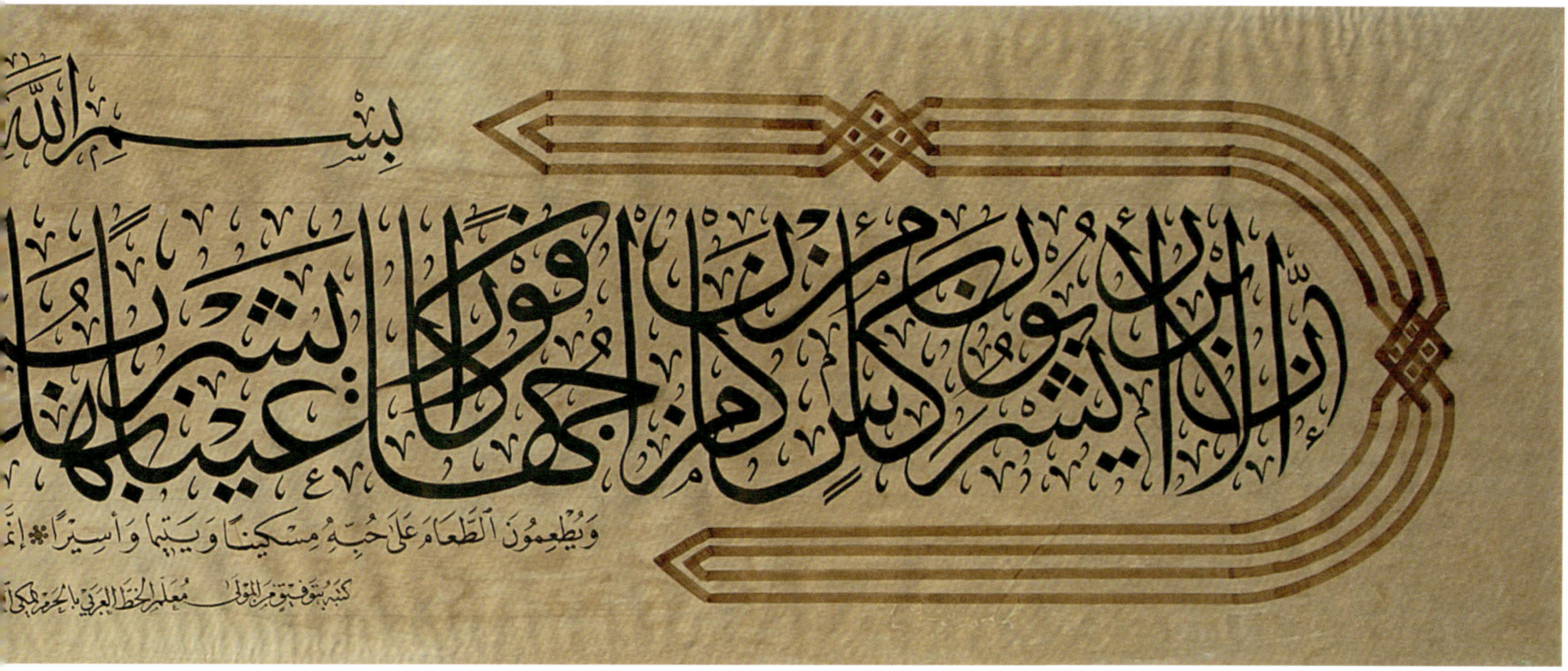
وَيُطْعِمُونَ الطَّعَامَ عَلَىٰ حُبِّهِ مِسْكِينًا وَيَتِيمًا وَأَسِيرًا

CAT. 67

Sundial with qibla indicator and cotton hat, 1328 AH / 1909 AD

21 × 17 cm (case)
Collection of the Ministry of Culture, Saudi Arabia
inv. IA 2021.25

The upper part of the case contains a *qibla* compass; the lid is attached to the case by a leather tie. Its metallic needle indicates the direction of Mecca and the cardinal points are filled in with red ink. The cotton cap is inscribed in black ink with surah *al-Ahzab*, verse 56, which reads: "Indeed, Allah showers His blessings upon the Prophet, and His angels pray for Him. O believers! Invoke Allah's blessings upon Him and salute Him with worthy greetings of peace".

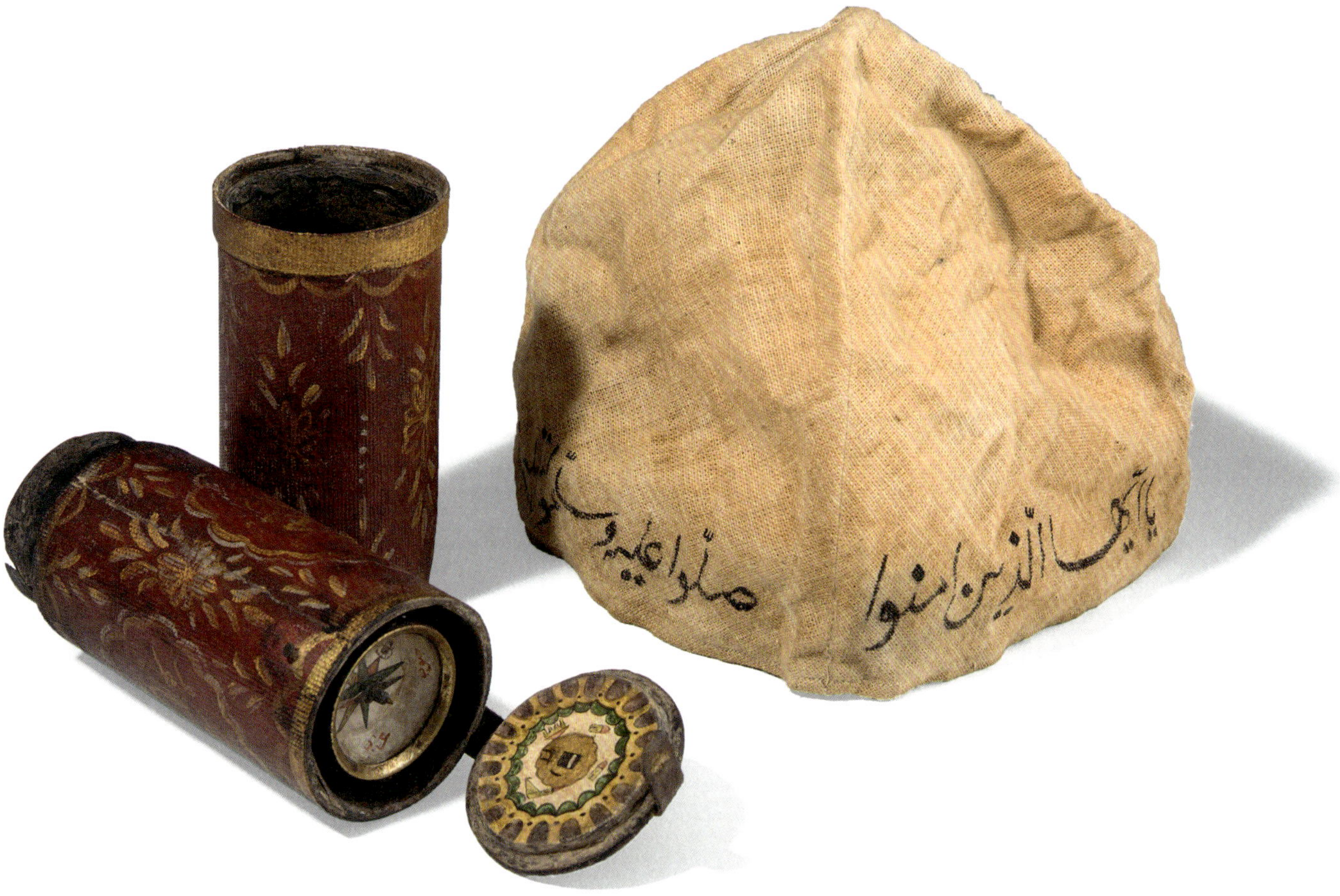

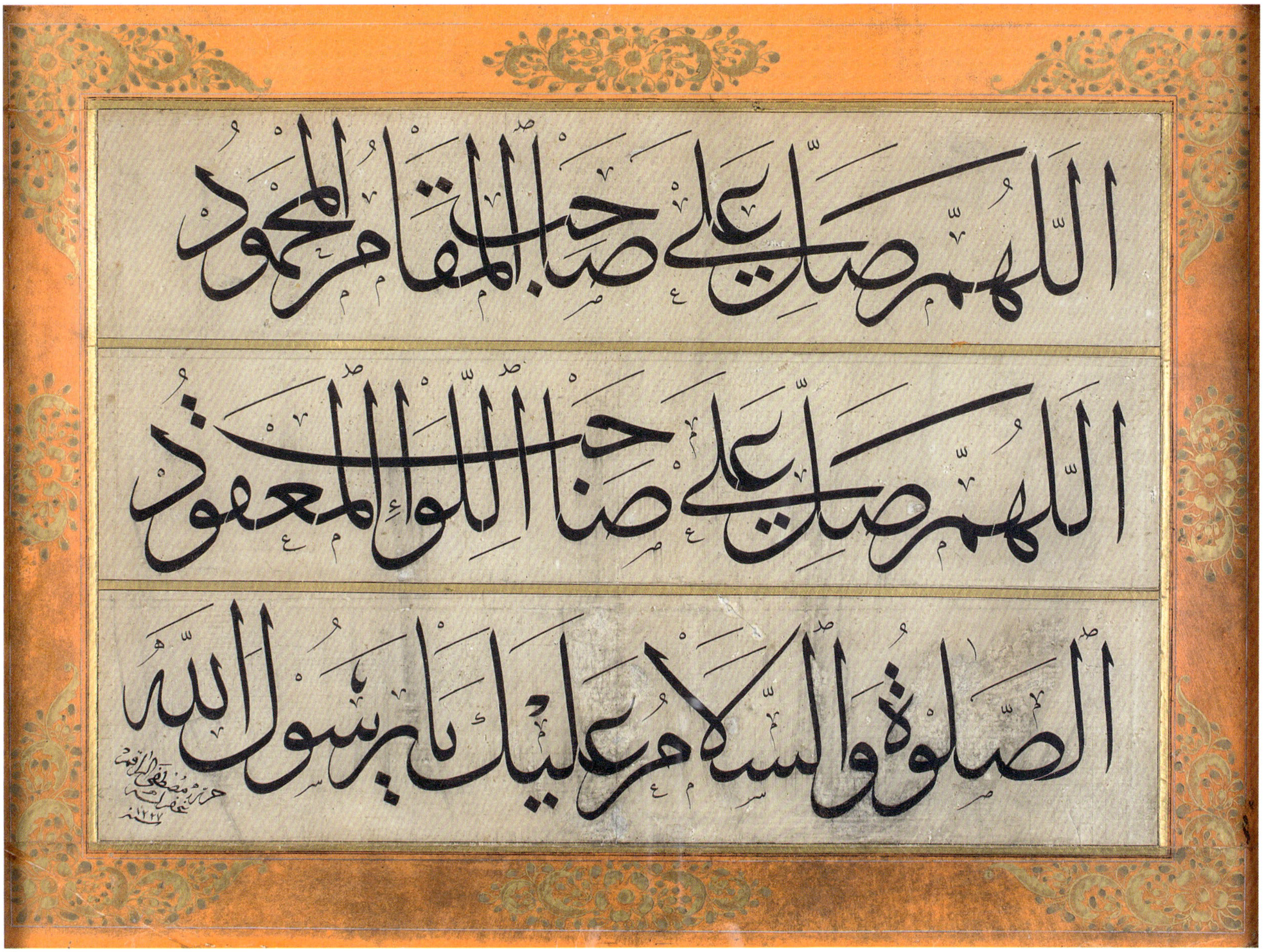

CAT. 68

Mustafa Rakim

Levha, 1227 AH / 1812 AD

Ink on paper
Written in *jaly thuluth* script
44.5 × 33.5 cm
Collection of the Ministry of Culture, Saudi Arabia
inv. IA 2021.27

This calligraphic panel is a prayer to the Prophet (PUBH) written with black ink in a delicate *jaly thuluth* style. Composing it in three lines, the calligrapher has balanced the length of each section of the prayer to create a harmonious overall composition. The symmetry at the beginning of the first two lines is repeated in the final *dal*, written in its isolated form, creating a lifting effect to the lines. The three initial *'ains*, written with the upwards lifted eyebrow (known as the "snake" stroke), as well as the elongation of the letter *ba'* across the middle, add dynamism and a particular flavour to the piece. Mounted onto the traditional *Muraqqa'*, it is illuminated by simple baroque motifs, gold on an orange background, which are characteristic of the nineteenth century. The signature appears at the bottom left corner: "Hararahu Mustafa Rakim, Ghafara Allahu lahu, Sanat 1227" (Completed in 1227 by Mustafa Rakim).

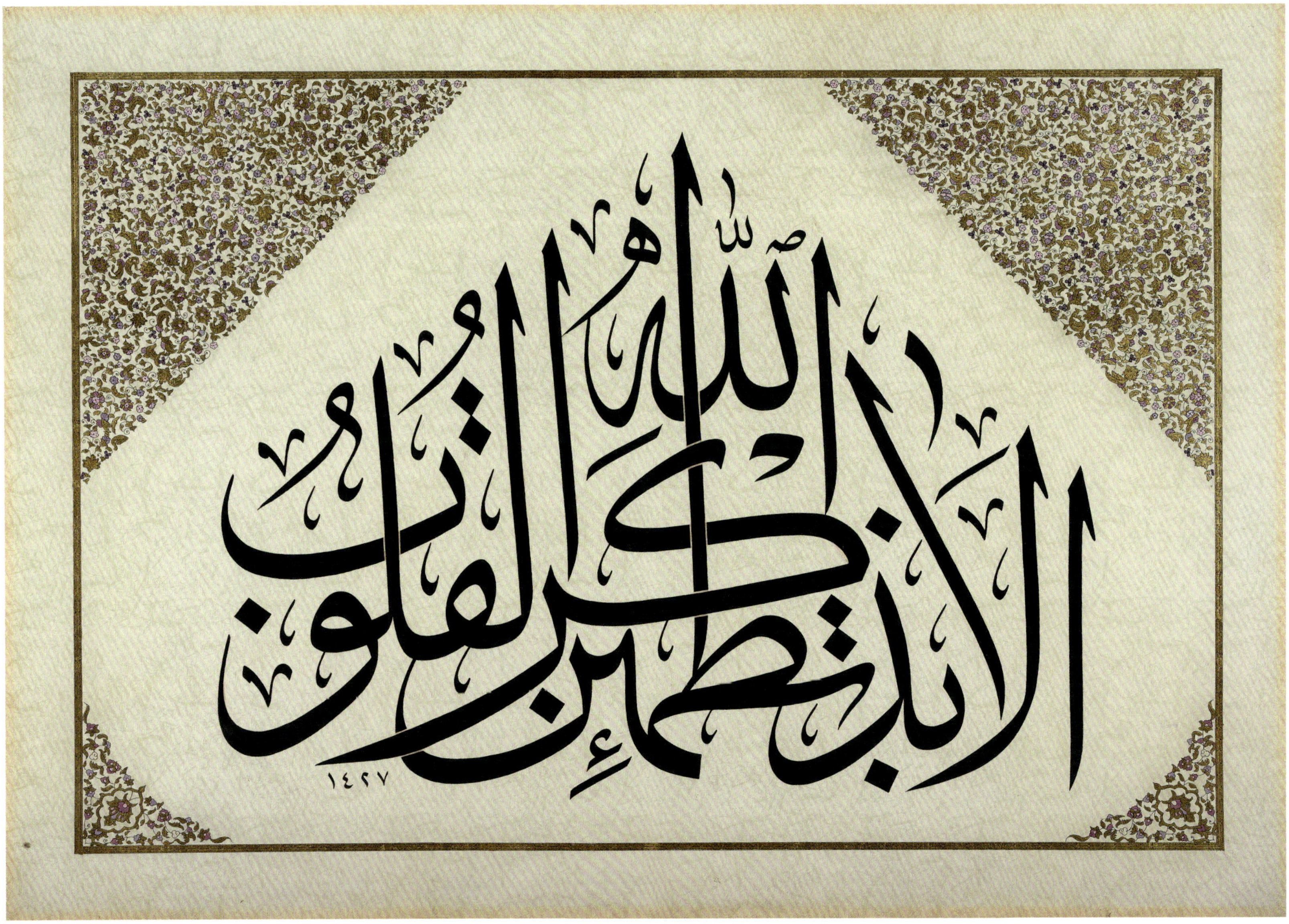

CAT. 69

Khodeir El-Borsaidy
The Hearts Find Peace Only in the Remembrance of Allah, 2006

Surah *al-Ra'd*, part of verse 28
Ink on paper
Written in *jaly thuluth* script
77 × 107 cm
Collection of the Ministry of Culture, Saudi Arabia
inv. IA 2022.13.8

A painting written in *jaly thuluth* representing the Qur'anic verse: "The hearts find peace only in the remembrance of Allah" (surah *al-Ra'd*, part of verse 28). The word Allah placed at the top of the painting is a sign of the divinity's preeminence. The sides are ornamented with gilded curlicues.

CAT. 70

Khodeir El-Borsaidy

At Least for the Favour of Making Quraysh Habitually Secure – in Their Trading Caravan to Yemen in the Winter and Syria in the Summer – Let Them Worship the Lord of This Sacred House, Who Has Fed Them Against Hunger and Made Them Secure Against Fear, 2009

Surah *Quraysh*, verses 1–4
Ink on paper
Written in *thuluth*, *jaly thuluth* and *naskh* scripts
95 × 70 cm
Collection of the Ministry of Culture, Saudi Arabia
inv. IA 2022.13.4

A painting carrying at its centre a graphic construction of the Kaaba using the surah *Quraysh* in free *naskh* script. A simple composition, complemented with colours and ornamentation to fill empty spaces on the sides and between writings.

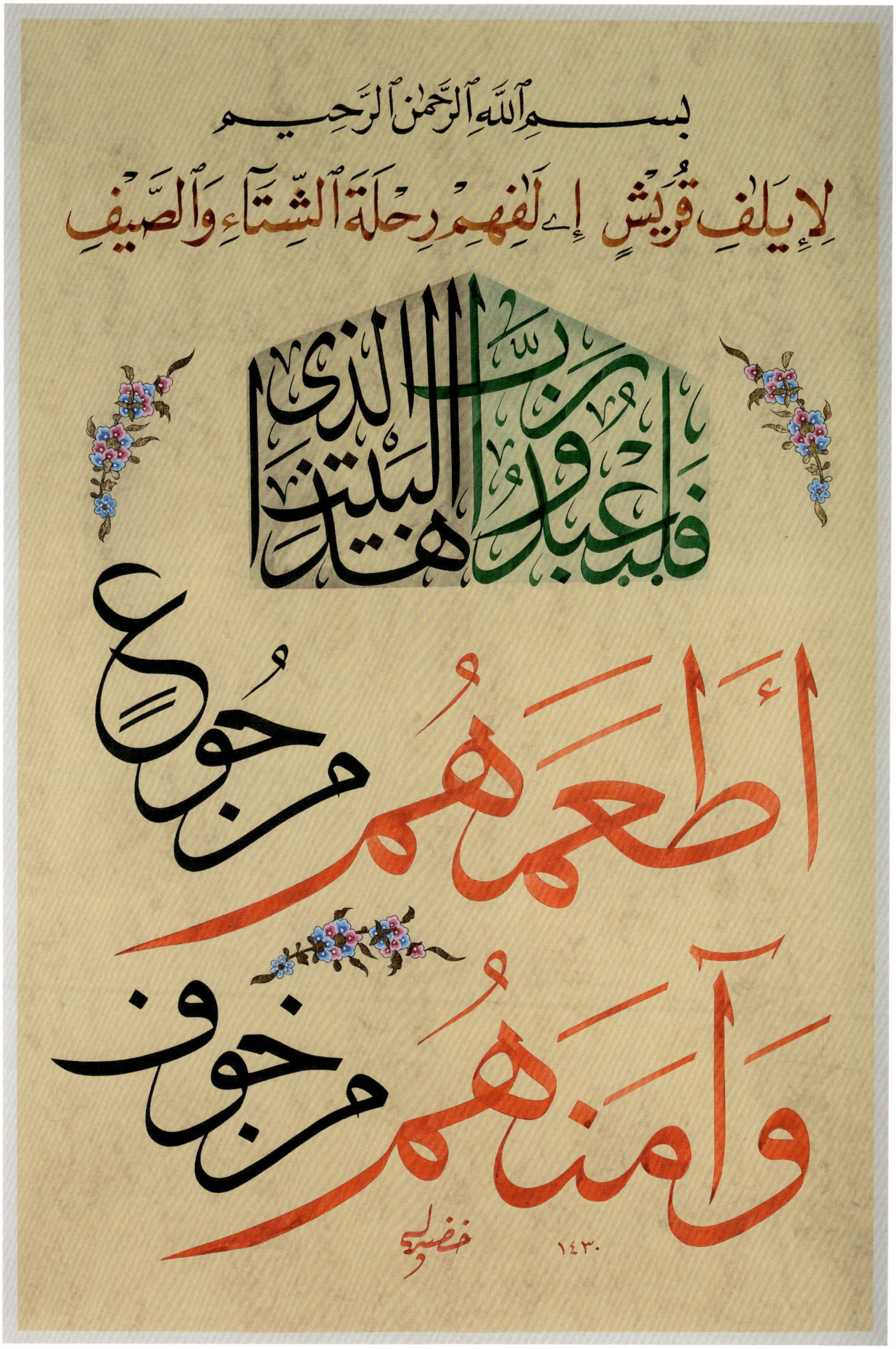

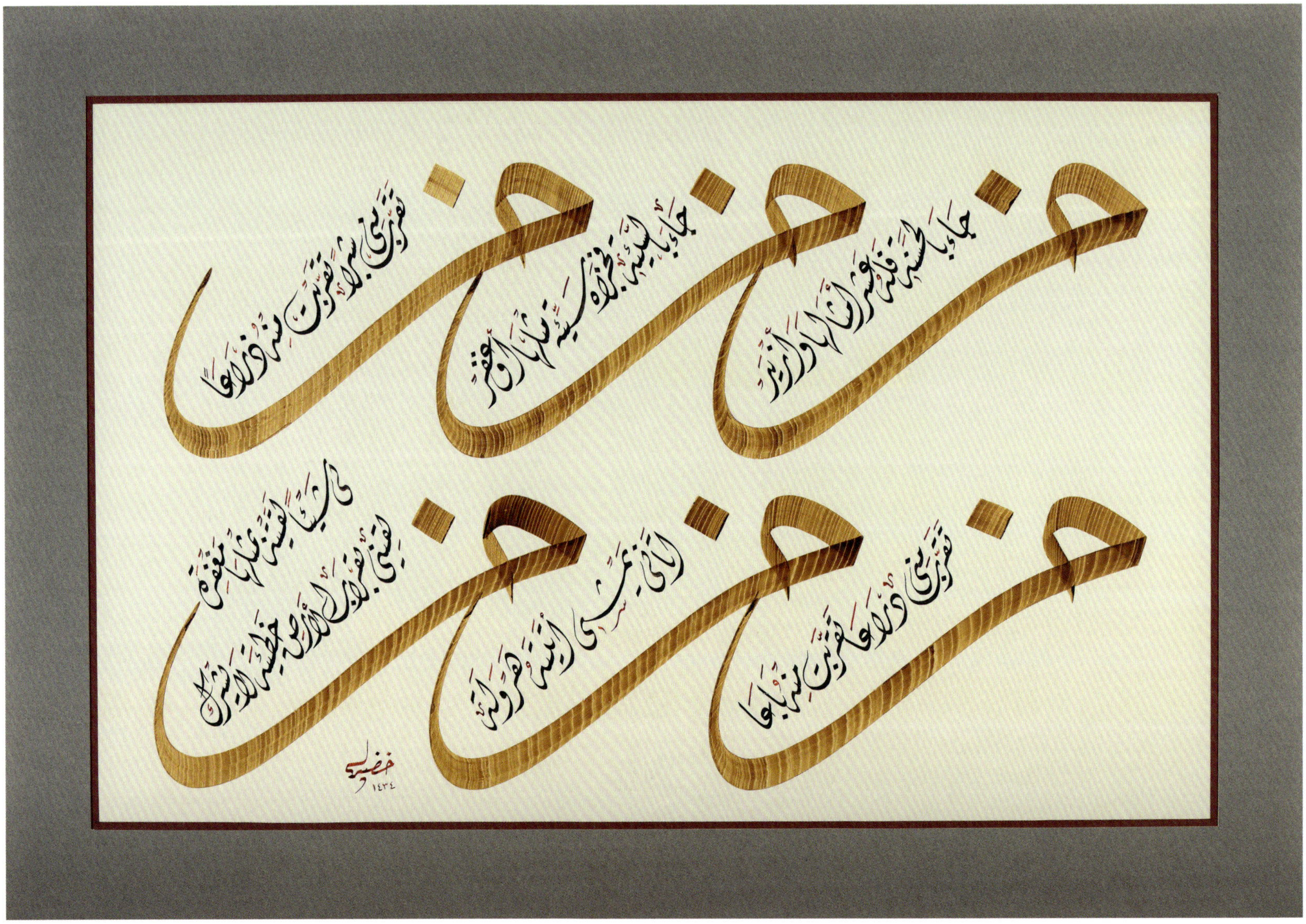

CAT. 71

Khodeir El-Borsaidy
Who Who, 2012

Ink on paper
Written in *thuluth* and *diwani* scripts
50 × 70 cm
Collection of the Ministry of Culture, Saudi Arabia
inv. IA 2022.13.5

A painting written in *thuluth* and *diwani* with the word *man* (He who), written in *thuluth* script, set as the primary component and creating a repetitive visual pattern. The remaining part of the six sentences is inserted within the curve of the *man* in smaller *diwani* script.

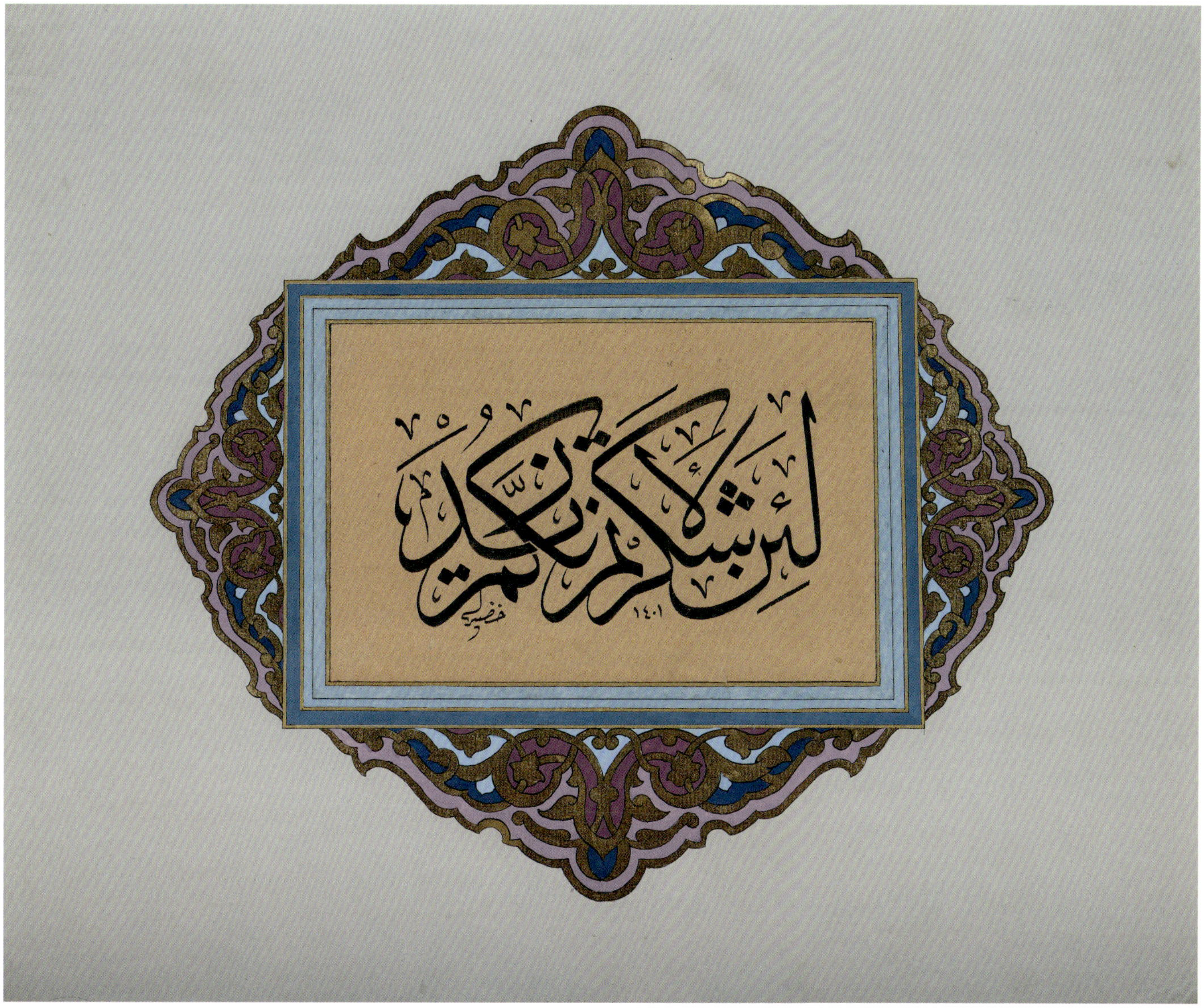

CAT. 72

Khodeir El-Borsaidy
If You Express Gratitude, I Shall Certainly Give You More, 1980
Surah *Ibrahim*, verse 7
Ink and illumination on paper
Written in *thuluth* script
28 × 35 cm
Collection of the Ministry of Culture, Saudi Arabia
inv. IA 2022.13.6

A painting written in *thuluth* script set within a traditional Arabic ornamented frame surrounding the following Qur'anic verse: "If you express gratitude, I shall certainly give you more" (surah *Ibrahim*, verse 7). The use of the two *kaf* letters as pillars upon which the rest of the simple composition is built creates a compelling visual and aesthetic dialogue.

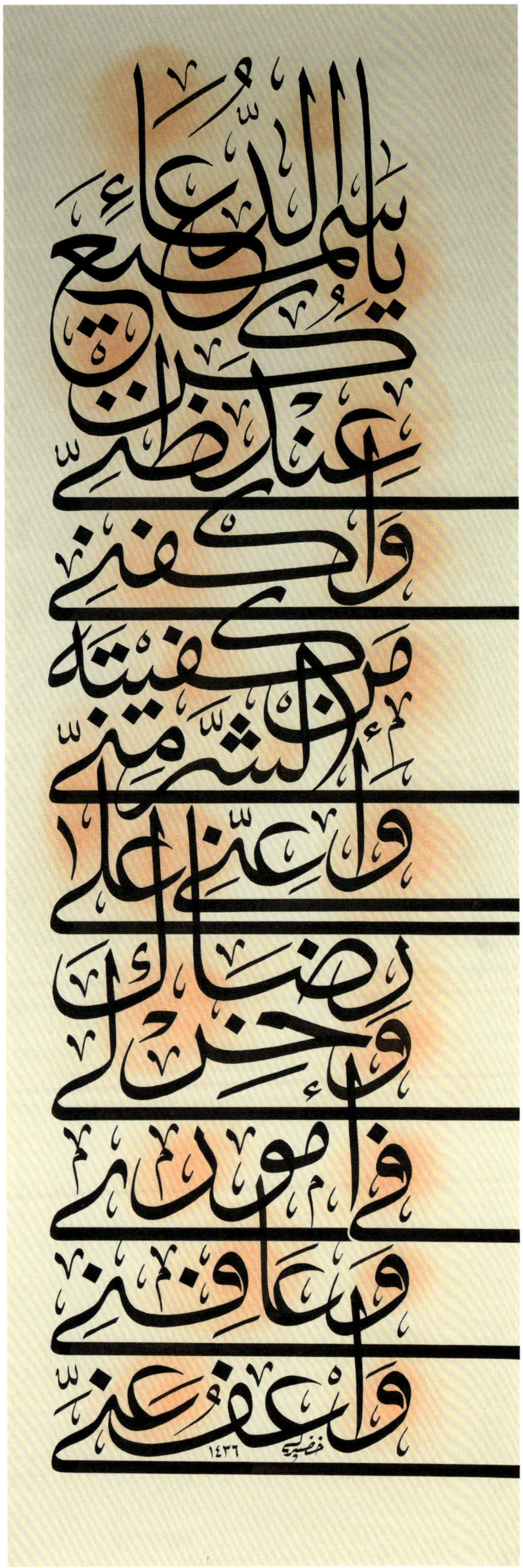

CAT. 73

Khodeir El-Borsaidy
Invocation of Prayers, 2014

Ink and illumination on paper
Written in *jaly thuluth* script
160 × 50 cm
Collection of the Ministry of Culture, Saudi Arabia
inv. IA 2022.13.7

A vertical composition for a long *du'a'* (prayer of invocation), where the letter *ya'*, considered to be a reference point, appears multiple times in the text. These elongated, horizontal *ya'* mark the work in gradual steps. Vertical compositions are considered modern constructions in Arabic calligraphy.

CAT. 74

Jamal Al Kebasi

Wherever You Are O Prophet, Turn Your Face Towards the Sacred Mosque. And Wherever You Believers Are, Face It, so that People Will Have No Argument Against You, Except the Wrongdoers Among Them. Do Not Fear Them; Fear Me, so that I May Continue to Perfect My Favour Upon You and so You May Be Rightly Guided, 2022

Surah *al-Baqarah*, verse 150
Ink on paper
Written in *jaly kufi* script
100 × 70 cm
Commissioned by the Ministry of Culture, Saudi Arabia
inv. IA 2022.7

Al Kebasi chose this verse from surah *al-Baqarah*, "Wherever you are O Prophet, turn your face towards the Sacred Mosque. And wherever you believers are, face it", because it captures the spiritual and existential link between a worshipper and his God, when man turns towards the *qibla*, towards the Holy Mosque in Mecca, and stands before the Almighty with no intermediary. Seeking to achieve a balanced composition as he began to write, he laid words and letters at the bottom of the frame, where elements complete one another, to embody the meaning of the verse, as one has to reach from below and rise towards the Almighty. The two mirrored curved designs in the middle symbolize the *mihrab* in the mosque. At the centre of the composition, as the orant prays and gives thanks, the grouped *alif* and *lam* intertwine inside the *mihrab* space before rising harmoniously in vertical lines to the top of the frame, a symbol of devotion towards God. Repetitive small and large ornamental units are scattered within the curves of the *mihrab* and above their upper crest to symbolize the dialogue and spiritual communication between God and His creation. The power of this *du'a'* (prayer of supplication) is such that flowers rain on the composition to express and visualize joy and spread in the sky near the supplication and around the *mihrab* with their gilded colours.

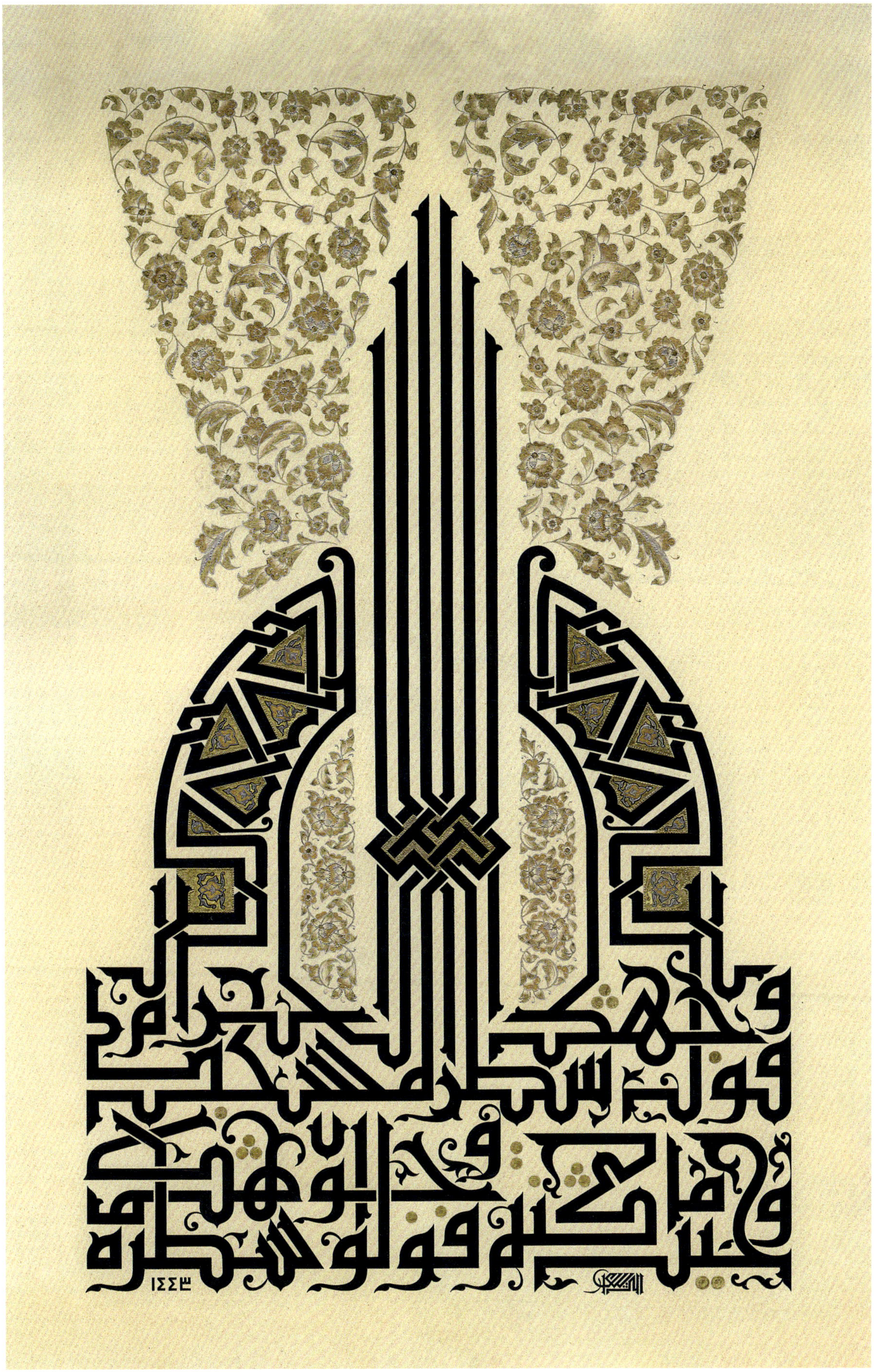

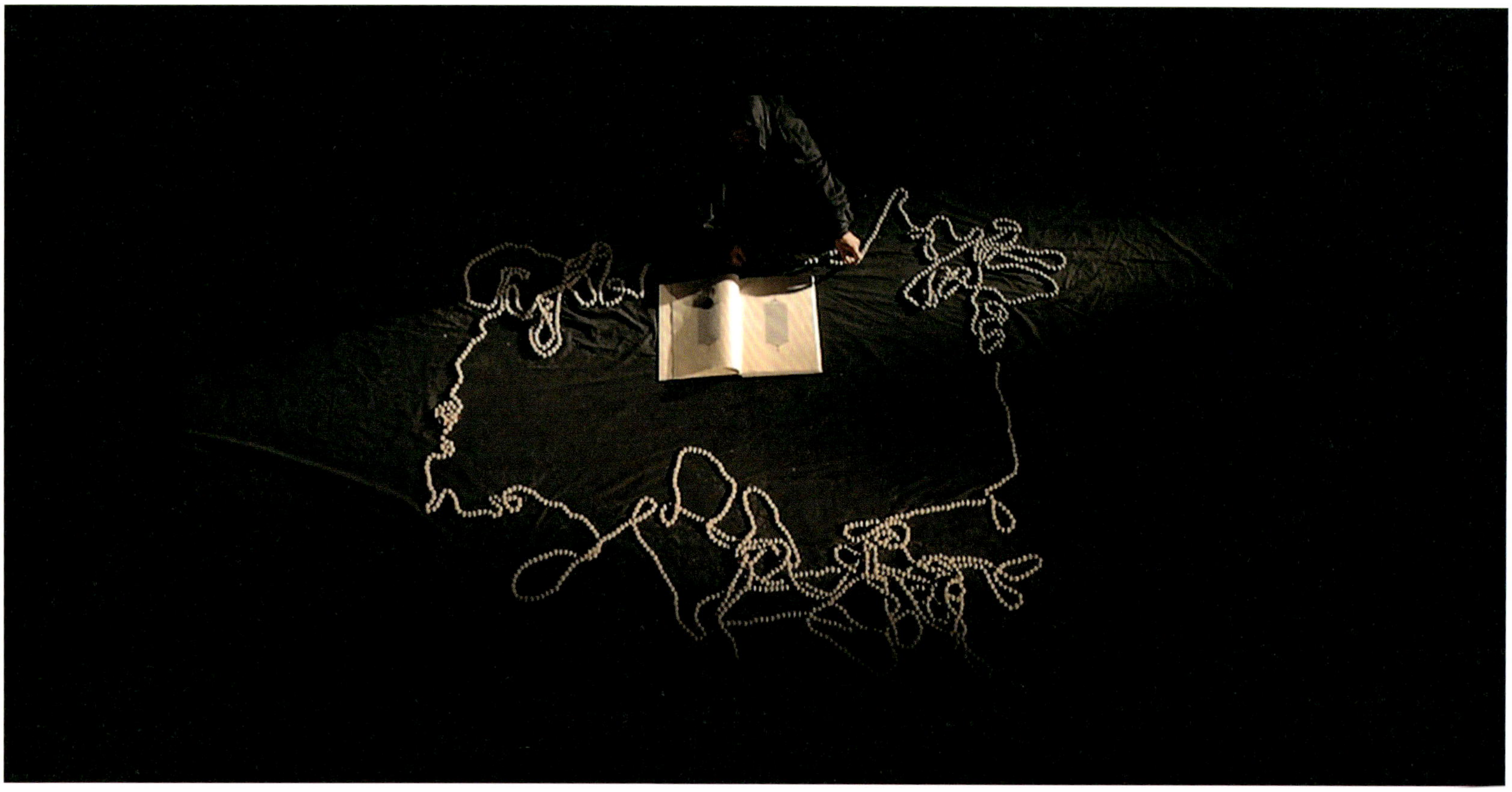

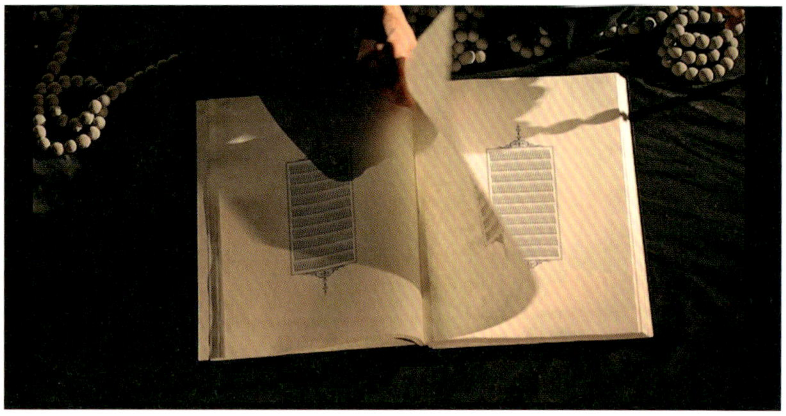

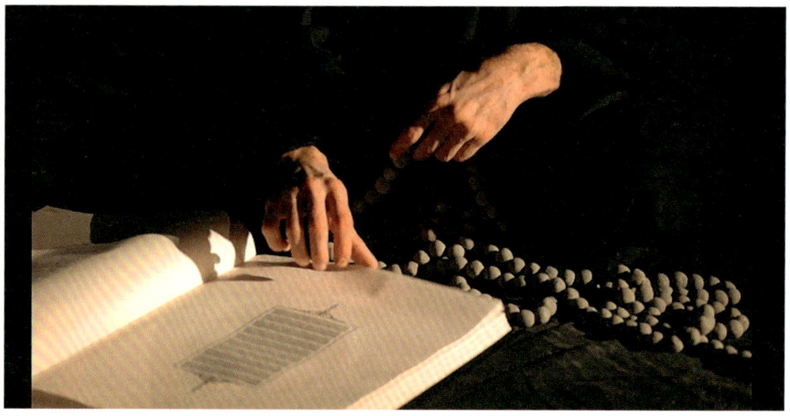

CAT. 75

Faig Ahmed

The Alif and Rhythm, 2016

Book, rosary and video
Collection of the Ministry of Culture, Saudi Arabia
inv. CA 2022.9

The Alif and Rhythm is a video installation focusing on a large hand-made book where the *alif* is repeated like a mantra over a hundred pages. *Alif*, the first letter of the Arabic alphabet, is a vertical mark with a curl at the top right end and a slight wavy declination to the right at its bottom end. It is the primary symbol from which the rest of the alphabet derives; in recognition of this, the artist chose to fill an entire book with its presence. A large rosary of clay beads lies on the ground; above, on the opposite side, a fixed video camera projects the image of the artist seated at the centre the frame, counting off an endless rosary while browsing the book. No words are written in the book, and yet it has the potential to hold the world's knowledge. According to the artist, "Touching the beads aligns the inner rhythm and gradually leads the practitioner into a state of altered consciousness and total peace of mind, followed by the perception of a uniform frequency throughout the universe. The book, which usually serves as a source of knowledge, becomes here a set of rhythmically repetitive symbols that turn into a kind of mantra when being read. Reading the book while touching a bead becomes a new *Dhikr* (remembrance)".

CAT. 76

Hazem El Mestikawy

Aequalis, 2014/2022

Cardboard, newspapers and glue
122 × 82 × 82 cm
Collection of the Ministry of Culture, Saudi Arabia
inv. CA 2022.21

From Latin, meaning "equal to", *Aequalis* is a quest for balance and equal representation for all humans, as all (HE and SHE) are created equal, carry the same values and should be entitled to the same rights, resources, opportunities, respect, education, trust, voice, as well as social, economic, and political participation, decision-making power, and protection. In *Aequalis* the words HE (*Huwa*) and SHE (*Hiya*) appear a total of four times, according to different combinations on the four sides of the tower piece (HE–SHE, HE–HE, SHE–HE, SHE–SHE), creating a square calligraphy pattern that rises from the base of the pillar in straight lines towards the top, where lines bend to meet in a net of nine squares. Made from recycling material (cardboard and daily Arabic newspapers), *Aequalis* invites us to rethink and recycle our old beliefs, ideas and words to go beyond the gender binary. This treatment of space and the careful construction suggest the complementarity of masculine and feminine, as much as of the human and the divine.

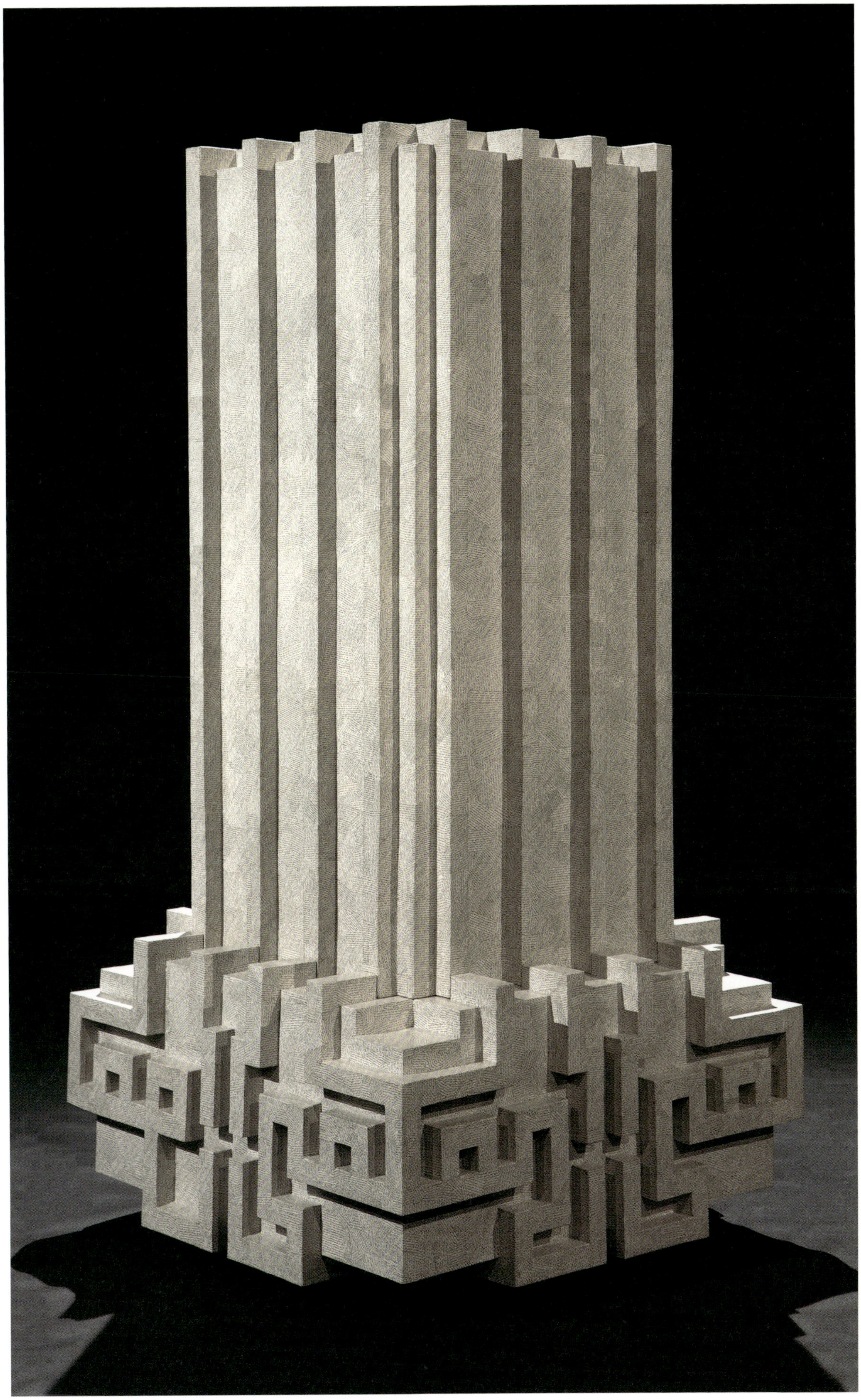

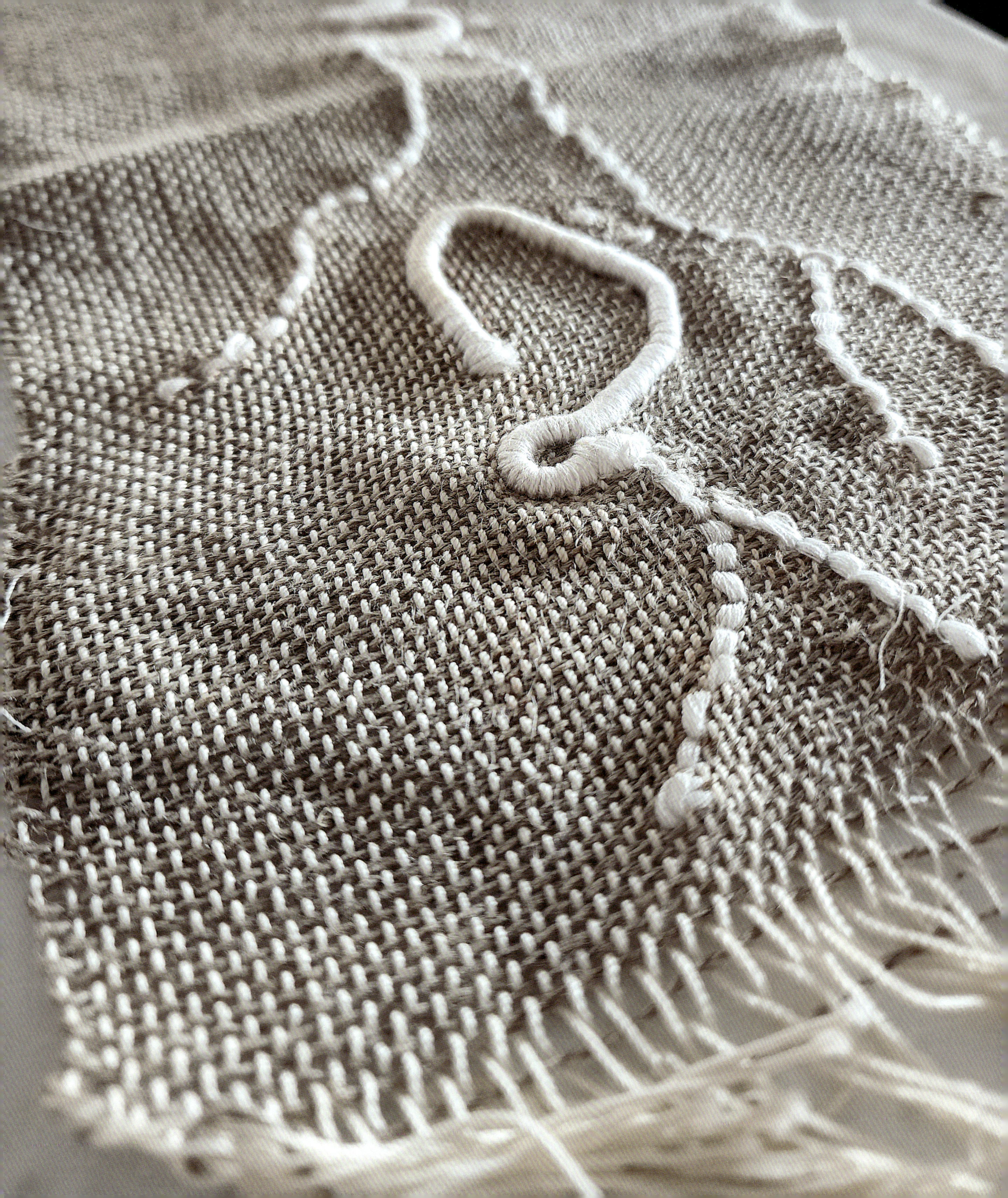

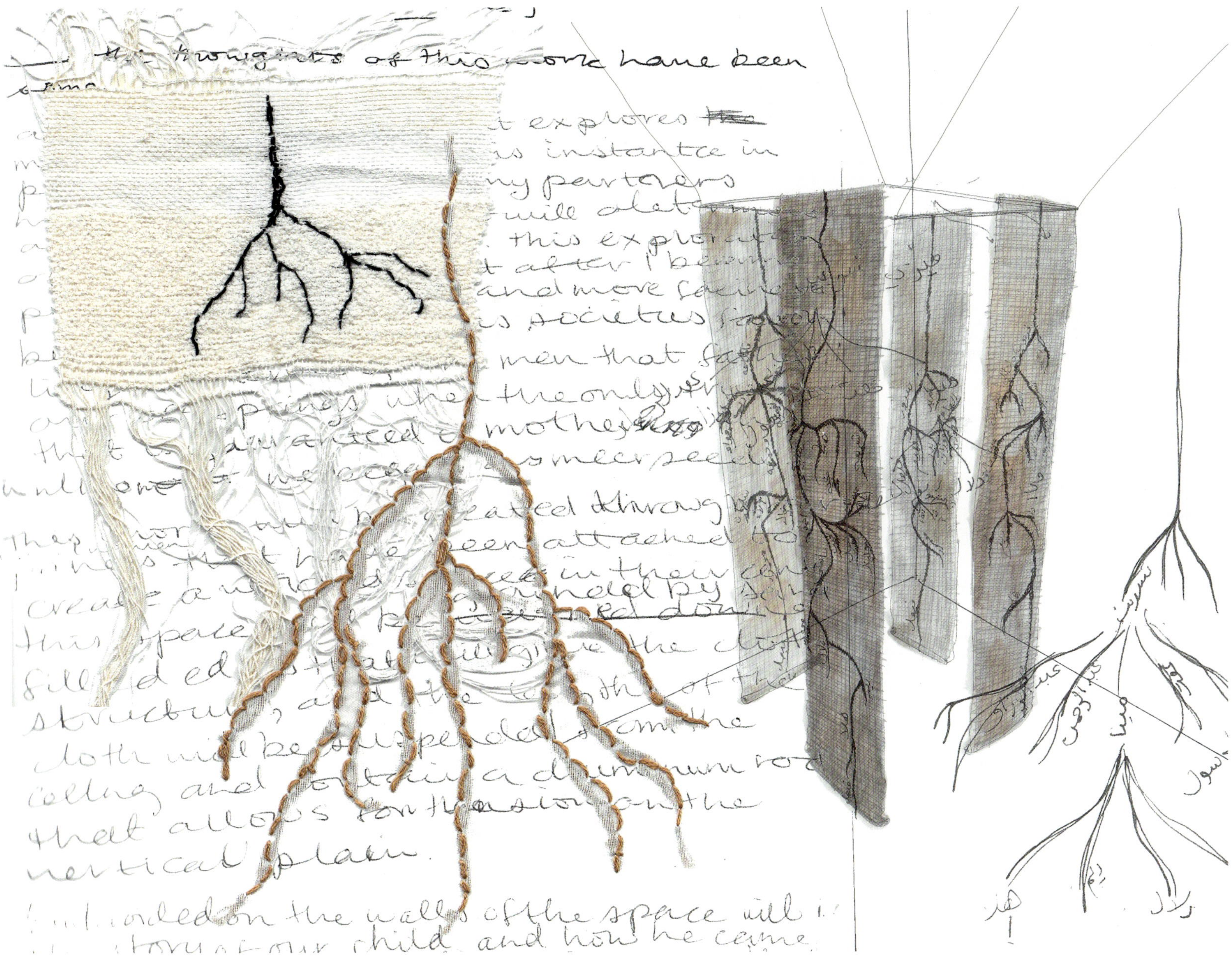

CAT. 77

Hala Kaiksow

Al-Thureya, 2022

4 hand-woven panels
Cotton, linen and naturally dyed hand-woven panels
300 × 80 cm each
Commissioned by the Ministry of Culture, Saudi Arabia
inv. CA 2022.25

Four hand-woven panels are hung down to create a semiprivate space; at the centre, an opening invites viewers to enter and interact with the fabrics, which are suspended and held by aluminium rods. Embroidered on the walls is the story of a child and how he came into being through generations of women who carried him in their minds and bodies, so that he and future beings would come into existence. Names and stories are inscribed on the walls to give roots to a floating soul on its way to earth.

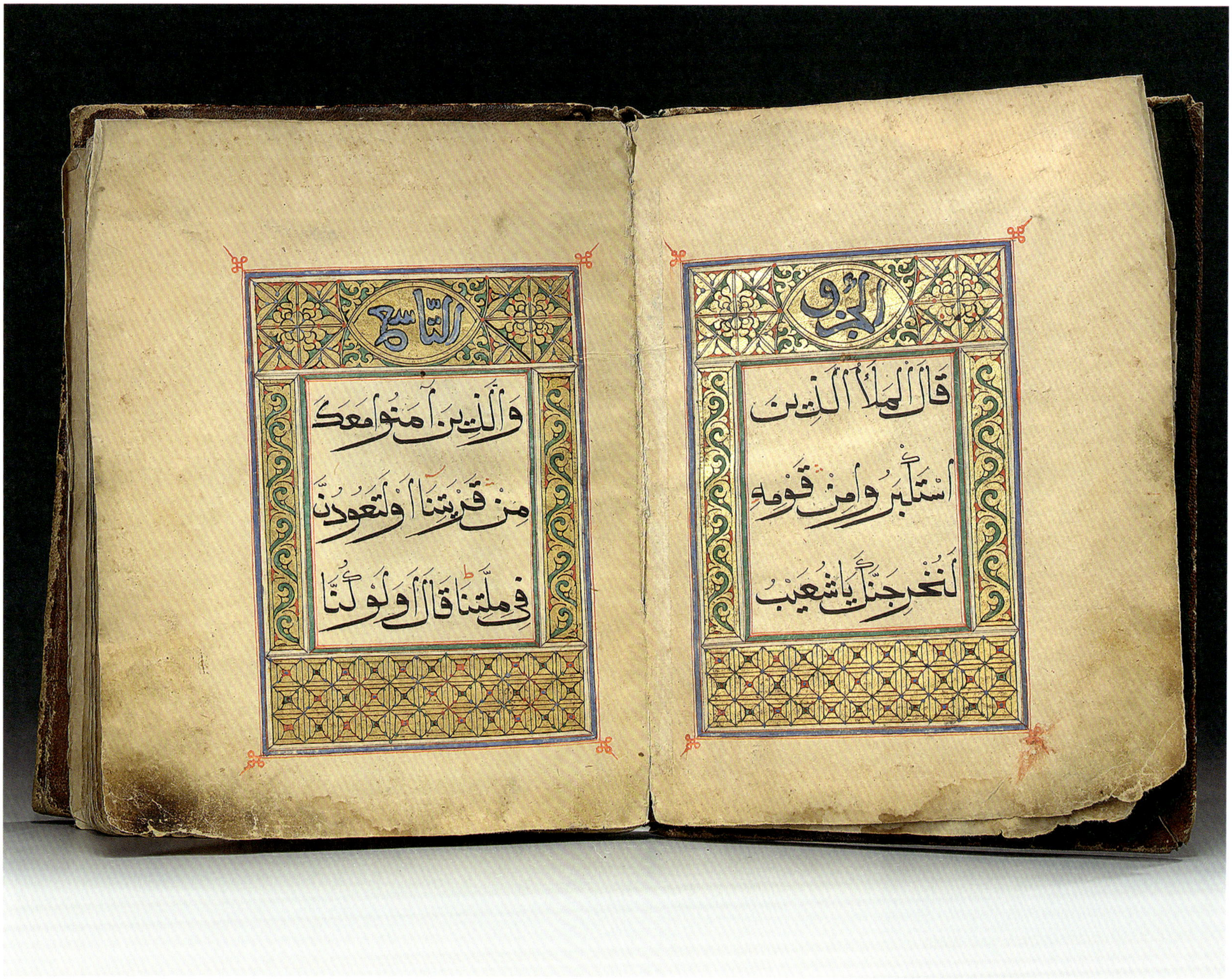

CAT. 78

The Holy Qur'an

China, twelfth century AH / seventeenth century AD

Ink on paper
Written in Chinese *muhaqqaq* script
28 × 25 cm (closed)
Collection of the Ministry of Culture, Saudi Arabia
inv. IA 2020. 2 (a)

Chinese copy of the Holy Qur'an written in Chinese *muhaqqaq* script with red outer rule, corrections in red, opening and final bifolio with polychrome and gold floral decoration, with gold and polychrome shams to opening and closing flyleaves, in original blind-stamped binding, folio.

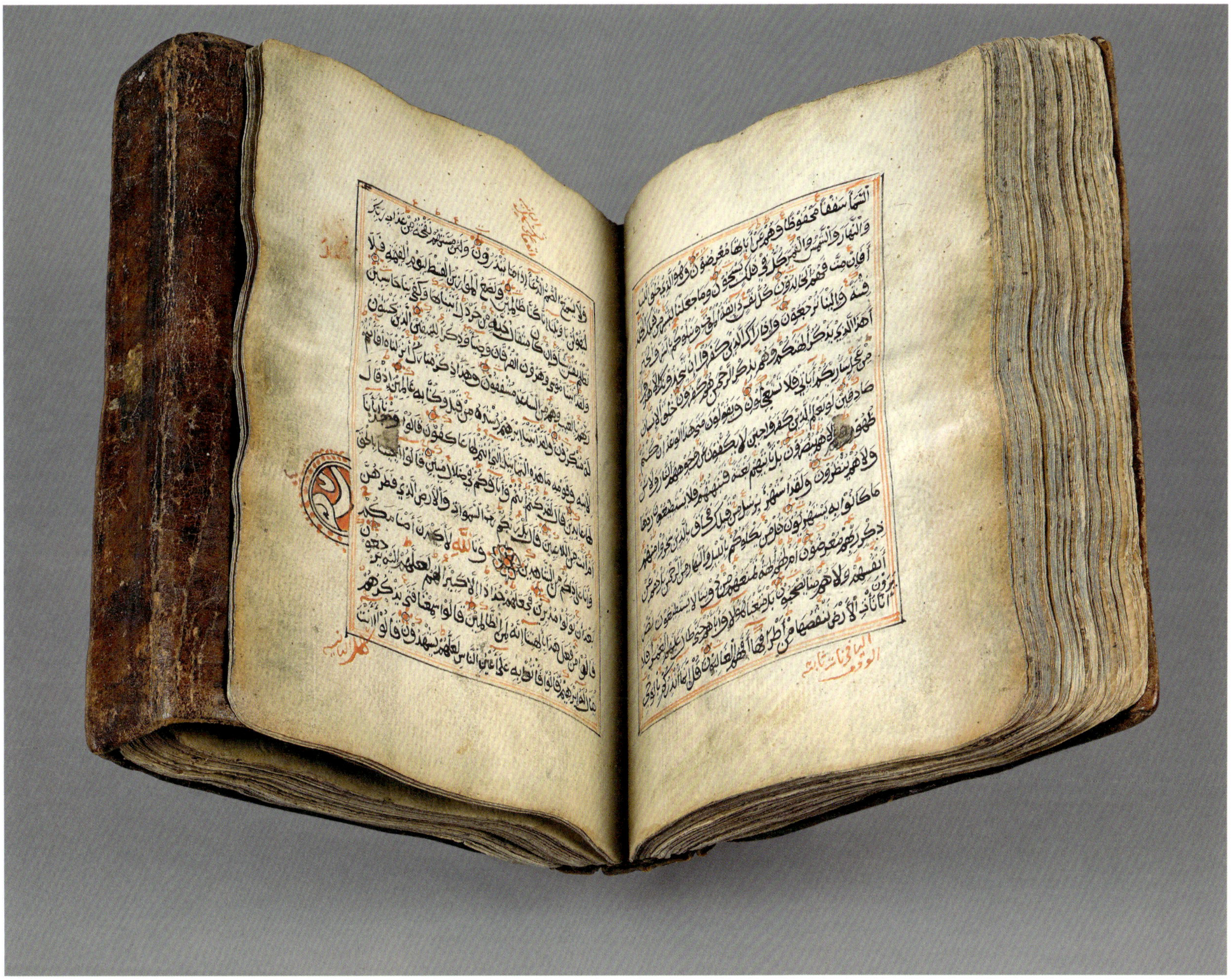

CAT. 79

The Holy Qur'an
Southern Arabia,
1205 AH / 1790 AD

Red and black ink, yellow pigment on paper, leather binding
23 × 17.5 × 6 cm (closed)
Collection of the Museum of the Institut du Monde Arabe, Paris
inv. AE 84-1

Copied in southern Arabia by Muhammad ibn Ya'qub al-Suri, the first two pages of this Holy Qur'an are decorated with geometric motifs and interlace painted in yellow and red.

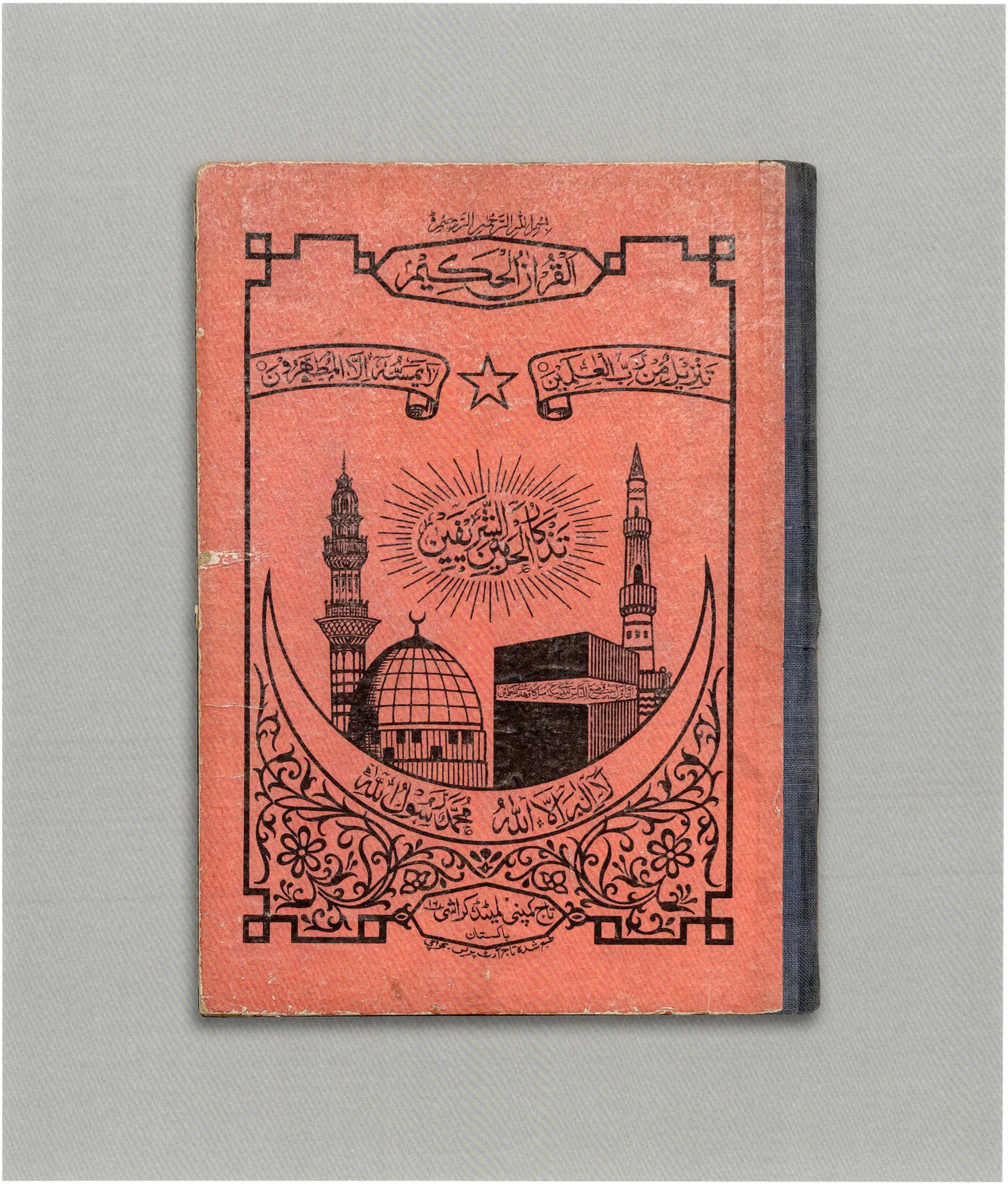
بسم الله الرحمن الرحيم
القرآن الحكيم
تنزيل من رب العلمين
لا يمسه الا المطهرون
تذكار الحرمين الشريفين
لا اله الا الله محمد رسول الله
تاج کمپنی لمیٹڈ کراچی
پاکستان

CAT. 80

Three copies of the Holy Qur'an

Ink on paper

Commissioned and printed in Pakistan and distributed as a souvenir in the Two Holy Mosques
24.5 × 18 × 2.7 cm

Dating back to the twentieth century, acquired at the Bab Al Salam market in the Al Haram district of Mecca
30 × 22.2 × 4.2 cm

1315 AH / 1897–98 AD, published by the Karimi printing house, commissioned by the late Qadi Abdul Karim Flabandri
25.3 × 17.5 × 2.5 cm

Collection of Hasab Allah Bugis

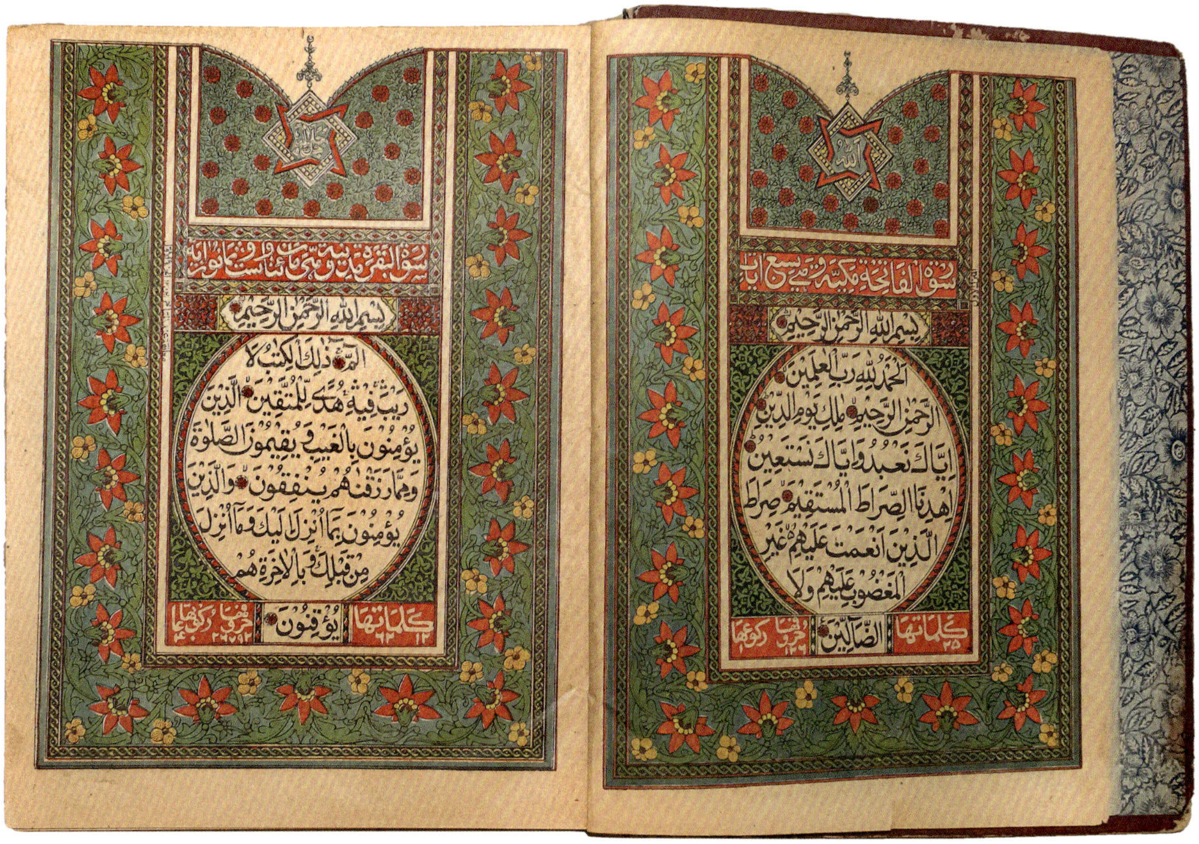

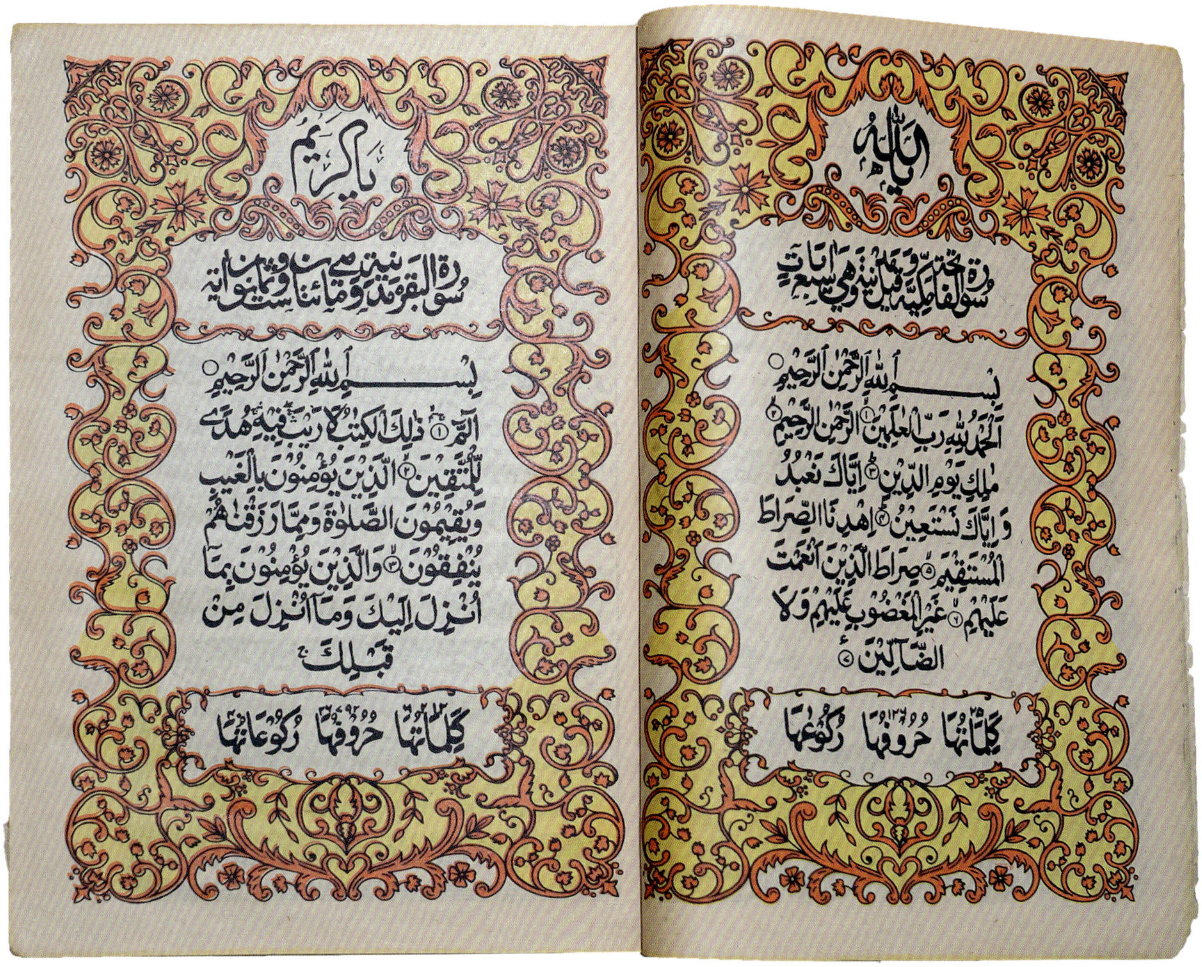

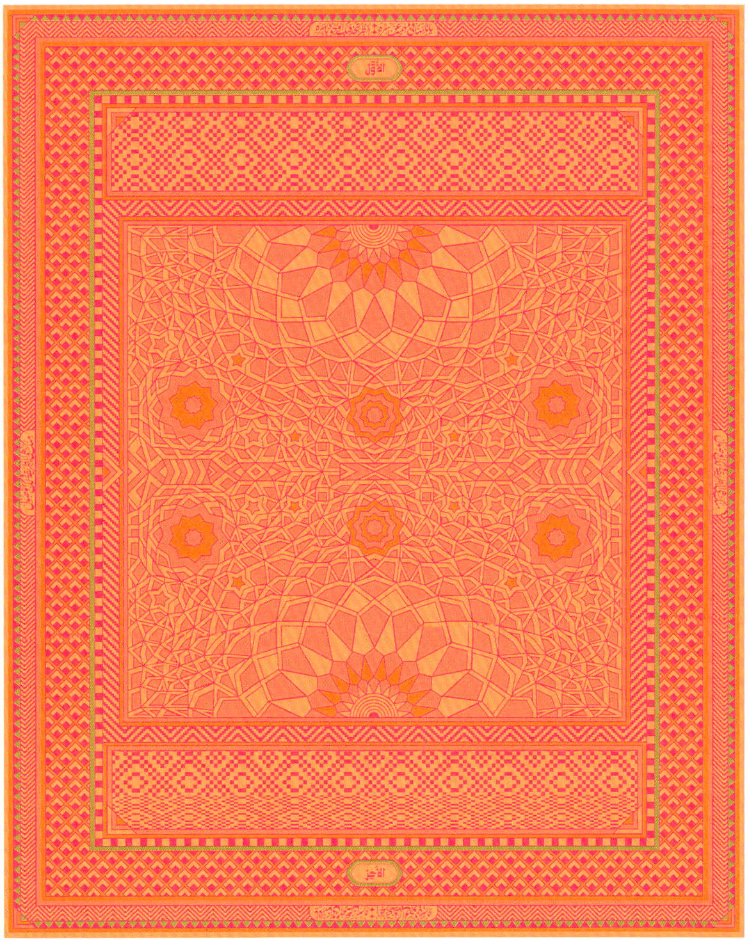

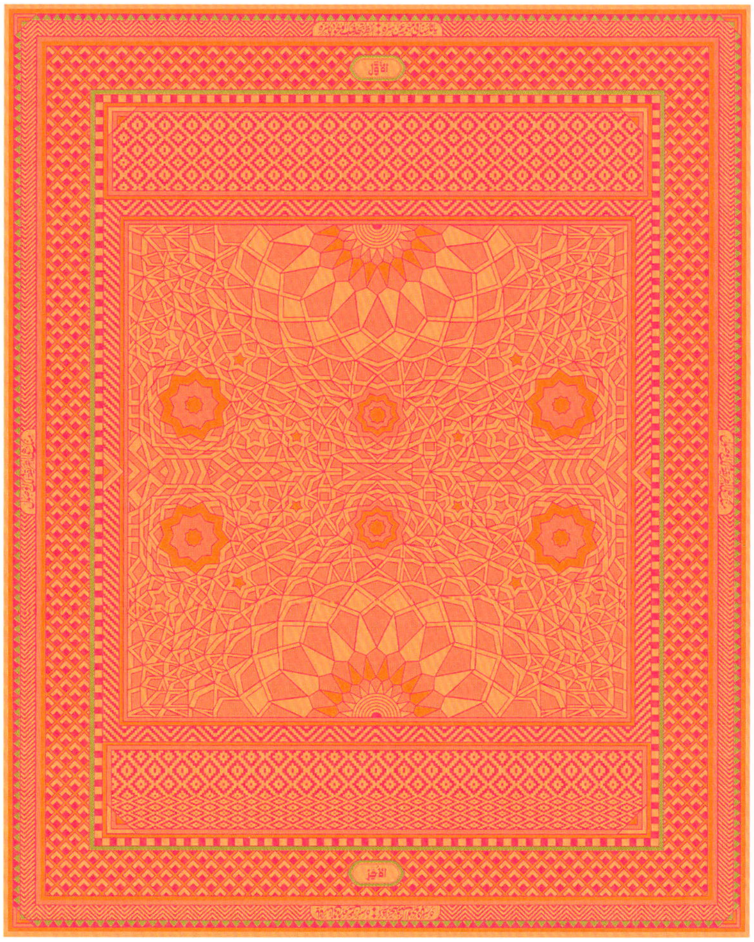

CAT. 81

Yusef Alahmad

Guide to Goodness, 2022

4 silkscreens, 5 colours on Coventry Rag
320 gsm archival paper
89.3 × 70.8 cm each
Commissioned by the Ministry of Culture, Saudi Arabia
inv. CA 2022.18

This is a limited-edition screen print inspired by *Dala'il al-Khayrat* (Guidelines to the Blessings and the Shining of Lights, giving the saying of the blessed prayer over the Prophet) (PBUH), a manual of devotions for prayers and blessings upon the Prophet (PBUH). Carrying the manuscript and reciting the prayers it contains is thought to provide *baraka* (blessing), good luck and protection.

A number of variations of this text exist across different artistic schools in the Islamic world where *Dala'il* manuscripts were produced. This work uses a limited palette of colours and emphasizes the reinterpretation and combination of visual elements commonly found in this type of manuscripts, such as geometric interlaced patterns, illustrated iconography and fluid prayer passages.

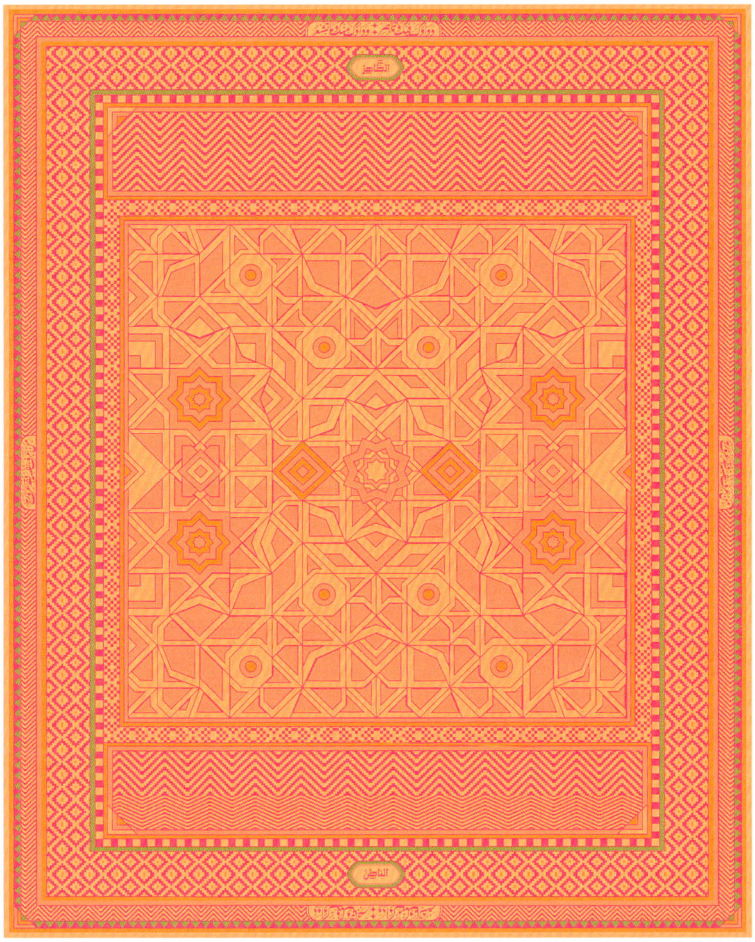

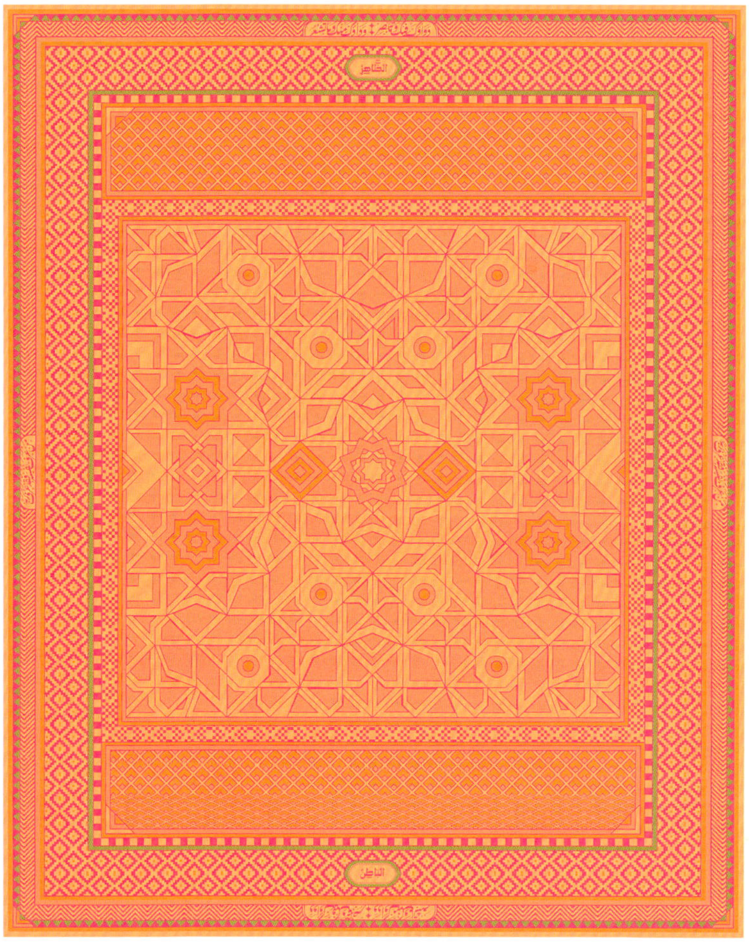

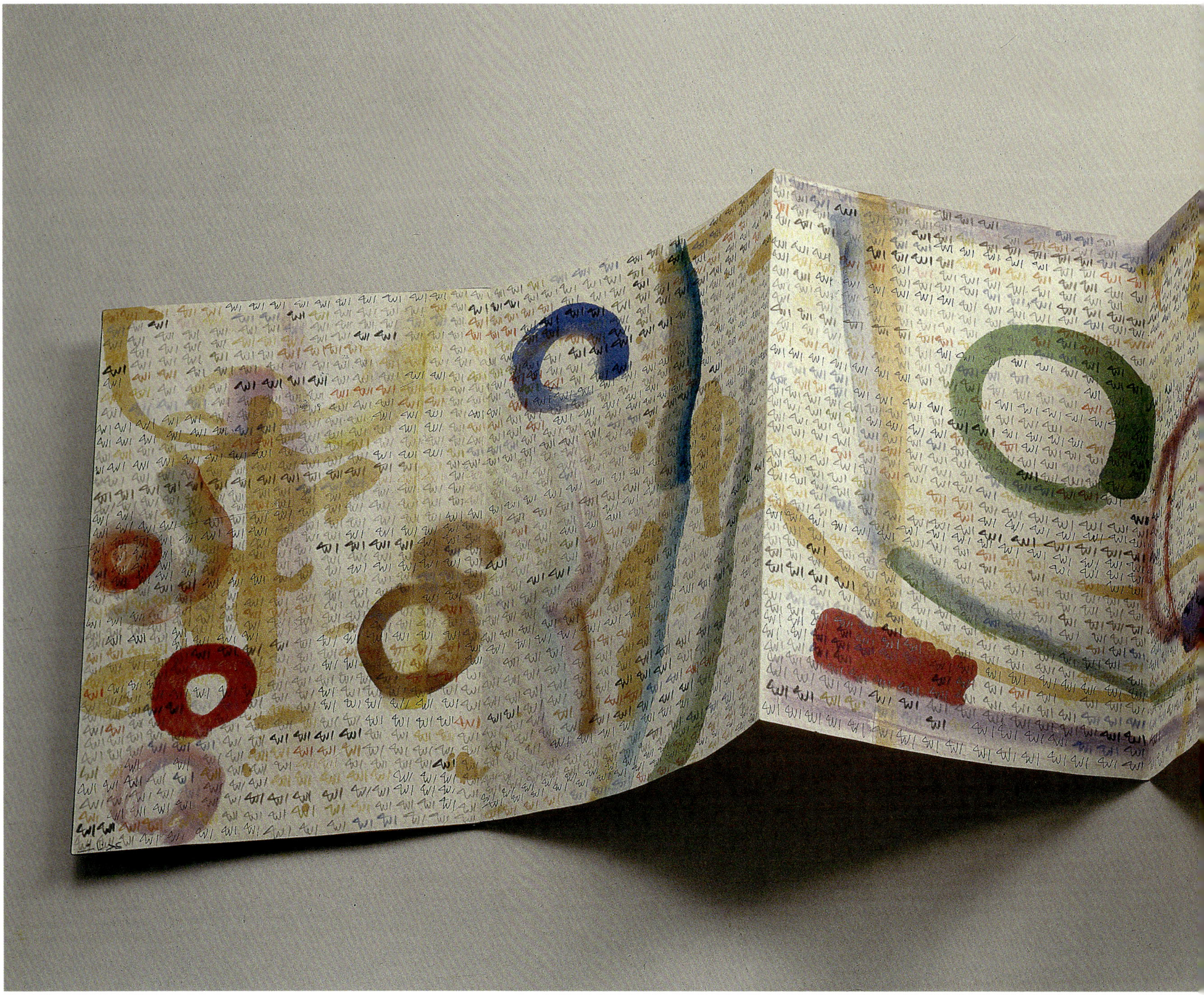

CAT. 82

Etel Adnan

Dhikr, 1978

Watercolour, coloured pencils and black pencil on Japanese folded notebook (*leporello*)
30.3 × 21 cm (closed)
30.3 × 950 cm (unfolded)
Collection of the Museum of the Institut du Monde Arabe, Paris
inv. AC 01-01

Etel Adnan never really mastered the art of writing the Arabic alphabet, but this did not prevent her from exploring the intrinsic possibilities of this script, which she practised more as drawing. *Dhikr* is unique amongst her works, which often drew from contemporary Arab poets. Here, Adnan copied the name of God (Allah) more than 2,500 times, combined with coloured lines and circles, making this exercise a journey into the depths of her being, during which she added the prompt from verses 41–42 of surah *al-Ahzab*: "O, believers! Remember God often. Glorify him morning and evening!"

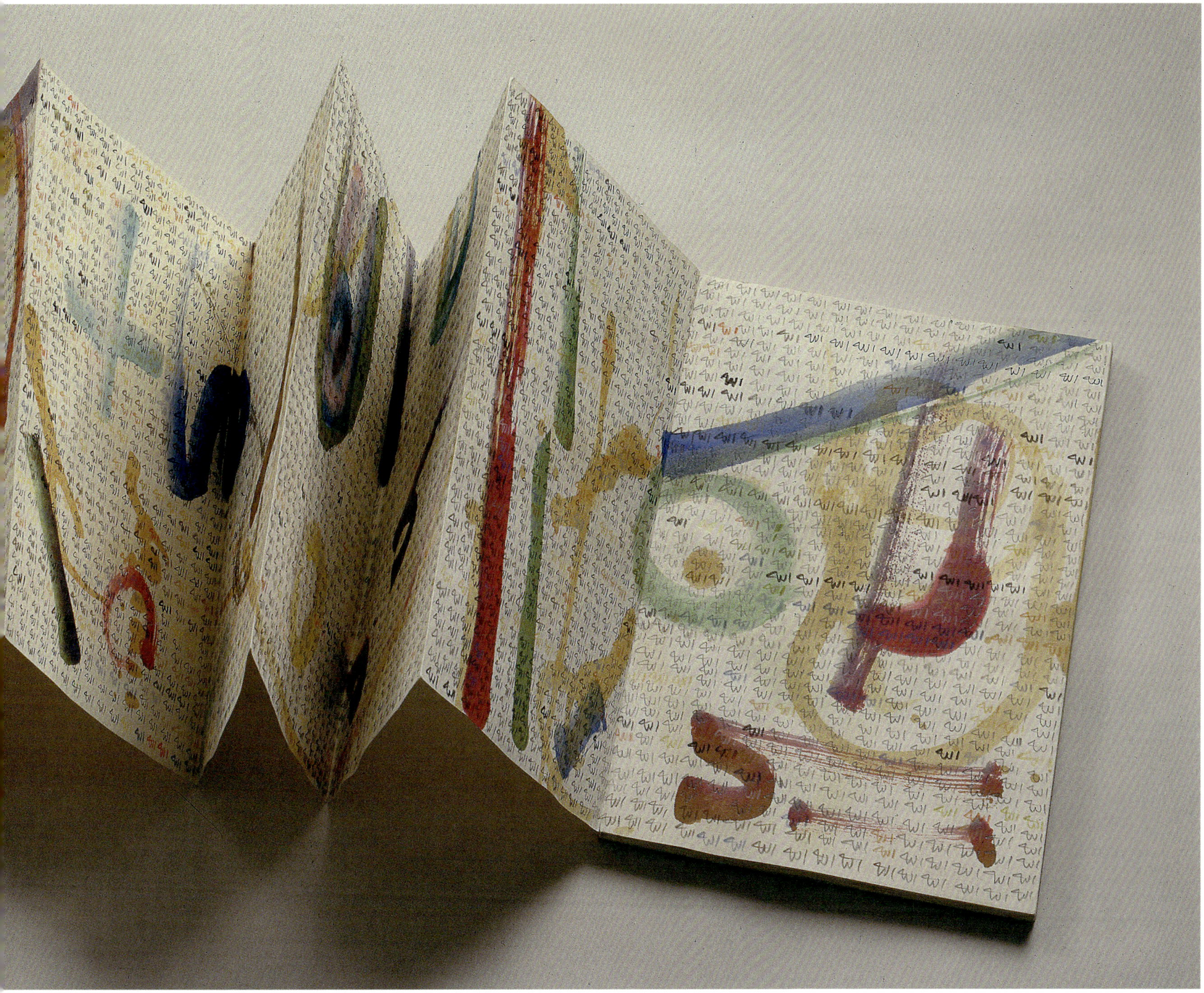

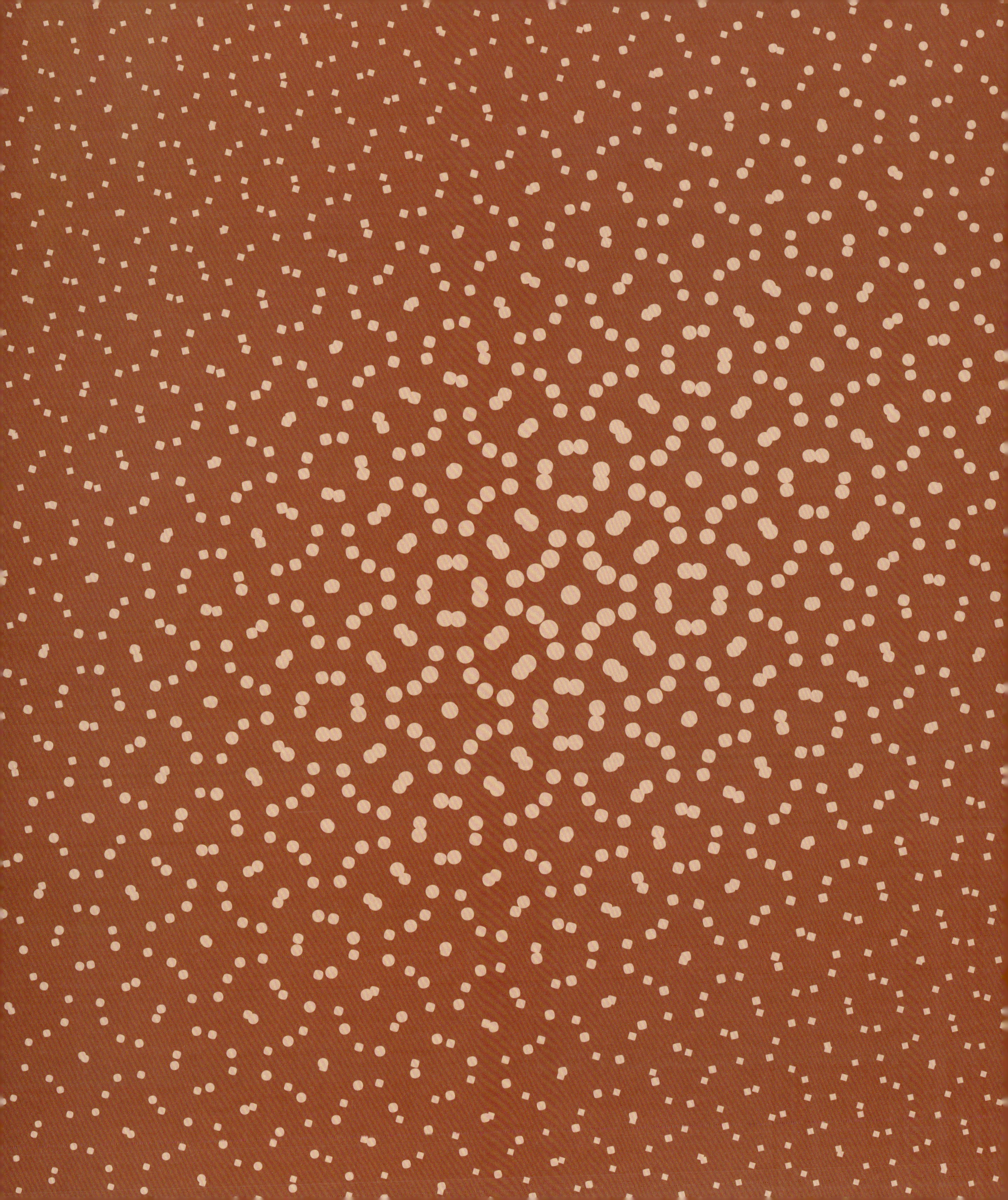

POETRY

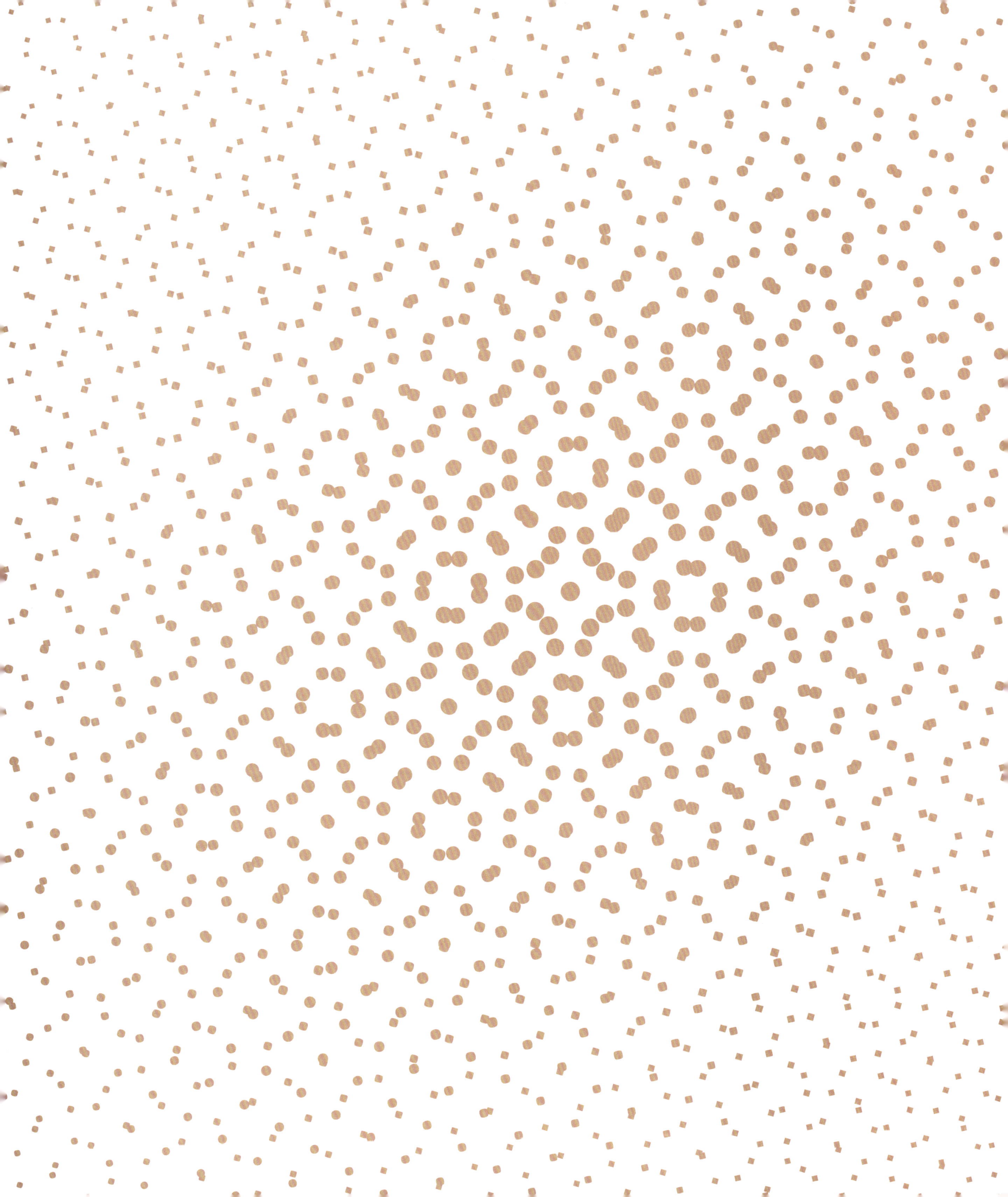

The society that witnessed the advent of Islam favoured the arts of language, especially poetry, rather than architecture or the plastic arts. It is in this context that the Qur'an was revealed in classical Arabic. The mastery of one's language is essential for the perfect understanding of the Revelation. Thus, Muslim scholars have collected everything in oral expression, in particular poetic declamation, which allowed them to refine their knowledge of the vocabulary and grammar of the Arabic language. The inimitability of the Qur'an, in its subject as well as in its form, often in rhyme, has not restricted the rise of poetry as a vehicle of the ideals, the sensitivity and the imagination of Arabs and Muslims. Along with the Qur'anic text and the hadiths, the musicality, rhythm and multiple meanings of the play on words in poetry have always inspired and continue to inspire calligraphers in search of the most beautiful compositions in order to transmit their spirit and aesthetics. The norms of classical calligraphy in no way prevent them from steady experimentation. Since the 1960s, artists have, for their part, explored the integration of the heritage of classical calligraphy and modern art as part of a movement known as *hurufiyya*. They manipulate the shape of the letters in search of a pan-Arab visual language. Many of them have returned to the medium of the book, in which they give primacy to artistic expression rather than semantics: thus they create a poetry of shapes and colours.

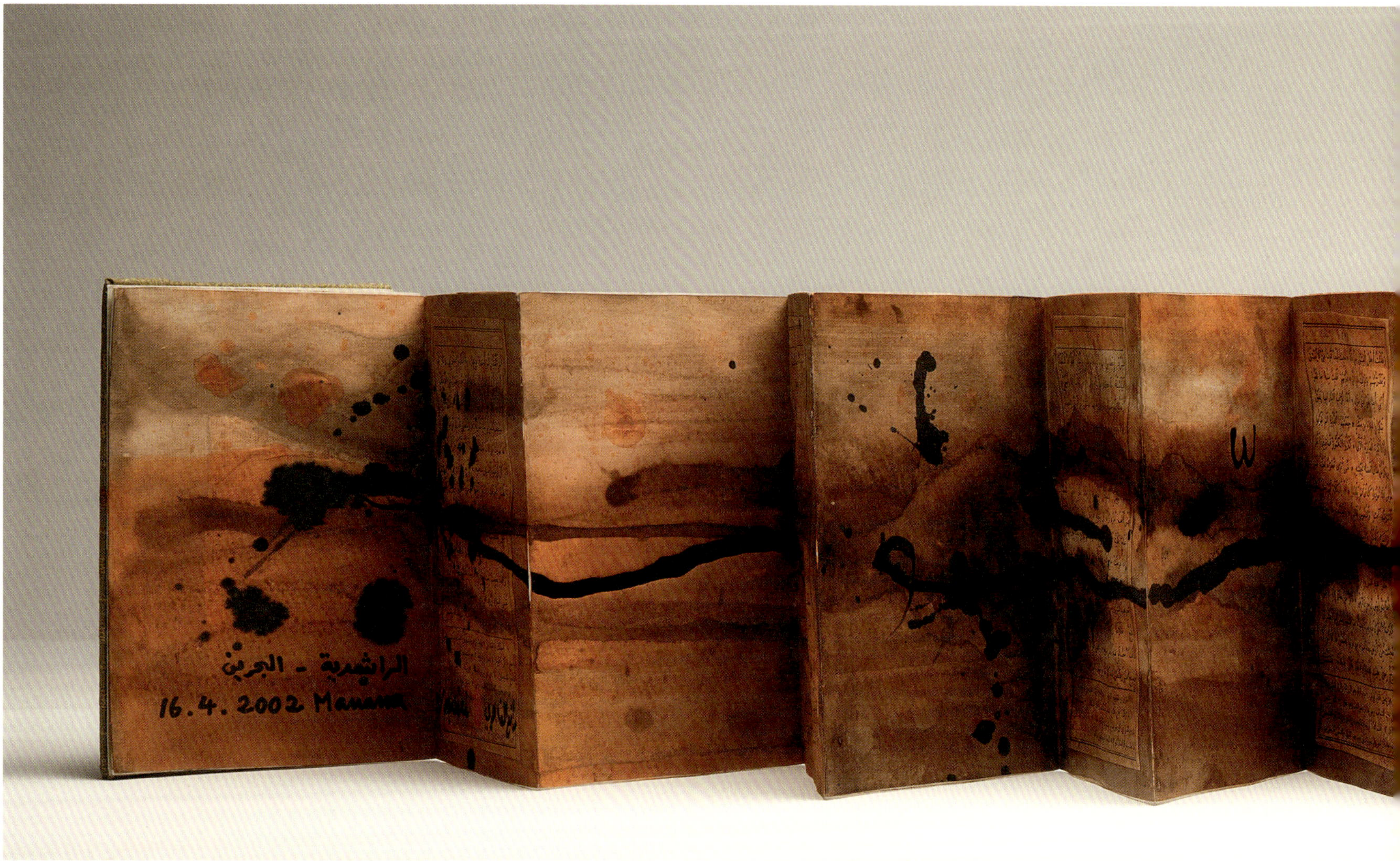

CAT. 83

Rafa al Nasiri
***Homage to Al Mutanabbi 3*,**
2002
Edition 1/3
Collage and inks on Chinese rice paper book (fold-out)
16.5 × 12 cm (closed)
16.5 × 306.5 cm (open)
Collection of the Ministry of Culture, Saudi Arabia
inv. CA 2022.23

Homage to Al Mutanabbi 3 is a handmade book, part of a series, using different techniques, and inspired by Abu Al Tayyed Al Mutanabbi (a miniature of the *Amine Hindiyya*, printed in Cairo in 1923 and then published by the Arab Center for Research and Publications in 1980). Al Nasiri was entranced by the design of the collection, the shape of the old, printed letters and the yellowish colour of old, aged paper. Captivated by Al Mutanabbi, whose words express so well notions of distance and exile, when one is far from friends, family and country, al Nasiri initiated a long inner dialogue with his own inspiration, seeking new ways to establish a connection that would bridge the centuries separating them. Over the course of seven years, he produced several works with different textures, sizes and techniques including drawing on paper, engraving on zinc, drawing on fabric, and writing on handmade folded notebooks he himself crafted. He used a collage technique to glue full or half pages on a rice paper base, like physical witnesses to the composition, before adding his personal touch. Perhaps this is why al Nasiri seeks to get closer to Arab Islamic books and chooses texts belonging to the Arab modern and classical heritage expressing exile and nostalgia. His notebooks testify to the fusion between the artist and Islamic manuscripts, as he uses illumination with Chinese ink, then acrylic paints, to turn this classical form of art into a contemporary one with new codes.

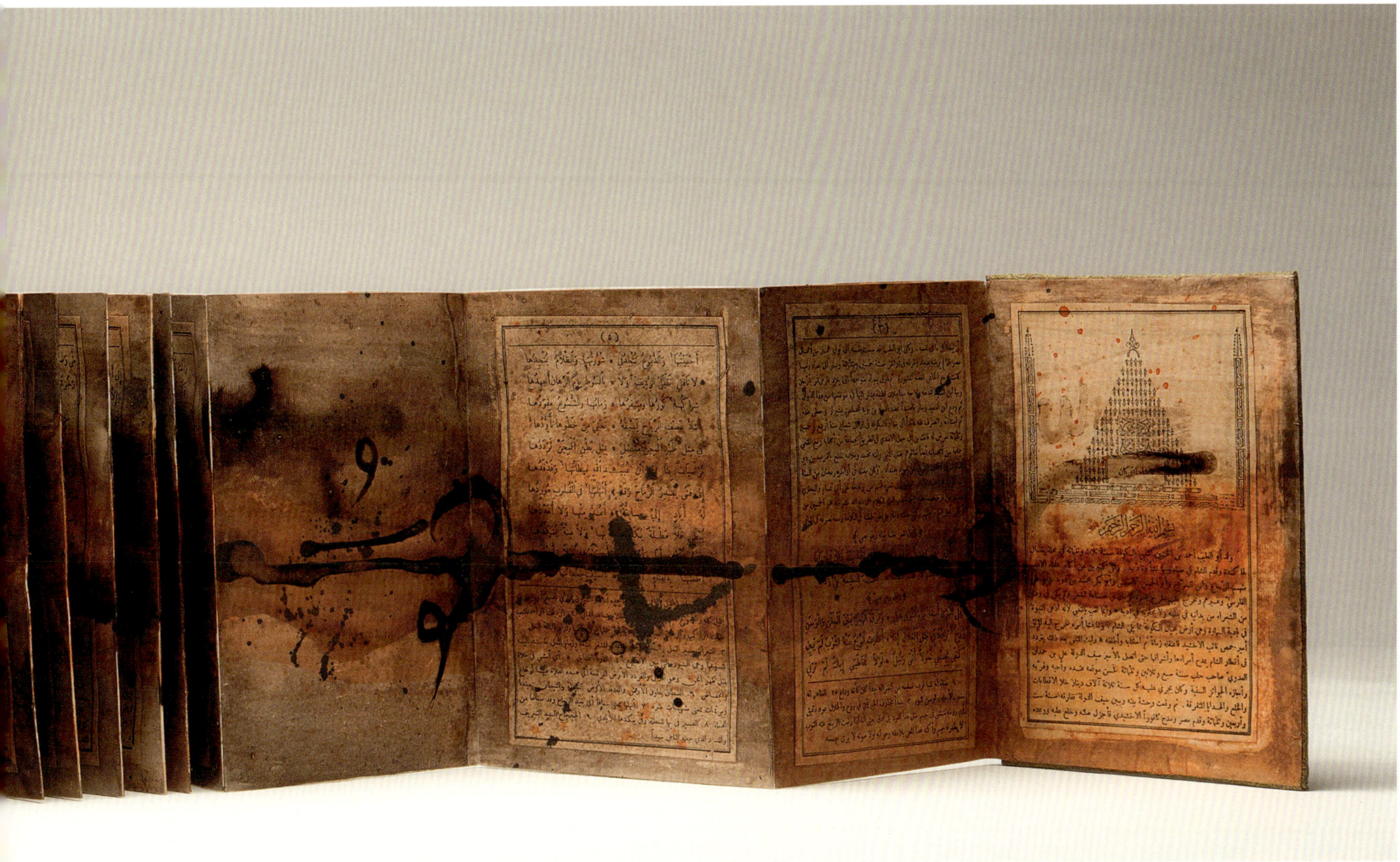

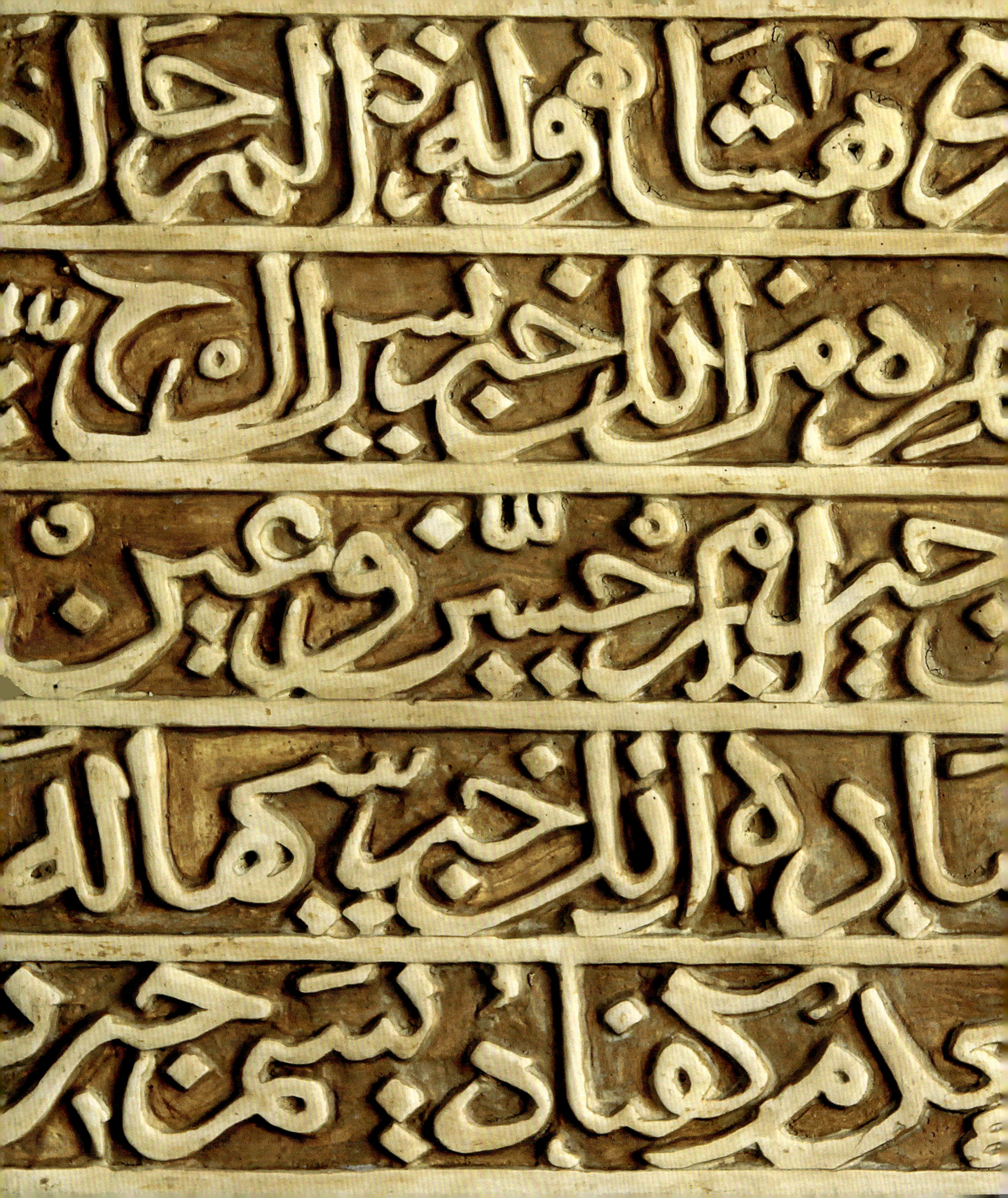

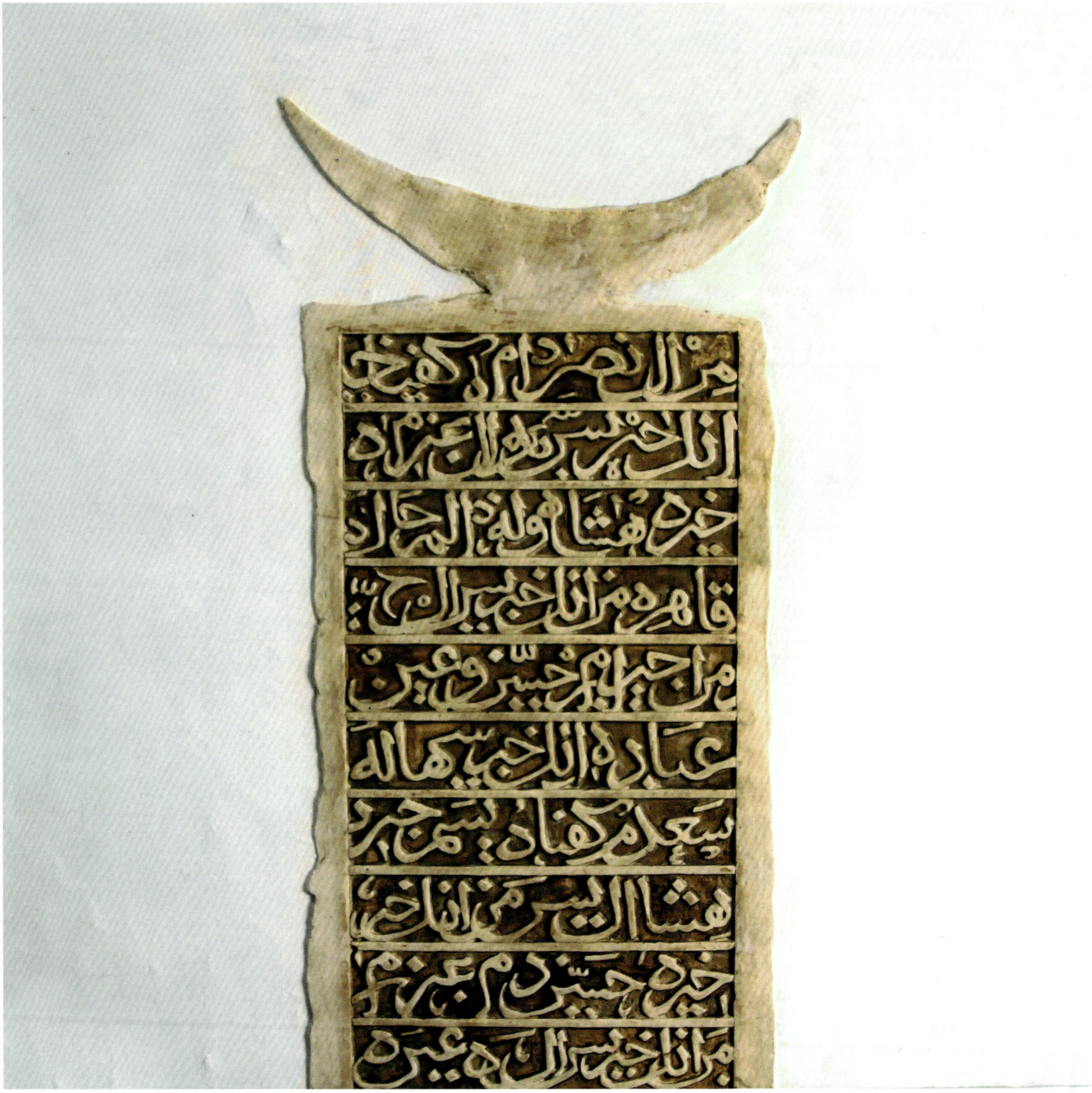

CAT. 84

Yazid Kheloufi
Naffas, 2016

Gypsum on wood, mud and ink, using ancient Andalusian technique
100 × 100 cm
Collection of the Ministry of Culture, Saudi Arabia
inv. CA 2022.15

Naffas (breath) is part of a collection called "Silence and Emptiness", where Yazid Kheloufi tackles the concepts of void and emptiness in Islamic art, knowing well that void carries aesthetic value. As he worked on letter groupings, he progressively felt the need to disembody letters from their meaning, since they carry their own significance, identity and status within themselves, as seen in the stand-alone letters adorning the beginning of certain surahs of the Qur'an. Letters need to be heard, because inside their curved shapes, they carry the pain of the universe and hold visible and invisible worlds . . . voices emerging from the depths of the self, where breath meets the soul. Therefore *Naffas* focuses on the soul as the entire universe breathes. Man breathes. His body breathes. His soul and his lungs breathe. Breath is the air that breathes in nature. The soul is therefore breath.

CAT. 85

Farah Behbehani
***The Conference of the Birds*, 2009**

Text by Farid al-Din Attar
One book and four limited-edition silkscreen prints
Written in *jaly diwani* script
32.8 × 22 cm (book), various dimensions (silkscreen prints)
Courtesy of Farah Behbehani

The Conference of the Birds is a Persian twelfth-century allegorical poem written by Farid al-Din Attar; it tells the story of the birds of the world flying on a quest to search for their mythological king. This illustrated calligraphed version, written in *jaly diwani* script, is designed to enable readers to understand the meaning and read the direction and flow of calligraphy, offering greater insight into the intricacies of Arabic script. The book was published by Thames & Hudson, London, in June 2009.

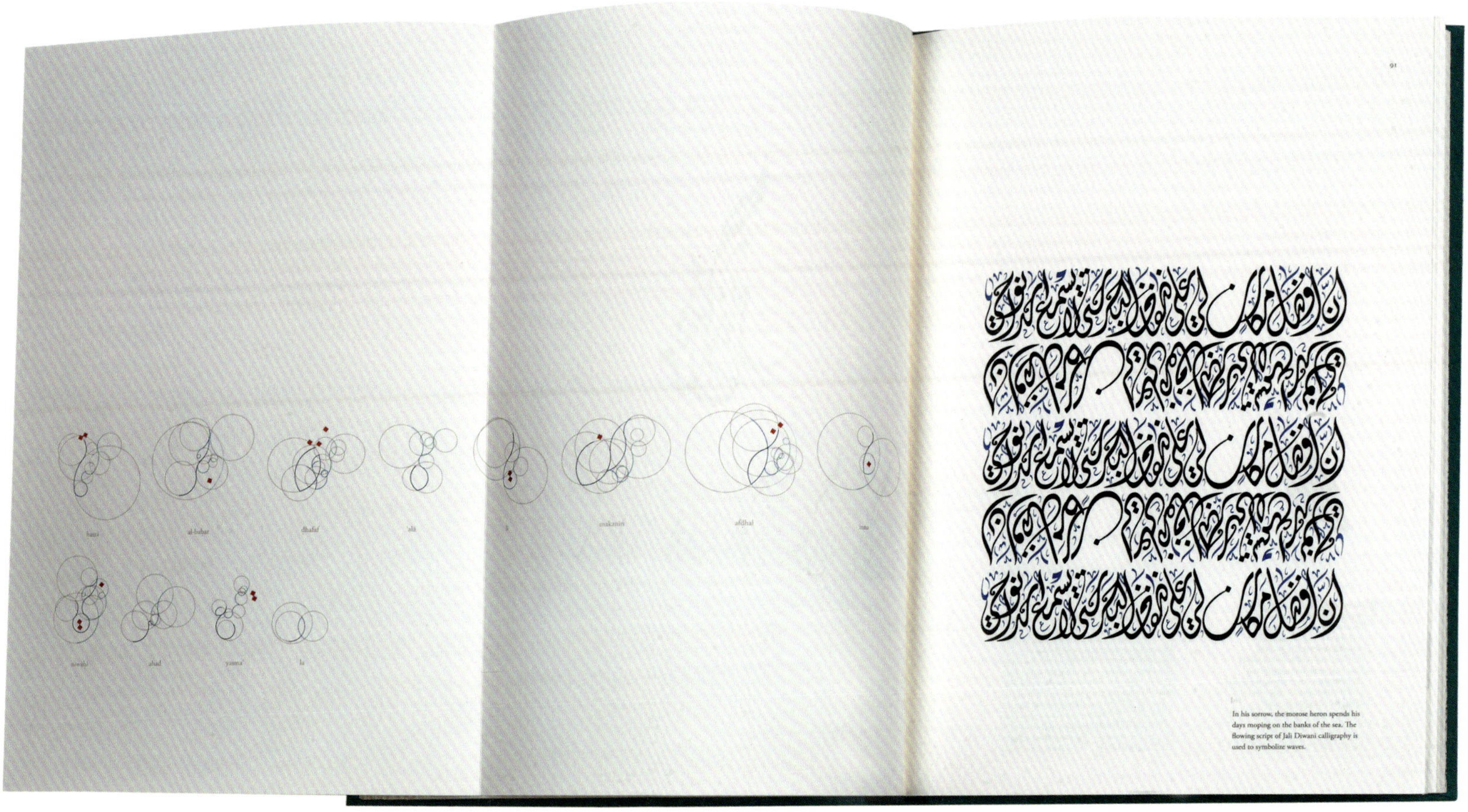

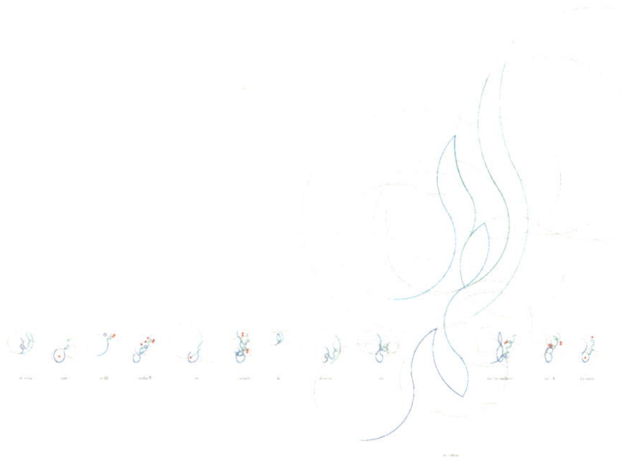
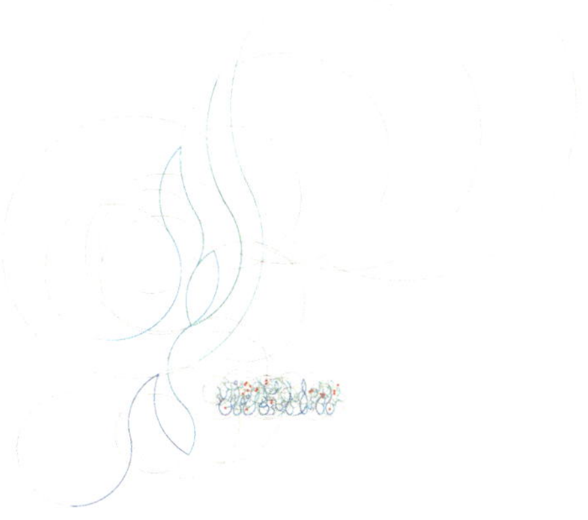
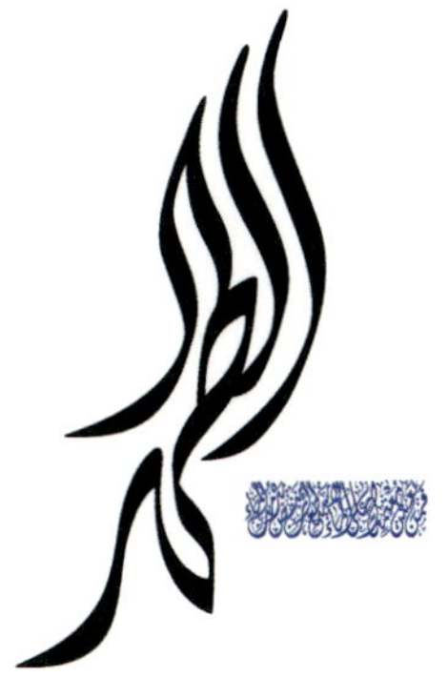
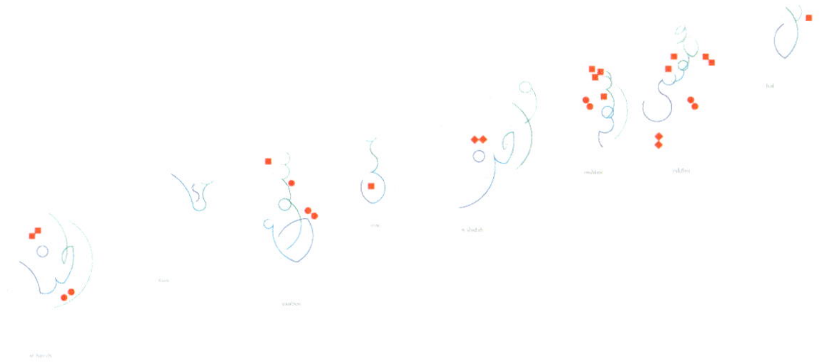
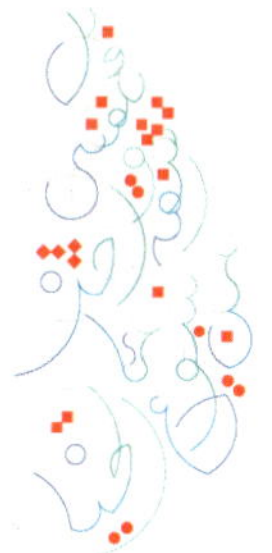
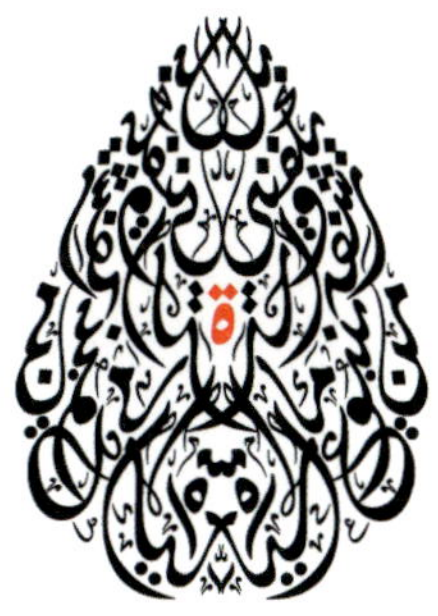
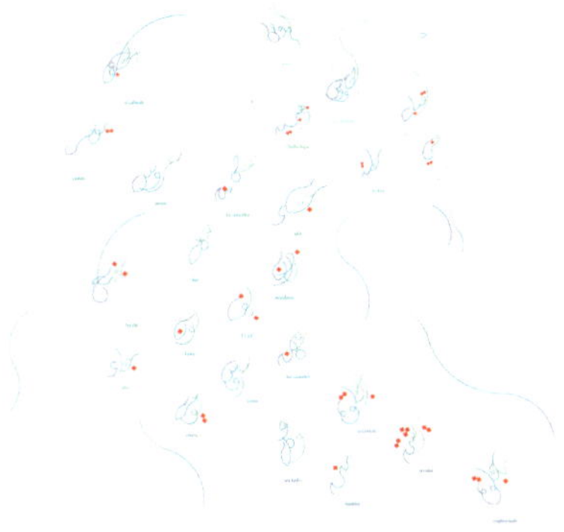
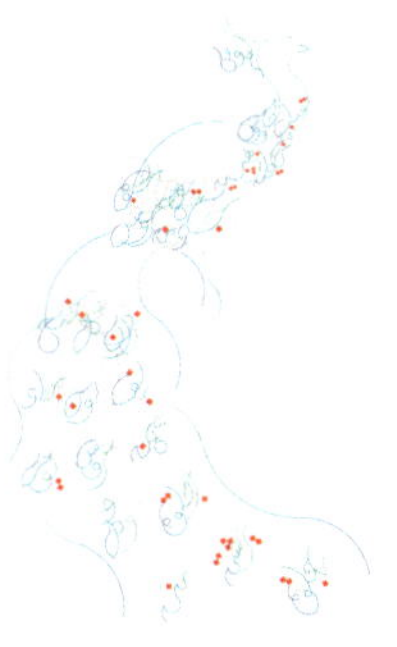
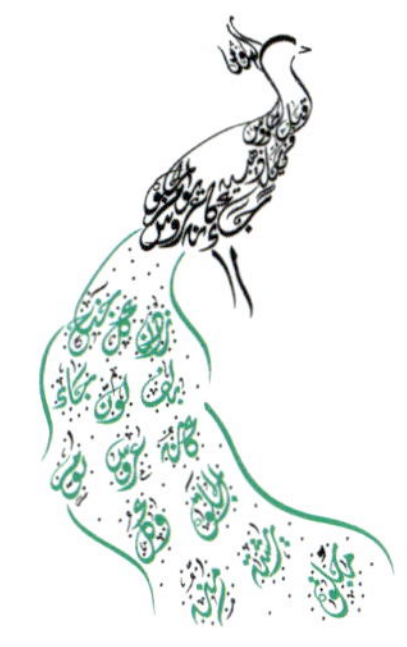
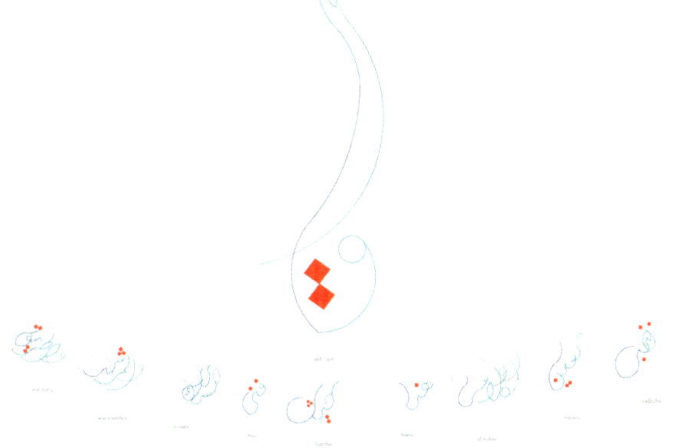
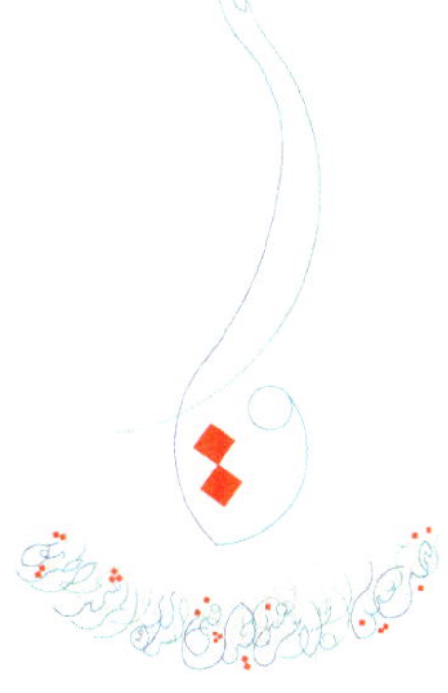
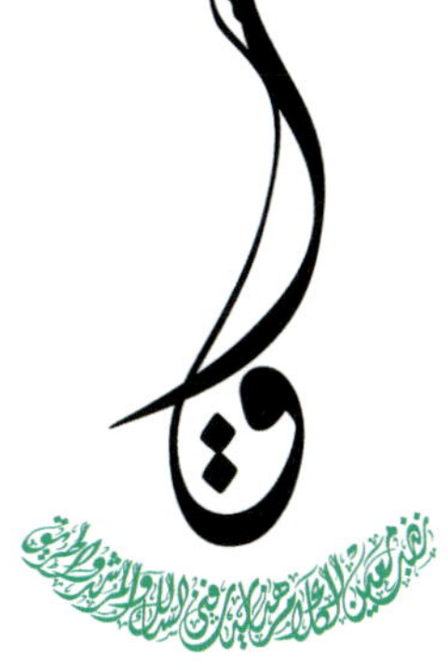

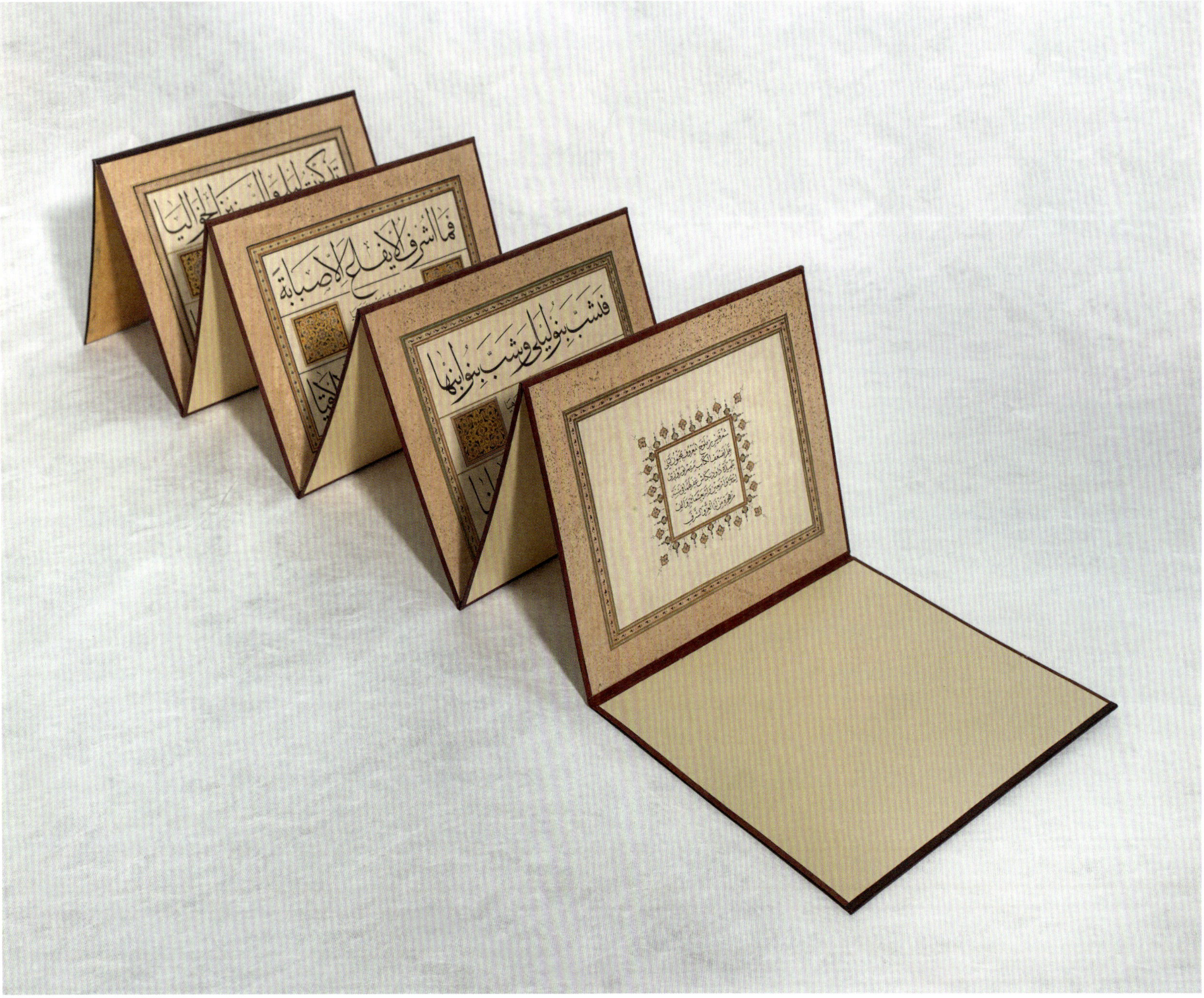

CAT. 86

Maryam Norouzi
Layla and Majnun, 2020

Poetry by Qays ibn al-Mulawwah
Muraqqa' (fold-out book) bound in leather with seven separate *qit'as* (fragments)
Ink, colour and gold on *ahar* paper
Written in *muhaqqaq* and *rayhani* scripts
29.5 × 34.8 cm each *qit'a*
Collection of the Ministry of Culture, Saudi Arabia
inv. IA 2020.35

This album contains a selection from the famous poem *Layla and Majnun* by Qays ibn al-Mulawwah, a celebrated Arab poet from the first century AH / seventh century AD. The poem is written following the traditional album (*Muraqqa'*) layout, conceived as a calligraphic masterpiece meant to be read and contemplated at the same time.
The poem is written with black ink on traditional *ahar* paper in delicate *muhaqqaq* and smaller *rayhani* script. Following the order of the poem, from top to bottom, the calligraphy has then been mounted onto the cardboard backing and bound in accordion form. This format allows for the display of all pages at once, as well as for easier access to each individual section or *qit'a*. Beautifully illuminated by Selcen Belgin, the poem comes to life as it unfolds gradually from page to page.

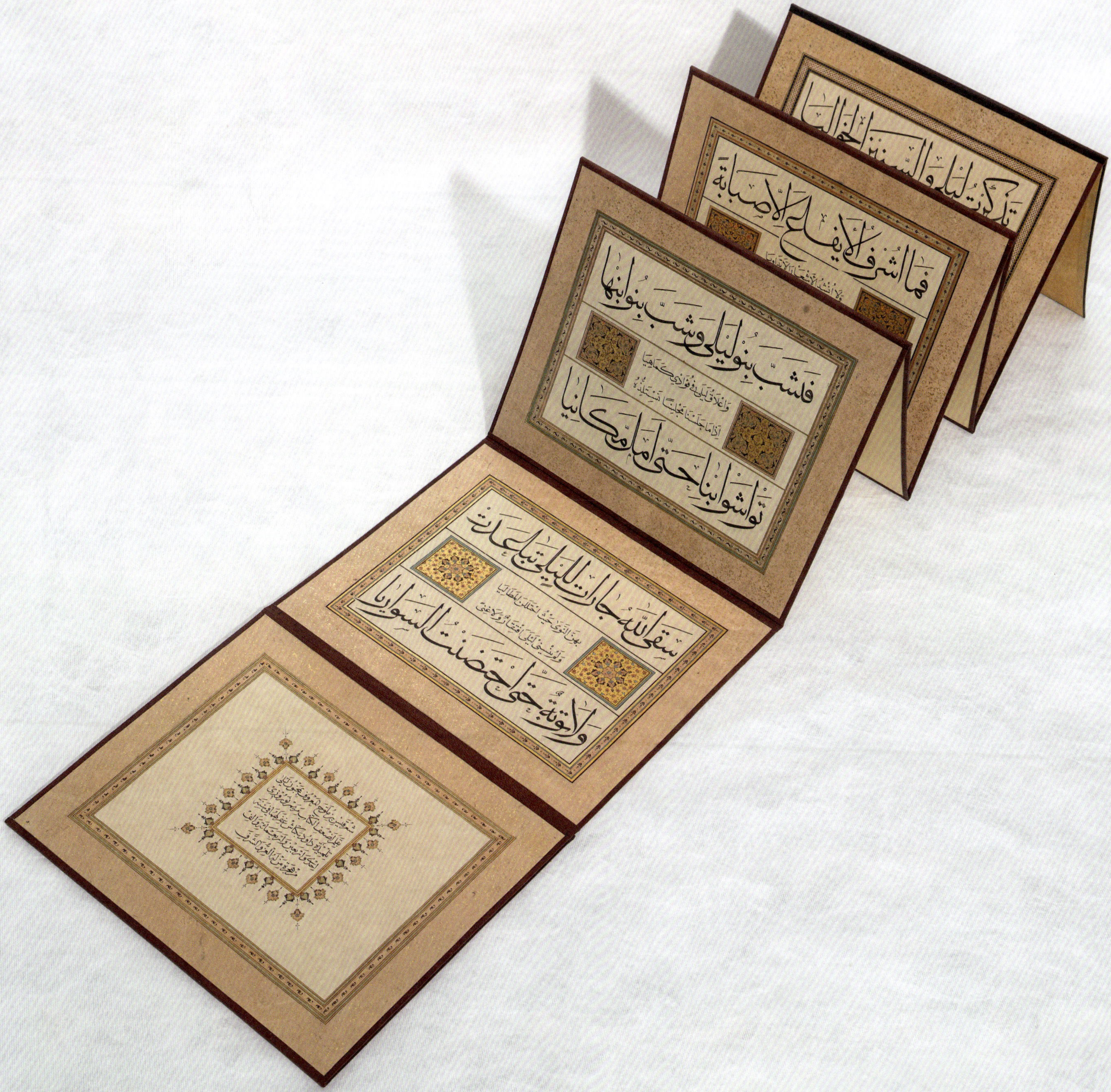

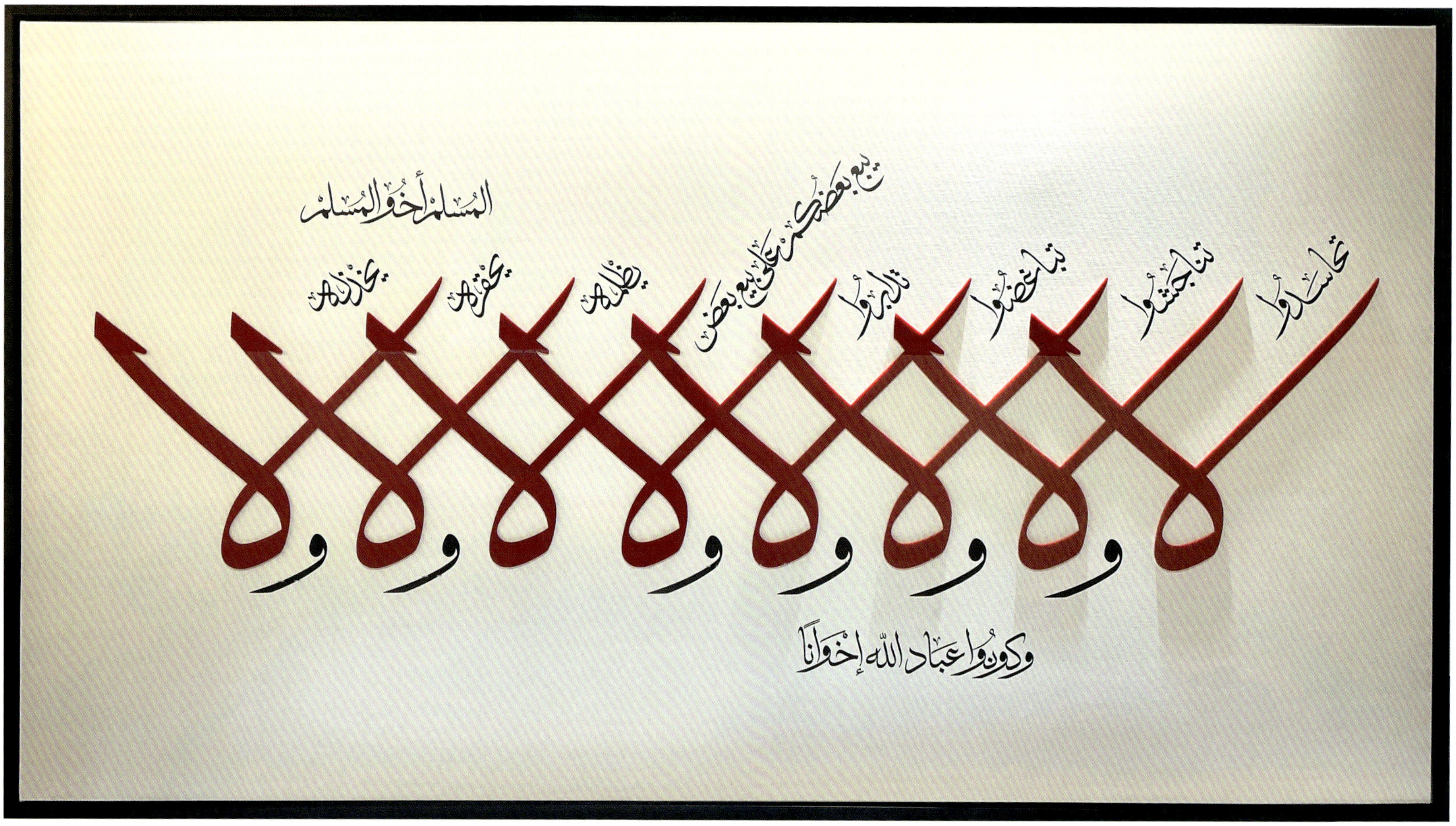

CAT. 87

Ahmad Jeddawi
The Eight "Las", 2022

Acrylic cut-outs on acrylic board
120 × 200 cm
Commissioned by the Ministry of Culture, Saudi Arabia
inv. CA 2022.17

This artwork gives life to the text of the Holy Qur'an as transmitted in the 35th hadith of the Prophet (PBUH): "The Messenger of Allah said, 'Do not envy one another, and do not inflate prices for one another, and do not hate one another, and do not turn away from one another, and do not undercut one another in trade, but [rather] be slaves of Allah and brothers [amongst yourselves]. A Muslim is the brother of a Muslim: he does not oppress him, nor does he fail him, nor does he lie to him, nor does he hold him in contempt'". It is characterized by a repetition of the *la* (do not) of prohibition: eight interconnected *las* emphasize compassion, attachment, and the rejection of hatred, injustice and envy. The repetition is increasingly emphasized by the artist as he gradually thickens the line of the *la*, lending the calligraphy a new artistic dimension.

CAT. 88

Ayman Hassan

Soliloquy, 2022

Muraqqa' (fold-out book) bound in leather with twelve separate *qit'as* (fragments)
Ink, colour and gold on paper
Written in *thuluth* and *nasta'liq* scripts
30 × 20 cm each *qit'a*
Commissioned by the Ministry of Culture, Saudi Arabia
inv. IA 2022.8

This is a *Muraqqa'*, a type of album whose pages, belonging to different (and sometimes distant) eras and written in various calligraphies, are assembled and bound together. As pages unfold, scripts and illuminations come to life, lending their beauty to this anthology of the Arabic poetry heritage on divine love and shedding light on the importance of calligraphy during the Golden Age. These pages from different sources, bound together in a unique work, are a testimony to the passion people held for books and poetry in ancient times. Written in elegant *thuluth* and *nasta'liq* scripts, this *Muraqqa'* contains a selection of verses and divine invocations drawn from the poems of Imam al-Shafi'i and a number of other poets celebrating divine love.

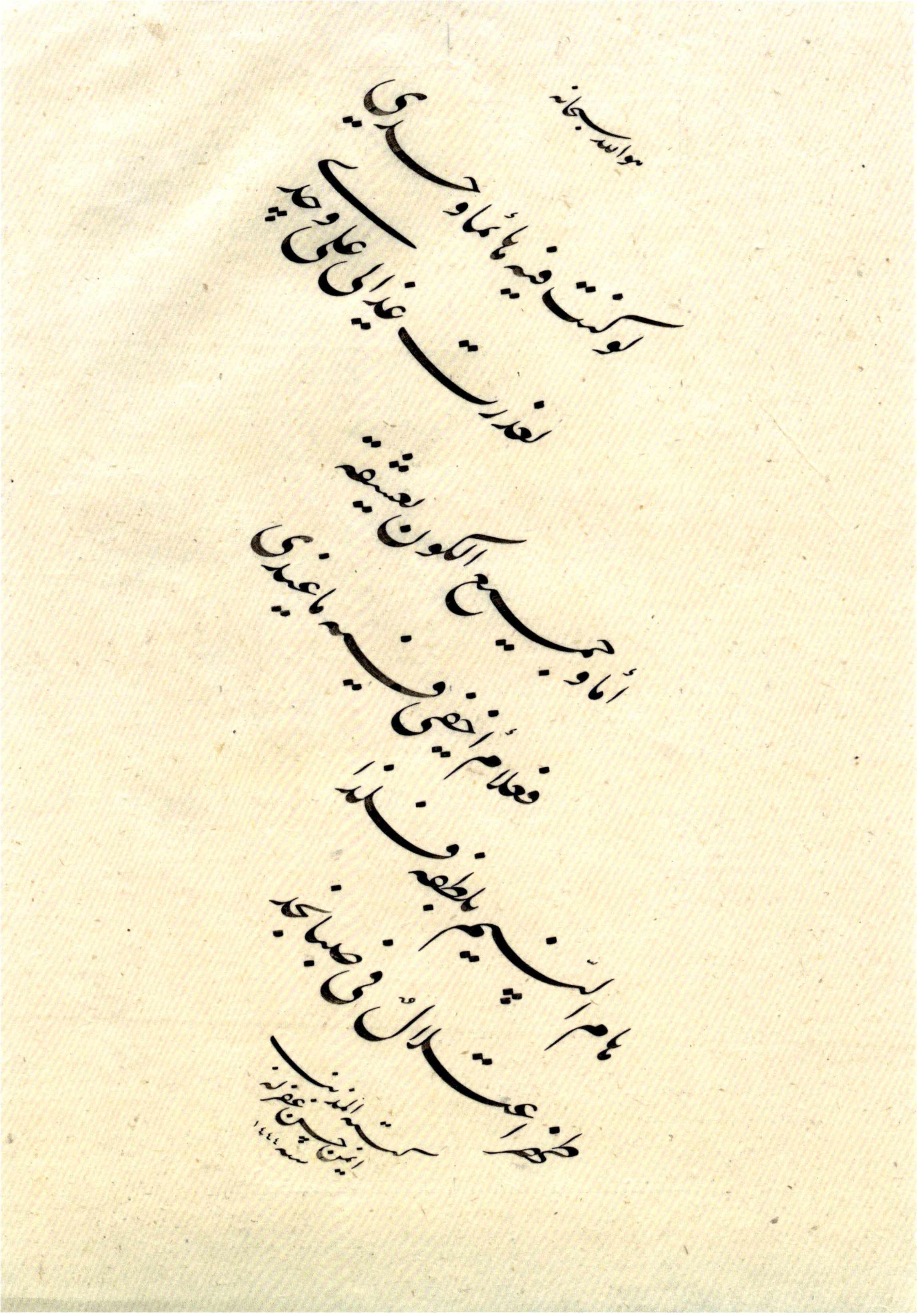

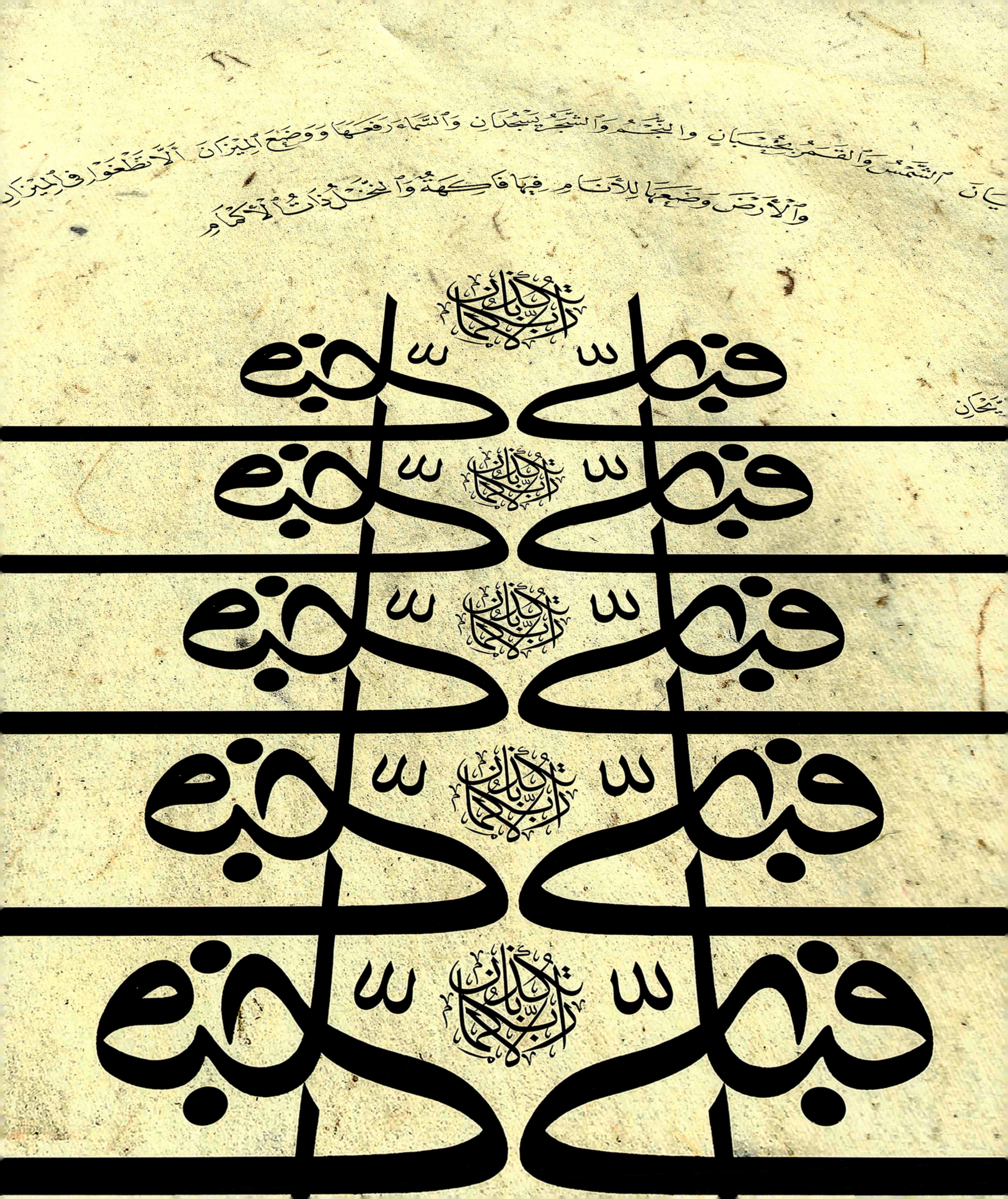
الشمس والقمر بحسبان والنجم والشجر يسجدان والسماء رفعها ووضع الميزان ألا تطغوا في الميزان
والأرض وضعها للأنام فيها فاكهة والنخل ذات الأكمام

CAT. 89

Zaki Al Hashimi
Surah ar-Rahman, 2022

Ink on paper
Written in *jaly thuluth* and *naskh* scripts
220 × 90 cm
Courtesy of Zaki Al Hashimi

With its symmetrical composition, this original piece carries a sense of harmony and aesthetic balance while preserving the non-recurrence of verses. The two most famous scripts used in the writing of the Holy Qur'an invite themselves onto this art piece, which is one of three original numbered copies in which the abbreviated word *fa-bi-ayyi* ("so which / so in what / then in what") is emphasized. The impact of this repeated question, when used in the surah *ar-Rahman*, is truly exceptional, as every verse in the Holy Qur'an holds the essence of its meaning.

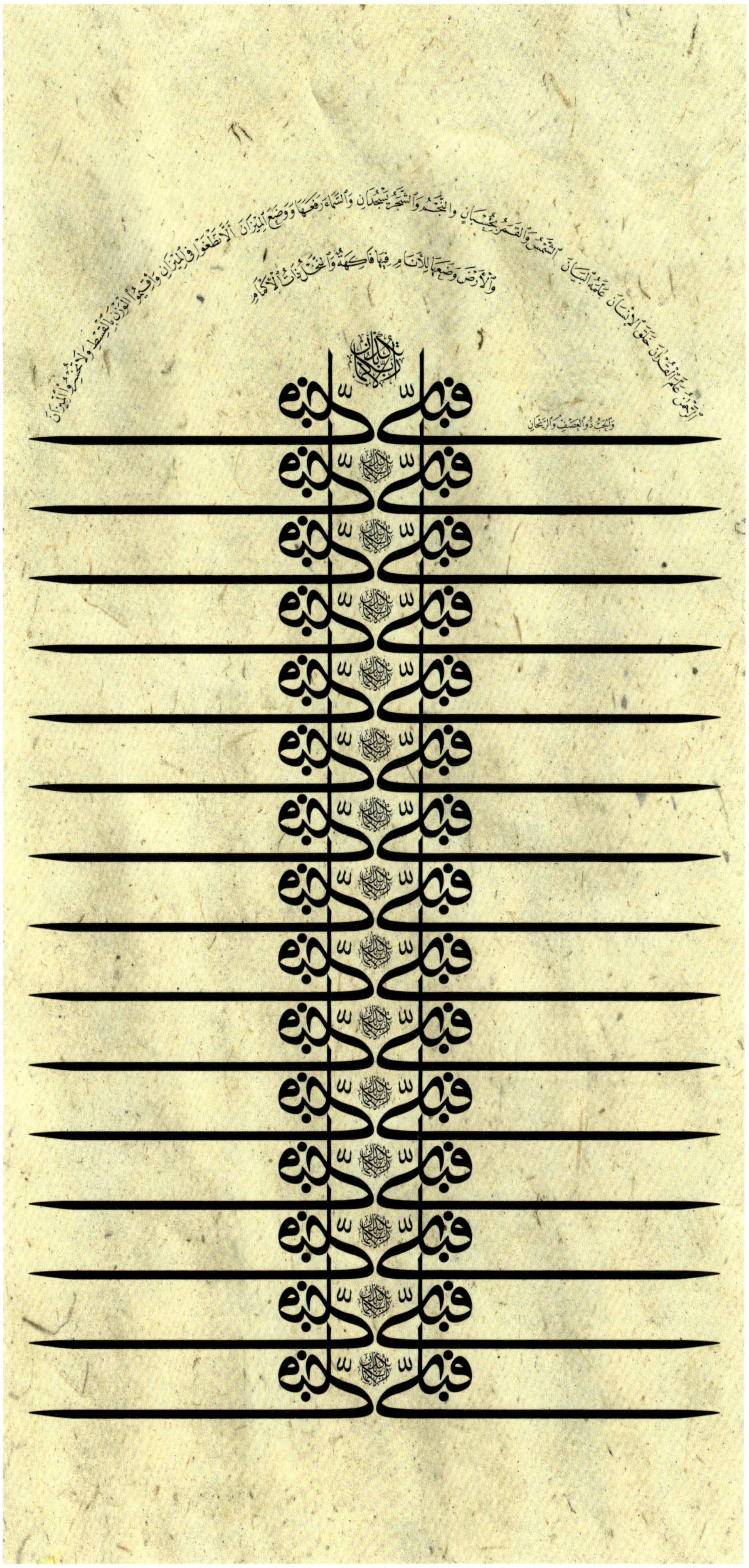

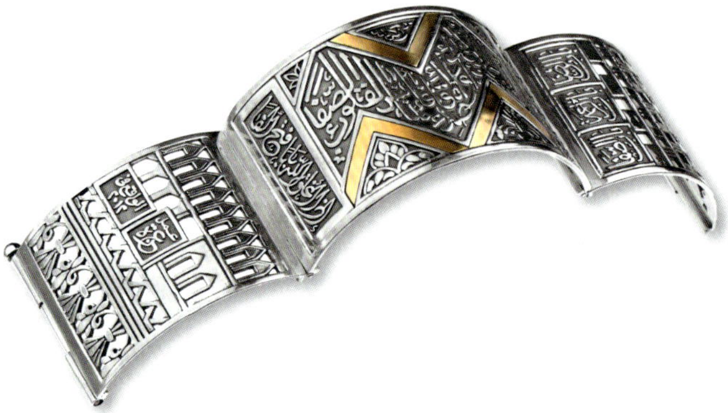

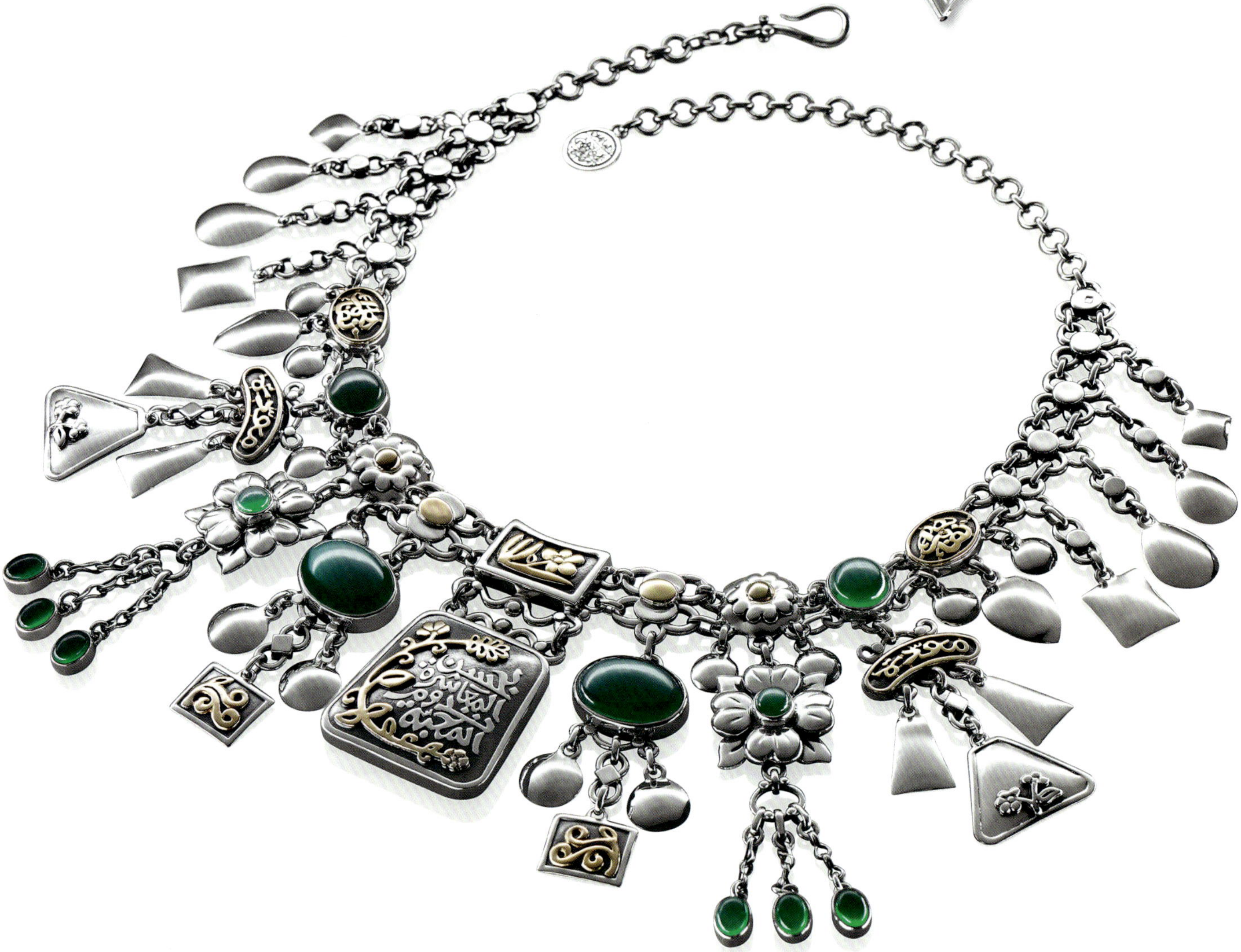

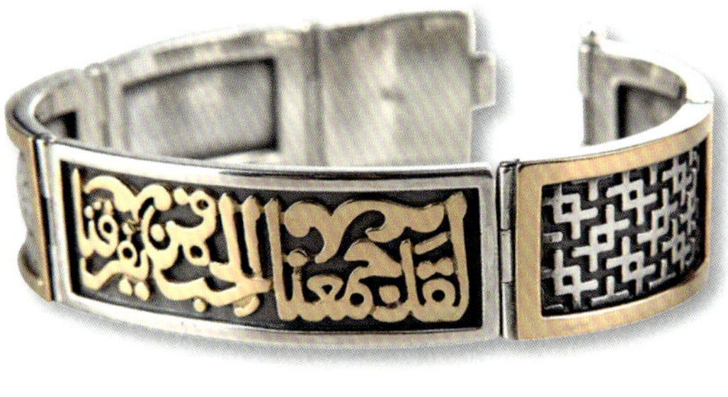

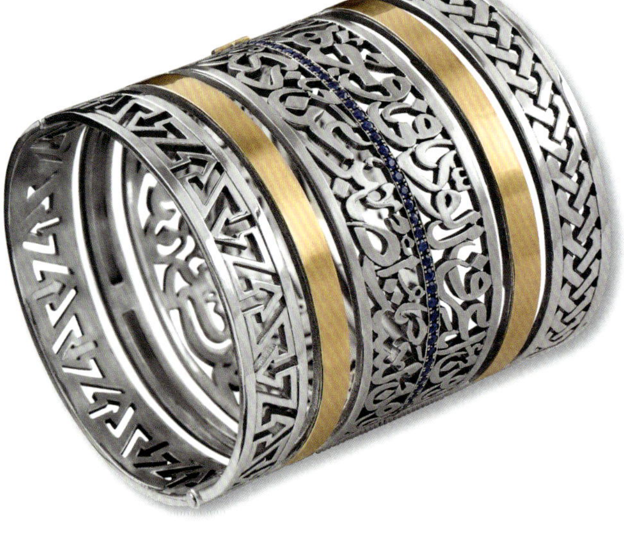

CAT. 90

Azza Fahmy
Poems Around the Neck, 2022

Jewellery pieces, jewellery stamps and video
Dimensions variable
Courtesy of Azza Fahmy (for the jewellery pieces)
Collection of the Ministry of Culture, Saudi Arabia
inv. CA 2022.24 (stamps only)

A passion for writing and poetry, a strong love for design and calligraphy and acquaintances among writers and poets took Azza Fahmy on a 50-year long journey whereby she fused her calligraphy into jewellery design. Having researched and studied the various scripts, delving into their specificities and historical variations, she designed a creative way to insert them into her pieces with stunning success, writing positive words into her creations such as Happiness, Joy, Love. "I love poetry and old Arabic sayings. Early on in my artistic journey, I realized this heritage had to be a part of the jewellery I make. This would be my message to the world: to convey the beauty of Arabic philosophy and literature", says Fahmy. The collection presented is unique, as every piece is unique, one being of Mameluke construction, the other engraved with Islamic poetry… Some of her pieces contain information about Hajj rituals. Each one is adorned with different styles of Arabic calligraphy, mixed with engraved ornamentation and cast with precious stones. Arabic calligraphy is either engraved or inlaid on jewellery and art pieces. The artist uses a combination of old and modern scripts, some typical of a given period or civilization, such as handwritten *kufi*, *maghribi*, *diwani* and lastly, Fahmy's own calligraphic style.

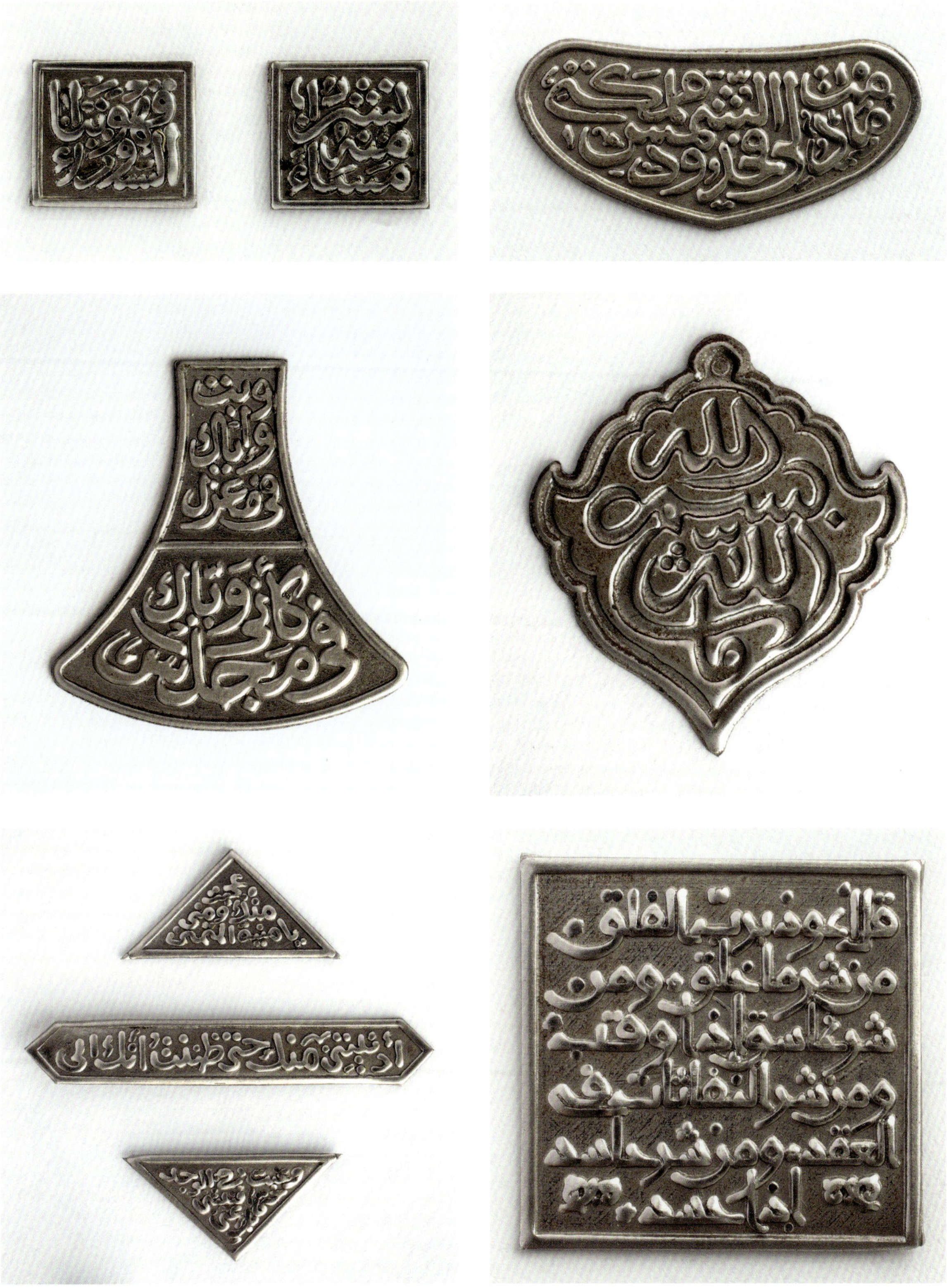

CAT. 91

Mohanad Qaisi

He Is Allah – There Is No God Worthy of Worship Except Him: Knower of the Seen and Unseen. He Is the Most Compassionate, Most Merciful. He Is Allah – There Is No God Except Him: The King, the Most Holy, the All-Perfect, the Source of Serenity, the Watcher of All, the Almighty, the Supreme in Might, the Majestic. Glorified Is Allah Far Above What They Associate with Him in Worship, 2020

Surah *al-Hashr*, verses 22–23
Japanese ink, 22k yellow gold and white gouache on natural banana leaf
Written in *thuluth* script
88 × 61 cm
Collection of the Ministry of Culture, Saudi Arabia
inv. IA 2022.6

The word "He" is repeated in every direction for five times, interspersed with eight golden circles bearing eight names of God. Surrounding the sacred text, the latter correspond to the eight angels who carry the throne of the All-Merciful God, as mentioned in verse 17 of surah *al-Haqqa*.

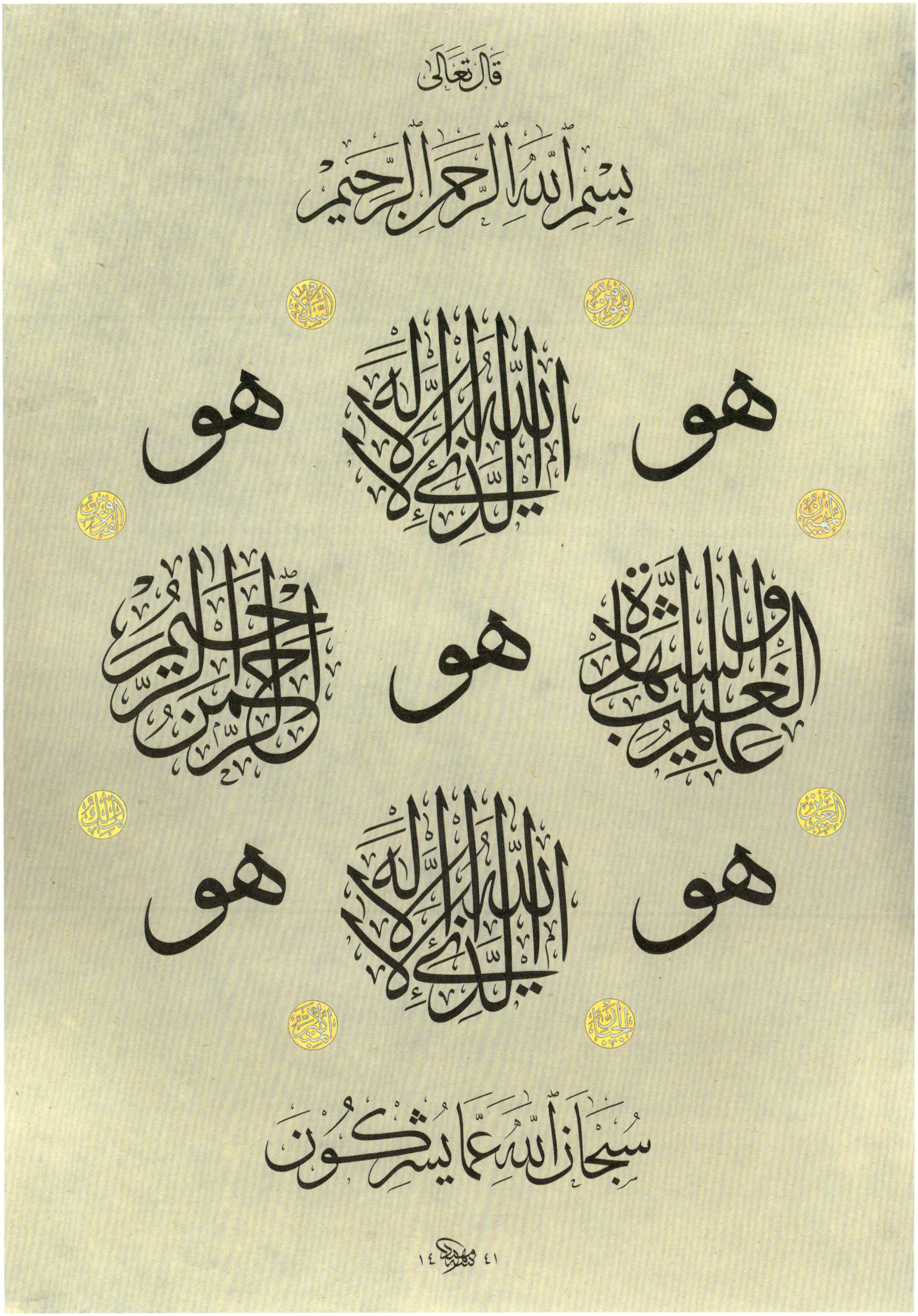
قال تعالى
بسم الله الرحمن الرحيم
هو الله الذي لا إله إلا هو
عالم الغيب والشهادة
هو
الرحمن الرحيم
هو الله الذي لا إله إلا هو
سبحان الله عما يشركون

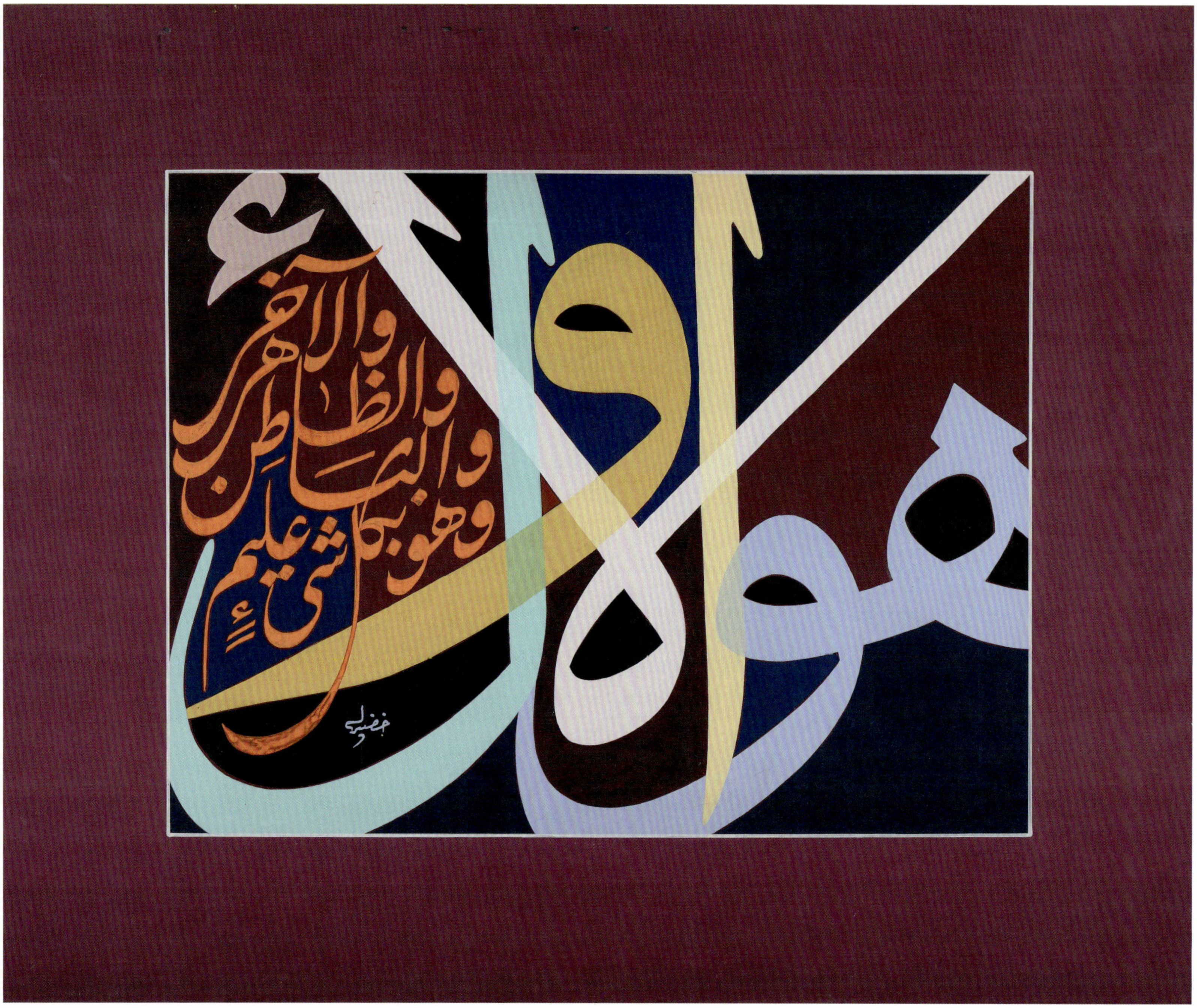

CAT. 92

Khodeir El-Borsaidy
He Is the First and the Last, and the Outward and the Inward; and He Is Knower of All Things, 1979
Surah *al-Hadid*, verse 3
Coloured ink on paper
Written in *diwani* and *nasta'liq* scripts
80 × 96 cm
Collection of the Ministry of Culture, Saudi Arabia
inv. IA 2022.13.9

A modern painting representing the following Qur'anic verse: "He is the first and the last, and the outward and the inward; and He is knower of all things" (surah *al-Hadid*, verse 3). This is a modern composition in terms of colour and script, as the first two words of the verse are written in *diwani* while the rest in an innovative mix of *diwani* and *nasta'liq*.

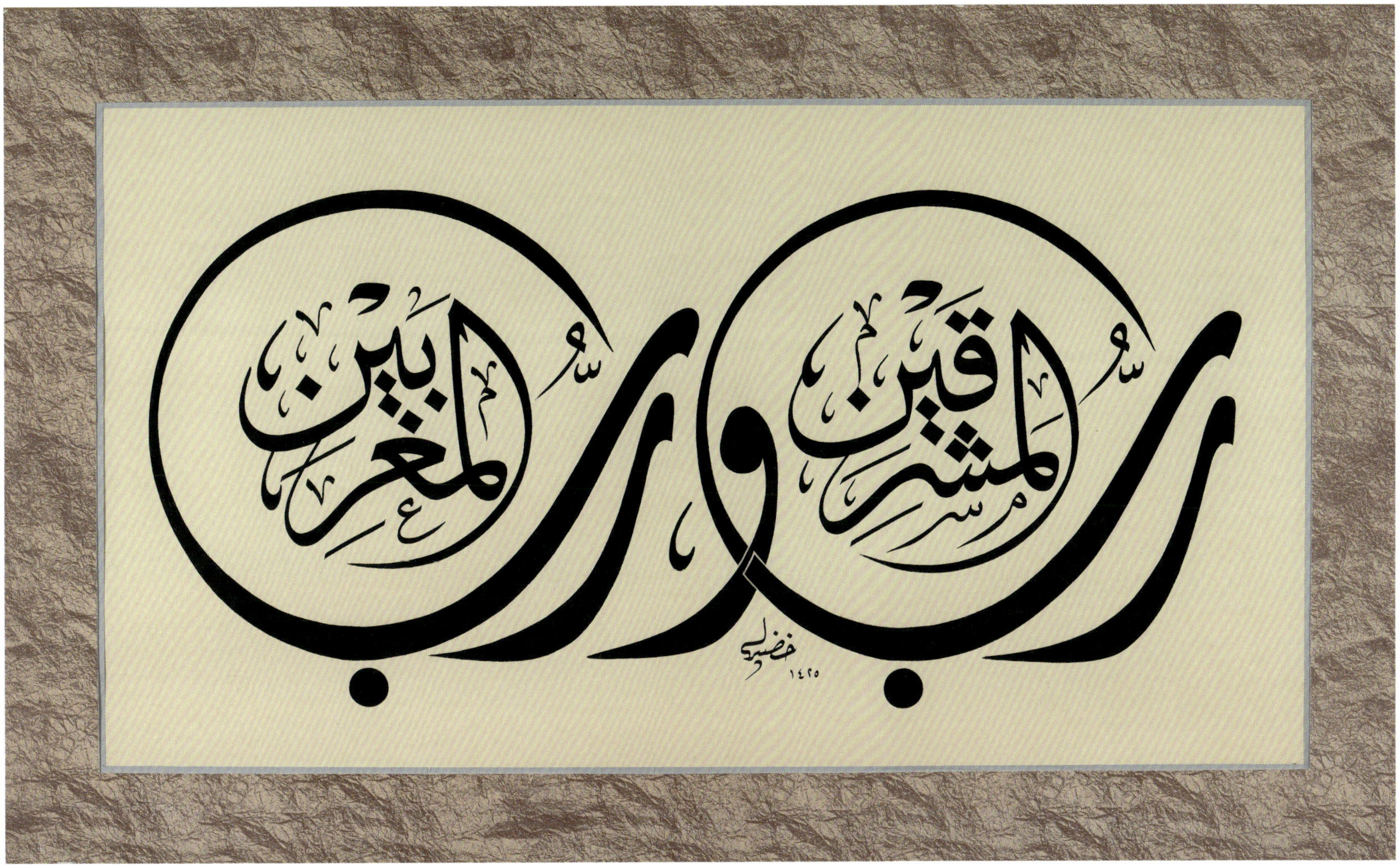

CAT. 93

Khodeir El-Borsaidy
Lord of the East and West, 2006

Ink on paper
Written in *thuluth* and *diwani* scripts
64 × 104 cm
Collection of the Ministry of Culture, Saudi Arabia
inv. IA 2022.13.10

A painting written in *thuluth* and *diwani* scripts forming the Qur'anic verse: "Lord of the two Easts and Lord of the two Wests" (surah *ar-Rahman*, verse 17), with the word *Rabb* (God) appearing two consecutive times in larger letters. The letter *ba'* elongates and curves to form a circular shape representing the all-encompassing divinity. As a result of the movement intrinsic to letters, no ornamentation was deemed necessary.

CAT. 94

Sameh Ismael
Untitled, 2022

Mixed media on paper
Diameter 140 cm
Collection of the Ministry of Culture, Saudi Arabia
inv. CA 2022.19

Executed in acrylic paint on canvas, this piece depicts a circle representing a cosmic pole, a passageway for the truth. An invisible ocean emerges under the artist's brush, suggesting questions with multiple answers. The blue indigo bursts on the scene amidst a cosmic dust of ochre and dark grey. Geometric white bands cut through the circular frame, adding both meaning and direction.

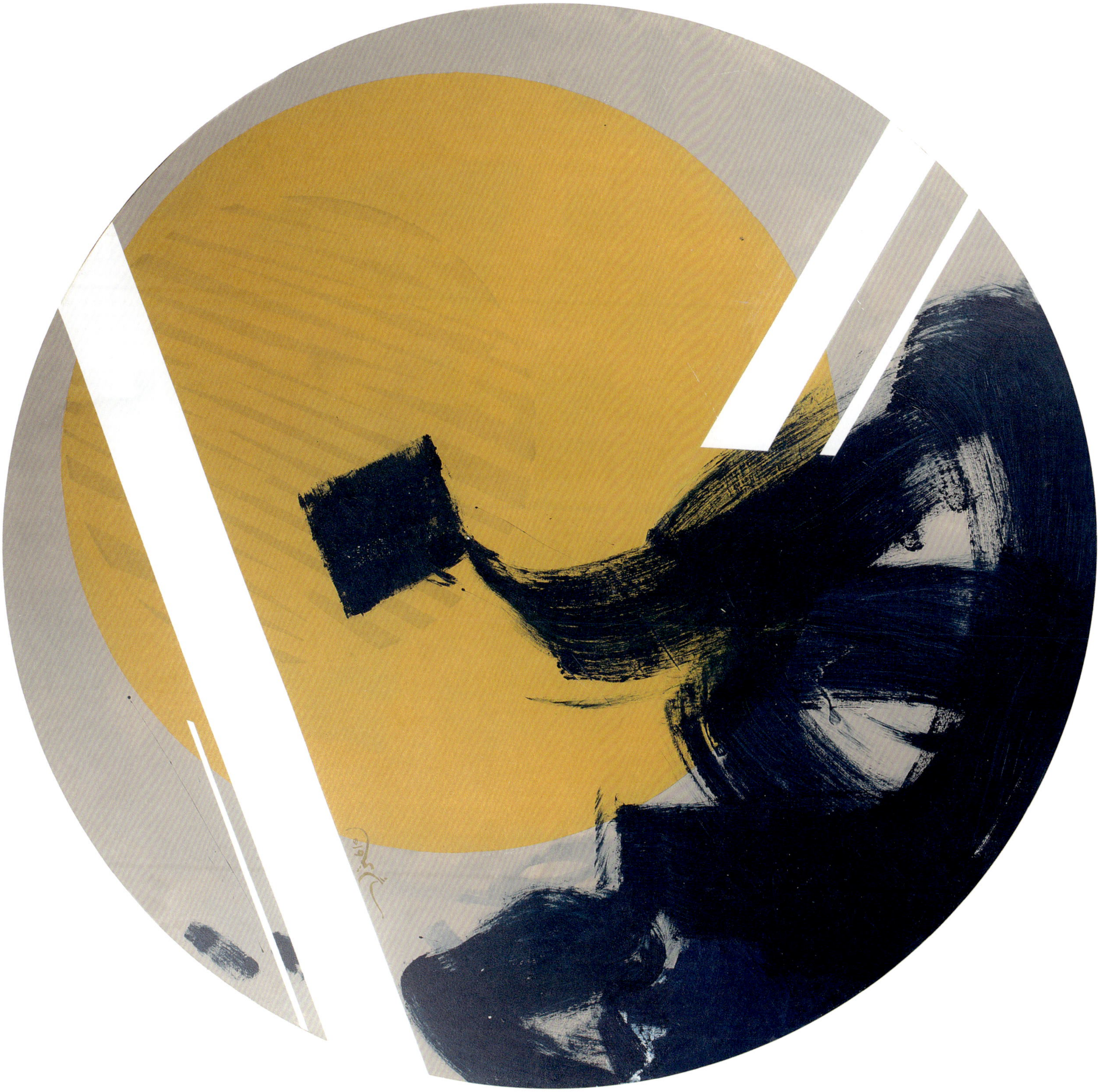

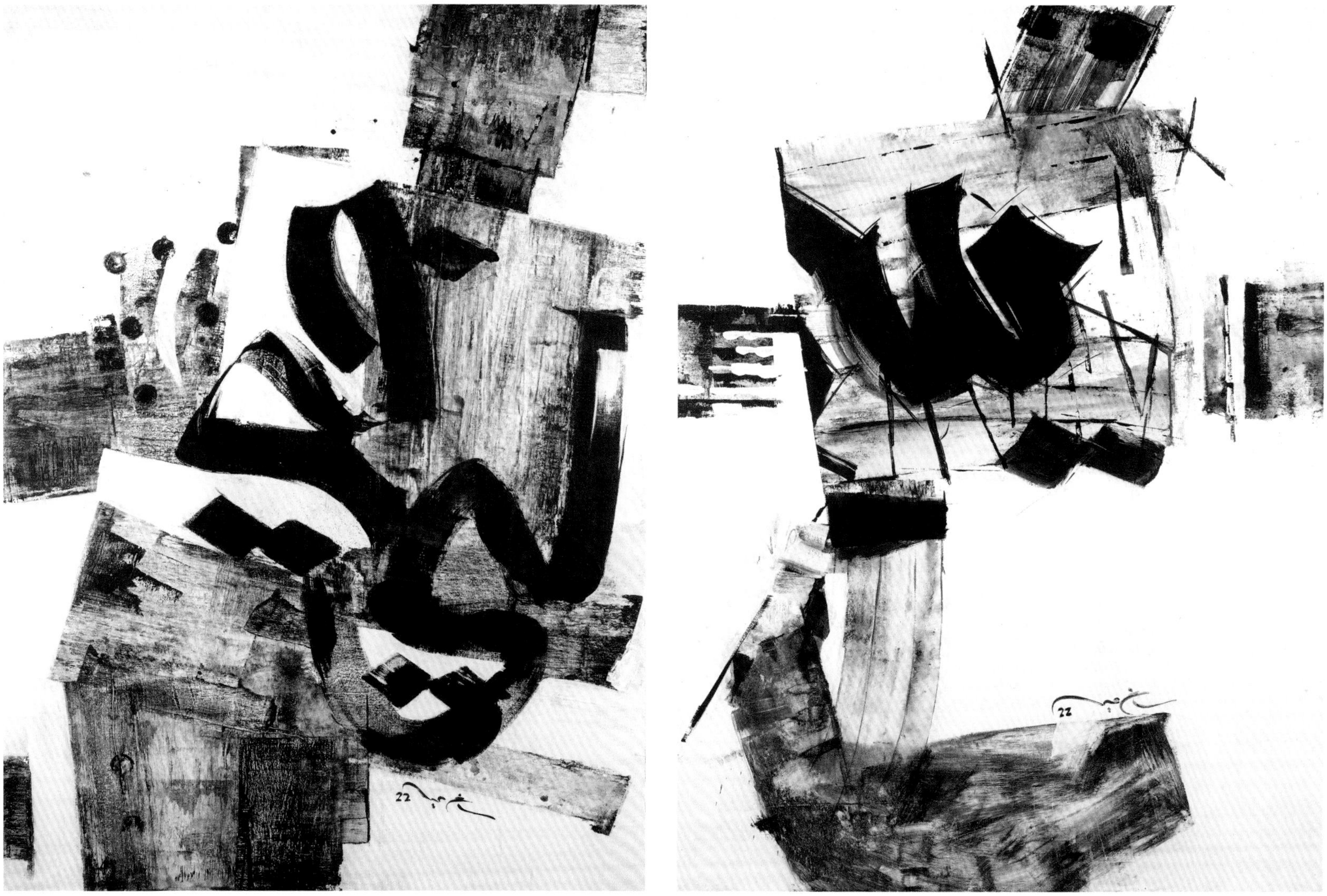

CAT. 95

Sameh Ismael

Untitled, 2022

Mixed media on paper
4 panels, 100 × 40 cm each
Collection of the Ministry of Culture, Saudi Arabia
inv. CA 2022.20

The composition consists of four panels in which Arabic letters arise like heroes enunciating words of wisdom. In the quatrain, the black and white tones emerge like an ascetic Sufi wrapped in the darkness of the night and the blackness of the eye, suggesting a visual revelation of an Arabic calligraphic text.

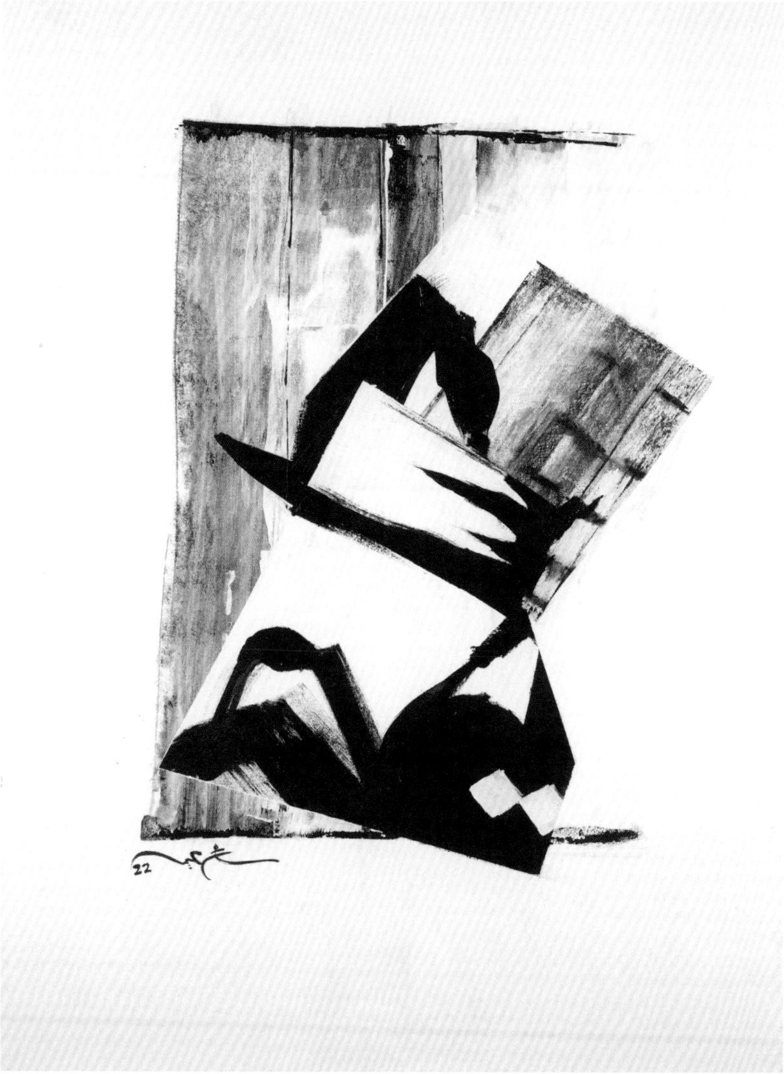

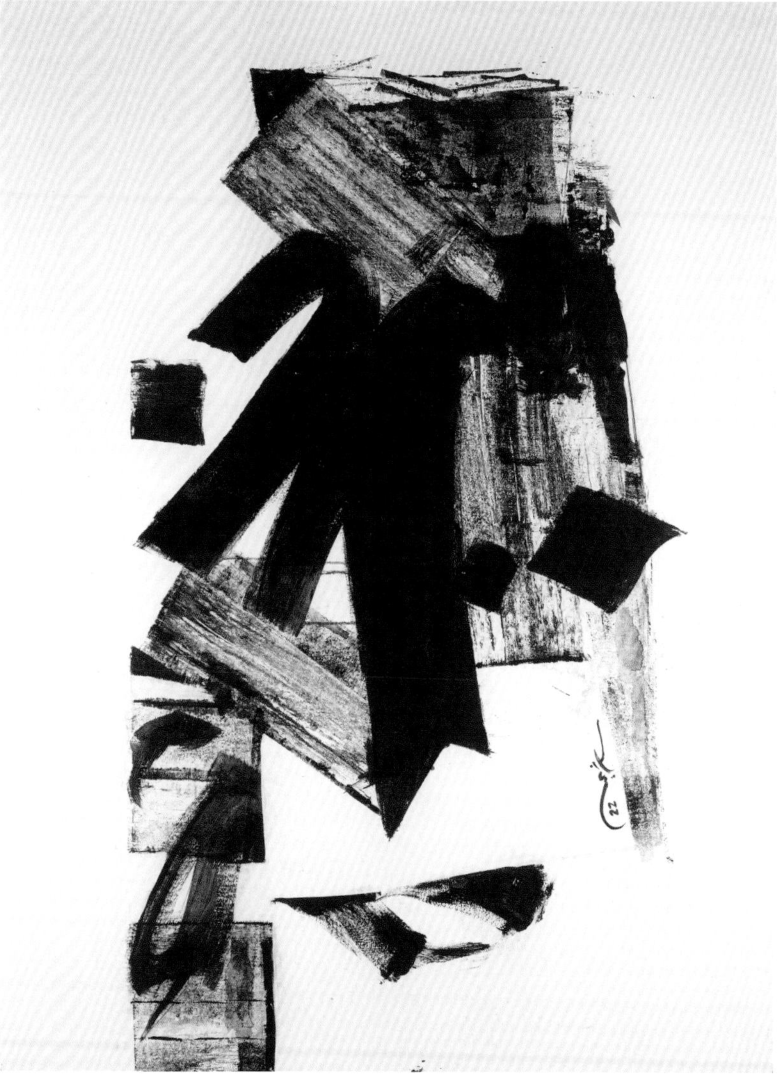

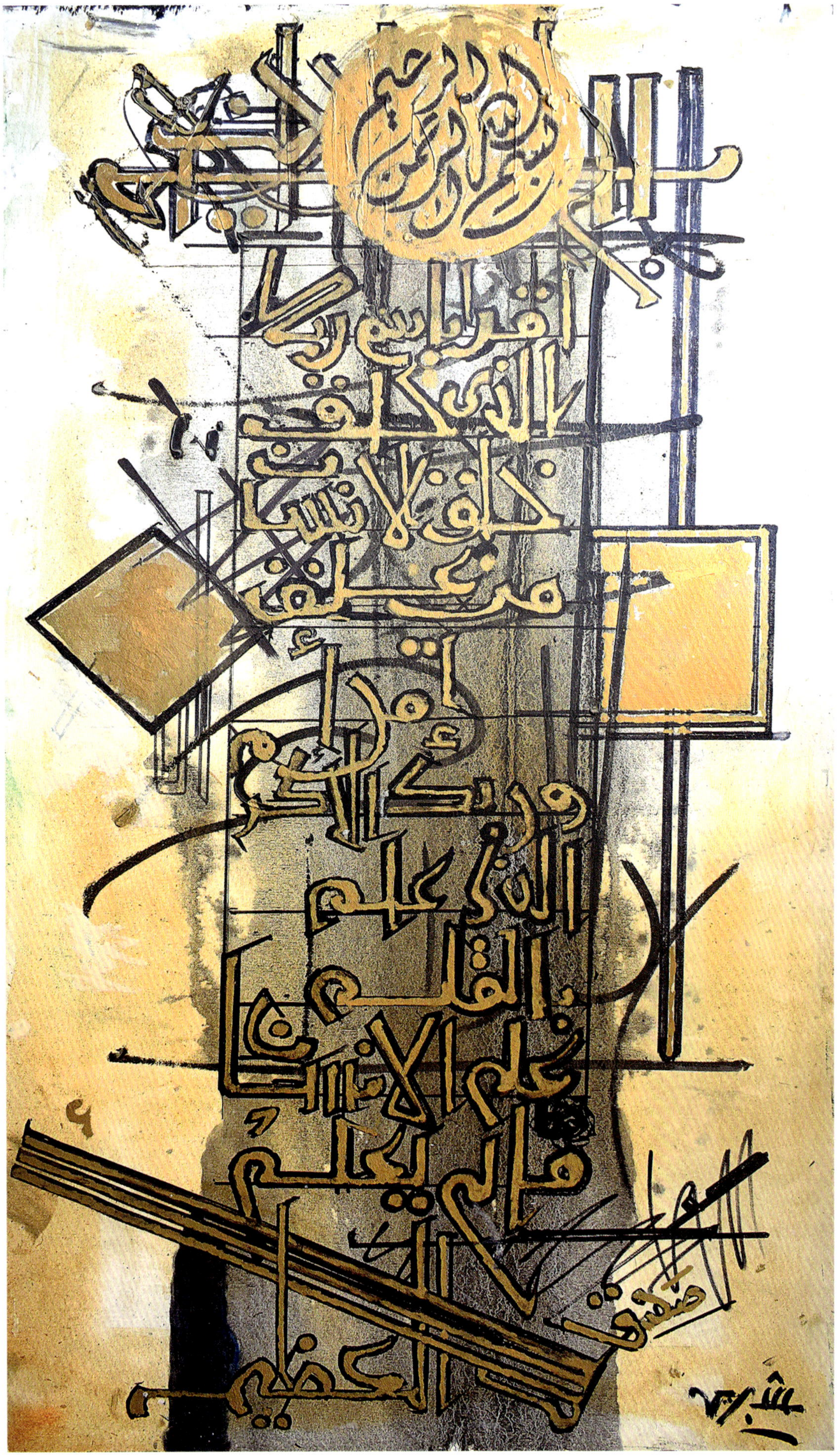

CAT. 96

Ahmad Shibrain

Untitled, 2006

Oil and gold colours on wood board
144 × 96 cm
Collection of Muhammad Ali Shibrain

Painted on a wooden support, *al-'Alaq*, the first revealed surah of the Holy Qur'an, displays a proud spiritual attachment to the Holy Book and a commitment to honour the Arabic language. Using Arabic cursive lines and abstractions to build a modern artwork through sound composition and aesthetic movement, letters of diverging forms intertwine, their curves and lines shaped according to different scripts such as the *riqa'* and *kufi* (heavily present in Shibrain's work). This piece shows a new awareness of perspective and all the dynamic potential intrinsic to modern Arabic letters and space: a new wholesome, thriving talent carrying within its folds a composition of old Islamic engravings and an elegant Arabic composition, as well as an enchanting African sense, whereby Arabia and Africa meet and generate a new vision and new forms of expression. It's a symbolic visual language made of shape and colour, with emphasis placed on blacks and greys. As black and sepia tones merge to evoke the Sudanese landscape, the elongation of black letters, their curved beauty and their coloured bodies introduce a sense of abstraction. To Shibrain, calligraphy is bound by no rules except those of beauty, which is deeply felt and represented in this vertical composition, a realm of free colours and simple shapes reminiscent of a journey initiated long ago with the Holy Book. Letters in various shades of black, from raven black to délavé, pervade an elongated rectangular board, a reminder of the *Khalawi* practice board in Sudanese Qur'anic schools. Simple squares flank both sides of the work, evoking a balcony, with frame ornamentation in pale gold colour. Shape, movement and colour combined as letters, geometric shapes and ornaments intersect while retaining their own specificities, whispering to the imagination, becoming a source of inspiration, and spontaneously communicating in this language of beauty, nature, depth and authenticity.

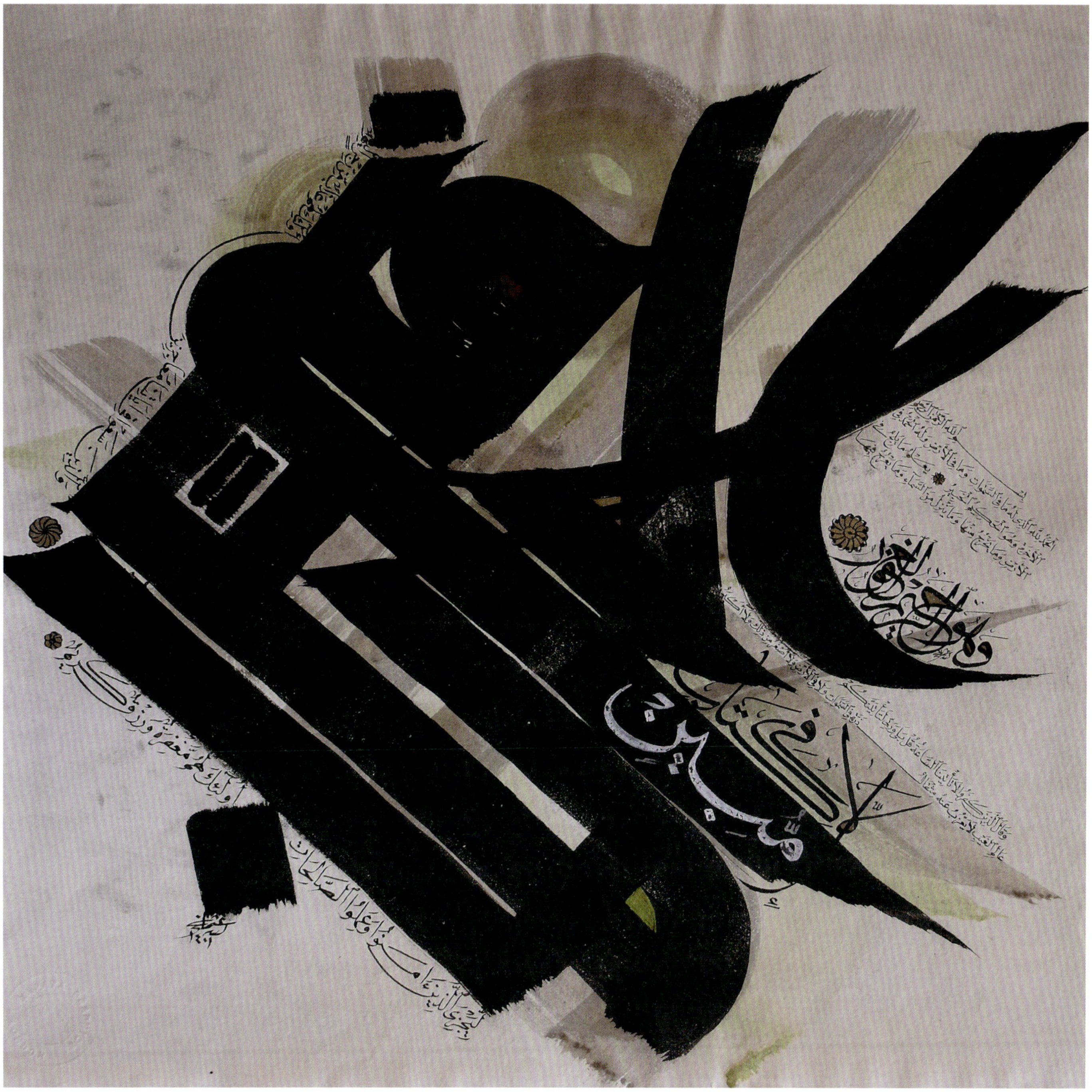

CAT. 97

Osman Waqialla
Who Gives You Provision from the Heavens and the Earth, 1981

Surah *Saba'a*, verses 1–5 and 24
Ink on paper
Written in *kufi*, *naskh* and *thuluth muhaqqaq* scripts
45 × 45 cm
Collection of Hana Waqialla

The artist used the verse *illa fi kitab* ("but it is written in a clear book") in the old *kufi* script with a balanced slanting structure as the main element of the painting.
In the background, in smaller *naskh* and *thuluth* script, an image of the *bismilah* revolves around it, and the word *mubin* (clear) is added in white. A coloured shadow of the initial text moves dynamically in the background, endowing the painting with balance and emphasis.

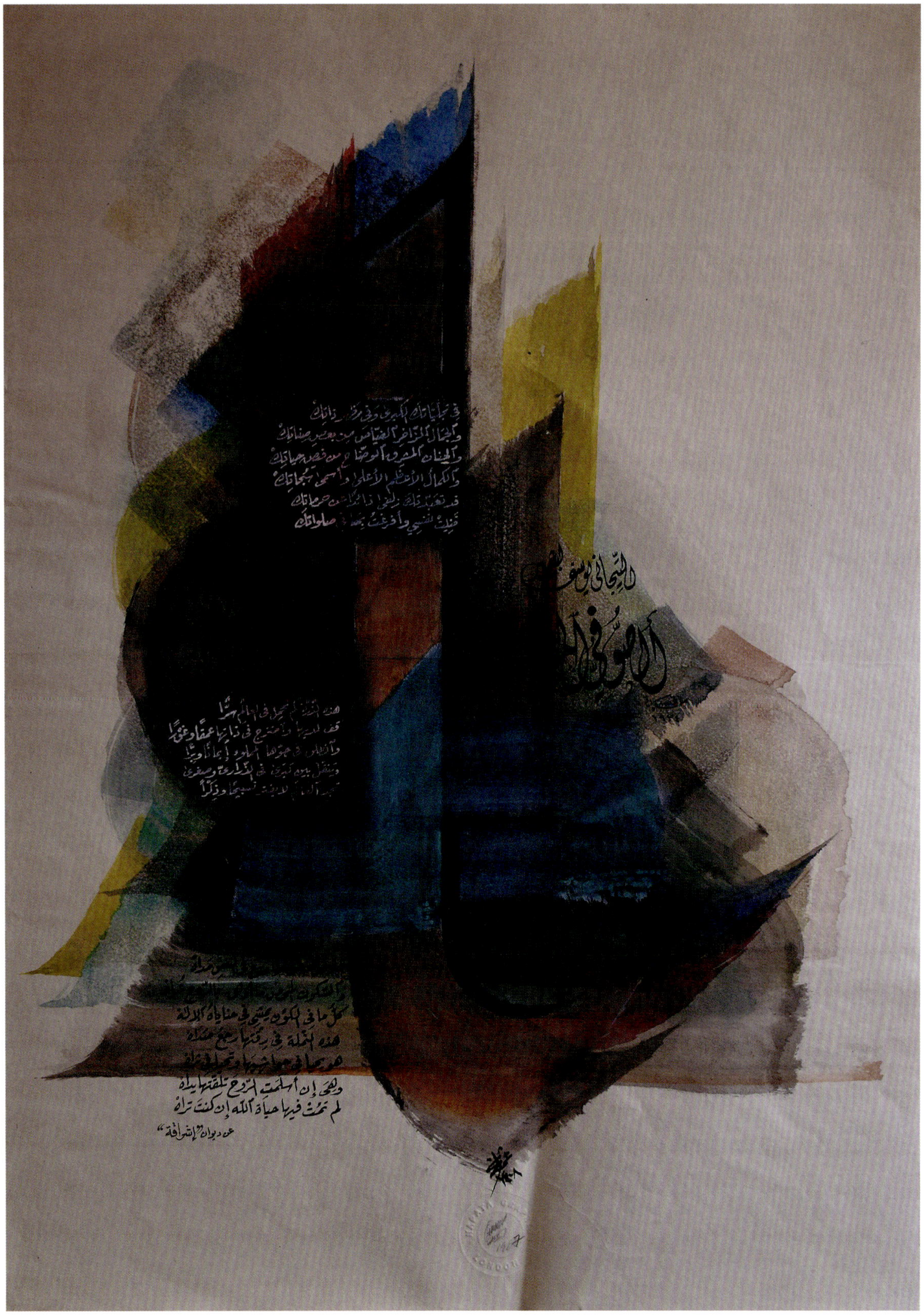

CAT. 98

Osman Waqialla

Tormented Mystic, 1987

Ink on paper
Written in *kufi*, *riqa'* and *diwani* scripts
58 × 41 cm
Collection of Hana Waqialla

One of Waqialla's distinguishing works, this painting represents his vision of the poem *The Tortured Sufi* by the Sudanese poet Al-Tijani Yusuf Bashir, included in his *Ishraqa* collection. With its interlocking coloured configurations, the panel has a multi-dimensional appearance. The shaded backgrounds present coloured, translucent and large letters of the old *kufi* script.
The segments of the three verses are written prominently in white *riqa'* script. On the right of the painting, the name of the poet and the title of the poem appear in a medium-sized *diwani* script, evoking a beautiful musical harmony. The painting is rich in scripts and colours that reflect the artist's love for poetry, which is expressed in his unique visual language.

CAT. 99

Osman Waqialla

***Surah al-'Ankabut*, 1987**

Ink and colour on paper
Written in *kufi*, *naskh* and *thuluth* scripts
49 × 31.5 cm
Collection of Hana Waqialla

The painting is composed of balanced interlockings of various verses of surah *al-'Ankabut*. The verses always start in small *naskh* script, then the painting is topped by the letters *kha* and *ta* in translucent black. This allows the appearance of part of a verse in *thuluth* script, *wa la takhtuhu bi-yaminika* ("nor could you write it with your own hand"). It is written within a black *ta* letter in order to endow the diverse black shadows and the variety of Arabic fonts with visual richness, emphasizing the meaning of the verses. Coloured gilded shadows of the letters *ta* and *kha* move in the background of the painting to achieve visual balance and add emphasis.

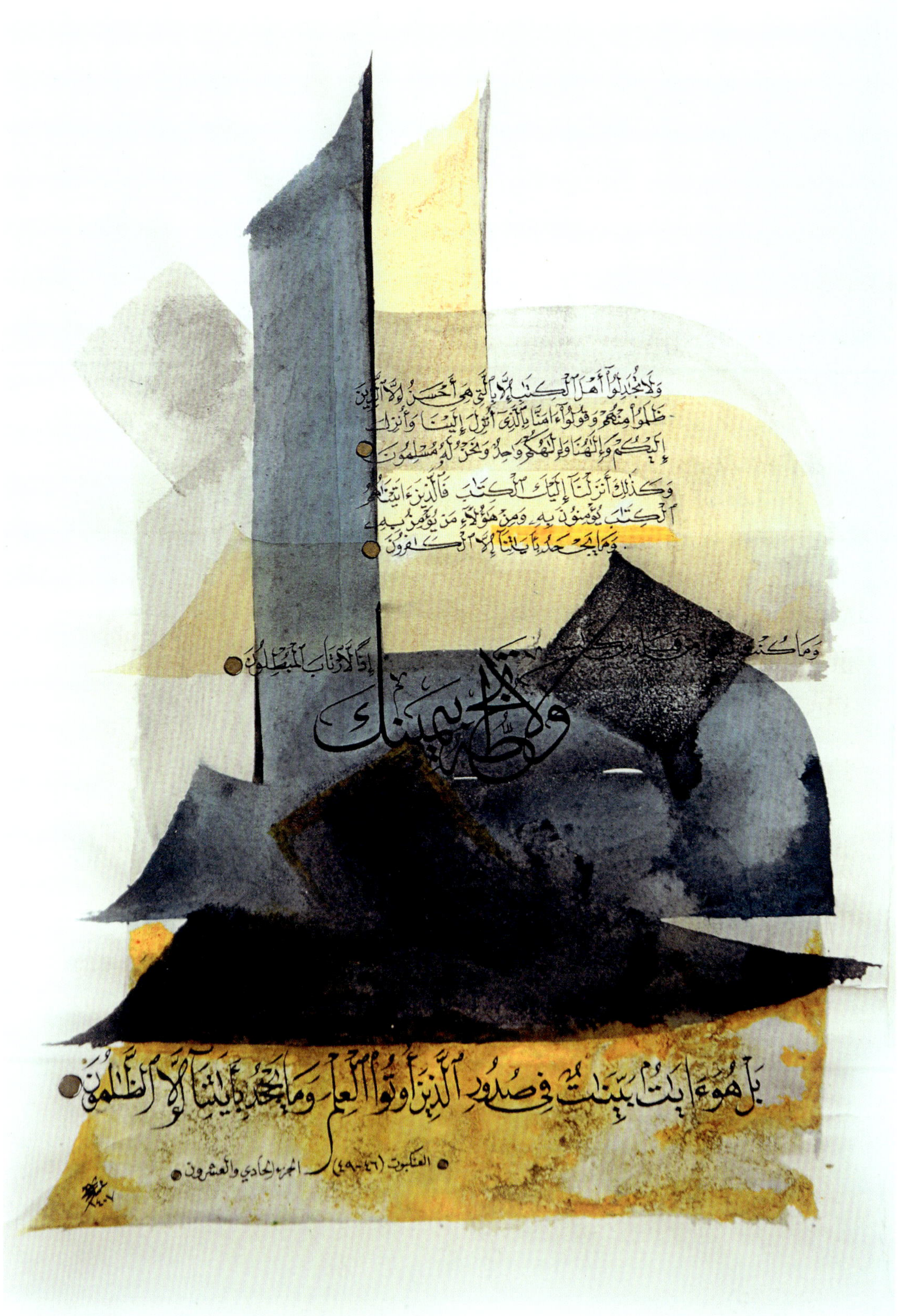

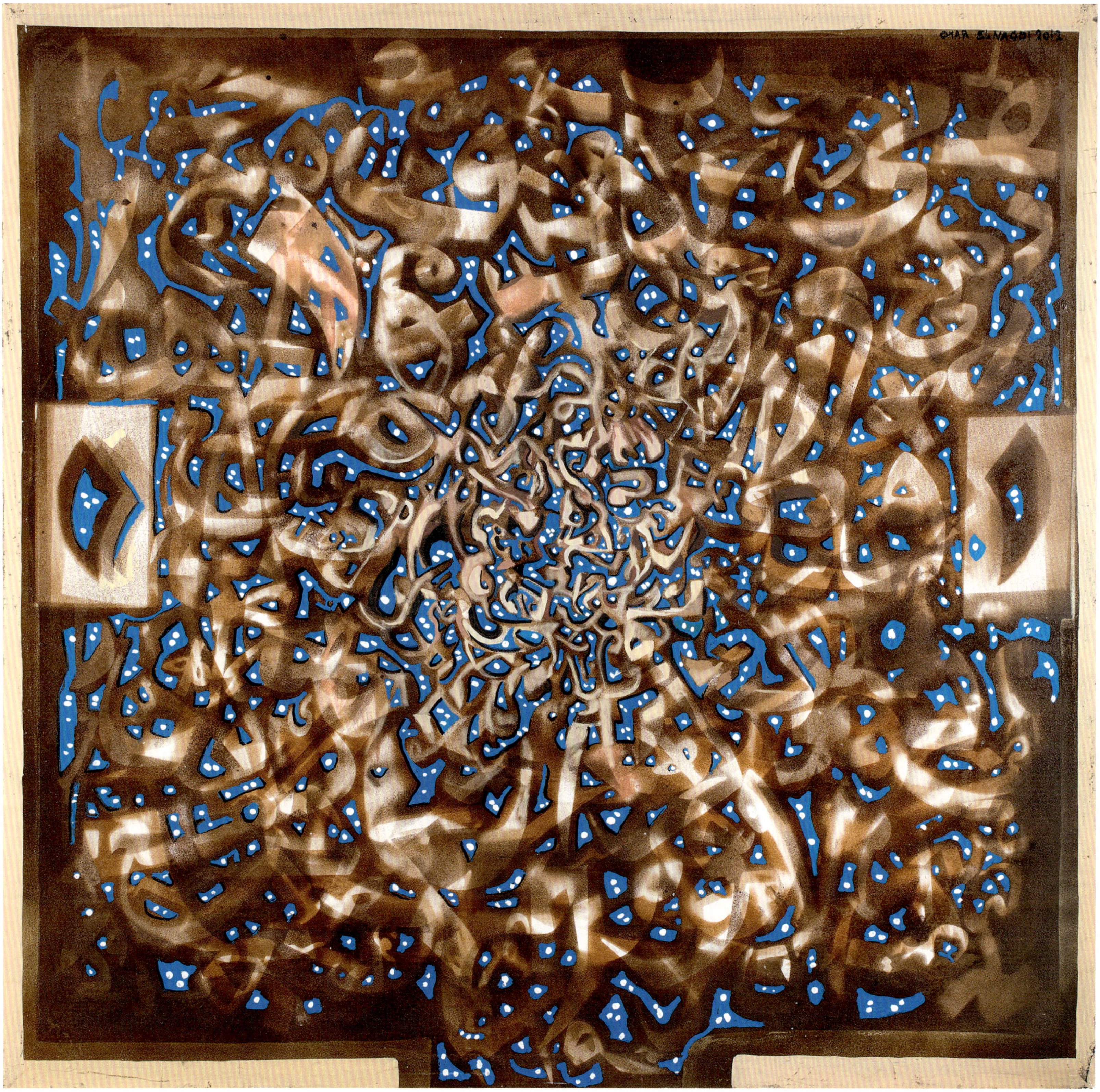
OMAR EL NAGDI 2012

CAT. 100

Omar El-Nagdi

***From the Kingdom of God*, 2012**

Oil on canvas
150 × 150 cm
Collection of Islam O. El-Nagdi

This graphic oil painting is a combination of intertwining Arabic letters and words in brown and sepia, representing the majesty of the Unique, the Only, the One God. In the space of the canvas, the letters *ha'* and *alif* float across the dark blue outer space of this perpetual universe that knows no beginning and no end. Adopting different sizes and proportions, the letters take shape, combine and intertwine so as to give the illusion of a relief in arabesque shape that opens up towards the sky of this wide universe, following the procession to hail the One God, Creator of the Universe.

CAT. 101

Nasser Alaswadi

***Love*, 2012**

Oil on canvas
194 × 114 cm
Private collection

Nasser Alaswadi sees calligraphy as a way of expressing thoughts and feelings without them being necessarily tied to language. His creativity feeds on a wide variety of styles and media as he finds his inspiration in Arabic letters, words, forms, religion and music. In this piece, letters and words are drawn neither on a straight line nor horizontally. Identical and yet tangled and lost in the imaginary space of the painting, they are painted and stacked separately. Alaswadi exhausts any style of Arabic writing to create a world in which his abstract work expresses itself beyond language. Inspired by everyday events and at the same time making use of the energy and light inherent in calligraphed words, he puts writing at the heart of his work as he forces letters to stray from their everyday usage, inviting viewers into a world of sign and visuality.

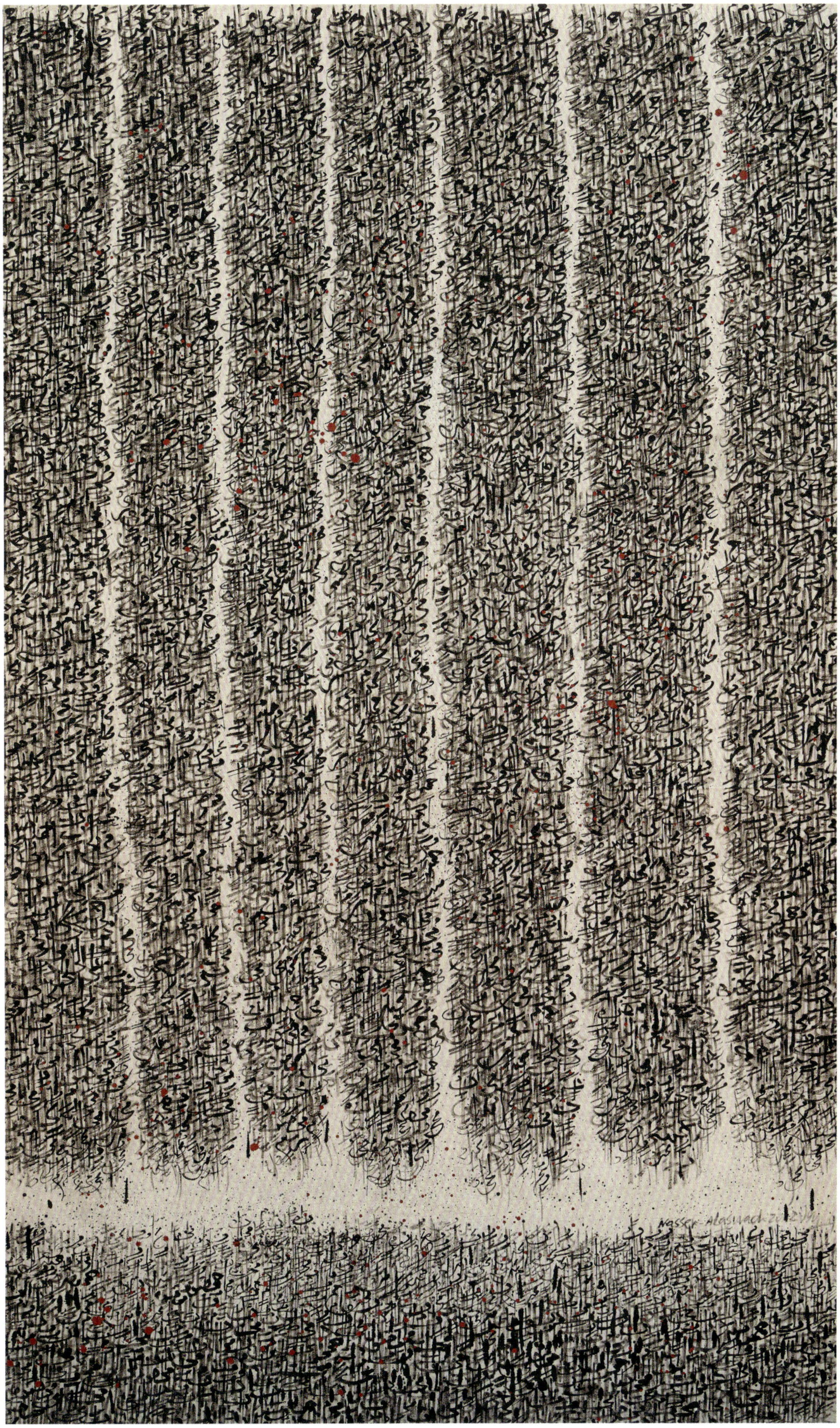

In Praise of Visual Poems

Ghassan Al-Khunaizi

Oh, wouldn't it be better if you followed these words until the end,
until the beginning,
if, with a pure heart, you cast your eyes less on meaning,
and more on flourishes within these lines.

Those common words borrowed,
and then released into this shared ether,
in this deafening clamour,
stealthily,
amble back to you
like an echo,
contaminated with places seen,
polluted by their own nature
uttering all that is plain and ordinary
like a chorus line.

Oh that we knew! Did we
give birth to a new creation, or
were we the receptacle of scrolls of old,
devoid of any new vision
under an all-encompassing sky,
devoid
of any new words
to be bequeathed to others.

Unseen, unfelt and yet
Seen and felt,
carvings, in the olden cave of childhood,
at times, deaf, by nature,
at others,
insignificant in the towering face of destiny,
prompt
a first step,
free from any destination
towards a path of becoming.

Oh they whose sole concern is to accompany those,
whose meditative steps
meandered
between a budding leaf here,
and a dying leaf there,
tracing
this story
that says all,
that
says naught, and yet
leaves on
the lips a lingering bitter
and sweet taste.

Here, you find yourself in no need

of

fallen

words

even though

at this moment

you are travelling

wherever

the wind

blows,

like you did

the moment

of your inception.

APPENDIX

Artists' biographies

SARA AL ABDALI

Sara Al Abdali was born in Jeddah in 1989. Her art is a means of transmitting Arab culture and Islamic philosophy through graffiti, comics and paintings. She attended a master's programme at The Prince's Foundation School of Traditional Arts, London, where she experimented with various traditional crafts from the Islamic world: woodwork, ceramics, miniature painting, mosaics, and plaster carving. One of Saudi Arabia's first graffiti artists, she likes to say that "Street Art is the perfect medium to experiment with". She took part in international art festivals such as RHIZOMA at the 55th Venice Biennale (2013) and #COMETOGETHER by Edge of Arabia, East London (2012).

LAMA ABDULRAHMAN

Born in 1999, Lama Abdulrahman is a self-taught Saudi artist whose passion for Islamic geometry earned her recognition across the world. In 2021, the Athr Gallery in Jeddah devoted an exhibition to Abdulrahman displaying one of her innovative signature pieces, *Tranquility*, where Arabic calligraphy proportions and ratios (*wazn* and *thogol*) morphed into a geometric construction. Today, as part of her mission to preserve this form of art, she seeks to teach Islamic geometry to the public, while also working on the advancement of this form of traditional art.

ETEL ADNAN

Etel Adnan (1925–2021) was an artist, poet and writer, born in Beirut to a Syrian father and a Greek mother. Adnan completed her studies at the Sorbonne Université, Paris and Harvard University in the United States. Then she taught philosophy of art in California. In the 1960s, the discovery of Japanese accordion notebooks led her to explore a mode of expression that intertwined writing, drawing and painting. The format of these *leporellos*, which can be spread over several metres, combines the temporal dimension of the creation with a narrative that is continuously reconstructed. The *leporello* pattern implies working in a small, flat format, resulting in Adnan's recurrent backache. She also wrote poetry, novels and plays. Her works are part of many private collections and museums around the world, including Tunis Museum of Modern Art, Moderna Museet in Stockholm, Sursock Museum, Beirut, Institut du Monde Arabe, Paris, The British Museum, London, the World Bank Collection and the National Museum for Women in the Arts, Washington, DC.

FAIG AHMED

Faig Ahmed is an Azerbaijani artist, born in Sumqayit in 1982 and living in Baku. He graduated from the Sculpture Department of the Azerbaijan State Academy of Fine Arts in 2004 and represented his country in 2007 at its inaugural pavilion at the Venice Biennale. His versatility prompted him to work on many art forms; however, he is most famous for his surrealist sculptural textiles. His conceptual creations, manufactured by a group of skilled weavers using traditional Azerbaijani techniques, transpose a traditional decorative craft and the visual language of carpets into contemporary artworks built according to his own design and vision. Faig Ahmed is part of a new wave of contemporary artists who revisit traditional arts innovatively. He has contributed to establishing the principles of conceptual works that break away from tradition and push the craft into the context of global contemporary art.

YUSEF ALAHMAD

Yusef Alahmad is a Saudi artist and designer born in 1983 and living in Washington, DC. He earned a Master of Fine Arts degree in graphic design from the Academy of Art University, San Francisco in 2016 and a bachelor of Fine Arts in liberal studies, with a focus on fine arts and graphic design, from Marymount University. His work is a vibrant and futuristic exploration of Middle Eastern heritage, portraying cultural and traditional elements in non-traditional ways. By incorporating visuals from his upbringing in Saudi Arabia and blending these design archetypes with his ever-changing environment, he seeks to create visual connections between cultures. Alahmad was the inaugural resident artist at the King Abdulaziz Center for World Culture Ithra's Majlis residency program in New York City. His work has been exhibited at numerous institutions worldwide.

NASSER ALASWADI

Born in 1978, Nasser Alaswadi grew up in Taiz, Yemen. At the age of 16, he started his training in architecture at the Fine Arts Institute in Sanaa and exhibited his first works in 2001. Always keen to translate his experience into artistic creation, he selects a writing style that helps him convey passion and meaning to his paintings as he draws inspiration from daily realities, rural landscapes, architecture and crowds on the streets. As calligraphic shapes take form on his canvas, he finds in them a way to express feelings, emotions and thoughts, yet without resorting to their semantic meaning. He finds his source of inspiration in Arabic letters, words, forms, religion, and music.

SARA ALHARBALI

Sara Alharbali is a Syrian architect and urban designer, born in 1990 and raised in Dubai, UAE. She holds a bachelor's degree in architecture from the American University of Sharjah and a master's degree in urban design from the University of California, Berkeley, USA. Alharbali is the founder of the Tajrid Design brand where her various interests converge – from industrial art and material fabrication to her passion for cities' morphology and the impact of urbanism on civilizations. She was the first artist to introduce the spectrogram as an expression of spiritual art for the recitation of the Holy Qur'an, an innovation for which she won the Grand Award for Emerging Artists Prize at the World Art Dubai 2021. In her *Revelation Spectrogram* series, she revives Arabic calligraphy as a spiritual form of art that also reflects the Arabic character, culture, and civilization; she thus disseminates into the world an unconventional way of expressing the blessings of the Holy words. Her art products are abstract depictions of verses from the Holy Qur'an in different formats, such as wall art, lighting pieces and jewellery. Each of her artworks narrates a deep story and carries a message that is always inspiring.

MAJID ALYOUSEF

For over 30 years, Saudi-born calligrapher Majid Alyousef has dedicated himself to the practice of his art, whereby he combines intricate craftsmanship with experimental composition. To him, "calligraphy depends on the anatomy of letters, words, their composition and the ties to other design-related disciplines". He holds a bachelor's degree in Fine Arts from Iraq and a master's degree in interactive design and game development from the Savannah College of Art and Design (USA). Following a career as a design director, he left the corporate world to focus on art. His exhibitions have travelled far and wide and his works are included in prestigious collections across the globe.

IBRAHIM AL ARAFI

For the past 17 years, Ibrahim Al Arafi has been teaching Arabic calligraphy at the Holy Mosque in Mecca. A renowned calligrapher himself, he is the author of *Mashq, Teaching the Balance of Arabic Calligraphy*. Viewers have come to recognize him, over 128 episodes, as the producer and presenter of the *Mashq TV Show* on the Saudi Cultural Channel. Not one to shy away from challenges, he presided over several competition juries in Saudi Arabia, such as the prestigious Okaz International Awards for Arabic Calligraphy. Ambassador of Arabic calligraphy, he is also a reference for Arabic calligraphy designers in Saudi Arabia.

LARA ASSOUAD

Lara Assouad is a Lebanese-Canadian graphic and type designer born in 1977 and living in Dubai. She holds a bachelor's degree in graphic design from the American University of Beirut and a master's degree in Arabic scripts and type design from the Atelier national de recherche typographique in Nancy (France). Her mentor, calligrapher Samir Sayegh, taught her Islamic art and arabesque. For "Typographic Matchmaking", a project initiated by the Khatt Foundation, she developed with Fred Smeijers *Fresco Arabic*, which won the Certificate of Excellence in Typography (2008) from the Type Directors Club (TDC) in New York. In collaboration with Dar Onboz and Aswat al Abjadiyyah, she worked on two children's books that were both exhibited in Munich at the Haus der Kunst in 2010 and then at the Agial Art Gallery in Beirut at the end of the year. *Tabati*, the typeface developed for the two books, was also awarded a Certificate of Excellence in Typography in 2011 from the Type Directors Club in New York. Lara Assouad was longlisted for the Jameel Prize 4 in 2016 for her "Modular Arabic Typography" project. In 2019, she held her first solo exhibition, *Alphabets*, at Grey Noise Gallery in Dubai. Through her art, she explores the physicality and symbolism, modularity, and rhythm of the Arabic alphabet, beyond its function as a language and cultural signifier.

BAYAN BARBOUD

Born in 1975, Bayan Barboud is a Saudi calligrapher and graphic designer. Barboud started her journey in Arabic calligraphy in 2009 studying under master calligrapher Ibrahim Al Arafi and then after 2012 under Hussam Al-Matar, focusing on six different types of scripts. Her participation in several local art exhibitions does not prevent her from focusing on her own vision: to integrate drawing, calligraphy and graphic design in one single artistic practice. Inspired by the Montblanc M pen, she teamed up with the company, along with eight other Arab artists, to celebrate the art of calligraphy. She facilitated many workshops and calligraphy trainings in Jeddah, Riyadh, and Khobar between 2010 and 2019.

IBRAHIM BATCHELDER

Born in 1975, since his childhood artist Ibrahim Batchelder was fascinated by nature and its harmony, by its indications of the accuracy of the cosmic order; nature continues to inspire him to this day. He attended the Putney School of Art and Design, where he explored drawing, painting, printmaking, sculpture in wood, stone and steel, metal working and jewellery making. In 1994, he travelled to Istanbul where he began his apprenticeship with master woodcarver and inlay artist Husamettin Yivlik. He completed a bachelor's degree at the Istanbul Mimar Sinan University, with a major in traditional bookbinding and a minor in illumination (*tezhip*). Currently residing in the UK, Batchelder pursues his multi-disciplinary work by incorporating various exotic materials and using his many skills such as illumination design and painting, carving, engraving, turning, jewellery making and woodworking. His unique artworks and designs are known throughout the Middle East and beyond, especially his innovative and original prayer beads (*misbahas*) featuring combinations of contrasting materials and detailed engravings.

MOHAMMAD SALEM BAJNAID

Mohammad Salem Bajnaid (1937–2019) is famous for using the *thuluth* script in writing verses from the Holy Qur'an and noble hadiths, with unique calligraphic compositions aimed at bringing forth not only the meaning but also the spiritual essence of the verse. He contributed to the design of the *Kiswa* (curtain) of the Kaaba, then, in 1982, he designed and installed a 7-metre frame housing the Kaaba door curtain, a gift from the Kingdom of Saudi Arabia to the United Nations headquarters in New York. Bajnaid was a member of the Jeddah Chamber of Commerce and Industry Committee on Fine Arts, member of the Jeddah Governorate Street Naming Committee, and member of the Ministry of Culture and Information delegation to the Arabic Calligraphy exhibition in Tunisia, 2005. When the city of Rabat, Morocco, was chosen in 2003 as capital of the Islamic culture, Bajnaid was as a member of the General Presidency for the Youth Welfare. He took part in the Art of Arabic Calligraphy International Forum, Sharjah, 2004. His work is featured in many Arabic calligraphy exhibitions.

FARAH BEHBEHANI

Farah Behbehani is a Kuwaiti artist and designer born in 1981. She achieved a master's of arts in communication design with distinction from Central Saint Martins College of Art and Design, London, in 2007. She worked on several architectural projects in her native Kuwait and collaborated with the American architectural firm SOM to design "veils" that would serve as shading structures for the Kuwait University seven administration buildings. Her work incorporates Arabic calligraphy into traditional Islamic geometric patterns, creating unique designs that reflect the purpose and structure of the buildings. Behbehani's work focuses on Arabic letters, continuously investigating their layered meanings and exploring the boundaries of their physical form. She has experimented with a variety of media, from paper and canvas to weaving and beading, as well as large-scale metal and wood structures: her *Tree of Life* installation, created with suspended wooden letters, explores the endless variations of calligraphic script. This piece, exhibited in 2012, was granted the Distinction Award at the Sharjah Biennial of Calligraphy. In 2009, Farah Behbehani published a book, *The Conference of the Birds*, based on Farid al-Din Attar's twelfth-century allegorical poem. Illustrating Attar's poetry with *jaly diwani* calligraphy, she created a design system to enable non-Arabic readers to comprehend the meaning and fluency of the calligraphic forms. Her work aspires to shed light on her rich cultural heritage, creating a bridge between East and West.

KHALED BEN SLIMANE

Khaled Ben Slimane is a Tunisian artist born in 1951. He studied at the Escola Massana of Barcelona and the Technological Institute of Art in Tunis. Khaled is a multi-disciplinary artist whose practice includes painting on paper, canvas and wood and bronze sculptures, although he is mostly known for his ceramic work, a synthesis of East and West in a distinctive style. Slimane's first Tunisian exhibition in 1982 propelled him on the international stage with exhibitions in Tunis, Baghdad, Rabat, London, Paris, Rome and New York, including the Musée National d'Art Moderne, Centre Pompidou and the Institut du Monde Arabe in Paris, and the British Museum in London. In 2004 and 2005, his exhibition *From Earth to the Sky: Ceramics and Paintings*, curated by the Badisches Landesmuseum, travelled across five different museums in Germany. His artworks can be found in numerous private and public collections, such as the British Museum, the Smithsonian Institution (Washington, DC), the Idemitsu Museum of Arts (Tokyo), the Benaki Museum (Athens), the Jordan National Gallery of Fine Arts (Amman), the Badisches Landesmuseum (Karlsruhe) and the Museu de Ceràmica (Barcelona).

KHODEIR EL-BORSAIDY

Called the "master of all Egyptian calligraphers", Khodeir El-Borsaidy is a painter and calligrapher who owes his name to the province of Port Said, where he was born in 1942. He took his first steps in calligraphy under the tutelage of his elder brother, Mohammed Khodeir. He wrote anti-occupation slogans on walls and roads and drew his first advertisements at the age of 10. He earned his *ijazah* (calligraphy certification) at the Tanta School and then specialized at the Khalil Agha School in Cairo. He counts major Egyptian calligraphers as his teachers, including Mohammed Hosni, Sayyid Ibrahim and Mohammad Abdel Kader. He is known for his superlative, magnificent attention to detail and for paintings that incorporate calligraphy. His signature came to be known in the cinema industry as he wrote titles and billboards for major movies and series. He was awarded the honorary encouragement prize by the State of Egypt, the Egyptian Opera House prize during the 6th Festival of Arabic Music (1997), the Ministry of Culture Festival for Arabic Calligraphy prize (1995), the Kazma International Festival gold medal in Kuwait (1996) and the Islamic Art prize in China in 1996.

KAMAL BOULLATA

Kamal Boullata (1942-2019) was a Palestinian artist and writer. In 1965 he graduated with a diploma in fine arts from the Accademia di Belle Arti, Rome, and from 1968–71 pursued his studies at the Corcoran School of Art, Washington, DC, where he received an MFA. Boullata's early silkscreen works focused on the *kufi* script, an ancient form of Arabic calligraphy with which he created colourful, geometric compositions on paper. Evoking his childhood spent in Al-Quds, much of Boullata's later paintings turned to abstraction while exploring themes of identity and exile by drawing from the rich decoration of the Dome of the Rock as well as the distinctive embroidery of his native Palestine. He had solo exhibitions staged at

Meem Gallery, Dubai, 2017; Berloni Gallery, London, 2015; Wiensowski & Harbord, Berlin, 2013; Musée du Château Dufresne, Montreal, 2002. He participated in group exhibitions at Whitechapel Gallery, London, 2015 and 2016; Barjeel Art Foundation, Sharjah, 2014; Institut du Monde Arabe, Paris, 2008; British Museum, London, 2006.
Boullata's paintings, silkscreens and artist's books were displayed in Europe, the US, France, and the Middle East. His work can be found in a number of private and public collections including the British Museum, London; Institut du Monde Arabe, Paris; New York Public Library, New York; Barjeel Art Foundation, Sharjah; Khalid Shoman Foundation, Amman; Alhambra Islamic Museum, Granada; Sharjah Art Museum, Sharjah; Bibliothèque Louis Notari, Monaco, and Mathaf, Museum of Modern Arab Art, Doha.
His publications include *Palestinian Art: From 1850 to the Present* and his selected essays appear in *There Where You Are Not*, edited by F. B. Flood. After his extended stays in the USA, Morocco and France, he moved to Berlin where he was elected in 2012–13 a fellow of the Institute of Advanced Study.

DOA BUGIS

Doa Bugis is a cross-disciplinary creative artist based in Jeddah. She graduated from Dar Alhekma University with a bachelor's degree in graphic design. Trained by Mughal miniature painting masters from India and Pakistan, she has been practising Islamic arts since 2017, specializing in storytelling through traditional painting that incorporates Indian miniature techniques in order to explore topics such as immigration, hybrid identities, healing, grief, loss, the manifestation of everyday human encounters, and individuals' relationships with their surroundings.

NABEEL BUKHARI

A biology teacher by training, Nabeel Bukhari was born in 1981 in Saudi Arabia. His artistic career took off in 2019 when he met Abdulaziz Al Rashedi, who taught him digital processing art, graphic design, and the square *kufi* script. His projects are many, most notably the processing of frescoes of Quba Avenue (a historical landmark of Medina) in 2018 and the *Sayyid al-Shuhada* project in a Medina historical neighbourhood. His commercial designs are in high demand among companies and academic establishments. His graphic design projects were featured in the *3 Bunt* exhibition for Abdulaziz Al Rashedi in 2018 and the Artists Exhibition (Medina, 2019). The Athr Gallery in Jeddah hosted a collection of his works in square *kufi* script in 2021.

PABLO CASADO

Born in 1982, Pablo Casado's personal and academic growth took place under his native Madrid sun. Despite a long-standing attraction towards Arabic calligraphy shapes, it was only in 2008 that he encountered a reed pen as part of a brief introductory course to Arabic calligraphy: enough to awaken a deep interest in him. He later met renowned calligrapher Nuria García Masip, who became his master and mentor. Under her guidance, in 2009 he travelled to Istanbul for the first time and studied under the supervision of master calligraphers Davut Bektaş, Hassan Çelebi and Ferhat Kurlu. In 2014, having devoted himself entirely to his art, he received his *ijazah* (calligraphy certification) in both *thuluth* and *naskh* scripts by the Research Center for Islamic History Art and Culture (IRCICA).

NADA DEBS

Born in 1963 in Kobe, Japan, Nada Debs is a Lebanese designer based in Beirut, Lebanon. Her work spans across scales and disciplines: from product and furniture design to one-off commissions across crafts, art, fashion, and interiors. Nada grew up in Japan, studied at the Rhode Island School of Design in the United States and spent significant periods of time living and travelling the world, investigating connections between different cultures. What ties her work together is her ability to distil culture and craftsmanship to create pieces of emotional resonance: she calls her approach "handmade and heart made". Her work is driven by a belief in the power of design to cross time and borders, to touch individuals on a primal level. She describes it as an expression not merely of form and function, but of feeling too. Nada Debs opened her first showroom in the Beirut Saifi district in 2003. Today her gallery and design studio comprise a team of 15 from a range of disciplines. Together, they work on annual collections of furniture and accessories and provide interior design concepts and services as well as artworks, jewellery, and installations.

ABDELRAHMAN ELSHAHED

Born in 1993, Abdelrahman Elshahed is a Saudi artist based in Jeddah with a master's degree in architecture from King Abdulaziz University. After receiving his *ijazah* (calligraphy certification) in 2012 at the Holy Mosque in Mecca, he became a calligraphy teacher. His teaching practice, together with his interest in art, paved the way for lectures and workshops on Islamic art as well as the publication of several research papers. As a creative director, Elshahed organized many exhibitions and artistic programmes. He was a consultant on the Saudi Ministry of Culture *Year of Arabic Calligraphy initiative* (2020–2021). His work is primarily focused on spiritual geometry as he seeks to express vital ideas, concepts and values through hybrid mediums and deep symbolism. He sees Calligraphy and Architecture as intrinsic components of contemporary artistic expression. During the Jeddah International Book Fair in 2016, Elshahed designed one of the largest calligraphy gates in the world. He joined other artists in group exhibitions across the world, among others, at the Sharjah Islamic Arts Festival and the Canadian Museum of Nature in Ottawa. His awards include the Okaz International Prize for Arabic Calligraphy (2011), the Qadasah International Short Film Award (2013) and the Building Planning and Design local prize from The Saudi Umran Society (2016). His works adorn many organizations and institutions such as the UNESCO headquarters in Paris, France and, in Saudi Arabia, the Prince Mohammed bin Salman Global Center for Arabic Calligraphy, the Prince Mohammed bin Abdulaziz International Airport in Medina and the Royal Commission for Jubail and Yanbu.

AZZA FAHMY

Azza Fahmy is an Egyptian jewellery designer born in 1944. Fahmy holds a bachelor's degree in interior design and jewellery craft education from the City of London Polytechnic. Her journey began almost 50 years ago as an apprentice in Khan El Khalili, Cairo's ancient jewellery quarter, where she rose to become one of the most esteemed jewellery designers in the Middle East region. With a strong sense of purpose, Azza Fahmy has taken on the role of translating regional and international art and historic references into contemporary jewellery designs that reflect her unique research approach and the preservation of traditional craftsmanship. Celebrated as Egypt's first luxury multi-national brand, Azza's craft has captured the attention of cultural and fashion experts. Her company is recognized for having established Egypt's luxury market and today employs over 200 people across the world. A few years ago, she independently funded and established the successful DSAF (Design Studio by Azza Fahmy), the first design education hub of its kind in the region.

RANDA FAHMY

Born in 1951, Egyptian designer Randa Fahmy received a bachelor's degree in Fine Arts from Helwan University in 1975 and a degree in General Metal Work Studies from London Polytechnic. Specialized in lighting design, she created lighting and furniture settings for more than 40 hotels, resorts, restaurants, palaces and houses in Egypt, Palestine, UAE, Saudi Arabia, USA, Jordan, Bahrain, Kuwait, Oman, and Lebanon. Although Randa focuses on a range of Arabic designs and motifs, from expansive glass and metal chandeliers for mosques and ballrooms to highly intricate bronze *mashrabiyya*, she also carries out projects in other styles. "If you can work with Arabic designs, you can do anything", she says, adding that her projects encompass Art Deco, Art Nouveau, and ultra-modern aesthetics. Randa Fahmy has grown from a small workshop to a renowned company and continues to design and create products that blend Islamic and Arab heritage with traditional techniques.

JASSIM MIRAJ AL-FAILAKAWI

Jassim Miraj Al-Failakawi is a Kuwaiti artist born in 1982. He holds a degree in chemical engineering from Kuwait University and a master's degree from the Faculty of Islamic Arts in Jordan (2008). He studied calligraphy with Waleed Al-Farhood, then with Davut

Bektaş, and in 2002 with Hassan Çelebi. He received his *ijazah* (calligraphy certification) in the *thuluth* and *naskh* scripts in 2007. He was part of many international exhibitions and festivals and won prestigious awards in international calligraphy competitions. He is currently the vice-president of the Kuwait Islamic Art Centre.

MOHAMAD GABER

Born in 1988, Mohamad Gaber is an Egyptian designer and artist. He holds a bachelor's degree in Specific Education from Mansoura University as well as a degree in Arabic script. In 2007, he was given his *ijazah* (calligraphy certification) by Ahmed Fares Rezq. He took part in many competitions and international forums: the Dubai International Forum for the Holy Qur'an Calligraphy (2015 to 2017), the Dubai International Arabic Calligraphy Exhibition (10th edition), the Sharjah Islamic Arts Festival, the Sharjah Forum 2020, the Kuwait International Forum (2016) and the Journey of the Noble Qur'an exhibition (Kuwait, 2015). He was awarded at the Al-Burdah International Competition and Festival (2017 and 2022, UAE) for his *thuluth* and *naskh* scripts, the Al Baraka International Competition (2018) and the IRCICA International Competition of the Organization of the Islamic Conference (2019) for his *muhaqqaq* and *diwani* scripts. He also won a prize at the Dubai Qur'an Calligraphy Forum (2016).

NURIA GARCÍA MASIP

Born in 1978, Nuria García Masip grew up between Spain and the USA. In 1999, after completing her university studies in literature and philosophy, she travelled to Morocco where she developed an interest in Islamic art. She studied calligraphy with masters Mohamed Zakariya, Hassan Çelebi and Davut Bektaş. In 2007, she received her *ijazah* (calligraphy certification). She holds a master's degree in Art History from the Sorbonne University and won prestigious awards in international calligraphy competitions. Her work is collected by many museums and adorns private art collections. She organized numerous workshops and conferences to promote the art of calligraphy internationally.

ZAKI AL HASHIMI

Zaki Al Hashimi, born in 1982, holds an *ijazah* (calligraphy certification) in Arabic calligraphy from Hassan Çelebi, Mumtaz Dordu and Ferhat Kurlu. He is an art consultant at the King Abdulaziz Foundation in Riyadh and an expert on Arabic calligraphy at UNESCO. He was part of many group exhibitions, such as the International Exhibition for Arabic Calligraphy in Algeria, 2013, 2014 and 2016, Kuwait, 2016, Sharjah, 2015–2017, Morocco, 2017, Medina, 2018, Riyadh, 2019, Dubai, 2019 and Aqaba, 2019. He held solo exhibitions in Qatar, 2019, Terengganu International Exhibition of Calligraphy, Malaysia, 2016, the Istanbul Biennial, Turkey, 2021 and the London Art Exhibition, UK, 2018–2022. Al Hashimi is the author of the 25-volume collection *Thanaya el-Rouh* (Folds of the Soul) on the *naskh* script, as well as a 24-volume series for teaching Arabic writing to non-Arabic speakers in Spain, in addition to an educational video series on Arabic calligraphy.

AYMAN HASSAN

Born in Syria in 1980, Ayman Hassan's interest in calligraphy can be traced as far back as his early years when, at the age of eight, he met master Hassan Çelebi in Kuwait. He began his studies in the *thuluth* and *naskh* scripts, continued under Davut Bektaş in 2002, then worked on the *nasta'liq* script under Ali Alparslan. Having earned his *ijazah* (calligraphy certification) in 2003, he felt it would be an enriching experience to study with different teachers, including Waleed Al-Farhood, Adnan Al-Sheikh Othman from Syria, Ahmad Zia Ibrahim and Nasser Al Maymoun from Saudi Arabia. Based in Kuwait, Hassan took part in many international exhibitions and festivals and has received numerous international awards.

SUSAN HEFUNA

Susan Hefuna, a German-Egyptian visual artist born in 1962, works with a variety of media, including drawing, sculpture, installation, video, photography, and performance. Enriched by her Egyptian-German roots, her artwork, focusing on cross-cultural codes and personal experiences of living within different cultures, is widely exhibited. In 2013 she received the international Daniel and Florence Guerlain Drawing Award in Paris. Since the 1990s, Susan Hefuna has been observing the combined effect of filtered light and *mashrabiyya* screens: typical of Islamic art and architecture, their function of allowing women to see out to the street yet remain unseen is a fitting structure for Hefuna's exploration of visibility versus invisibility and the dynamics of human interactions.

SAYYID IBRAHIM

Calligrapher Sayyid Ibrahim was born in the Citadel district of Cairo in 1897. He began teaching calligraphy in Egyptian schools in 1918, then at the Royal School of Calligraphy in 1935, the Faculty of Arts (1938 to 1959), the American University of Cairo (1970 to 1977) and the Arab University. For over 70 years, he trained countless calligraphers and Orientalists such as Abu Bakr Sass, the Libyan founder of the Muqla calligraphy school, Hashem Al Baghdadi, head of the International Calligraphy Committee in Istanbul, Nasser Al Maymoun from Saudi Arabia, Dr. Mohammed Said Charifi, Boutheliga Mohammed, Abdel Kader Boumalah from Algeria, Burhan Kibara and Mohsen Fotouni from Lebanon, Sheikh Bashir al Adli from Syria, Anne Royal from the US and Abdel 'Ilah al Arab from Bahrein.
At the Academy of Arts, he saw his students from Egypt and the Islamic world graduate, such as Saudi Minister of State Dr. Abdel Aziz al Khoweitir, poet Faruk Shosha, Dr. Abdallah Shahata, Dr. Abdel Sabour Shaheen, Dr. Kamal Bashar, Dr. Said Badawi, former Minister of Culture Dr. Ahmad Shebli, Dr. Ahmad Haykal, and other major cultural figures of Egypt and the Arab world.

SAMEH ISMAEL

Born in 1974, Sameh Ismael is an Egyptian visual artist, calligrapher, and musician. He graduated from Helwan University in 1997 with a bachelor's degree in Fine Arts. His work introduces the visual elements that are connected to sound. As a painter, Ismael explores the role of Arabic letters as a recognized form of culture; according to him, Arab calligraphers are still trapped inside mosque walls and places of worship, although many have tried to develop Arabic calligraphy through their artistic works. Throughout his research in calligraphy, he has concluded that Arabic letters are not to be used as a decorative motif, but rather they must embody a meaningful sentence. His creations and technique are deeply inspired by his multi-layered Arab, Islamic, Mediterranean and African culture.

AHMAD JEDDAWI

During his childhood at the Ibn Salah primary school in Jeddah, 1990-born Ahmad Jeddawi discovered a passion for Arabic calligraphy, which he nurtured for years under the teachings of Ibrahim Al Arafi at the Holy City of Mecca. He earned an architecture degree in 2013 at the King Fahd University for Petroleum and Minerals.
His passion for Arabic calligraphy and architecture, coupled with a keen interest in graphic design, lighting and project management, help him explore, through calligraphy, new ways to highlight and embody deep concepts into words and sentences. He seeks to redefine the relationship between Arabic calligraphy and architectural spaces in contemporary works.

AMOR JOMNI

Born in Jbel Jloud (Tunis) in 1957, calligrapher Amor Jomni graduated from the School of Graphic Arts and is a researcher in History. He was awarded the Tunisian Order of Cultural Merit while working as a graphic designer at Tunisian newspaper *El Bayan*. Since 1987, he has taken part in numerous national, regional and international festivals and symposia. He won the golden medal at the Sharjah Calligraphy Biennial and the first prize at the Contemporary Arabic Calligraphy Festival (Algeria, 2009). He published a book of calligraphy illustrations to poems by Abu El-Kacem Chebbi, *Lahn el-Kayinet*. His talent was called upon by the Tunisian government, for whom he designed the national currency banknotes and coins. His calligraphic artwork includes several scripts such as *al-mujawhar, jaly maghribi thuluth, zamami.*

HALA KAIKSOW

Hala Kaiksow is a Bahraini textile designer, born in 1990 and living in Manama. Her journey as a designer finds its roots in the ability of human hands to imbue garments with a sense of soul. A twenty-first-century artisan, her thoughtful approach to craft encompasses hand-woven fabrics, natural dying techniques and handmade buttons and fasteners. Inspired by the beauty residing in everyday objects and by a utilitarian approach to dressing, she deconstructs garbs from the past and present to create clothing infused with feminine strength. A trained artist and sculptor, her creative process is driven by experimentation and the thrust to explore the endless possibilities of garment construction. On her loom, raw linen, silk, and hemp are woven into otherworldly patterns and textures, embellished with fragments of metal, wood, latex and mother-of-pearl. Thus, her vision is brought to life, reflecting her artisanal approach to thoughtful luxury, informed by her passion for transforming unexpected materials through age-old craft traditions. Hala Kaiksow's work was internationally recognized in 2016 at the International Fashion Showcase in London and the Paris Grand Palais, as a part of a group exhibition in 2018. More recently she was shortlisted for the Jameel Prize in its fifth edition.

JAMAL AL KEBASI

Born in Saudi Arabia in 1950, Jamal Al Kebasi pursued his professional training in calligraphy as a fine art in Baghdad, where he earned his *ijazah* (calligraphy certification) in 1974. He trained under great masters such as Hashim Mohammad Al Baghdadi and Sadig Al Dori. He is the author of *Creative Design in Kufi Calligraphy.*

YAZID KHELOUFI

Yazid Kheloufi is an Algerian visual artist and graphic designer born in 1963. Fascinated with calligraphy from an early age, he sees writing as an inexhaustible source of creation, whether it is considered as the transmission of meaning, of forms, or even as the inheritance of thousands of "writers" from the past. From cuneiform script to Arabic, letters have turned Kheloufi into the descendant of scribes from ancient civilizations. Highlighting the power of the Arabic alphabet, he freely adopts different orientations, sizes and formats in his artwork, thus reflecting various phases of human existence while perpetuating the predominance of spirituality.

NASSER AL MAYMOUN

A self-taught calligrapher born in Saudi Arabia in 1957, Nasser Al Maymoun has earned his place among major contemporary masters of Arabic calligraphy such as Sayyid Ibrahim, Kamil Al-Baba and Abdullah Ridha. His work brought him worldwide recognition culminating in 29 awards in national and international competitions. He is a board member of the Saudi Society of Arabic Calligraphy and has worked for the Saudi Ministries of Media and Culture. In addition to his talent as a calligrapher, he taught Arabic at the Riyadh Chamber of Commerce and the Society of Art and Culture. On the 100th anniversary of the establishment of the Kingdom, his talent was called upon to design the celebration logo, which he did by setting the name of Saudi Arabia in a calligraphic design. His works adorn numerous collections across the world – in Malaysia, Kuwait, Qatar, and the UAE, to name a few.

HAZEM EL MESTIKAWY

Born in 1965, Hazem El Mestikawy is a Swiss-Egyptian artist. With a bachelor's degree in Art Education from Minia University, he has been part of many group exhibitions since 1989 and had solo shows in Egypt, Dubai, Sharjah, Doha, Switzerland, Austria, Germany, Japan, and the USA. His style revolves around architecture, design, sculpture, and the art of optical illusion. Initially trained as a sculptor, as he gives shape to his pieces he toys with light and shade, volume, and the surrounding space. He believes in pushing the boundaries of sculpture to create site-specific installations both inspired and influenced by architecture.

OMAR EL-NAGDI

Omar El-Nagdi (1931–2019) was a renowned Egyptian artist, musician, and philosopher whose career was crowned by a large number of local and international prizes. Known as a multi-disciplinary artist, he experimented with sculpture, calligraphy, mosaic, watercolour and oil painting. In March 2016, he broke a record when his 15-metre painting *Sarajevo* was sold at Christie's Dubai. El-Nagdi drew his inspiration from the cultural diversity of his native Egypt, as he intertwined

Pharaonic and Islamic arts and experimented with traditional languages, using Eastern forms with an outstanding handling of colour, texture, and symbolic elements. He has been known since the 1960s for incorporating Arabic calligraphy into his work. His captivating pieces result from his unique vision and feature a rhythmic abstraction built on Arabic letters and numerals.

RAFA AL NASIRI

Rafa al Nasiri (1940–2013) was an ingenious, dedicated Iraqi painter, printmaker, graphic designer, and author. He studied art in Baghdad, specialized in graphic arts in Beijing and was also trained at the Associação de Gravura in Lisbon. His prolific heritage includes paintings, book binding, art books and graphic design. He published four books on Arabian art and artists, including an autobiography. He displayed his work in international solo exhibitions in Asia, Europe, USA, and Latin America. Considered to be one of the leading modern innovators in Iraq and the Arab world, al Nasiri's artworks travelled far beyond the borders of his native Tikrit (Iraq) and found their place in museums across the world.

TIMO NASSERI

Timo Nasseri was born in 1972 and is based in Berlin. He received his diploma in photography from the Lette-Verein Berlin in 1997. Nasseri explores themes such as geometry, mathematics, architecture, calligraphy, and most recently, camouflage. Combining Islamic and Western cultural heritages, his work is inspired by specific memories and religious references as well as by universal archetypes springing from language and mathematics, the bearers of inner truths of form and rhythm. Through natural science, his work opens a perspective on the poetic and fantastic. His practice tackles the subject of infinity and aims to solve puzzles, from historical mysteries to mathematical theorems, to see an overarching order emerge from the chaos of existence. Nasseri held many solo exhibitions and was the winner of the Abraaj Capital Art Prize in 2011.

OBAID AL NOFAEY

Born in 1985 in Saudi Arabia, Obaid Al Nofaey holds a bachelor's degree in Arabic Language from the College of Teacher Education and an *ijazah* (calligraphy certification) in Arabic calligraphy delivered by Nasser Al Maymoun in 2013. He widened his horizon by studying different calligraphic scripts such as the *naskh*, *riqa'* and *thuluth* in different establishments. Al Nofaey was part of local and international exhibitions, forums and festivals. He is a founding member of the Asala Harf Group for Arabic Calligraphy and the Riyadh Education Department Arabic Calligraphy Club.

MARYAM NOROUZI

Born in 1986, Maryam Norouzi received her *ijazah* (calligraphy certification) in *thuluth* script from master calligraphers Hassan Çelebi and Davut Bektaş in 2014. Her work was featured in a number of international exhibitions in Saudi Arabia, Morocco, Malaysia, and France. She was awarded prizes for her work in the *thuluth* and *muhaqqaq* scripts.

SARA OUHADDOU

Born in 1986, Sara Ouhaddou lives and works between Morocco and France. She studied at the École Olivier de Serres in Paris and has participated in numerous exhibitions. Born in France in a traditional Moroccan family, her dual cultural affiliation informs her practice. She strikes a balance between traditional Moroccan art forms and the conventions of contemporary art, aiming to place the forgotten cultural continuities of artistic creation into new perspectives. She works *in situ*, producing works based on encounters with communities, craftsmen, and researchers, while exploring heritage sites and objects. Each of her works is a project of learning, knowledge or exchange channelled through an intimate or universal story.

MOHANAD QAISI

Born in 1982 in Jordan, Mohanad Qaisi received a bachelor's degree in 2009 and a master's degree in Islamic Art in 2013. He earned his *ijazah* (calligraphy certification) in 2010 after training under Hassan Çelebi, Davut Bektaş and Mohamed El-Behairy. In 2009, while still a student, Qaisi completed his *ijazah* piece in *jaly thuluth* script, following which he took part in the Algeria Festival for Islamic Arts (2010 and 2014). He calligraphed letters and created designs and decorated ornaments for the Jordanian Hashemite Fund; he also contributed to the writing of King Hussein bin Talal's *Mushaf* in *muhaqqaq* script (*Suhrawardi* style) in 2010. Mohanad Qaisi delivers specialized courses in the art of Arabic calligraphy and decoration in many cultural and artistic centres. His teachings are recorded on the electronic *Shaghafi* (My Passion) platform of the Jordanian Ministry of Culture.

SADEK RAHIM

Algerian artist Sadek Rahim was born in 1971. In the late 1990s, he travelled and lived in Syria, Jordan and Lebanon, where he graduated from the Académie Libanaise des Beaux-Arts in Beirut; then, in 2004, he graduated from the prestigious Central Saint Martins College of Art and Design in London. Afterwards, while developing an international career, he chose to live and work in Algeria. Depending on his project, Rahim works with a variety of media including drawing, painting, sculpture, installation, photography, and video. He exhibits all over the world and is very active on the Algerian cultural landscape. In 2012, he was the first artist to present the first ever contemporary drawing solo exhibition in Algeria; then, in 2013, he was one of the founders of the first contemporary drawing art fair in his country. In the summer of 2019, his solo show *Gravity*, curated by Marie Deparis-Yafil, opened at the Musée d'Art Moderne in Oran, Algeria: the first major monographic exhibition of contemporary art in the museum, whose space of over 3,000 square metres was filled with some thirty works in all media produced specifically for the occasion.

MUSTAFA RAKIM

Mustafa Rakim (1757–1826) is considered one of the greatest masters of the late eighteenth century. Originally from Unye on the Black Sea, he moved to Istanbul at a young age to study calligraphy under his brother, calligrapher Ismail Zühdi Efendi, and with master Dervis Ali Efendi III. He was also an accomplished painter, and soon became well-known for his mastery of the large-scale scripts, especially *jaly thuluth*, and his large-scale compositions. His meticulous treatment of the letters and mastery of composition and balance in monumental pieces marked an important aesthetic shift in calligraphy, often referred to as pre-Rakim or post-Rakim periods. One of his most noteworthy architectural compositions is in the Nusretiye Mosque in Istanbul and has been preserved to this day.
He also produced countless calligraphic panels (*levha*) and *qit'a*.

AHMED FARES REZQ

Egyptian calligrapher Ahmed Fares Rezq was born in 1980 in Saudi Arabia. He holds a bachelor's degree in Literature and Arabic Language. He studied in Turkey under the tutelage of Mehmed Özçay and received his *ijazah* (calligraphy certification) in 2014. Rezq was part of many local and international exhibitions and won numerous first prize awards. His work can be found in private collections and museums. He has published articles on the art of calligraphy.

NOOR SAAB

Born in 1981, Noor Saab is a Lebanese artist and graphic designer currently based in London. She earned her bachelor's degree in graphic design from the American University of Beirut and her master's degree in media and communications from Goldsmiths College, London. Under the mentorship of acclaimed artist Samir Sayegh, she explored the relationship between Arabic calligraphy and the human body in motion; this marked the beginning of a lifelong passion for this specific art form. Saab later joined BBC News, specializing in multilingual user experience design, with a strong expertise in Arabic scripts. Alongside her job, she has been building a substantial body of work in geometric *kufi* calligraphy. Strongly inspired by her rich cultural heritage, London's dynamic multicultural atmosphere and her multidisciplinary experience in graphic, motion, textile and accessory design, Saab adopts a contemporary experimental approach to ancient traditions, underpinned by an ever-evolving cross-cultural dialogue.

NASSER AL SALEM

Nasser Al Salem is a Saudi artist born in 1984, currently based in Jeddah. He pursued his undergraduate studies in architecture at the Umm Al-Qura University in Mecca. He also studied calligraphy at the Haram Al-Sharif, where he obtained his *ijazah* (calligraphy certification). He is co-founder of the Jeddah-based artist collective Al-Hangar, a member of the National Guild of Calligraphers, and an active fellow of Saudi Arabia's Arts and Culture Group. His artistic practice challenges the boundaries of traditional Islamic art forms; as regards calligraphy, he re-contextualizes it in unconventional mixed media thus releasing its conceptual potential through minimalist and architectural methods. Al Salem's work has been part of numerous national and international group exhibitions. His work is featured in the British Museum (London), the Los Angeles County Museum of Art and the Centre Pompidou (Paris). In 2013, he was shortlisted for the Jameel Prize at the Victoria and Albert Museum (London). In 2018, his work was part of The Royal Commission for AlUla (Saudi Arabia).

SAMIR SAYEGH

Samir Sayegh, born in 1944, is a Lebanese artist, critic, and poet. Driven by a deep interest in the formal power of letters, Sayegh sought to liberate calligraphy from language and meaning, choosing to focus instead on the aesthetic properties of the written word, as part of an effort to create a universal visual language.
Sayegh studied art history at the École nationale supérieure des Beaux-Arts in Paris. His research on traditional calligraphy, combined with his interest in contemporary design, led him to create new calligraphic typefaces and design several logos.
A prolific writer, Sayegh penned many articles and essays on art and aesthetics. Between 2003 and 2007, he was a lecturer at the Architecture and Graphic Design Department at the American University of Beirut. By combining ornamentation with calligraphic script, Sayegh has developed a distinctive style. Through formal elements of line and space, he abstracts Arabic letters and words into dynamic geometric compositions, often covering the entire surface.

AHMAD SHIBRAIN

Ahmad Shibrain (1931–2017) was a painter and graphic artist from Sudan. He studied at the Khartoum College of Fine and Applied Arts and then, in 1957, entered the London Central School of Arts & Crafts. In 1970, he became the Head of the Graphic Design Department at his former college before being promoted to Dean in 1975. He founded the Shibrain Art Centre, which showcases and promotes Sudanese artists. Alongside his influential contemporaries Ibrahim El-Salahi and Kamala Ishag, Shibrain was one of the founders in the 1960s of the Khartoum School, an artistic movement that cultivated a new visual style called *Sudanawiyya*, which sought to express local and Pan-African traditions alongside Western influences. Through the use of calligraphy, the aesthetics of *hurufiyya* (transforming Arabic letters into abstract shapes) and Islamic motifs, the movement attempts to convey the cultural fabric of Sudan.

HANI AL-TAWEL

Born in 1980, Hani Al-Tawel is the calligrapher of the Holy Qur'an Museum in the Prophet's Mosque in Medina. He got his *ijazah* (calligraphy certification) from masters Ahmad Diya' El-Din Ibrahim, Dr. Uthman Taha (calligrapher of the *Mushaf*) and Dr. Abdulaziz Mustafa Najat El-Din. He has a perfect command of both *naskh* and *diwani* scripts as well as six other types of calligraphy. His work has been acknowledged in exhibitions in Istanbul, Qatar, Paris (UNESCO), Cairo (the Egyptian Opera House), and the Research Centre for Islamic History, Art, and Culture (*jaly thuluth* script). He was awarded a certificate of appreciation by the Saudi Association for Arts and Culture and the Opera Aida medal for Excellence in Arabic calligraphy.

IHAB THABET

Jordanian artist Ihab Thabet was born in 1968 and taught himself calligraphy at a young age. He received his *ijazah* (calligraphy certification) from Mehmed Özçay in 2021, as his work began to travel across the world. Thabet took part in several exhibitions: the Arabic Calligraphy Exhibition (Jordan during the 1980s), the Baghdad Festival (1998), the Dubai Calligraphy Exhibition (2004, 2010, 2015, 2017, 2019) and the Frankfurt Exhibition of Arab Art (2004). He is one of the artists who contributed to writing the largest Holy Qur'an in the world, *Mushaf Alsham* in 2006.

OSMAN WAQIALLA

Osman Waqialla (1925–2007) was a Sudanese painter and calligrapher. He graduated from the School of Design at the Gordon Memorial College in Khartoum in 1945, before joining the former Camberwell School of Arts and Crafts in London. He was trained under master calligrapher Sayyid Ibrahim at the Cairo School of Arabic Calligraphy. In his paintings, Waqialla explores the expressive and compositional possibilities of Arabic calligraphic forms. He became one of the first artists to free Arabic calligraphy from its historical relationship with sacred texts and propose it as a veritable resource for modern art. Waqialla was part of a group of Sudanese artists, later to be known as the Khartoum School, searching for a new artistic identity drawn from their own culture and heritage.

HAYTHEM ZAKARIA

Born in 1983, Haythem Zakaria is a France-based transdisciplinary artist. Profoundly influenced by cosmogony and spirituality, his work is a constant experimentation with the possible conjunctions between various systems and disciplines (sociology, economy, ethnography, etc.). By rooting his aesthetic practice in a cross-disciplinary approach, Zakaria uses a considerable variety of tools and techniques. In a continuous quest for archetypal figures, each time he explores new methods through advanced technologies, such as interactive programming and art installations, but also through more traditional media like photography, video, drawing and sculpture. In his latest work, for which he received the Grand Prize of the Japan Art Media Festival, he resorts to simpler and more basic tools, while always preserving the digital aspect of his art. Due to the simplicity of its forms, the work of Haythem Zakaria is as hermetic as "reality" could be; it only allows to grasp its multi-layered meanings when observed thoroughly and patiently.

Bibliography

N. Abbott, *The Rise of the North Arabic Script and its Ḳur'ānic Development. With a full description of the Ḳur'ān manuscripts in the Oriental Institute*, Oriental Institute Publications of the University of Chicago, vol. 1 (Chicago: University of Chicago Press, 1939).

G. Miles, "Early Inscriptions near Ṭā'if in the Ḥijāz", in *Journal of Near Eastern Studies* VII (1948): 241.

F. Rosenthal, "Abū Ḥaiyān al-Tawḥīdī on Penmanship", in *Ars Islamica* 13–14 (1948): 10.

D. S. Rice, *The Unique Ibn al-Bawwab Manuscript in the Chester Beatty Library* (Dublin: Emery Walker, 1955).

Calligraphers and Painters, a Treatise by Qadi Ahmad, Son of Mir Munshi, trans. V. Minorsky (Washington, DC: Freer Gallery of Art, Smithsonian Institution, 1959).

R. Ettinghausen, *Arab Painting* (Geneva: Skira, 1962).

Ibn Khaldūn, *The Muqaddimah: An Introduction to History*, trans. F. Rosenthal (Princeton: Princeton University Press, 1967).

E. Dodd, "The Image of the World", in *Berytus* 18 (1969).

Ibn al-Nadīm, *The Fihrist of al-Nadīm*, trans. B. Dodge (New York: Columbia University Press, 1970).

A. Grohmann, *Arabische Paläographie*, t. II: *Das Schriftwesen. Die Lapidarschrift*, series of the Österreichische Akademie der Wissenschaften, Philosophisch-Historische Klasse, Denkschriften, 94/2, Forschungen zur Islamischen Philologie und Kulturgeschichte, II (Vienna, 1971).

Abū l-Faraj al-Iṣbahānī, *Kitāb adab al-ġurabā'*, ed. Ṣalaḥ al-Dīn al-Munǧid (Lebanon: Dār al-kitāb al-ǧadīd, 1972).

E. Atil, *Art of the Arab World*, exh. cat. (Washington, DC: Freer Gallery of Art, Smithsonian Institution, 1975).

R. D. Talbot, *Islamic Art* (London: Thames & Hudson, 1975).

U. Vogt-Göknil, *Mosquées* (Paris: Chêne, 1975).

K. Critchlow, *Islamic Patterns: An Analytical and Cosmological Approach* (London: Thames & Hudson, 1976).

A. Ḥ. Šaraf al-Dīn, "Some Islamic inscriptions discovered on the Darb Zubayda", in *Atlal. The Journal of Saudi Arabian archaeology* I (1977): 69.

H. S. Yasin, *Islamic Calligraphy* (London: Thames & Hudson, 1978).

Calligraphy in the Arts of the Muslim World, ed. A. Welch, exh. cat. (New York: The Asia Society, 1979).

The Arts of the Book in Central Asia, 14th–16th Centuries, ed. B. Gray (Paris: UNESCO and London: Serindia Publications, 1979).

Ibn al-Haytham, *Kitāb al-manāzir*, ed. A. Sabra (Kuwait: Sabra, 1983).

M. al-Fa'ar, *Taṭawwur al-kitābāt wa l-nuqūš fī l-Ḥiǧāz munḏu faǧr al-Islām ḥattā muntaṣaf al-qarn al-sābi' al-hiǧrī*, series Rasā'il ǧāmi'iyya, 23 (Jeddah, 1984).

B. Moritz, *Arabic Paleography* (Cairo, 1905; reprint Osnabrück, 1986).

S. A. Fahmī, "Naqshāni jadīdāni min Makkah al-Mukarramah mu'rikhan bi-sanat thamānīna hijrīyya", in *Al-Manhal* 53 (1987): 348–49.

Ibn al-Jawzī, *Funūn al-afnān fī 'uyūn 'ulūm al Qur'ān* (Beirut, 1987).

S. H. Nasr, *Islamic Art and Spirituality* (Albany NY: SUNY Press, 1987).

D. James, *Qur'ans of the Mamluks* (London: Alexandria Press, 1988).

S. Ory, "Aspects religieux des textes épigraphiques du début de l'Islam", in *Revue du monde musulman et de la Méditerranée* 58 (1990): 30–39.

A. Schimmel, *Calligraphy and Islamic Culture* (London: I. B. Tauris, 1990).

F. Déroche and The Nasser D. Khalili Collection of Islamic Art, *The Abbasid Tradition: Qur'ans of the 8th to the 10th centuries AD* (London: The Nour Foundation & Azimuth, 1992).

C. W. Ernst, "The Spirit of Islamic Calligraphy: Bābā Shāh Iṣfahānī's *Ādāb al-mashq*", in *Journal of the American Oriental Society* 112, 2 (1992): 279–86.

B. Gruendler, *The Development of the Arabic Scripts: From the Nabatean Era to the First Islamic Century according to the Dated Texts*, Harvard Semitic Series no. 43 (Atlanta GA: Scholars Press, 1993).

M. b. 'Alī Al Rāwandī, "Faṣl fī ma'rifat uṣūl al-khaṭṭ min al-dā'ira wa al-nuqat", in *Kitāb-ārāyī dar tamaddun-i islām*, ed. N. Māyel-Hirawī (Mashhad, 1993), pp. 1–9.

A. Khatibi and M. Sijelmassi, *L'art calligraphique de l'Islam* (Paris: Éditions Gallimard, 1994).

S. A. al-Rashid, *Kitābāt islamiyya min Makkah al-Mukarramah* (Riyadh, 1995).

O. Grabar, *Penser l'art islamique. Une esthétique de l'ornement* (Paris: Albin Michel, 1996).

N. Safwat, M. Urbik Zakariya and The Nasser D. Khalili Collection of Islamic Art, *The Art of the Pen: Calligraphy of the 14th to the 20th centuries* (London: The Nour Foundation & Azimuth, 1996).

S. S. Blair, *Islamic Inscriptions* (New York: New York University Press, 1998).

N. Çetin, "The Rise and Development of the Art of Calligraphy", in *The Art of Calligraphy in the Islamic Heritage* (Istanbul: IRCICA, 1998).

M. U. Derman and N. M. Çetin, *The Art of Calligraphy in the Islamic Heritage*, series Islamic Cultural Heritage no. 1 (Istanbul: IRCICA, 1998).

Art of Islam: Heavenly Art, Earthly Beauty, ed. M. B. Piotrovski, exh. cat. (Amsterdam: De Nieuwe Kerk, 1999).

M. al-Baqamī, *Nuqūš islāmiyya šāhidiyya bi-Maktabat al-Malik Fahd al-waṭaniyya: dırasa fı Ḫaṣa'iṣı-ha al-fannıyya wa taḥlīl maḍāmīni-hā* (Riyadh, 1999).

M. Bayani-Wolpert, A. Contadini, T. Stanley and The Nasser D. Khalili Collection of Islamic Art, *The Decorated Word: Qur'ans of the 17th to 19th centuries* (London: The Nour Foundation & Azimuth, 1999).

Golden Pages: Qur'ans and Other Manuscripts from the Collection of Ghassan I. Shaker, ed. N. Safwat (Oxford: Oxford University Press & Azimuth Editions, 2000).

N. Safwat, *The Harmony of Letters: Islamic Calligraphy from the Tareq Rajab Museum* (Singapore: National Heritage Board, 2000).

L'Art du livre arabe, du manuscrit au livre d'artiste, eds. M. G. Guesdon and A. Vernay-Nouri, exh. cat. (Paris: Bibliothèque nationale de France, 2001).

G. Necipoğlu, *Word of God, Art of Man: The Qur'an and its Creative Expression* (Oxford: Oxford University Press, 2003).

F. Déroche, *Le Livre manuscrit arabe. Préludes à une histoire* (Paris: Bibliothèque nationale de France, 2004).

S. S. Blair, *Islamic Calligraphy* (Edinburgh: Edinburgh University Press, 2006).

A. George, "The Geometry of Early Qur'anic Manuscripts", in *Journal of Qur'anic Studies* IX, 1 (2007): 78–110.

Purs décors? Arts de l'Islam, regards du XIXe siècle, eds. R. Labrusse, S. Makariou and E. Possémé, exh. cat. (Paris: Les Arts décoratifs et Musée du Louvre, 2007).

A. I. Ghabban, "The Inscription of Zuhayr, the oldest Islamic inscription (24 AH / AD 644–645): The Rise of the Arabic script and the nature of the early Islamic state", in *Arabian Archaeology and Epigraphy* 19 (2008): 217.

G. Necipoğlu, "The Dome of the Rock as Palimpsest: 'Abd al-Malik's Grand Narrative", in *Muqarnas* XXV (2008): 17–107.

N. Rabbat, "Design without Representation in Medieval Egypt", in *Muqarnas* XXV (2008): 147–55.

M. U. Derman, *Eternal Letters from the Abdul Rahman Al Owais Collection of Islamic Calligraphy, Sharjah* (Sharjah: Sharjah Museum of Islamic Civilization, 2009).

A. George, *The Rise of Islamic Calligraphy* (London: Saqi, 2010).

Routes d'Arabie. Histoire et archéologie du royaume d'Arabie Saoudite, eds. B. André-Salvini and C. Juvin, exh. cat. (Paris: Musée du Louvre & Somogy, 2010).

The Aura of Alif. The Art of Writing in Islam, ed. J. W. Frembgen, exh. cat. (Munich: Museum für Völkerkunde, 2010).

F. Imbert, "L'Islam des pierres: l'expression de la foi dans les graffiti arabes des premiers siècles", in *Revue du monde musulman et de la Méditerranée* 129 (2011).

Calligraphy and Architecture in the Muslim World, eds. M. Gharipour and İ. C. Schick (Edinburgh: Edinburgh University Press, 2013).

O. Grabar, *L'Ornement. Formes et fonctions dans l'art islamique* (Paris: Flammarion, 2013).

A. Moustafa and S. Sperl, *The Cosmic Script. Sacred Geometry and the Science of Arabic Penmanship* (Rochester NY: Inner Traditions, 2014).

M. al-Ṯunayān, *Nuqūš al-qarn al-hiğrī al-'awwal (al-qarn al-sābi' al-milādī) al-mu'arraḫa fī l-Mamlaka al-'arabiyya al-sa'ūdiyya (Dirāsa taḥlīliyya ğadīda)*, series Silsila dirāsāt 'ilmiyya maḥkama, 4 (Riyadh, 2015).

C. Dagher, *Arabic Hurufiyya: Art and Identity*, original ed. 1990 (Milan: Skira, 2017).

J. M. Puerta Vílchez, *Aesthetics in Arabic Thought* (Leiden: Brill, 2017).

'Abdul-Raḥmān al-Sa'īd, "Al-nuqūsh al-sha'riyya fī kitāb 'Aḥğār al-ma'alā al-shahidiyya bi-Makkah al-Mukarramah' wa-qīmatuha al-'adabiyyah", in *Mağallah dārah al-malik 'Abdul 'Azīz* 43/2 (2017).

N. B. Azzouna, *Aux origines du classicisme: Calligraphes et bibliophiles au temps des dynasties mongoles (Les Ilkhanides et les Djalayirides 656–814 / 1258–1411)* (Leiden: Brill, 2018).

J. Hamoudi, "About the Letter . . . A Response (1973)", in *Modern Art in the Arab World: Primary Documents*, eds. A. Lenssen, S. Rogers and N. Shabout (Durham NC: Duke University Press, 2018).

S. H. Al Said, "Contemplative Art Manifesto (1966)", in *Modern Art in the Arab World: Primary Documents*, eds. A. Lenssen, S. Rogers and N. Shabout (Durham NC: Duke University Press, 2018).

N. Shabout, "Transregional Solidarity: The Arab Biennial in Retrospect", in #5 *Refractions of Socialist Solidarity*, Mezosfera's fifth thematic issue, ed. E. Szakács, May 2018.

M. Umar, "Arabic Calligraphy: An Inspiring Element in Abstract Art (1949–50)", in *Modern Art in the Arab World: Primary Documents*, eds. A. Lenssen, S. Rogers and N. Shabout (Durham NC: Duke University Press, 2018).

N. Shabout, "*Dafatir*: Testimonies of Forgotten Times", in *Theater of Operations: The Gulf Wars 1991–2011*, exh. cat. (New York: MoMA PS1, 2019).

S. M. Hassan, "When Identity becomes 'Form': Calligraphic Abstraction and Sudanese Modernism", in *Taking Shape: Abstraction from The Arab World*, eds. S. Takesh and L. Gumpert, exh. cat., Grey Art Gallery, New York University, New York, 2020 (Munich: Hirmer Publishers, 2020).

S. Al-Rashid, *Medieval Routes to Mecca: A Study of the Darb Zubaidah Pilgrim Trail*, ed. P. Webb (London: Gilgamesh Publishing, 2020).

N. Shabout, "Mediating Abstraction through the Arabic Letter", in *Taking Shape: Abstraction from The Arab World*, eds. S. Takesh and L. Gumpert, exh. cat., Grey Art Gallery, New York University, New York, 2020 (Munich: Hirmer Publishers, 2020), pp. 41–49.

U. Bongianino, *The Manuscript Tradition of the Islamic West* (Edinburgh: Edinburgh University Press, 2022).

This publication accompanies the exhibition
Scripts and Calligraphy: Paths to the Soul
presented at Irqah hospital, Riyadh
from 10 June to 2 September 2023
and then at Madina Arts Center, Medina
from 15 October to 23 December 2023.

We would like to thank Madina Arts Center for hosting the exhibition in Medina

Lenders
The Ministry of Culture would like to thank all the lenders for their generosity:

Elmarsa Gallery, United Arab Emirates and Germany
Institut du Monde Arabe, France
King Abdulaziz Complex for Endowment Libraries, Saudi Arabia
Raqqada Museum of Civilization and Islamic Arts, Tunisia
Bashar Abubaker Alowh, Saudi Arabia
Ibrahim Al Arafi, Saudi Arabia
Jassim Miraj Al-Failakawi, Kuwait
Salem M. Fawzi Bajnaid, Saudi Arabia
Farah Behbehani, Kuwait
Doa Bugis, Saudi Arabia
Azza Fahmy, Egypt
Zaki Al Hashimi, Saudi Arabia
Nasser Al Maymoun, Saudi Arabia
Islam O. El-Nagdi, Egypt
Nasser Al Salem, Saudi Arabia
Mohamed Al Mohamed Shibrain, Sudan
Hanaa Waqiallah, Sudan

Credits for the photographs in the exhibition
Abdullatif Al Fozan Award for Mosque Architecture, Saudi Arabia
Institut du Monde Arabe, France
Sumaya Dabbagh, United Arab Emirates
Saïd Nusseibeh, United States of America
Ieva Saudargaitė, Lebanon

Catalogue
Edited by the Ministry of Culture, Saudi Arabia and Skira editore

Project coordination
Yassmeen Tukan (Ministry of Culture, Saudi Arabia)
Edoardo Ghizzoni, Emma Cavazzini, Eva Vanzella (Skira editore)

Book design
Naji El Mir (Studio Nem)
Anna Cattaneo (Skira editore)

Copy editor
Emanuela Di Lallo

Book layout
Antonio Carminati

Design of the exhibition logo
Wissam Shawkat

Translations
Sara Noss, Malcolm Williams and Nancy Roberts on behalf of *Scriptum*, Rome

We would like to thank
Maya Chidiac for writing the captions
Dr. Issa Makhlouf for the revision of the Arabic translations

Published by

The Ministry of Culture, Saudi Arabia
King Faisal Road
Al Diriyah, PO Box 3424
13711 Riyadh, Kingdom of Saudi Arabia

Skira editore spa
Palazzo Casati Stampa
via Torino, 61
20123 Milano
www.skira.net

Printed and bound in Italy. First edition

ISBN: 978-88-572-5071-7 (Ministry of Culture)
ISBN: 978-88-572-4881-3 (Skira editore)

Distributed in USA, Canada, Central & South America by ARTBOOK | D.A.P.
75 Broad Street, Suite 630, New York, NY 10004, USA.
Distributed elsewhere in the world by Thames & Hudson Ltd., 181A High Holborn, London WC1V 7QX, United Kingdom